Cases on Information Technology Entrepreneurship

Jose Aurelio Medina-Garrido
University of Cádiz, Spain

Salustiano Martínez-Fierro
University of Cádiz, Spain

Jose Ruiz-Navarro
University of Cádiz, Spain

IGI PUBLISHING

Hershey • New York

Acquisition Editor:	Kristin Klinger
Senior Managing Editor:	Jennifer Neidig
Managing Editor:	Sara Reed
Development Editor:	Kristin Roth
Copy Editor:	Jeannie Porter
Typesetter:	Amanda Appicello
Cover Design:	Lisa Tosheff
Printed at:	Yurchak Printing Inc.

Published in the United States of America by
IGI Publishing (an imprint of IGI Global)
701 E. Chocolate Avenue
Hershey PA 17033
Tel: 717-533-8845
Fax: 717-533-8661
E-mail: cust@igi-global.com
Web site: http://www.igi-global.com

and in the United Kingdom by
IGI Publishing (an imprint of IGI Global)
3 Henrietta Street
Covent Garden
London WC2E 8LU
Tel: 44 20 7240 0856
Fax: 44 20 7379 0609
Web site: http://www.eurospanonline.com

Library of Congress Cataloging-in-Publication Data

Cases on information technology entrepreneurship / Jose A. Medina-Garrido, Salustiano Martinez-Fierro & Jose Ruiz-Navarro, editors.
    p. cm.
  Summary: "This book provides a cutting-edge look into how IT can be the structural foundation of an entrepreneurship, and describes specific examples of IT as the base of a start-up company--providing insight into the successes and failures of applying IT in innovative ways"--Provided by publisher.
  Includes bibliographical references and index.
  ISBN-13: 978-1-59904-612-9 (hardcover)
  ISBN-13: 978-1-59904-614-3 (ebook)
 1. Information technology. 2. Entrepreneurship. 3. New business enterprises. I. Medina Garrido, José Aurelio. II. Martinez-Fierro, Salustiano, 1973- III. Ruiz Navarro, José.
  HC79.I55C365 2008
  025.04068'1--dc22
                              2007022431

British Cataloguing in Publication Data
A Cataloguing in Publication record for this book is available from the British Library.

Cases on Information Technology Entrepreneurship

Table of Contents

Section I: Entrepreneurs

Alfonso Miguel Márquez-García, University of Jaén, Spain
María Teresa Garrido-Álvarez, University of Jaén, Spain
María del Carmen Moreno-Martos, University of Jaén, Spain

Andrea Bikfalvi, Universitat de Girona, Spain
Christian Serarols, Universitat Autònoma de Barcelona, Spain

Salustiano Martínez-Fierro, University of Cádiz, Spain

Andrew N. Garman, Rush University, USA
Mayur Patel, Rush University, USA
Rod Hart, Advantage Health LLC, USA

Section II: Corporate Entrepreneurship (Intrapreneurship)

Foreword

In recent years it is possible to detect an increasing interest in entrepreneurship development worldwide. Governments and all kinds of institutions are asking for information about entrepreneurs' characteristics, behaviors, and everything related to them, the aim being to understand their mechanisms for creating wealth and to foster entrepreneurship among the population. The saturated labor market in developed countries, the need to create jobs in underdeveloped ones, migration processes, the loss of certain values, and other issues are making it advisable to pay close attention to the kind of individual that can assume personal risk, has interesting and innovative ideas, and has the courage to start up a business.

It is true that information, studies, and analysis of entrepreneurs' characteristics and behavior can help policy makers design adequate public policies to foster entrepreneurship among the population, but what about helping individual people to become entrepreneurs?

For this purpose other kinds of tools are needed, especially educational ones. Schools, universities, and other organizations are providing several programs to help potential entrepreneurs acquire the knowledge they need to become real entrepreneurs. Thus, in many countries it is now possible for interested individuals to learn how to develop an idea, how to make a business plan, how to deal with bureaucracy, how to determine if the business is viable or not, and how to learn all of the details needed to start up. All the abovementioned organizations—schools, universities, Chambers of Commerce, business associations, and others—can assess people and help them develop a good idea into a real business.

But now, despite all these programs, which are improving day by day, there are persistent problems that cannot be solved so easily. One of these problems is how to come up with original business ideas and another is how to decide if an individual is really prepared to become an entrepreneur, if they really know what this entails.

Books like the one presented here are tools that can help people to understand the real process of being an entrepreneur because they show real cases and experiences that no one, apart from an entrepreneur, can live and explain. Examples are the best way to show how others had a clever idea and translated it into a profitable, growing business.

The case study method allows interested people to step figuratively into the shoes of a particular entrepreneur. It gives an accurate description of the business, its situation, the problems faced by the entrepreneurs, the kind of decisions the entrepreneurs have to make, and the challenges and opportunities the entrepreneurs are considering for the future. Thus, apart from actually living alongside an entrepreneur for a period, cases come closest to transmitting the experience of what it feels like to be an entrepreneur.

This book, by examining entrepreneurs' actual experiences, will help solve some of the real problems that arise in firm creation, but it offers something more: the cases focus on businesses involved in Information Technology.

As mentioned, another common problem for potential entrepreneurs is how to find a good and original idea. It is very difficult to be original and to discover a "unique" product or service in practice. Brainstorming sessions and other educational methods can help individuals generate new ideas, but another alternative is to look at the market and be a good observer of what is going on around and where the opportunities are.

And that is what makes this book a very interesting contribution. It presents cases involving what is currently one of the most recommended fields for potential young entrepreneurs: the Information Technology sector.

This sector has enormous potential, offering a large number of business opportunities for potential young entrepreneurs trained in a large number of specializations. Information Technology influences the way firms organize their production, distribution, customer and supplier relationships, accounting, human resources, and all branches of their activity. Firms need good solutions for dealing with all of these matters, and the IT industry is creating them continuously. Moreover, things can be done in a wide variety of different ways, and there are enough business opportunities to allow diversity. Information technology is also critical in marketing, advertising, market research, and related sectors. All conceivable business activities now involve some use of information technology. The cases presented in this book explain how some entrepreneurs jumped over the barrier and went inside a sector that can frighten at first but where there is a lot of work to do.

One of the keys of technology-based entrepreneurship is to take into account that it is probably necessary to create multidisciplinary teams to start up. In other words, a person who has a technical idea but does not have expertise or knowledge in business management will have to search for the right people to deal with the managerial part of the initiative. Another important factor to consider is location, and seeing whether there is a possibility of joining a business cluster of the same sector. It is also critical to work in this sector in order to understand that if the firm is going to offer technical solutions to other firms, it is essential to know and analyze the interaction of technology with all aspects of the firm that will buy the products. This brings us back to the need for a good and adequate multidisciplinary team.

Cases on Information Technology Entrepreneurship discusses all these issues, and it will undoubtedly prove very useful, in two ways, to students who have not yet chosen their professional future. On one hand, it should convince many students of the attractiveness of the entrepreneurial option, and, on the other, it should persuade them to give serious consideration to the IT sector as a possible area in which to work, regardless of their particular branch of study. All branches are relevant, given the need for multidisciplinary teams when creating new businesses in this field.

Alicia Coduras, PhD
Technical Director of the GEM Project in Spain
Instituto de Empresa (IE)

Preface

Role of Information Technology in Entrepreneurship

All authors agree that the firm creation phenomenon is important for growth and economic development, particularly since the work of Schumpeter (1942). Entrepreneurs are vital for economic growth and prosperity. Today, millions of men and women, young and not so young, of all ages and ethnic groups, are currently involved in entrepreneurial activities: starting up new businesses, buying failed businesses, revitalizing family firms, or innovating (Osborne, 1987). A reflection of the importance of the entrepreneurship phenomenon can be found in the GEM consortium,[1] which is made up of research teams from more than 30 countries dedicated to analyzing entrepreneurship at the national, and in some cases, regional level. A large number of works have studied the determinants of entrepreneurship. Many of these have investigated the characteristics of successful entrepreneurs. These studies have tried to explain firm creation by analyzing the characteristics of these individuals, including their personality, educational level, or ethnic origin (Storey, 1994), factors associated with new firm creation (Armington & Acs, 2002; Reynolds, Miller, & Maki, 1993), the geographic, industrial, and organizational factors associated with entrepreneurship (Reynolds et al., 1993; Saxenian, 1999), and the effect of new firm creation on regional growth and development (Kirchhoff, Armington, Hassa, & Newbert, 2002; Storey, 1994).

Others studies analyze the influence of competitive factors such as innovation or technology on the creation of new firms. Innovation and creativity are key ingredients for providing more and better products and services. One of the first writers to discuss entrepreneurs was Schumpeter (1942), who defined the entrepreneur as a person who introduces new technologies into the production process. Schumpeter argued that entrepreneurship boosts innovation, the introduction of new products, or processes (services were not considered goods at that time). These individuals are coordinators of innovation, engineers of imagination and ideas, and, at the same time, managers of ambiguity and uncertainty (Osborne, 1987).

This book focuses on information technology, since this is a factor that favors competitiveness, innovation, and, presently, the creation of new firms.

This preface describes the entrepreneurship process and stresses the important role of innovation in firm creation, the role of the technology entrepreneur, and the capacity of information technology to be a source of competitive advantage and value creation for the firm. This is followed by some practical recommendations on how to generate value. The section concludes by analyzing the changes that the adoption of these technologies is causing in the traditional structures of organizations.

Entrepreneurship Process

An analysis of the entrepreneurship phenomenon first requires an understanding of the characteristics of the entrepreneurship process. There is some consensus in the literature that the firm creation process consists of various stages (Reynolds, Bosma, Autio, Hunt, de Bono, & Servais et al., 2005; Veciana, 1988). These stages include gestation, creation, launch, and consolidation. Understanding each of these stages may shed light not only on the firm creation process itself but also on the entrepreneurs' characteristics and the problems they face.

In the gestation stage, various factors influence the decision to create a firm, among which the future entrepreneur's professional background is particularly important. Individuals who create technology-based firms normally have a technical university education. Although this type of entrepreneur also tends to have previous professional experience in the field, they usually have less experience than non-technical entrepreneurs. What seems to influence the decision to create a firm in this type of person is the business organization in which they work. These entrepreneurs tend to create firms using the technology or knowledge they have acquired previously, so although these are technology-based firms, they are not innovative firms. These entrepreneurs often create their firms after a trigger event (getting fired, failing to get promoted or recognized, etc.).

The creation stage begins with the entrepreneurs identifying a business opportunity in the market or in their environment. They must then produce a business plan detailing all the information relevant to the idea, the product or service, and the market. The plan must also include an economic-financial analysis with projected earnings and profits for the first few years in the life of the firm. This stage ends with the firm's incorporation.

In the launch stage the entrepreneurs must find the right people to work in the organization, and obtain the resources they will need to operate. Technology has a very important role in this stage, since fewer people may be required to work in the organization if new technologies are used effectively. This might, on the other hand, require highly qualified technical personnel. In any case, the entrepreneur will have to assess the long-term profitability of any investment in technology very carefully. Choosing the wrong technologies (problems of incompatibility or standards, obsolescence, rejection by the market, the technology is untested, etc.), or not using technologies correctly (poor planning, inconsistency with the firm's overall plan, poor implementation, resistance and opposition to the technologies from organization members, no control over compliance with the proposed objectives, etc.), could lead to failure. But firms will inevitably suffer declines in short-term productivity due to their lack of experience, as they are in the first stage of a learning curve of how to use the technologies effectively. These negative short-term effects are related to the concept known as the technology productivity paradox (Bruque & Medina, 2002). According to the productivity paradox, greater investment in information technology is associated, unexpectedly, with lower productivity.

The final stage is the consolidation of the firm. Consolidation occurs if the market has accepted the firm's products or services and the entrepreneurs have overcome any difficulties they faced in the early stages of the process. Personal problems often arise between the partners and some may leave the project as a result. The entrepreneurs are then effectively starting afresh at this point, because this is when they start making decisions concerning the growth and expansion of the firm. Investments in IT are at a stage that is close to maturity. The organization has gained a certain experience, and this helps it use the technology more efficiently and rectify initial errors. The entrepreneurs begin to realize that there are new ways of exploiting the technology investment made and that new business opportunities are beginning to be more clearly discernible.

Technology-Based Entrepreneurs

Economists and politicians began to pay more attention to the creation of technology-based firms from the 1990s onward. These firms contribute to job creation, and fast-growing startups, particularly in high-tech sectors, play a crucial role in renewing the economic system. In the past quarter century, the computing industry has grown much more quickly than the economy in general, although with some ups and downs. These firms, particularly those from sectors of the so-called new economy, such as software, e-commerce, and communications equipment, have competitive advantages based on innovation. The Internet has become commonplace in practically all firms, not just the new ones but also the already consolidated ones. New technology adoption began in firms in the United States, but quickly spread to Europe and the rest of the world.

The Internet is now regarded as a powerful tool that can help firms overcome physical and managerial barriers to internationalization. This is particularly important for the smallest entrepreneurial firms, given their well-known initial limitations in terms of financial and human resources, international experience, and knowledge of global markets (Sinkovics & Bell, 2006). Thus, small firms that use information and communications technologies (ICT) tend to be more involved in internationalization activities and tend to perform better (Nieto & Fernandez, 2006).

The tendency in the current century is for information and the information technologies to continue transforming our homes and businesses, changing the way companies compete and consumers behave. Products and services based on information will expand and will have a high level of innovation (Osborne, 1987). ICT has changed the fundamental principles of traditional trade, but if firms handle the technologies properly they can be a source of competitive advantage (Porter, 1985). Nieto and Fernandez (2006), in contrast, argue that ICT on its own is not necessarily a source of competitive advantage; the technologies are complementary with some of the firm's other strategic resources. ICT is modifying the processes in all the firm's functional areas. Specifically, the Internet's impact can be seen in all the organizational areas: marketing, distribution, business processes, and so forth (Loane, 2006). With regard to the impact of ICT on firm creation, when a new technology appears, a large number of business opportunities are frequently seen shortly after.

Information technologies have proved to be innovative and are constantly being reinvented, creating shorter product life cycles, a higher level of automation, and faster obsolescence, in both products and services (Osborne, 1987). For entrepreneurs and the entrepreneurial process, the information era is a magnificent opportunity. The early 21st century is a time of considerable expectations for the technology entrepreneur, due to the excellent business opportunities available to technology-based firms and the fact that the ICT sector is still maturing.

In this context, the concept of e-entrepreneurship arises. This is rather more than simply applying technologies to the firm. In fact, it is the interaction between technology, business strategy, and business processes. E-entrepreneurship involves the application of ICT by entrepreneurs to create value from the entire value chain of business processes by acquiring, sustaining, and enhancing business competitiveness (Mahmood & Yu, 2005).

Researchers have examined whether entrepreneurs starting up technology-based firms have different profiles from other entrepreneurs. In general, Osborne (1987) finds that entrepreneurs are well-educated people, knowledgeable and experienced, and excellent students of human behavior and observers of consumer habits. Entrepreneurs starting technology-based firms tend to be younger than other entrepreneurs and tend to have a higher educational level in the case of high-tech manufacturing startups (Autio, Kanerva, Kaila, & Kauranen, 1989; Donckels, 1989; Jo & Lee, 1996; Licht, Nerlinger, & Berger, 1985; Westhead & Storey, 1994), but a lower educational level in the case of startups directly or indirectly involving the Internet (Colombo & Delmastro, 2001). For many entrepreneurs, starting up technology-based firms is their first professional experience. But this usually depends on the type of technology firm involved. High-tech start-ups strongly depend on the founder's knowledge and skills, so these entrepreneurs are likely to have considerable previous experience from working in technology and experience of the market relevant to their firm (Colombo & Delmastro). This is even more the case when the firm is from the ICT manufacturing sector. Nevertheless, technology entrepreneurs starting up firms offering Internet services very often have less experience.

Two complementary explanations may explain why entrepreneurs have different characteristics in function of their activity in the high-tech sector (Colombo & Delmastro, 2001): first, the advent of the new Internet paradigm and the consequent appearance of new markets opening up new business opportunities and giving rise to many new enterprises; second, the technological and managerial knowledge and skills associated with previous work experiences quickly become obsolete, and repeating consolidated knowledge patterns may endanger the success of the business. This is why the founders of firms providing Internet services generally have lower educational levels and less previous experience than entrepreneurs from the ICT manufacturing sector. These latter firms are in the maturity stage of their life cycle and are consequently subject to less market turbulence. The competencies acquired during their education and previous work are consequently critical to the entrepreneurs with these firms.

Another characteristic of IT-intensive firms is that they tend to employ fewer people than firms from other sectors. Thus, their entrepreneurs typically need fewer financial resources to start their firms than entrepreneurs from other sectors.

Entrepreneurs who use IT undoubtedly have a different profile from other entrepreneurs. But technology entrepreneurs also have specific characteristics that influence their decision to start a business. The decision to start a business is conditioned to a greater or lesser extent by three factors. The first factor is the motivation to start a business. Technology entrepreneurs are more motivated to start out projects and put their innovative ideas into practice than other entrepreneurs. They tend to be driven by the need for achievement and self-realization and the desire to implement their projects; their motive is not purely economic.

The second factor is the entrepreneur's capacity or ability to create a business in the chosen sector. The competencies required to start up a firm come within the so-called managerial capacities. These are as necessary for entrepreneurs starting up a technology-based firm as they are for other entrepreneurs. But if the new firm needs to use information technologies intensively, either in its processes or in its products, the entrepreneur must possess technical competencies. Entrepreneurs can hardly apply IT efficiently if they lack knowledge or experience in the area.

The third factor that strongly conditions the decision to start a business is the entrepreneur's perception that there are business opportunities that they can exploit. Clearly, whether there are more or less business opportunities is important, but more important still is the entrepreneur's ability to see them. Technology entrepreneurs tend to have a refined analytical capacity developed during their technical education. Moreover, the constant evolution of these technologies and the possibility of applying them to various unforeseen uses provide fertile ground for the proliferation of opportunities.

Information Technology as a Source of Competitive Advantage

The motivation to start a business, possessing the competencies required to do this, and the perception that there are business opportunities all encourage firm creation, but they cannot guarantee success. The interest in studying the creation of firms that use IT in their products or processes lies in the fact that the technologies are frequently a source of competitive advantage for the firm.

Many researchers mention ICT as a source of competitive advantage (Barney, 1991; Clemons & Row, 1991a; Feeny & Ives, 1990; Mata, Fuerst, & Barney, 1995; Porter & Millar, 1986; Powell & Dent-Micallef, 1997), and this section now discusses this question.

One of the most important possibilities offered by ICT, from an internal perspective, is the impact of these technologies on the firm's processes, products, and services. For example, ICT can favor the creation of products with a greater informational content, or of services added to the product, for example, via the Internet.

With regard to improving the firm's processes, ICT can help create, modify, or destroy activities and links in the value chain (Porter & Millar, 1986), or restructure current business processes (Hammer & Champy, 1993). In fact, ICT allows firms to apply many of the principles of business process engineering. For example, firms can use the technologies to control or self-control the results of processes and transmit the results to management and to the workers concerned; workers carrying out tasks can simultaneously process the information that they generate, thereby lightening the workload of the administrative structure; information can be made available directly to whoever needs it in their work; and the firm no longer captures information more than once, so anyone who needs certain information can access the database that stores it, regardless of which company unit produced the database. In this way, the firm integrates independent systems with the consequent benefits in terms of synergies and scale economies (no redundancy of data or information, consistency of information, minimum cost of updating data, savings in data storage, and quality of data).

Many contributions in the literature examine the advantages obtained by the increased switching costs that ICT can generate (Clemons, 1986; Clemons & Row, 1991b; Feeny & Ives, 1990; McFarlan, 1985).

According to Mata et al. (1995), the literature recognizes five attributes of ICT as potential sources of sustainable competitive advantages: customers' switching costs, capital requirements, ownership of the technology, technical skills in ICT, and ability to manage the ICT. Their analysis, which is carried out under the resource-based perspective, concludes that only the last attribute is a likely source of sustainable competitive advantages. The generation of switching costs may dissuade future customers, who will prefer to use alternative standards that avoid investment in specialist technologies (and their concomitant switching costs). Capital requirements may exclude some firms if substantial investments in technology are required, but a large number of firms have enough capital to make such investments. Reverse engineering and the high level of obsolescence in information technologies make basing the firm's competitive advantage on its ownership of technologies alone unwise. And technical skills in the use of ICT are accessible on the market, either by employing qualified people or through training courses. With all this, the ability to manage the ICT is the only attribute that can give rise to sustainable competitive advantage. This will require a continuing evolution and learning for a more efficient and dynamic use of the ICT, for the firm's processes, and for the products and services it offers. It will mean that the firm needs to adapt continuously and proactively to the needs of its customers, suppliers, partners, and, indeed, to its own needs. These management skills imply that the technology firm is first and foremost a firm; the fact that it uses technologies is secondary. In fact, more than one technology firm has failed as a result of giving too much weight to the technology side and not enough to its essential nature as a firm. In the particular case of e-business, concentrating too much on technology aspects has blinded many firms to the fact that as businesses they must generate value, in other words, profits. Earle and Keen (2000) refer to this phenomenon using an inspiring phrase: firms must "pass from .com to .profit."

Some work in the ICT literature has focused on the role of these technologies in knowledge management. It is important to note that when the environment and the organization are highly complex, information systems and knowledge management become more important (Nonaka & Takeuchi, 1995). ICT, which supports the information system, plays a decisive role in this context (Davenport, De Long, & Beers, 1998; Lowendahl & Revang, 1998).

According to Garud and Nayyar (1994), the creation, maintenance, and development of a mass of technological knowledge will form the basis of future competencies.

From an external perspective, Porter and Millar (1986) argue that information has acquired a strategic value, since it can modify the structure of a sector, create new competitive advantages, and even lead to the creation of new businesses that were not feasible before. Cash and Konsynski (1985) and Porter and Millar (1986) stress that firms can use ICT to develop generic cost-leadership, differentiation, and segmentation strategies. Rackoff, Wiseman, and Ullrich (1985) add innovation, growth, and external alliances to these strategies.

Nolan and Gibson (1974) and Nolan (1981) write that investments in ICT are dynamic in nature. Applying the product life-cycle philosophy to the introduction and development of ICT in the firm, these authors develop a six-stage model relating ICT investment with its organizational and strategic impact using a standard model of development and learning. The final stages of the model (information management and maturity) correspond to situations where the information system is evolving and it has a strategic role for the firm, but for which it has been necessary to evolve initially from previous stages facilitating learning.

McFarlan (1985) also stresses the strategic role of the systems and of the ICT, but arguing, from a more contingent perspective, that the role of these may differ from one company to the next. Thus, this author differentiates between firms whose current systems and systems in development depend to a great extent on ICT, and firms where they do not. It is therefore necessary to analyze whether ignoring the importance of a future technological development could leave the firm at a competitive disadvantage. Firms in this situation need to be aware of the strategic importance of ICT in the firm's planning. A serious error in the organization's information system plan can threaten its very survival.

ICT can undoubtedly represent a source of competitive advantage for the firm. But for this to happen, the company needs people who know how to manage it correctly (Mata et al., 1995). This management capacity is useful both to improve the processes and products of already existing companies and for the creation of new firms. The technology entrepreneur's role is critical here. As mentioned above, being a technology entrepreneur is more than just applying technologies to the firm. This type of entrepreneur is able to apply ICT efficiently at all steps in the value chain of the business processes, improving the firm's competitiveness (Mahmood & Yu, 2005) both in its internal operations and in its relationships with other organizations.

ICT offers entrepreneurs an enormous number of business opportunities in sectors like ICT infrastructure, Internet infrastructure, Internet intermediation, and e-commerce (Mahmood & Yu, 2005).

Activities relating to the ICT infrastructure include, for example, the supply of products and services involving software, hardware, communications, network support, and Internet services.

With regard to the Internet infrastructure, this includes services and programs such as Internet consultancy, e-commerce applications, multimedia programs, Web site development software, search engine software, online education, consultation of online databases, Web site support and hosting services, and transaction processing services.

Internet intermediation gets around the limitations of physical intermediation in the old economy in which firms achieved an efficient distribution by cutting transaction costs, in turn achieved by locating goods and services close to the customers. The need for intermediaries on the Internet arises from the information asymmetries that exist between suppliers and customers, and also to aggregate supply or demand. But Internet intermediation can fail if the activity is limited to the traditional concept of bringing together the supply of some parties with the demand of others. Internet intermediaries need to generate value added for the providers, the buyers, or both. There is an important potential to start up new firms offering intermediation services in areas such as online travel agencies, online brokerages, content aggregators, portal content providers, Internet advertising brokers, and virtual malls.

Finally, e-commerce involves the commercialization, via the Internet or other networks, of products and services delivered either off-line or online (for purely digital products). E-commerce opens up business opportunities throughout the entire commercial process: marketing, promotion, distribution and logistics, procurement and purchasing, supply-chain management, sales, customer-relationship management, customer service, and provision of complementary information with products.

Practical Guidelines to Create Value

Nowadays, the technology firm par excellence is one that uses technologies to carry out its operations, to generate or offer its products and services, or to communicate with its customers and other firms. This type of firm is commonly known as an e-business.

Amit and Zott (2001) conclude, after their empirical study, that an e-business must create value if it is to be successful. The authors identify four interdependent dimensions that can potentially generate value in this type of business: efficiency, complementarities, lock-in (of customers and partners), and novelty.

Firms can become more efficient by cutting the cost of transacting with other firms and their production or service-delivery costs. Information technologies have contributed to reducing transaction costs between firms. On one hand, firms can use the technologies to quickly search for available providers and the supply becomes more transparent. On the other, after selecting the providers, or when transacting with customers, the technologies improve both formal and informal communication, and tools such as electronic data processing, electronic data interchange, and electronic fund transfer help automate the transactions. Similarly, systems such as computer-aided manufacturing, flexible manufacturing systems, computer-aided design, and computer-aided engineering help reduce production costs. The technologies also improve service delivery by facilitating an efficient and quick access to global markets through the Internet, cell phones, satellite communications, and so forth.

Complementarity means that a set of resources or capabilities provides more value working together than working separately. In this respect, individual information technologies have no value in isolation. If a firm could buy all the technological assets of a successful firm but lacked the complementary resources and capabilities required to make them work properly, it would inevitably fail. In this sense, Powell and Dent-Micallef (1997) ask why some companies encounter difficulties while others prosper when using the same IT, and why IT-based advantages dissipate so quickly. They suggest that IT and complementary human resources and business capabilities must be integrated. Thus, IT requires complementary human resources, such as open organization and communication, consensus, top management commitment, flexibility, and experience in strategic-IT integration. In addition, with regard to complementary business capabilities, IT requires a close relationship and IT connections with suppliers, suitable IT training and planning, redesigning processes, orientation towards teamwork, and benchmarking capabilities (see Table 1).

With regard to the recommendation to lock in the customers, a valuable strategy commonly adopted by e-businesses is to encourage customers to make repeat transactions rather than occasional ones. On one hand, trapping customers in the relationship generates value. On the other, firms want to dissuade their partners from opportunistic behaviors that go against the spirit of the alliance. Firms can achieve both these objectives when switching providers or partners generates costs that dissuade such a decision. Nevertheless, this "captivity" should ideally be the result of a relationship that has value for the customer or partner, rather than due to the existence of switching costs. The threat of embarking on a transaction when switching the provider or partner is costly may dissuade them from entering the relationship in the first place. In this respect, adding value to the relationship, offering the customers or partners resources and capabilities that are complementary to their own, developing trust by tightening the links in the relationship, and consolidating the reputation that an honest and non-opportunistic behavior can be expected from the firm, are all potentially ways of attracting customers and partners. Moreover, the fact that the relationship maintained with these is stable and lasting means that routines can develop over time, and the information technologies used by the

Table 1. Complementary human resources and business capabilities (Source: Adapted from Powell and Dent-Micallef, 1997)

Human resources	Business capabilities
• Open organization	• Relationship with suppliers
• Open communication	• Connect IT with suppliers
• Consensus	• IT training
• Commitment of top management	• Redesigning processes
• Flexibility	• Orientation towards teamwork
• Strategic integration/IT	• Benchmarking
	• IT planning

two organizations can become more integrated and coordinated. This discourages customers and partners from terminating the relationship, since they would have to learn new routines and adapt to new technologies with other firms. Moreover, a positive and valuable experience with the current relationship creates obstacles to terminating it in favor of another relationship that is full of uncertainties.

Novelty, in other words continuous innovation, also generates value in e-businesses. In fact, e-businesses usually obtain advantages if they are the first mover. Technologies can help in the most traditional continuous innovation—innovation in the firm's internal processes, and innovation in products and services. In fact, technologies are increasingly making products and services more ubiquitous and more virtual. But technologies are also enabling another type of innovation—creating new ways of carrying out transactions. Thus, they are innovating the way sellers and buyers are brought together, or innovating the way the purchase process takes place (e.g., Internet auction sites, or reverse markets), or integrating all the agents of the same sector (e.g., buyers, sellers, finance companies, and insurance companies). These are just some examples of how transactions can be restructured in novel ways.

If an e-business cannot generate value with its strategy, it will not be rewarded with improved earnings or a stronger competitive position. The firm must build a strong position in at least one of the four value creation formulas discussed above. But as was mentioned above, the four dimensions are all highly interdependent.

E-businesses must develop strategies to generate value if they are to be successful. This contrasts with the generalized belief that it is enough to be on the Internet, and that being on the Internet is just to support the traditional physical business. Many firms that think like this have Web sites that simply direct customers to their traditional sales channels.

Other firms do exploit the digital economy, but they are lost in a sea of .coms that only work because they are linked to popular portals or search engines. But in this last case achieving a transaction is costly, and does not necessarily guarantee customer loyalty after a sale. Thus, each new transaction incurs the same customer acquisition costs.

The challenge is to go from being present on the Internet to being profitable. For this, firms must turn occasional commercial transactions into stable customer-firm relationships by giving the customers value and being profitable at the same time. When Internet businesses are managed only from the perspective of the technology infrastructure, they end up being run by technical people. In short, it is essential that entrepreneurs run their e-businesses as the businesses that they are, and that the managers manage the firm from a business, and not just a technical, perspective.

On the other hand, going it alone is unwise in both business and technology. The firm should work with customers, product and service providers, technology providers, and even competitors. But it must not forget that it is only as strong as its weakest partner. Badly chosen, inefficient partners that do not add differentiation to the firm's products or services do not add value—quite the opposite.

Some authors offer practical guidelines to create value in e-businesses (Earle & Keen, 2000; Shapiro & Varian, 1999). There follows some recommendations on how to run firms as businesses rather than as technological infrastructures:

- Cultivate stable relationships with your customers. By building a critical mass of loyal customers firms can avoid customer acquisition costs for each transaction. The idea is to build a solid relationship with a strong bond. With this in mind, some firms offer free services in their Web sites, such as specialized information (grants, congresses, trips, etc.), discussion forums, e-mail accounts, space on their server, and so forth.

- Build a powerful brand. On the Internet, the brand concept becomes redefined. It is a relationship brand, rather than a product brand. Customers cannot see the product physically, as they would do in a supermarket, or leaf through the book that is of interest, as they would do in a bookshop. Thus, firms wishing to commercialize products or services on the Internet have no option but to establish a brand, a reputation (Shapiro & Varian, 1999). This reputation takes a long time and is costly to build, but it can be acquired rapidly by partnering with an organization that has one already.

- Improve your logistics. Firms that distribute physical products need to have first-rate logistics. In fact, many Internet start-ups fail because of logistics problems. Getting the logistics right creates synergies with many of the firm's other processes and allows the firm to increase its marketing actions, reduce prices, or improve its services. At the same time, it puts the firm in a good position to exploit other e-commerce opportunities, by using its now developed logistics capabilities. The evidence is clear: firms that have superior logistics perform better than their competitors.

- Harmonize your channels in the name of the customer. Customers choose the communications channel that offers them the most advantages. Firms must give their customers the option that best builds and maintains the relationship, and this choice is for the customer to make, not the firm. In this respect, some firms with an Internet presence operate a myriad of communication channels (Web forms, e-mail, telephone, fax, ordinary mail, combination of physical and virtual branches, etc.).

- Become an intermediary that adds value, or use one that does. In spite of all the evidence suggesting that the Internet would lead to an increasing disintermediation of markets, the coming era of business on the Internet will be dominated by hubs, which some authors call cyberintermediaries, such as portals with powerful brands and other intermediaries bringing together the supply and demand. These intermediaries will control the interaction between providers and customers by virtue of their role as coordinators of information, and they will advise customers where to go on the Internet to find the products or services they are looking for. Only those intermediaries that provide value to consumers and firms will thrive. If a firm does not provide value as an intermediary, it must use an intermediary that does if it wants to be profitable.

- Information has the special characteristic that obtaining and processing it is costly, while it can then be copied indefinitely at practically zero cost, and subsequently be distributed quickly and with no logistical problems in an electronic market. At the same time, consumers do not consume information when they buy it. This is a more attractive opportunity on the Internet than manufacturing and selling physical products. It is important to analyze how much is invested in producing and selling the information. The electronic trade of data allows firms to distribute information globally enjoying scale economies, which reduce unit costs and so make the product cheaper. This last aspect also boosts the demand for such information services.

- Finally, scale, flexibility, and speed of entry and exit are all critical when competing in a commodities market. In this type of market, firms must:

  o Enter at the right time. The firm must weigh the advantages of being a pioneer. It is not always worthwhile (e.g., before a price or standards war).

  o Seek substantial market share and exploit scale economies to produce at low cost.

  o Exit at the right time or change activities, before the business becomes unprofitable.

Information Technology as a Factor of Organizational Change

Nowadays, entrepreneurs are finding that ICT helps them create and manage their firms. Nevertheless, ICT's role in the firm has evolved over time along with developments in the technology. Firms' incorporation of ICT can be divided into three stages (Arjonilla & Medina, 2002), characterized by the technological advances and organizational changes experienced. The first stage runs from the 1960s to the mid-1970s. This stage saw the introduction of centralized computer systems and database systems in firms. The only objective was to automate and organize basic internal administrative tasks. The application of ICT in this stage had practically no influence on how work was done or the organization was structured.

The second stage began in the 1980s, with the advent of personal computers and local area networks. This is the stage when information technology began to modify the nature of the work and the structure of the organization. ICT allowed managers to flatten their organizations, which required fewer levels of managers responsible for transmitting information, instructions, and control reports. An effective use of databases required a reorganization of the functional barriers between departments. Cooperative software (groupware tools) produced important changes in how the organization's members interacted with each other.

The expansion of the Internet in the 1990s marks the third stage. ICT accelerated the transformation of organizations by eliminating the organizational barriers between companies. Internal and external activities became integrated, and firms connected better with their customers, suppliers, and other firms (Antonelli, 1992; Bradelley, Hausman & Nolan, 1993; Jarvenpaa & Ives, 1994; Kambil & Short, 1994; Lucas & Baroudi, 1994; Malone & Rockart, 1991).

The advances in ICT have been widely recognized as having a substantial impact on the organizational structure. But firms' use of the technologies has evolved over time. ICT's role ranges from passively supporting the firms' operations to a more active role redesigning organizational structures. Initially, the rudimentary systems of index cards and memos between offices allowed bureaucracies to develop, making it possible to coordinate and control the components of the organization (Yates, 1989; Yates & Orlikowski, 1992). Later, the telephone, telegraph, and mail systems enabled distributed organizational forms and interorganizational communications (Chandler, 1977; Pool, 1983). Organizational forms were designed to adapt to the needs of communication. For example, self-contained units were created to reduce environmental uncertainty (Galbraith, 1973; Thompson, 1967; Tushman & Nadler, 1978). Conversely, ICT was designed to adapt to the organizational forms in place. For example, workflow systems were developed to support the matrix organization (Fulk & DeSanctis, 1995).

Beniger (1986, 1990) argues that ICT and the organization are equivalent forms. ICT creates new options for organizational design; and the new organizational forms, in exchange, offer new opportunities for the design of technology. This is consequently a more active vision of ICT's role in organizational design. In fact, designing ICT and designing the organization have become the same task (Lucas & Baroudi, 1994).

In 1958, Leavit and Whistler (1958) wrote a controversial article predicting that the combination of management science and ICT would lead to a reduction in the number of middle managers and an increased decentralization of the organization. Since the publication of their article, numerous authors have studied the relation between ICT and organizational structure. Some support the thesis that firms should use ICT to centralize the decision-making process and consequently cut the number of middle managers (Whistler, 1970). Other researchers see the possibility of increased decentralization. They argue that ICT provides timely and relevant information that could enable decentralized decision-making and the delegation of power (Arjonilla & Medina, 2002). Nevertheless, there is general recognition that ICT is changing the way people work, the structure of their organizations, and indeed the structure of entire sectors (Neumann, 1994; Zuboff, 1988).

There is also consensus that ICT is improving the control and self-control of workers, which reduces the number of hierarchical levels needed and makes organizations less formalized (Daft, 1995; Drucker, 1990; García, 1998).

Firms can also use ICT to establish either a greater centralization or a greater decentralization, depending on management's preferences, improving coordination with offices, warehouses, and plants distributed around the world (García, 1998).

ICT influences the organizational structure via the firm's organizational design parameters, which, according to Mintzberg (1979), are: job design, design of the superstructure, design of the lateral linkages, and design of the decision-making system. With regard to job design, ICT can be used to reduce the vertical and horizontal specialization of jobs. Workers can then assume more self-control and their jobs become more creative, motivating, and multifunctional, making organizations more organic. All this occurs because ICT can assume the routine tasks that traditionally dictated a horizontal specialization of the jobs, a formalization of the task, and more bureaucratized structures. This new way of looking at the division of labor favors team work over the traditional individualist work typical in highly specialized jobs.

ICT also influences the design of the superstructure, in other words, the authority that defines the criteria for grouping the units. The reduced vertical specialization, together with the teamwork, cuts the number of managers required as well as the number of hierarchical levels. Another reason why fewer managers are required is that ICT can take on many of their communication, coordination, and control functions, as well as widening their span of control. All this leads to flatter organizations.

With regard to unit size, enriched jobs mean that fewer people are required for a given set of functions, so the units will be smaller.

According to Mintzberg (1979), organizations use lateral linkages to coordinate themselves. These elements are planning and control, which standardize the outputs, and linking mechanisms, which facilitate the necessary mutual adaptation when direct supervision and standardization are insufficient. ICT affects each and every one of these lateral linkages. In the case of planning, ICT improves analytical and design capacities, and increases access to information, making it easier to capture, prepare and handle information in flexible formats that are easy for the decision-makers to use (Arjonilla & Medina, 2002). With regard to control, ICT makes it easier to access the results being controlled, calculate more sophisticated indicators, detect the reasons for deviations from the expected results, conduct ad hoc control as continuously as is necessary, and control by exception. The new technologies also improve coordination and mutual adaptation by providing more effective communication systems.

Finally, the design of the decision-making system defines the level of centralization or decentralization in the decision-making. ICT can support centralization processes, by providing enhanced organizational transparency and giving top managers greater control capacity. But equally, it can also support decentralization processes, or at least selective decentralization, since information becomes rapidly accessible at any point in the organization. Thus, ICT allows organizations simultaneously to exploit the advantages of both centralization and decentralization. According to Daft (1995), ICT leads either to increased centralization or increased decentralization, depending on what management decides to do.

Organization of This Book

This book describes 14 real cases of firm creation involving information technologies.

The cases presented in this book are grouped in two parts: entrepreneurs and corporate entrepreneurship. The first section includes cases 1 to 10. These are firms created by physical people, either one individual or a group of partners, who began an entrepreneurial process after a particular trigger event, and this process eventually culminated in the creation of a new firm.

The second section runs from cases 11 to 14, which involved the creation of firms or development of projects by already existing firms. This type of entrepreneurial behavior is known as corporate entrepreneurship. This entrepreneurial behavior does not always end in the creation of a new firm. It often generates an innovative process that leads to new projects and entrepreneurial initiatives that remain in the organization. In other cases this entrepreneurial initiative does in fact end in the creation of a new firm that is distinctive from the original one.

A brief description of each of these cases follows:

Chapter I looks at the revolution created by FON. Its objective is to create a universal and unified Wi-Fi network that allows the members of its community to share not only bandwidth, but also experiences and ideas. FON is a virtual community of Wi-Fi users worldwide making use of spare bandwidth from customers' broadband connections. This enormous Wi-Fi network, practically free of charge, is a new project from Martin Varsavsky, an entrepreneur who has created seven innovative businesses in the past 20 years, nearly all in the high-tech sector.

Chapter II explains the creation process of Remote Internet-Based Supervision Systems, S.L. (RISS), a spin-off of the University of Figueres. It describes all the phases, from its creation to the present day, and the problems and challenges faced by the entrepreneurial team composed of academics and industry professionals. Starting in a lab shared by two computer engineers finishing their PhDs, their friendship later turned into a new science-based venture.

Chapter III analyzes the case of BookingFax. This firm acts as an intermediary between wholesalers of tourism offers and retailers, in other words, the travel agencies. The main objective of this case is to examine how information technologies have provided the basis for this firm-creation idea in the tourism sector. BookingFax has used information technologies to enter a market that had no apparent room for more intermediaries. The key to its success is that it creates value and offers cost savings to all the parties involved. Increasing the critical mass of users of its information systems will be crucial to reduce the threat of new entrants and imitation by the sector's wholesalers.

Chapter IV examines the case of ShiftMarket, an example of IT entrepreneurship in the health care sector. ShiftMarket is a startup company developing and promoting technology-driven solutions for staffing hard-to-fill hospital shifts. Started without angel or venture-capital funding, ShiftMarket negotiated a strong beginning by pursuing technology transfer in collaboration with a U.S. hospital rather than building from scratch. At the time of this case study, ShiftMarket is facing some key changes in the market, including new entrants and new alliances, and has begun evaluating what strategic adjustments may be warranted.

Chapter V analyzes different factors in the entrepreneurship process in a company that exploits the business opportunities offered by open-source software. Blobject connects opportunities for local development, use of open-source technologies, and new social trends in many consumers. The case shows the integration process of the different technologies, which connect through a digital infrastructure.

Chapter VI illustrates, in a holistic way, the different components that affect recognition of the technological venture opportunity—the environment, attributes that characterize technology-based entrepreneurs, the type of organization created, and the type of technology used to build the venture—and the interactions that take place between those components, which ultimately result in the market innovation. NTC, an emerging business, offers a clear example of how the entrepreneur, technology, and the accumulation of experience and knowledge interact to give rise to a technology-based venture.

Chapter VII focuses on the case of Waleli. Waleli is a high-tech company that uses the latest technological developments in wireless communication to bring innovations to the market. The firm aims to develop wireless communications to solve simple communication needs, both between people and between machines.

Chapter VIII is about Workcenter SGD. This company was born on the basis of following the same idea and services that Kinko's® created successfully in the United States, with nearly 1,300 retail stores devoted to reprographic services. Nevertheless, in 4 years the company went far ahead of the original idea, developing new technologies that helped manage its growth, control its operations, and reduce its costs.

Chapter IX describes the entrepreneurial process in the case of Europrint, a manufacturer of Printed Circuit Boards (PCBs), from 1991 until 2006. It offers an entrepreneurial perspective on the European PCB landscape, highlights the manufacturer's successful launch of a dot.com in the highly competitive B2B environment, and illustrates the manufacturer's transition to an e-business to break the product commodity cycle. As a final point, the case also reveals how the manufacturer's off-line and online business activities were consolidated and leveraged for maximum impact across Belgium, Hungary, and India.

Chapter X is about Cember.net. This online business networking start-up based in Turkey provides a platform through which its members can locate potential economic exchange partners. Cember.net differentiates its business model from those of major online competitors by incorporating ways of fostering social interactions and exchanges. Cember.net, with its continually growing membership base, presents networking opportunities to its members by advancing not only the quantity but also the quality of the relationships.

Chapter XI, which examines the firm Comitas Comunicaciones, is a clear example of corporate entrepreneurship in the telecommunications sector. This firm was created to offer telecommunications services in general, and telecommunications services applied to telemedicine in particular. Comitas Comunicaciones exploits the business opportunities opened up by market demands not currently being adequately attended to by other firms. The role of the incubator firm is particularly important in this case, since it provides the company with resources, capabilities, and technological knowledge.

The purpose of Chapter XII is to describe a real story where key issues related to the business expansion process of a young IT-based applied research center (ARC) are discussed. The start-up ARC develops visual and interactive communication technologies in the field of computer-aided graphics. The expansion of this IT-based organization was original—it involved the creation of two spin-offs during its infancy period. This chapter highlights the general concerns associated with knowledge management and the capacity of innovation that emerged during the business expansion process. These concerns can be classified in three main theoretical areas: entrepreneurship, interpreneurship, and intrapreneurship.

Chapter XIII analyzes how various stakeholders—a university, an innovation and technology transfer institute, and private and public client organizations—acting in concert, create multiple opportunities for the application of technology to real-world problems, and how some of those projects originate spin-offs. This chapter presents a real-life example of one such company, which develops software for mobile applications. It spun off from a project with a big cell-phone service provider 5 years ago, incubated for 3 years at the institute, and moved out in 2004. The authors draw on their experience in assisting the creation of 70 technology-based start-ups to provide practical recommendations and point out key success factors.

Chapter XIV concludes and focuses on a pharmaceutical distribution firm. This case explains the process of discovering and applying new information technology-based opportunities. It is a mature firm, which, during the course of the last few years, has been able to adopt information technologies in innovative ways thanks to the intrapreneurial spirit of its managers.

Editors,
Jose Aurelio Medina-Garrido, PhD
Salustiano Martinez-Fierro, PhD
Jose Ruiz-Navarro, PhD
Cadiz (Spain)
May 2007

References

Amit, R., & Zott, C. (2001). Value creation in e-business. *Strategic Management Journal, 22,* 493-520.

Armington, C., & Acs, Z. (2002). The determinants of regional variation in new firm formation. *Regional Studies, 36,* 33-45.

Autio, F., Kanerva, R., Kaila, M., & Kauranen, J. (1989). *New technology-based firms in Finland.* Helsinki: Sitra Publication Series.

Barney, J.B. (1991). Firm resources and sustained competitive advantage. *Journal of Management, 17*(1), 99-120.

Beniger, J.R. (1986). *The control revolution: Technological and economic origins of the information society.* Cambridge, MA: Harvard University Press.

Beniger, J.R. (1990). Conceptualizing information technology as organization, and vice versa. In J. Fulk & C. Steinfield (Eds.), *Organizations and communication technology.* Newbury Park, CA: SAGE Publications.

Bradelley, S.P., Hausman, J.A., & Nolan, R.L. (1993). *Globalization, technology and competition: The fusion of computers and telecommunications in the 1990s.* Boston: Harvard Business School Press.

Bruque, S., & Medina, J.A. (2002). The technology paradox: Characteristics, causes and implications for IT management. *International Journal of Information Technology, 8*(1), 75-94.

Cash, J.I., & Konsynski, B.R. (1985). IS redraws competitive boundaries. *Harvard Business Review, 63*(2), 134-142.

Chandler, A.D. (1977). *The visible hand: The managerial revolution in American business.* Cambridge, MA: Harvard University Press.

Clemons, E.K. (1986). Information systems for sustainable competitive advantage. *Information & Management, 11*(3), 131-136.

Clemons, E.K., & Row, M.C. (1991a). Sustaining IT advantage: The role of structural differences. *MIS Quarterly, 15*(3), 275-292.

Clemons, E.K., & Row, M.C. (1991b). Information technology at Rosenbluth travel: Competitive advantage in a rapidly growing service company. *Journal of Management Information Systems, 8*(2), 53-79.

Colombo, M.G., & Delmastro, M. (2001, May): Does Internet made a difference? *Small Business Economics, 16*(3), 177-190.

Daft, R.L. (1995). *Organizational theory and design.* West Publishing.

Davenport, T.H., De Long, D.W., & Beers, M.C. (1998). Proyectos exitosos de gestión del conocimiento. *Harvard Deusto Business Review, 85,* 4-19.

Donckels, R. (1989). *Tech versus common starters: Comparison by means of 32 case studies.* Brussels: Small Business Research Institute.

Drucker, P.F. (1990). *The new reality.* New York: Harper & Row.

Earle, N., & Keen, P. (2000). *From .com to .profit. Inventing business models that deliver value and profit.* San Francisco: Jossey-Bass, Inc.

Feeny, D., & Ives, B. (1990). In search of sustainability: Reaping long-term advantage from investments in information technology. *Journal of Management Information Systems, 7*(1), 27-46.

Fulk, J., & DeSanctis, G. (1995). Electronic communication and changing organizational forms. *Organization Science, 6*(4), 337-349.

Galbraith, J. (1973). *Designing complex organizations.* Reading, MA: Addison-Wesley.

García Calderón Díaz, L. (1998). *A PLS model of strategic networks and organizational performance: Based on environmental turbulence, information technology, and transaction costs.* Doctoral thesis, Instituto Tecnológico y de Estudios Superiores de Monterrey.

Garud, R., & Nayyar, P.R. (1994). Transformative capacity: Continual structuring by intertemporal technology transfer. *Strategic Management Journal, 15,* 365-385.

Hammer, M., & Champy, J. (1993). *Reengineering the corporation.* New York: Harper Business.

Jarvenpaa, S.L., & Ives, B. (1994). The global network organization of the future: Information management opportunities and challenges. *Journal of Management Information Systems, 10*(4), 25-57.

Jo, H., & Lee, J. (1996). The relationship between an entrepreneur's background and performance in a new venture. *Technovation, 16,* 161-171.

Kambil, A., & Short, J.E. (1994). Electronic integration and business network redesign: A roles-linkage perspective. *Journal of Management Information Systems, 10*(4), 59-83.

Kirchhoff, B., Armington, C., Hassa, I., & Newbert, S. (2002). The influence of R&D expedintures on new firm formation and ecnomic growth. Retrieved May 16, 2007, from http://njit.edu/old/News/Releases/finalreport_10_02_02.pdf

Leavit, H.J., & Whistler, T.L. (1958). Management in the 1980s. *Harvard Business Review, 36*(6), 41-48.

Licht, G., Nerlinger, E., & Berger, G. (1995). *Germany: NTBF literature review.* Mannheim, Germany: ZEW.

Loane, S. (2006). The role of the internet in the internationalisation of small and medium sized companies. *Journal International of Entrepreneurship, 3*(4), 263-277.

Lowendahl, B., & Revang, O. (1998). Challenges to existing strategy theory in a postindustrial society. *Strategic Management Journal, 19*, 755-773.

Lucas, H.C. Jr., & Baroudi, J. (1994). The role of information technology in organization design. *Journal of Management Information Systems, 10*(4), 9-23.

Mahmood, A., & Yu, C.M. (2005). E-entrepreneurship in knowledge economy: Implications for the Asian-Pacific economies. *The Business Review, 4*(1), 153-160.

Malone, T.W., & Rockart, J.F. (1991). Computers, networks, and the corporation. *Scientific American, 265*(3), 128-137.

Mata, F.J., Fuerst, W.L., & Barney, J.B. (1995). Information technology and sustained competitive advantage: A resource-based analysis. *MIS Quarterly, 19*(4), 487-506.

McFarlan, F.W. (1985). La tecnología de la información cambia el modo de competir. *Harvard Deusto Business Review, 22*(2), 43-50.

Mintzberg, H. (1979). *The structuring of organizations.* Englewood Cliffs, NJ: Prentice Hall.

Neumann, S. (1994). *Strategic information systems: Competition through information technologies.* Macmillan College Publication Company.

Nieto, M.J., & Fernández, Z. (2006). The role of information technology in corporate strategy of small and medium enterprises. *Journal International of Entrepreneurship, 3*(4), 151-262.

Nolan, R.L. (1981). Cómo comprender y controlar la evolución del proceso de datos. *Harvard Deusto Business Review, 1,* 5-18.

Nolan, R.L., & Gibson, C.F. (1974, January-February). Managing the four stages of EDP growth. *Harvard Deusto Business Review*, 76-91.

Nonaka, I., & Takeuchi, H. (1995). *The knowledge-creating company. How Japanese companies create the dynamics of innovation.* New York: Oxford University Press.

Osborne, A. (1987). Understanding entreprenuership. *Business Forum, 12*(4), 12-13.

Pool, I.D.S. (1983). *Forecasting the telephone: A retrospective assessment.* Norwood, NJ: Ablex.

Porter, M. (1985). *Competitive advantage.* New York: The Free Press.

Porter, M.E., & Millar, V.E. (1986). Cómo obtener ventajas competitivas por medio de la información. *Harvard Deusto Business Review, 25,* 3-20.

Powell, T.C., & Dent-Micallef, A. (1997). Information technology as competitive advantage: The role of human, business, and technology resources. *Strategic Management Journal, 18*(5), 375-405.

Rackoff, N., Wiseman, C., & Ullrich, W. (1985). IS is for competitive advantage: Implementation of a planning process. *MIS Quarterly, 9,* 285-294.

Reynolds, P., Bosma, N., Autio, E., Hunt, S., de Bono, N., Servais, I., et al. (2005). Global entrepreneurship monitor: Data collection, design, and implementation 1998-2003. *Small Business Economics, 24*(3).

Reynolds, P., Miller, B., & Maki, W. (1993). Regional characteristics affecting business volatility in the United States, 1980-1984. In C. Karlsson, B. Johannison, & D. Storey (Eds.), *Small business dynamics* (78-115). New York: Routledge.

Saxenian, A. (1999). *Silicon Valley's new immigrant entrepreneurs.* San Francisco: Public Policy Institute of California.

Schumpeter, P. (1942). *Capitalism, socialism, and democracy.* New York: Harper Torchbooks.

Shapiro, C., & Varian, H.R. (1999). *Information rules. A strategic guide to the network economy.* Boston: Harvard Business School Press.

Sinkovics, R.R., & Bell, J.D. (2006). Current perspectives on international entrepreneurship and the Internet. *Journal International of Entrepreneurship, 3,* 247-249.

Storey, D. (1994). *Understanding the small business sector.* New York: Routledge.

Thompson, J.D. (1967). *Organizations in action: Social science bases of administrative theory.* New York: McGraw-Hill.

Tushman, M., & Nadler, G. (1978). Information processing as an integrative concept in organizational design. *Academy of Management Review, 1,* 613-624.

Veciana, J. (1988, May-August). Empresario y proceso de creación de empresas. *Revista Económica de Cataluña, 8.*

Westhead, P., & Storey, J. (1994). *An assessment of firms located on and off science parks in the U.K.* London: HMSO.

Whistler, T.L. (1970). *The impact of computers on organizations.* New York: Praeger Publishers.

Yates, J. (1989). *Control through communication: The rise of system in American management*. Baltimore: Johns Hopkins University Press.

Yates, J., & Orlikowski, W. (1992). Genres of organizational communication: An approach to studying communication and media. *Academy of Management Review, 17,* 299-326.

Zuboff, S. (1988). *In the age of the smart machine: The future of work and power*. New York: Basic Books.

Endnote

[1]   For more information on the GEM project, see www.gem-consortium.org.

Acknowledgment

The editors would like to acknowledge the help of all those involved in the collation and review process of this book, without whose support the project could not have been satisfactorily completed. A further special note of thanks goes to all of the staff at IGI Global, whose contributions throughout the whole process from inception of the initial idea to final publication have been invaluable.

Deep appreciation and gratitude is due to Consejeria de Innovacion, Ciencia y Empresa (Junta de Andalucia), for its ongoing sponsorship in terms of financing.

Thanks goes to all those who provided constructive and comprehensive reviews.

Special thanks also go to the publishing team at IGI Global. In particular, to Kristin Roth, who continuously prodded via e-mail to keep the project on schedule.

In closing, we wish to thank all of the authors for their insight and excellent contributions to this book. We would also like to thank Frank Callan for his invaluable and professional collaboration in the edition of this book. Finally, this book would not have been possible without the ongoing professional support of Mehdi Khosrow-Pour, Renee Davies, Michele Rossi, and Kristin Roth at IGI Global.

Section I

Entrepreneurs

Section 1

Entrepreneurs

Chapter I

FON:
A Social Collaborative Technological Entrepreneurship

Alfonso Miguel Márquez-García, University of Jaén, Spain

María Teresa Garrido-Álvarez, University of Jaén, Spain

María del Carmen Moreno-Martos, University of Jaén, Spain

Abstract

FON is a revolution, or at least is defined as such on its Web page (http://en.fon. com) and the multiple posts that inundate the blogsphere. Its objective is to create a universal and unified Wi-Fi network that allows the members of its community to share not only bandwidth, but also experiences and ideals. FON is a virtual community of Wi-Fi users worldwide making use of spare bandwidth from customers' broadband connections. This enormous Wi-Fi network, practically free of charge, is the new project of Martin Varsavsky, an entrepreneur who in the past 20 years has created seven innovative businesses, nearly all in the high tech sector. The generalization of broadband connections and the development of Wi-Fi and WiMax wireless technologies will change the competitive landscape of the telecommunications sector, which will lead businesses to retool their business models, both with

relation to Internet and mobile telephones. With its visionary nature, FON is try-
ing to position itself in this new context and for this purpose has the financial and
strategic support of top companies such as Google, eBay, and Skype.

Background

In this chapter we present the new technological project of Martin Varsavsky, a natu-
ral-born and expert entrepreneur with previous national and international successful
initiatives. He is an enthusiastic entrepreneur who loves to bet on innovating projects
about which others only dare to think, accepting the risks derived from innovating
and proactive behaviors (Covin & Slevin, 1989; Lumpkin & Dess, 1996, 1997).

The creation of a firm is usually associated both with the detection of market opportunities or with the entrepreneur's survival needs. This case meets both motiva-
tions, although in a special way. As regards market opportunities, they are not only
detected but creatively constructed. As for the entrepreneur's survival needs, the
theme is not about economic satisfaction, but a vital need for a person who defines
himself as an entrepreneur and is able to project all his abilities towards being successful (McClelland, 1961) in each initiative he carries out.

As Drucker (1998) indicates, innovation is based on both creativity and ability
to associate a solution with a need and Martin declares that he creates innovative
companies to meet his personal needs. Varsavsky symbolizes the entrepreneur who
Schumpeter's (1911) early work established conceptually as innovator. According
to the literature, innovation becomes an important factor that characterizes entrepreneurial behavior (Covin & Slevin, 1989; Karagozoglu & Brown, 1988; Miller,
1983; Miller & Friesen, 1982; Zahra & Covin, 1995). Entrepreneurship contributes
to economic performance by introducing innovations, creating change (Audretsch,
1995), creating competition, and enhancing rivalry (Wong, Ho, & Autio, 2005).
That is what Varsavsky naturally does in his every day life.

Literature on entrepreneurship habitually differentiates between nascent and novice
entrepreneurs and habitual ones (Carter, 1999; Davidsson, Low, & Wright, 2001;
Westhead & Wright, 1999). The habitual entrepreneur sets up a series of businesses,
either in parallel (portfolio entrepreneurs) or in sequence (serial entrepreneurs);
therefore, we can talk about novice, serial, and portfolio entrepreneurs.

Varsavsky is a habitual entrepreneur, mainly a serial entrepreneur since his great
business projects have been sequentially made. Previous experience in the development of technological projects plays a prominent role in successful business opportunities recognition (Ardichivili, Cardonzo, & Sourav, 2003; Shane, 2000) in the
same field (Cooper, 1985; Roberts, 1972). However, empirical evidence confirms
that portfolio entrepreneurs have more diverse experiences and more resources

than either serial or novice entrepreneurs (Westhead, Ucbasaran, & Wright, 2003); therefore portfolio entrepreneurs appear to offer more attractive growth prospects than other entrepreneurs. Sometimes Martin Varsavsky also develops his main projects simultaneously with diversified investments in other sectors and firms; thus, he could be also considered a portfolio entrepreneur.

Varsavsky's recognized ability to create and develop innovating companies provides him with a smaller risk perception of his projects (Begley & Boyd, 1987) that he is able to transmit to his collaborators and the sector to involve them in his projects. In this case, according to Park (2005), we find the interaction of the elements that facilitate the entrepreneurial innovation process in high-tech start-ups: the founding entrepreneur, the knowledge and experience of the organization he builds around himself, and the technology.

This case aims to show the important role of habitual entrepreneurs in the process of identification and creation of new business opportunities in a global, technological, and increasingly competitive context (Ucbasaran, Wright, Westhead, & Busenitz, 2003). We also present an unusual case of social entrepreneur (Dees, 2001) and philanthropist. In addition, Varsavsky is a ground-breaking leader who knows how to project his vision of the project to his collaborators, how to attract the best professionals to jointly develop the business model, and how to motivate them to reach the highest performance levels. As a result, his businesses grow by the day. Also he has been able to transmit his enthusiasm for the project to some of the main companies of the technological sector that have become FON's financial partners.

It is a singular technological project that begins in Spain with international ambition and the aim of creating a universal and unified Wi-Fi network. From its inception and throughout its evolution, FON has faced technical, legal, and competitive challenges to make possible an idea about which many speak but nobody carries out anywhere in the world. The FON project does not represent a radical technological innovation because the technology already exists, and what is really relevant is Varsavsky's enterprising nature to get new forms of combining already existing resources (Amit, Glosten, & Muller, 1993; Zahra, Jennings, & Kuratko, 1999).

Another aim of this chapter is to illustrate the usefulness of using blogs as an instrument for supporting the creation and development of business projects. In this case, Varsavsky tells in his blog, which he calls the Blog of an entrepreneur, FON's process of creation and development, the challenges the firm faces, and the way it responds. The blog also provides stakeholders and the community communication with the firm, which generates new ideas that feed the innovation process.

An additional objective is to analyze the economic and financial viability of creating social technological ventures where everybody wins sharing. In this project, investments in infrastructure are not determining since FON uses already existing ones. FON has a business model based on collaboration both with suppliers and among clients. Without this collaborating community this project would not be possible.

Martin Varsavsky: The Journey of an Entrepreneur

In order to locate the beginnings of the FON business project reference needs to be made to its founder and promoter, Martin Varsavsky, who has an internationally acclaimed business background for having created seven businesses over the past 20 years, and especially for having led technological projects such as Jazztel (http://www.jazztel.com) or Ya.com (http://www.ya.com). Looking to better understand the entrepreneurial nature of the founder, it is worth going into his life history in order to try to find some of the reasons that help to explain his continuous creative entrepreneurial behavior and his tendency to develop projects in the realm of new technologies.

Born in Argentina and nationalized Spanish, he grew up in a family of intellectuals of Jewish origin that emigrated to the United States for political reasons when Martin was only 16 years of age. His father received a doctorate in astrophysics from Harvard and was a professor at the University of New York. At this same institution, Martin Varsavsky received a degree in Economics, and later obtained an MBA and a Masters in International Affairs from the University of Columbia. However, he directed his path toward the business world,[1] taking advantage of his entrepreneurial spirit fed by his personality: patient, persevering, tenacious, and not easily discouraged, which leads him to persist until he reaches a successful conclusion when believing in a project (Ganitsky & Sancho, 2002). He has a contagious vision and positive approach that inspires all who meet him, and he seeks the collaboration of those he considers valuable to the development of his projects as well as accepting criticism as an opportunity to learn and improve.

Martin Varsavsky declares himself to be a good entrepreneur but not a manager because he finds management boring. On numerous occasions he has declared that he likes to build an idea, a business. He loves to be an entrepreneur. He enjoys the moment of starting a business, he considers himself a visionary, able to detect business opportunities where others only see problems, has ground-breaking ideas, according to Schumpeter's (1934) creative destruction idea, and knows how to sell them. However, he prefers to seek managers much better qualified than he is to execute them, leaving operational decisions to them. Varsavsky says, "I will be the founder, the strategist, the shareholder, but not the CEO." He says he knows how to share benefits with his key employees,[2] delegate to the maximum (Oakey, 2003), and leave when necessary. His style as entrepreneur is far from normal, his personal availability and the importance that he gives to human resources in his businesses (he considers that he owes everything he has to his employees) give him an aura of a revolutionary businessman, which is also evident in the FON movement.

His enterprising character takes him to search for opportunities jointly with teams of professionals highly qualified and motivated by the personal vision that he stamps on his projects. He provides the idea but he tries to get many people, both internally within the organization and externally, to help him to develop it and to make it viable. A good example of this is the opening to clients, competitors, and so forth, as a means of getting information that allows him to improve as much the product as the business idea. As a result, his projects and companies are constantly highly innovative ones.

Varsavsky's business projects began in 1984, while studying at the university. He created Urban Capital Corporation, a company dedicated to the real estate business, which was one of the first promoters of the transformation of ruined and abandoned buildings in industrial areas of New York into the charming lofts that later characterized the urban development of the city. It is very illustrative of the tenacious character of Martin Varsavsky, the fact that he had to present the project for six months to more than 80 banks before obtaining the necessary financing for his business plan, because one after another rejected him, until finally he achieved success. In 1986, Varsavsky created Medicorp Sciences (http://www.medicorp.com), along with Argentinean scientists Claudio Cuello and the Nobel Prize winner for physiology and medicine in 1984, César Milstein. Medicorp Sciences is a biotechnology business based on the detection of opportunities around development of reagents to fight AIDS. However, the initiatives for which he is most renowned in the business world are related to information and communication technologies (ICT), computing, and the Internet.

Viatel (http://www.viatel.com), Varsavsky's third business, was founded in 1991, halfway between New York and London, and was initially dedicated to the delivery of call-back services for international calls as well as other data and voice telecommunications services. Today, Viatel provides companies of all sizes across Europe with a full range of managed voice and data communications services such as voice over IP, business broadband and DIA, private virtual networks and ethernet, managed hosting and co-location, and Internet security.

Since this project required him to spend a great deal of time in Europe, the Varsavsky family decided to move to Spain, a country with which Martin became acquainted thanks to Miguel Salís, a friend and fellow student at the University of New York. Since his move to Spain, his four latest, best known technological initiatives were developed: Jazztel, Ya.com, EinsteiNet AG, and FON.

In 1997, Varsavsky created Jazztel to take advantage of the liberalization of the Spanish telecommunications market planned to take place the following year. He declares that the fight against monopolies is one of his greatest business passions. His aspiration was to become the "first alternative local access provider of the Iberian Peninsula." He remained in this project until 2003, when Jazztel had a wide range of integrated services through its own fiber optic national network: metropolitan, provincial, interprovincial, international, and land to mobile voice services, value-added voice services, data and IP protocol services, and a wide range of Internet services, which range from simple access to hosting and e-commerce. Jazztel developed approximately 5,870 km of trunk network and 2,770 km of local access networks. It had more than 730,000 indirect access clients and more than 1,200,000 lines in service, of which 60% were businesses.

In October 1999, Varsavsky created Ya.com, the intelligent portal of Jazztel for the provision of Internet access. Creating it cost him 30 million euros and he sold it in September of the following year for 550 million euros to Deutsch Telecom AG, through its Internet affiliate T-Online International, one of the leading access and content providers in Europe, which acquired 100% of the company capital of Ya.com Internet Factory. Currently, Ya.com is consolidating its position as an operator within the Spanish market undertaking a high investment in the infrastructure of its own network.[3]

EINSTEINet AG was another of Varsavsky's fine accomplishments, founded in 1999 in Germany. This business distributed software applications through fiber optic broadband. Taking into account the possibility of the high speed interconnection offered by Internet, it was thought that if a fiber optic cable could reach an office and pass on much information and cheaply, it would not be necessary to have applications on hard disk, thus allowing PCs to be replaced by servers. However, this was the only business of Martin Varsavsky that failed; he did not find enough clients for his innovative applications service provider (ASP) technology. He lost 35 million euros because, according to Varsavsky, he was "too much" of a pioneer in the use of a technology that was before its time, but which is currently reemerging as a result of the enormous and unstoppable trend of maintaining programs and information on networks and less on the hard disk.

The latest initiative in which Varsavsky has become fully involved is FON. This business began at the end of 2005 with the objective of creating a universal Wi-Fi network access to the Internet, taking advantage of all that this technology offers. In order to better understand the idea of the FON movement, it is important to keep in mind the previous experiences with Jazztel and Ya.com. According to Varsavsky, "FON is telecommunications like Jazztel and a community like Ya.com. FON needs a network like that of Jazztel and a community like that of Ya.com. With FON, the fiber optic of Jazztel is filled and the communities of Ya.com become mobile."

Although he states that currently FON is everything in his life, he always finds enough time to get involved in other projects. Martin's business projects do not end with the case we are presenting. He is building the Moralejo wind farm. He has requested permits to construct a rural luxury hotel in Menorca. He financed an Argentinean airline called Southern Winds, which did not go well, and is now forming flyAZUL, a possible low-cost competitor for intercontinental flights. Other technological firms that have drawn Varsavsky's investing interest are Menéame, Technorati, Netvibes, Gspace, and so forth.

Varsavsky has assumed control of Proesa, a business holding with two brands: SyBilla (http://www.sybilla.es) and Jocomomola (http://www.jocomomola.com).

The entry into the world of feminine fashion and design was a new situation for this entrepreneur. The reason for his entry into the business was his conviction that the creation of value is increasingly in creativity and not in production and the business has the potential to sell all types of design products. The annual sales volume to the public of both brands is approximately 90 million euros. The main market is Japan, although the objective is to grow in other Asian countries and in Europe.

Varsavsky really thinks his firms are not only businesses but contributions to the community. In fact, his projects not only fit into the business realm, he is also a socially committed man who calls himself a "social entrepreneur," because he likes to "add my little grain of sand to create a better world." In this area he has promoted the Varsavsky Foundation (http://english.varsavskyfoundation.org), promoter of Educ.ar and Educarchile, and the Safe Democracy Foundation (http://english.safe-democracy.org).

The Varsavsky Foundation, created in May 2000, is a private and independent organization, financed entirely by Martin, which promotes education access for all children on Earth and encourages global dialogue and the exchange of opinions in order to live in a world of solidarity, peace, and democracy, a world in which all children can go to school, all schools have computers, and all computers become powerful tools for education. By means of this foundation, Varsavsky hopes to make reality all of the educational potential of technology and the Internet.

The Safe Democracy Foundation is an independent and non-profit Spanish organization that works to encourage the development of communication tools and opinions in order to obtain creative solutions to the problems facing democracy throughout the world.

The entrepreneurial work of Martin Varsavsky has been recognized on various occasions. Among the many awards he has received, those that deserve special mention include being finalist in the Businessman of the Year contest in New York City in 1995, European Businessman in Telecommunications of 1998, and European Businessman of the Year for ECTA in 1999. He was chosen Global Leader for Tomorrow by the World Economic Forum in Davos in 2000 and Spanish Businessman of the Year 2000 by iBest. He also earned the Columbia University Pickering Prize in 2003. In November of 2006, FON won the World Technology Award in the category "Communications Technology – Corporate." This award goes each year to the most innovative people and organizations in the science and technology world.

In the following section, we outline the current situation of information and communication technologies based on broadband, which is the development basis of the initiative we describe. Finally, we present a series of matters that may represent a challenge to the viability of this innovative project, which intends to create a world-wide community of broadband Internet access by sharing the Wi-Fi connections of users.

Setting the Stage

According to the "Worldwide Online Access 2004-2010" report of eMarketer, Internet access in the world reached a billion people in 2005. Of those, 845 million have regular Internet access (Mackin, 2006).

However, the development of a country is no longer measured by Internet penetration, but rather by the penetration of broadband. Recent studies carried out in the United States also indicate that those communities where the penetration of broadband is greater have an employment rate of one point higher than the rest; therefore, investing in broadband means investing in competitiveness, and to do so throughout the territory means investing in cohesion. The European Commission, in its first Annual Report on i2010, affirms that the countries within the European Union must revitalize their efforts to improve Internet access connections through broadband with the aim of obtaining the maximum benefit from information and communication technologies.[4]

The total number of broadband connections in the world is estimated at nearly 195 million at the end of 2005. We find differences by country among the most used access technologies (DSL, cable, etc.). Currently, the fastest download speed rates are in Japan and Korea through fiber to the home (FTTH) connections.

In Spain, the penetration of Internet home connections has continued to grow, in 2005 exceeding 5 million homes connected, 16% more than in 2004. The penetration of the total of homes of this key service in the development of the Information Society has thus passed from 30.8% to 33.9%, one in every three Spanish homes. The average for the UE-15 is 53%, compared to 46% in 2004, and over 70% in Holland, Luxembourg, and Sweden.[5]

The percentage of Spanish homes connected in relation to the number of homes that have some type of computer (8,059,547) reached 65.4%, which implies the current existence of a significant number of homes with computers able to connect to the Internet. In homes connected to the Internet, the desktop computer continues to be the most used terminal (89% of cases), although in recent years there is a growth tendency in the use of the portable computer (23%). The mobile telephone has lost penetration as the equipment for home Internet access.

With regard to the means of Internet connection, both telephone line and RDSI connections have decreased. The increase was produced primarily in ADSL connection and cable network, in greater measure in the former. From 2005 onward, the percentage of homes connected to the Internet by mobile telephones is estimated separately from other means, a ratio increasing to 4% in the second semester of the same year.

According to data from the Spanish National Institute of Statistics (http://www.ine. es)[6] corresponding to the second semester of 2005, only 22.5% of homes in Spain have broadband access (the average of UE-15 is 25%, although Holland reaches 54% and Belgium, Sweden, and Luxembourg approach 40%),[7] and for Internet connections at home, broadband represents 66.2% (53.4% ADSL and 13.1% cable). In 2005, there was an increase of nearly a million and a half of new homes with broadband connection with regards to 2004, which assumes that, for the first time, the majority of Internet connections at home are broadband ones.

In May of 2006, it was estimated that subscribers to the various broadband options approached 5.5 million, of which 1.2 million have cable access and the rest ADSL, according to the Spanish Telecommunications Market Commission.[8]

The majority of new broadband lines are established with wireless connection routers so that the Wi-Fi market is growing along with the number of Internet users. According to the second report of the Wireless Observatory, prepared by IWE-X (http://www.iwe-x.com), Spain currently has 15 million Internet users, of which 6 million are connected through a wireless network. Approximately 9 million are potential Wi-Fi users because they have equipment with wireless connection capabil-

Figure 1. Internet users and broadband households 2005 (Source: eMarketer, May 2006, retrieved April 28, 2007, from http://www.emarketer.com)

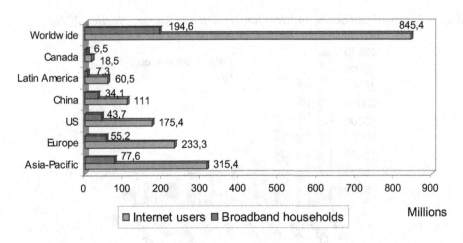

Note: eMarketer defines an Internet user as an individual aged 3+ who accesses the Internet at least once per month; a broadband household is a measure of only residential households with a broadband connection.

ity. The portable computer is not the only device used to connect to Wi-Fi; mobile phones, PDAs, video game consoles, desktop PCs, and so forth, also can or will be able to do so. The perspective for 2006 sets the number of internauts at 18 million and 8.5 million Wi-Fi users, and for 2007 they will be 11 million of a total of 22 million Internet users, which means that for the first time half of Internet users will be connected through Wi-Fi.

Figure 2. "Top Ten" broadband countries (Source: Mueller, 2006)

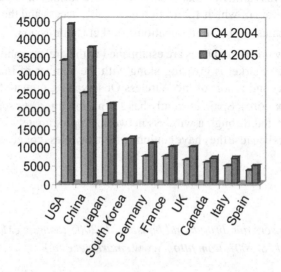

Figure 3. Broadband access in "Top Ten" countries (Source: Mueller, 2006)

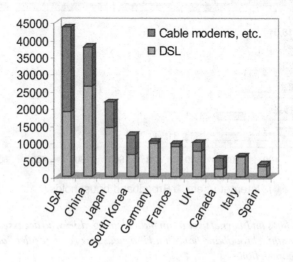

Figure 4. Homes connected to Internet (evolution) (Source: Spanish National Institute of Statistics, http://www.ine.es)

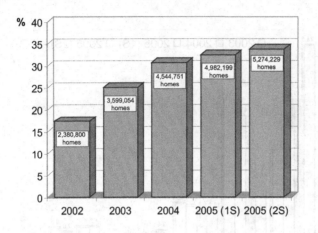

Approximately 80% of broadband line connections installed in Spain correspond to urban areas. There, one can choose from a multitude of offers for Internet access ranging from basic telephone network, ADSL, cable modem, Wi-Fi, and even PLC, while more than a million telephone subscribers do not have ADSL coverage.

According to the UE, the number of Wi-Fi users all over the world is 120 million people, of which 25 million are in Eastern Europe. The global figure may reach 500 million or even exceed that limit over the next three years, which would also facilitate the use of Wi-Fi for mobile telephones; therefore, access mobility to broadband and the Internet appear to be guaranteed by way of Wi-Fi and UMTS (3G).

The technological progress considered to have the greatest repercussion on the mobile and wireless communications business is the increase in available bandwidth in all types of access: cellular (UMTS with HSDPA and HSUPA, 802.20), wireless (Wi-Fi, WiMAX), and land (ADLS2+, VDSL, cable, etc.). Equally significant will be the migration of circuit switching networks to IP networks, and the increase in capacity and facilities of user terminals. The evolution of these technologies facilitates new business models.

In this scenario, Iber Band Exchange (http://www.iber-x.com) considers that 2006 will be the year for broadband through alternative networks such as Wi-Fi and "its big brother Wimax." Wireless technology, which allows Internet access at any time and place and without the need for cables, will bring about a true revolution, both for individual and business users.

There are already wireless access providers (WISP) and a broad experience in the creation of Wi-Fi spaces, both private (e.g., commercial hotspots) and public. Com-

Figure 5. Internet access forms at home (Source: Spanish National Institute of Statistics, http://www.ine.es)

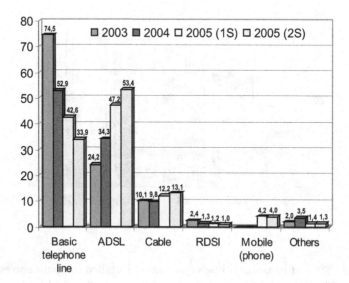

mercial initiatives tend to be oriented towards the itinerant professional market, offering connection possibilities in hotels, airports, train and bus stations, shopping centers, restaurants, coffee shops, and so forth, generating little islands of access in specific locations.

Public initiatives include the experiences of Wi-Fi cities that are proliferating all over the world, from those initiated in San Francisco and Philadelphia to many others in a great number of cities of all sizes. The objective of these Wi-Fi city projects is to create wireless broadband spaces through which, without charge, their citizens can connect to Internet and turn the Information Society into a reality by making use of the advantages that the ICT can offer. In this way, Internet access would not be limited to the home, workplaces, educational institutions, and spaces enabled for this purpose, but could be extended to any point of the city.

In some cases, these initiatives are planned to be offered as public services, as essential in the new society as public lighting was in the past. However, free Internet access through broadband would have a negative effect on Internet access providers (ISP), depriving them of clients in the regions in which the service is offered without charge.

Initially, the ISP business was based not only on Internet access, but also on connection time. Later, increased competition and technological evolution transformed the business model and connection time was no longer charged with the new "always on" access systems, so that income was linked to connection access. If in this new scenario access is obtained without charge, providers must link their profit to another factor that will allow them to stay in business. Speed, quality of service, and security are some of the factors considered to be potentially important for ISP business.

Therefore the projects related to the creation of local area Wi-Fi spaces, or even with a greater range, will facilitate the connection to broadband with a reduced speed (300 kbps), while those who desire greater speeds, greater reliability, and security in their connection will be able to request their own access with ISP or WISP.

Various initiatives have arisen as a result of expectations surrounding Wi-Fi technology development and its expansion, in the form of businesses, products, and services intended to take advantage of the possibilities derived from generalized broadband access. Thus, we find WISP that provide Internet access services with or without their own network, mobile telephones with Wi-Fi, GSM/Wi-Fi, UMTS/Wi-Fi and GSM/UMTS/Wi-Fi, which offer the possibility of lowering the cost of calls based on VoIP, and so forth.

Perhaps a good model of the commercial possibilities represented by wireless technology can be found in the project that Google is developing in some U.S. cities. Google offers free broadband Internet access in exchange for advertising. It has patented a system that describes changes in the appearance of the browser in the client device, when this is connected to a specific wireless access point, offering specific advertising related to the businesses near the geographic location of the user.

This "glocalization" initiative fits into the Web 2.0 movement, which positions the user as the central axis and attempts to develop useful applications, considering that the use of the Web is oriented towards interaction and the creation of social networks. Web 2.0 sites act more as meeting points, or user-depending Webs, than as traditional Webs. The Web 2.0 label is opening the door to projects based on the transformation of the user into supplier, editor, reviewer, judge, and jury.

This all gives way to a different project in the form of the FON initiative, overcoming the inconvenience of the reduced coverage of Wi-Fi technology to generate wide spaces with broadband access. All this through collaboration among users and a business model that is generating considerable interest in the blogsphere, with defenders and detractors of a project that Martin Varsavsky has been able to place in the center of the debate on the future not only of Internet access systems, but also of mobile telephones. Anyway, we can not forget the key role that public regulatory institutions play in this sector.

Case Description

What is FON?

The aim of this movement is to create a world Wi-Fi network among all ADSL users in the world, based on the idea of sharing connections, given that according to FON, broadband subscribers have excess capacity. Basically, FON is a bandwidth-sharing movement based on peer-to-peer principles. The idea is that if you are willing to share your bandwidth, that is, share the Wi-Fi access point for which you pay a subscription to a broadband provider, you can tap into a global network of users (called "foneros") who are also willing to share theirs. As Varsavsky says, "You pay for your bandwidth at home and can enjoy bandwidth wherever there are other foneros" or, if you prefer, you can also charge for your extra bandwidth.

Thus, the innovation of FON lies in the creation of a unique software interface, so that access is shared through a single network: the FON network. This software can be installed in a Wi-Fi router, converting that router into a FON hotspot. It can then be used to access the Internet and other data services by the connection owner and others, as allowed by FON. It is important to emphasize that FON not only allows the sharing of Internet access using ADSL, but also works with cable.

There are two ways in order to become a fonero: either buy a FON-ready wireless router or download a piece of Linux-based software that will rewrite the code of the existing router, adding access and billing layers and sharing the not-used bandwidth with the FON network, with a minimum of 512 Kb. The FON-ready wireless router is called La Fonera[9] and the second version, which will be called FON Liberator, has more memory and it is designed according to a full Bittorrent concept.

The FON router is considered a social router. That is because when the foneros activate their La Fonera, they become part of the FON Community. It is also a social router because the foneros can personalize the page that other foneros see when they log on to their FON Access Point; therefore, they can tell people a bit about themselves or their local area. La Fonera is partially financed by FON initially. In return, FON asks anybody buying La Fonera to take the Fonero Promise. This means they promise to be nice and activate their FON social router to share their WiFi, or to return the router to FON or give it to somebody else who can share instead.

FON's operation involves the existence of three types of users: as a Linus,[10] you allow any other fonero to use your bandwidth and in return can access that of anyone else in the network for free. As a Bill,[11] you sell bandwidth from your hotspot to a third category of users, the Aliens, who are not part of the network, and you also must pay to use somebody else's hotspot. As an Alien, you do not have bandwidth to share and you connect to the FON network paying economical rates (3€/day).[12] Says Varsavsky, "with this rate, we become the EasyJet (low-cost airline) of Wi-Fi."

The business is based on expected income for services offered to Bill and Alien users. The project begins with the existence only of Linus users who share their bandwidth and, in exchange, can connect at all access points of the FON Community. From June 2006, the Bills are receiving income generated by the Aliens for connecting through them (50%), being able to see at all times who is connecting to their router, how long they do so, and how much money they have earned selling access to the FON Community. Also, with this income, FON will install Wi-Fi access points in those places where there are fewer users to guarantee the extent of the service. However, the exact business model is still being fine-tuned day by day.

In addition to being a business project, the social nature of the FON movement is evident in the significant role that it gives to institutions, whether public, private, associations, political parties, universities, and so forth. A specific plan is being developed to provide Wi-Fi equipment without charge to all Universities that request it, in order to turn them into fonero Universities, with access accounts for all their staff and students.

Development of the Idea

The project was launched in November 2005, but the idea began to take form in July 2004 and, initially, was defined as an international project based on providing telephony and Internet access through its own WiMax infrastructure. Finally, FON abandoned the idea of selling Wi-Fi telephones, considering that this market was already covered by other businesses such as Peoplecall, and focussed on Internet access. According to Martin Varsavsky "mobile operators have failed in their attempt to offer mobile Internet" and with FON the intention is to stand up to UMTS and its high fees, especially in Europe and, in Spain in particular, where the mobile oligopoly generates untenable fees that, in general, duplicate the American ones.

Although the project was created in Spain with the objective of converting it into a Wi-Fi country, FON is a global project. In fact, most current users are from other countries and the scope has expanded to the entire world to create a universal and unified Wi-Fi network. For now, the business is said to have more than 110,000 worldwide registered foneros[13] who share their Internet access on a trial basis, in the process of buying their router or downloading the software, if they have compatible equipment. But this figure is changing continually, since the number of new foneros is growing exponentially. The business operates with Linus and Bill users but, obviously, the business is based on the Aliens, who must represent a sufficiently high number, given that the income they generate is needed for investments and to compensate ISP.

The current objective is to attain a million access points (users) in 2010. For this purpose, it is seeking entrepreneurs to lead growth in each country it is present in (currently more than 140 countries and Web sites translated into 11 languages). These affiliates are spread over the United States, the United Kingdom, and France; the list of countries where the "fonero leaders" obtain greater penetration each day grows continually, almost by the hour: Germany, Italy, China, Japan, Korea, Argentina, Sweden, Ireland, Holland, and so forth.

Varsavsky has personally invested 700,000 euros in the project. FON does not accept investments from small shareholders since according to Martin it is a highest risk project. He has attained great success for FON by obtaining the support, not only financial but mainly industrial, of Google, eBay, and Skype, as well as the two largest venture capital companies of Silicon Valley, Index Ventures and Sequoia Capital.[14] The global financing injection, according to what has been made public, is 18 million euros and it will be used to develop the software necessary for the connection to the network and international expansion and marketing of this world broadband Wi-Fi network project, since FON is not a conventional telecommunications company requiring major investments in network infrastructure. The network already exists and the business is based on its owners joining and sharing, as well as others paying for it. The difference to other Wi-Fi networks is that the fee will be much lower.

Although FON has not revealed in what percentage Google, eBay, and Skype participate, a good indication of the degree of their involvement in the project is the fact that FON was chosen by Google to become its first investment in a start-up company outside the United States. The intense relationship between both has led FON to buy the popular Firefox extension GSpace from Google. GSpace allows users to treat their GMail accounts as an online file storage locker. On the other hand, the important economic contribution made by Skype to the FON project justifies the presence of Niklas Zennstrom, CEO and founder of Skype, to the board of FON, since for Skype, collaboration with FON allows it to extend its commercial scope to all Wi-Fi connected devices, setting Skype in a privileged place to compete in the market of mobile IP telephony. In addition, Zennstrom and Varsavsky have not only great personal similarities, but their enterprising trajectories are also similar and both have a business philosophy based on sharing and making the most of the communication possibilities that IT offers. Also at the Board of FON we find Danny Rimer from Index Ventures and Mike Volpi from Sequoia Capital.

FON's Management Team

According to Kakati (2003), a diversified management team combining both managerial and technical skills contributes to successful ventures. The initial FON team was therefore made up of about twenty "star professionals" of considerable prestige in the telecommunications sector.[15] Currently, FON's human team is made up of 87 employees from all over the world, with many open selection processes.[16] Fon is directed by Martin and his management team, including a CFO, COO, International Business Developer, European Business Developer, and Asian Business Developer. Under these positions we find country managers and logistics and marketing directors. Further, there are a number of advisers and an International Team (see Appendix).

José Antonio Arribas is the FON's technical director. Jose Antonio has been an integral part of the development of the Internet in Spain over the last 10 years. For the past 5 years, he acted as Ya.com's Technical Director. Previously, he had worked in Retevisión as head of the Systems Department during the launch of the Alehop portal. Jose Antonio began his professional career in 1996 at Servicom S.A., one of Spain's first ISP.

Diego Cabezudo is the FON's vice president of operations. Diego was formerly strategy manager at O2 in Ireland, where he was, among others, the Business Sponsor leading the launch of the 3G network and was responsible for the first commercial WiFi hotspots in Ireland. He has also worked for a cable operator (TeleCable) in technical, marketing, and sales roles and in DMR/Fujitsu Consulting.

Antonio Fuentes is the FON's CFO. Formerly COO and the controller of Jazztel, and general manager of the investment holding company, Jazzya. He has extensive experience in the mobile and fixed telecommunications industry mainly in the financial areas, both in Spain and abroad, USA and UK.

Faisal Galaria is the FON's vice president of business development. Faisal has over 10 years of international experience in the telecoms and Internet industries. He joins from Skype where he was the European business development director and led the global online business development team. Previously, Faisal was one of the authors of Ofcom's Strategic Review of Telecommunications and spent a number of years in strategy consulting with Arthur Andersen and Cluster Consulting where he specialized in supporting many of the world's largest telecoms and Internet companies formulating M&A and growth strategies.

Robert Lang is leading the European Business Development for FON in Europe. Robert was founder and CEO of Germany's largest WiFi operator: WLAN AG was sold to Swisscom Group in 2003 and renamed as Swisscom Eurospot and is the current leader in the European hotel Internet access market. Before that, Robert was vice president of business development and finance for iobox Germany, a subsidiary of a Finnish Mobile Entertainment startup. It was sold in 2000 for 230M Euros to the Telefonica-Group and became one of the largest mobile entertainment portals in Germany with 1.8M users. He began his career as a consultant and worked for LEK Consulting in London, Paris, Munich and Australia.

Alexander Puregger is regional manager for FON Asia. Before joining FON, Alex worked for more than 8 years as strategy consultant for Booz Allen Hamilton (BAH). At BAH he focused mostly on strategic projects in the area of fixed/mobile telecommunications and media. Alex helped establish the BAH office in Vienna, Austria (which grew from 4 to more than 25 employees within 5 years) and recently led BAH's telecommunications team in Madrid, Spain. Alexander has worked in Europe, Asia, and the Middle East, and is fluent in four languages.

Antonio Saez is the CEO of FON Spain. From 1999-2004, Antonio was COO and board member of Ya.com. Previously, he worked for Telefónica as Telefónica Services and content administrator for the Internet which resulted in the launching of Terra. Antonio has also worked as marketing and sales director for Spain at IDG Communications, a United States multinational leader in IT publications.

So, we find that FON's team is made up of professionals with recognized prestige and experience in the technological sector who sometimes are also international entrepreneurs. Each one contributes to FON both his wide experience and his worldwide level network of contacts obtained throughout his professional trajectory.

FON's Management Style

The FON management style engages in the practices that its entrepreneur, Varsavsky, implements in any of his business projects and in which we find a series of factors in common, that result in highly innovative organizations: he likes to create organizations that are less hierarchical, rather flat, and with few organizational levels, delegating as much as possible, decentralizing the decision making at different levels, clearly communicating the strategic idea of the business, and leaving operational decisions to highly talented professional teams who Martin works to identify and select, not always through conventional channels (e.g., the signing of Brainslayer, the best hacker in the world, on firmware issues). His ability to sign up executives from competitors and other sectors is well known, as well as his ability to turn his critics into FON's supporters, which has happened with his main detractor, Ricardo Galli.

Martin admits to managing people in the fonero style, which is nothing but the Varsavsky style: "FON trusts its team to manage the objectives with little supervision from FON. The business is managed in the fonero style, in which I give ideas rather than directives or orders. The same occurs with the offices in France, Germany, Italy, United States, China, Japan, Korea, Argentina, Sweden, Ireland, and Holland; the fonero leaders test initiatives and decide whether they work." FON give them the freedom to explore opportunities in each market.

Martin is the driving force, inspiring the work force through his vision. He is very good at inspiring his employees to follow his lead. FON does not need a large staff. People get involved in the business and see it as their "baby." Martin is very good at motivating his staff and getting everyone involved and passionate. There are objective-based remunerative models which achieve more competitiveness; furthermore, there is a stock option plan for the employees. Martin admits that his employees want to make money, but this is not their primary target. They work for FON because they love the Internet and the idea of being an essential part of such a spectacular project.

Communication is direct at FON through Skype, e-mail (everyone is on-line 24/7 through their Blackberrys), and meetings to keep everyone up to date on the latest developments. Furthermore, statistics of progress are sent out on a daily and weekly basis.

Martin is very direct and demands that his employees do their job and reach their objectives. While others disappoint, he finds opportunities. In fact, he is very good at seizing opportunities and along the project development necessary changes are made to make the most of them as they arise, so the ideas that could benefit the success of FON will be implemented using a flexible approach.

The development of the business is greatly influenced by his vision of the Internet as a tool for communication, debate, and learning. For Martin Varsavsky, Internet is a way of life. He not only creates Internet businesses, but also shares his ideas over the Internet, communicates with his employees over the Internet, and in general he considers that the Internet is the best tool for improving democracy. For this entrepreneur, the Internet allows one to compare opinions, become informed, feed creativity, and learn to be critical. Martin is hyperactive using e-mail and that results in what a partner calls "all time productivity". It requires turning time into fractal time to find how to read and to answer e-mails, SMS, and to make fast decisions.

Taking advantage of "viral marketing" within the Web, the breadth of the project is growing exponentially day by day, thanks to the combination of three elements: a great idea, the power of communication through a blog, and the opening of the project to individual participation. This communication strategy means FON does not need to spend on advertising.

Confidentiality is not his style and Martin shares his ideas with internauts through the FON blog and his personal blog, informing them in detail—almost daily—about the development of the project, taking their suggestions and responding to the comments they make. By doing so, we can all be witnesses, almost directly, of the birth of the business and participate actively in this collaborative entrepreneurial experience through blogs, which is demonstrating a capacity not only to communicate, but also to unite interests and truly carry out a common project. There are few companies that actually allow clients, competitors, and so forth, to follow the progress of the company in real time. In addition to using blogs extensively as a reflection of the implementation of a Web 2.0 philosophy, Varsavsky also views FON as the Web 2.0 concept transferred to infrastructure.

Evidence of Martin's conviction of the need and usefulness of collaboration to develop any project is especially visible in the FON Community, in which each member becomes both a creator and beneficiary of the business, an aspect that contributes to strengthening its open and democratic nature.

FON is both an innovation and a source of innovations, first because it makes the most of an opportunity to satisfy a latent need of users to be able to have broadband access everywhere in the world, and second, due to its configuration and style of management.

Constantly changing technological environment is an inexhaustible source of innovation opportunities. Varsavsky is able to anticipate innovative alternatives identifying his own unsatisfied needs as an intensive IT user. For developing these projects he hires highly qualified people. Their wide experience in the sector and professional trajectories in prestigious IT companies make them suitable to collaborate with him to make real his ideas. We can find evidence that market innovation in the field of high-tech start-ups is a result of the interactive combination of the three components of the entrepreneurial process: people, technology, and environment (Park, 2005).

In order to achieve an innovation success, it is not enough to have the technical resources, nor to count on the necessary knowledge and competences to manage the process, but what is essential is to have an organization adapted to the level and specific features of the technological system and the specific team.

FON is organizationally shaped and managed to generate continuous innovation possibilities which arise as the project is developed. This is possible thanks to several factors that appear jointly and synergically: collaborators' entrepreneurship and exceptional technical qualities, along with Martin Varsavsky's enterprising ability; his extraordinary ability to inspire his partners with the motivation to contribute all to the project; his direct and open management style, decentralizing the decision making in those qualified collaborators in each area of decision; and the use of flexible and flat organizational structures to foster constant communication among all members of the team, partners, suppliers and anybody who wants to give ideas for the project development. We can find in this case the interaction of the four main factors that Gartner (1985) identifies in the process of entrepreneurship.

Current Challenges Facing the Organization

Like prior Varsavsky's initiatives, FON also arose from a market failure. Wi-Fi technology does allow a connection to Internet without cables, but its range is not wide enough; thus, these zones are connection islands and there is no wide Wi-Fi network to ensure a permanent connection anywhere. FON is an international grass-roots attempt, initiated in Spain, to reduce the main Wi-Fi weakness: spotty access. FON leads us to suppress the paradox that Wi-Fi networks exist everywhere, but each person only has it for himself.

Today it is believed that in a short time we will see, on a daily basis, people walking through cities connecting their portables to the Internet at any time or talking on their mobile Wi-Fi telephone with a flat fee, using the new digital cameras that send photos by Wi-Fi, or connecting their video game console anywhere. The growing tendency towards globalization and the improvement of transportation will favor the mobility derived from tourism and work mobility, generating demands for connection in places other than the home or usual workplace.

On the other hand, technological possibilities allow people access to an increasingly superior bandwidth at an ever lower cost, with the resulting oversizing of resources possessed, which means that the incentive to join the FON initiative may increase. The growing tendency to use the Internet to share applications and store information without the need to have them on a PC should be kept in mind.

These environment evolution perspectives represent an opportunity for the consolidation of the FON project. However, despite the above opportunities, the FON Community is facing a series of challenges to which it must provide solutions so that the challenges do not threaten future success possibilities.

Legal Challenges

The regulatory uncertainty in some countries in the realm of telecommunications represents a significant challenge for all businesses that intend to develop innovative business models, as is the case of FON. In this sense, public administrations should create the necessary conditions to guarantee a favorable legal environment for the development of initiatives allowing citizens to enjoy the advantages derived from ICT. Therefore, FON considers that the Spanish Telecommunications Market Commission must be "pro consumer" and pose no obstacles to users benefiting from the increased competition that this type of project bring to the sector, offering better services and prices.

The legal possibilities of sharing ADSL are restricted by some national legislation, so that in certain countries it is not legal to share ADSL connections since the providers forbid it expressly in their contracts or the public authorities hinder it. But, Varsavsky is convinced that ISP will change their mind once they realize the potential opportunity of obtaining synergies thanks to this initiative.

FON does not intend to create a network where everything is free, rather it seeks to create a network between those who already pay for their Internet access, and the others who wish to use it. According to FON, telecommunications operators would be protected, selling even more Internet access than before, since to enter the FON Community one must offer an access point, and these will continue to be sold by the ISP. Also FON will offer them part of the income collected from the Aliens. Varsavsky does not intend to take advantage of infrastructures created by others either. In FON it is not a matter of avoiding investment, but the fact is that the network already exists. It is a matter of investing in the improvement and maintenance of software and equipment. Another incentive for ISP to reach agreements with FON is the possibility of becoming mobile operators so that they can offer their clients the same as they are offering now, ADSL and Wi-Fi at home, but also in any other part of the world, and they can also receive a part of the income derived from it, at no additional cost to them.

However, as long as the prohibition persists, it may pose an obstacle for the project, legally impeding the users from sharing bandwidth. In any case, FON does have an option: to become a provider of Wi-Fi ADSL itself, granting their clients authorization to share their Wi-Fi. Although FON has an ISP licence from the Spanish Telecommunications Market Commission, some analysts question the economic viability of this alternative, since it lacks its own network and FON has clearly declared that it is not its business.

The most probable alternative, as has occurred in other countries (Sweden, France, etc.), appears to be to reach agreements with other ISP, when they become convinced, as FON affirms, that it would not damage their business but could even provide additional competitive advantages. Varsavsky has stated that his strategy is to negotiate with ISP and to increase their sales. "My heart is with the people who invest in networks. We understand each other when sharing the income." This has been recognized by numerous world ISPs with whom FON has signed agreements to sell ADSL with FON inside. The first was established with Glocalnet, the second Swedish ISP and principal competitor in ADSL of Telia Sonera, the primary telecommunications operator in the Nordic countries. There is also an agreement with Labs2, principal national fiber optic competitor of Telia Sonera. The agreement is incredibly simple: FON gives it the exclusive to sell ADSL with FON inside to Glocalnet, and the exclusive to sell it with fiber to Labs2, and these businesses accept that in all of their sales with Wi-Fi they will use the FON software.

Later, in April 2006, an agreement was reached with the French ISP Neuf Cegetel (http://www.cegetel.fr/), one of the primary access providers in France, with more than 1.2 million ADSL clients. The users of this company will have the FON software on their routers, so that they will be able to become FON points. In France, in contrast to what is occurring in Spain, for example, broadband services come with Wi-Fi and with a box that is the property of the operator and in which new characteristics and functions can be included. Neuf can also increase the bandwidth of its clients and flash them the FON software from their central offices, so that they can all become Neuf/FON access points and enjoy free roaming. Also, Neuf will soon offer Wi-Fi telephones and its clients will be able to make calls free or at very low cost in the majority of cities in France.

Similar negotiations are taking place in Germany, the United Kingdom, Israel, and many more countries. In Spain, a collaboration agreement has been signed with

Jazztel[17] to study the commercial possibilities of the services the latter offers, using the infrastructures of Jazztel. If this agreement prospers, Jazztel would become the "first Spanish fonero ISP" and both companies will develop an Internet access product to allow Jazztel clients to join the FON Community. In fact, on its blog, FON encourages Internet access with Jazztel, since they have the fastest ADSL connections of the Spanish market with the ADSL2+ product, up to 20 Megas. In this way, becoming part of the FON Community will not diminish the connection quality of the foneros due to sharing.

Technical and Security Challenges

Existing operators doubt the ability to maintain a sufficient level of quality in a free network by charging the Aliens for it. The reduced Wi-Fi range and coverage, until the WiMax technology is developed, make it difficult to ensure coverage, provide quality solutions to the problems of continuous interconnection and roaming, levels of interference, client authentication, and so forth, so they could be unlikely to be willing to pay for the service.

The FON investment plan takes into account the way to meet these challenges; therefore, FON is giving La Fonera for free to increase its coverage. Also, when WiMax technology is commercially available FON is intending to offer its foneros a change from the Wi-Fi router to the WiMax router, and thus the first WiMax network will be generated from one day to the next to make the continuous wireless network viable.

Another challenge is that connection speed would be reduced as a result of sharing bandwidth, mainly for users of P2P exchange networks. However, the fact that most users often use no more than a minimal percentage of the contracted bandwidth means this challenge is not a limitation for users to join the FON movement, especially given the progressive increase of the available bandwidth to connect to Internet offered by the ISP. Anyway, each fonero can choose the amount of bandwidth the fonero wants to share.

An additional challenge arose in relation to the need of setting the existing routers to join the FON community. Many ISPs did not guarantee the routers provided to their users if they rewrote the codes, which is required in order to download the software that converts them into foneros. To resolve this situation, Varsavsky recommends the acquisition of a totally compatible router designed by FON, La Fonera, in order to become a fonero immediately and without problems.

The enormous challenge of developing systems that sufficiently guarantee security when sharing a connection has arisen in order to ensure that no one can copy anyone's data when connecting to an open network, or that users will not be held responsible for any and all illegal activities undertaken through their connection.

FON discourages any inappropriate use of the connection by making sure that each user of the FON Community has registered and is identifiable by a username and password. In addition, each user can always know who is connected to the router, and from where. Although total security does not exist, FON stresses its solution as the safest of all viable Wi-Fi sharing projects. La Fonera offers two wireless network signals (SSIDs), a private and a public one. The private signal is encrypted and offers complete privacy. The public signal is accessible to foneros only. This signal is the one that turns each broadband connection into a FON Access Point.

Although the blogsphere emphasizes the need to specify security aspects in more detail, these security challenges are not exclusive to FON; they also affect the sector and the technology. Panda Software has carried out "wardriving" tests at an international level and the results show that nearly 60% of the networks lack any type of protection (Panda Software, 2006). Also, the investigation demonstrates the security deficiencies presented by the WEP (wired equivalent privacy) protocol, the most commonly used in Wi-Fi environments,[18] as well as the reasonable reliability of other more current systems, such as WPA or WPA-PSK.

Commercial Challenges

Another challenge for FON includes the need to reach a sufficient critical mass of those interested in connecting to it, as well as a sufficiently high number of users willing to pay as Aliens. For some, the viability of this business may seem uncertain when it must supply the equipment, invest in software, and pay the ISP with income based on a still undefined number of clients who would pay three euros a day. In an extreme situation where all users were Linus, according to Varsavsky there would not be business possibilities and FON would be a great NGO, although he thinks that perhaps it could be possible to make money with advertising.

In order to increase the growth of the FON Community, the company is subsidizing partially and even giving La Fonera. FON is also using a communication strategy through its blog in which it shows the exponential foneros growth that foster new users membership to a revolutionary social project based on ideas such as community and sharing. Also, work is being undertaken on the concept of Super Bills. They are entrepreneurs who operate in neighborhoods connecting access points and charge from many points. FON wishes to work with Super Bills, because it believes that the Bill spirit is necessary to create the Community. The model of FON users is not inflexible, and it is intended that, at least twice a year, the foneros will be allowed to move from being Linus to being Bill, if they want to earn some money, or from being Bill to being Linus, if they wish to travel.

For FON, the usefulness of having Linus foneros in isolated regions would be reduced, since they would have the possibility of access to Wi-Fi in other areas when they travel, while the bandwidth that they share in their home region would predictably be little used due to the low number of itinerant users in these peripheral and/or isolated residential areas. For the Bills situated in these same areas, the possibilities of making membership in FON profitable would be low, due to the few itinerant Aliens in the peripheral and/or isolated residential areas. A possible solution could come from the commercial development of Wi-Max routers.

However, these threats would depend on the enthusiasm that the Wi-Fi users show towards the FON movement in the future. At the moment, new memberships appear to predict exponential growth in users. According to Varsavsky one important issue that attracts people to FON is its global scope. Although currently FON loses 0'5 million euros monthly, Varsavsky hopes that the company will make a profit in 2008. The financial support of Google, eBay, and Skype, as well as of the more prestigious technological capital risk funds from Silicon Valley, not only provides scope for action until getting profits, but grants a strategic backup contributing to the project credibility.

Competitors

From the beginning, the FON project has had strong business and institutional competitors. Along with the collaborative model of FON, there are different kinds of Wi-Fi networks with regard to their financing and management models: solidarity networks, open municipal networks, alliances between public and private institutions, networks financed with publicity, citizen cooperatives, commercial network, and so forth.

The idea of sharing ADSL is not new. FON is not alone in the initiative of creating a community of access to broadband through sharing Wi-Fi. Numerous initiatives (hotspots, public authorities, and so forth) and businesses are working in many countries with a similar focus, such as Wibiki (www.wibiki.com/), UnitedWi-Fi, ShareMyWiFi (http://www.sharemywifi.com/), and Air Bites (http://www.air-bites.com/), although from different perspectives.

However, for FON, the current proposals for shared Wi-Fi are doomed to failure, both free and paid. The first, because everyone wants to use it and no one contributes; the second, because it is very expensive. According to FON, its proposal is reasonable: free access for Linus foneros and three euros per day for Aliens, who do not share, and for Bills who charge to share, and must pay to access. It is inexpensive enough to stimulate frequent use, for example, among tourists who visit us or workers who travel, but not so cheap that it is not worth giving up an ISP to permanently use a Linus' Wi-Fi.

Some free and solidarity initiatives to share Wi-Fi face the challenge of being efficiently managed but without resources and, as a result, have even greater problems of security, legality, and service quality. For example, SharemyWi-Fi.com is a free tool and a non-profit organization, so that the users of any operator can share Wi-Fi through a database that puts users into contact privately with others who are willing to share their connections. Using Google Earth, one may get graphic indications of the points where one may connect and register a request where one wishes to connect.

The major ISPs have invested in creating networks distributed in cities, hotels, restaurants, airports, stations, and so forth, and charge for their use. In Spain, Telefónica stands out, with over 2,000 access points, and Kubiwireless, a Vodafone's partner, with 250 access points. The main manufacturer of processors (Intel), an Internet search engine (Lycos), and a Spanish operator (Telefónica) have developed a free application (Sniffer) that enables the nearest hotposts to be identified, allowing a search for free providers or hotspots and payment access points. It appears that the focus of these hotspots is mainly towards the business traveller. Compared to them, FON has a more residential orientation, so that it may even complement these more professional networks. In any case, they cover very similar needs, and to compete with them, FON offers better prices. Besides, in the face of the fragmented character of the different existing initiatives, FON is the only sustainable project for creating a Wi-Fi network at a world level.

Many ISPs are carrying out initiatives to share their ADSL Wi-Fi areas, with the goal of permitting their clients to use the services of Wi-Fi access, irrespective of the company with which they are working. This is the case of the recent alliance between Telefónica, Portugal Telecom, and Telecom Italy, which other European telecommunications operators may join. Some interpret these initiatives as an attempt to be compared to the huge FON movement.

On the other hand, since providing free Internet access is becoming a very inexpensive alternative, and each day it will be even more so, there are initiatives that intend to offer free Internet connection networks in exchange for publicity. Google is behind one of these projects initiated experimentally in the city of San Francisco, with the collaboration of the company Feeva, and which intends to spread to the rest of the United States. This business has developed technology which is able to detect the localization of a Wi-Fi network user. With this, they can sell personalized publicity, based on the site where the user is located, which appears to be behind the Google publicity plan.

Many communities and municipalities all over the world have begun Wi-Fi initiatives (http://www.muniwireless.com/), and there are many more projects expected to be developed in the near future. There are development models of open access Wi-Fi networks and coverage of large geographic areas, from cities to whole countries.

If these initiatives to provide free Internet connection through Wi-Fi to large geographic areas lead to a reduction of the number of users who would contract their own Internet access to paid ISPs, this would imply a lower number of possible foneros to share their connections. However, it is possible that FON may establish agreements with these institutional providers to share clients and services. Although the free projects of Wi-Fi cities have not been successful, Varsavsky considers that if they could be possible it would be a great complement for FON, since FON goes from the house to the street and they go from the street to the house, so they could collaborate.

The FON project would become a great competitor for mobile operators because the creation of a wide Wi-Fi network will make them lose a great deal of business when the same service is offered through a Wi-Fi network at a lower cost than they can offer. Its presence and the support of large businesses within the sector will at least force land and mobile telephone companies and providers of Internet access to offer more and better services and prices in the market, ultimately benefiting consumers and accelerating the spread of this technology as well as the development of the Information Society.

According to Varsavsky, Wi-Fi is better than 3G and much better than GPRS because it is free, it is fast and it is cheaper. FON is beginning to compete with the 3G infrastructure of the large mobile operators, but its infrastructure is built day by day by the foneros, who enjoy it free of charge. The generalization of Wi-Fi connections, both within businesses and at home, combined with the current launching of GSM/Wi-Fi and GSM/UMTS/Wi-Fi hybrid mobile terminals, will cause part of the 70% of current mobile communications to no longer be processed by mobile operators. However, it must be kept in mind that this initiative may take some time to consolidate for this service.

FON has faced the outlined challenges, becoming a global project, receiving the attention and the recognition of the world-wide technological community and the financing and support of the main companies of the sector. All that can be seen as a guarantee of technical, technological, economic, and commercial viability. In spite of that, FON defines itself as an innovative project of highest risk that redefines its business model day to day.

Final Remarks

This case allows us to extract some of useful insights both for entrepreneurs and companies already established in the IT sector.

The FON case shows the possibility of developing business initiatives anticipating to the environment evolution, helping to construct and set the most desirable future for the company that is being created. The entrepreneur must believe in his idea, transmit his vision to his team, and jointly know how to face the unexpected challenges that will arise along the project development.

The case states that the entrepreneur added value is to think and develop new ideas, to lay the way where others will walk later. Also we can see how the entrepreneur's innovating spirit does not expire with the project creation and it allows him to constantly redefine the business. Also, we observe how the enterprising spirit and his ability to innovate constantly make Varsavsky leaves the created company in other hands and to initiate a new project in which he concentrates all his abilities again.

As we can see in the firms created by Varsavsky, it is not necessary that the entrepreneur be a good manager, since he can take people on who are better than he is in management tasks. Therefore, good staff selection and knowing how to choose a qualified team is very important. These people should be motivated by the entrepreneur's vision and charisma more than by the expectations of joining a big firm. In this case, the entrepreneur recognizes that he owes everything he has to his employees and he is aware of the need to distribute profits with them.

This case is a good model of what is considered a habitual entrepreneur in the IT realm, showing how to make the most of the experience and contacts previously acquired. The case could stimulate novice entrepreneurs to become serial or portfolio entrepreneurs since they can get synergic effects with past and current initiatives. It is more likely with human resources, because it is possible to count on them for each new project, either recruiting them for the new company, or collaborating with them thanks to the position they already have in other companies of the sector. This greater knowledge that habitual entrepreneurs could have about the business and their staff makes them less necessary to control the firm and facilitate delegating some management issues to the staff.

The FON project also shows how to create a new technological company with a minimum infrastructure investment, making the most of that available on the part of suppliers and clients. Also it illustrates how a world-wide company can be created with a small staff and getting an exponential growth through collaboration with other companies and professionals which can be competitors but that are able to join in an innovative project. This implies the usefulness of considering the entrepreneurship from a systemic perspective.

For the already established companies, the case illustrates the need and usefulness of maintaining the entrepreneurship tension along the project development, to favor the arising of new and potentially complementary projects. Also, this case contributes to the knowledge of firm creation, since it illustrates the collaboration among IT habitual entrepreneurs. Particularly, we observe how it is possible that a small company could attract some of the best professionals of the IT sector and to obtain the strategic and financial support of recognized great companies. This possibility of having highly qualified collaboration from different companies allows the creation of new initiatives that can be useful for their own business. This it is the case of Skype that can benefit from the creation of a universal Wi-Fi network to provide its clients services of mobile IP telephony.

Also the case represents an exceptional opportunity to state how internal and external communication through blogs can be used both as an innovation enhancer, and an effective commercial and advertising low cost tool. The entrepreneur's presence and availability in his blog to receive comments, suggestions and criticism, as well as the creation of FON's blogs in different languages facilitate a bidirectional communication that stimulates a perception of openness and a feeling of membership.

Taking into account all the favorable characteristics related to the entrepreneur, his management team, and the organization he is creating, and beyond the challenges that FON must face and that stimulate its collaborators' innovating skills, it is not possible to determine whether the FON project to create a world Wi-Fi Community will become reality in all its dimensions and revolutionize Internet access and its uses, but what is indisputable and widely acknowledged is that it is a revolutionary idea and a fascinating project.

References

Amit, R., Glosten, L., & Muller, E. (1993). Challenges to theory development in entrepreneurship research. *Journal of Management Studies*, *30*(5), 815-834.

Ardichivili, A., Cardonzo, R., & Sourav, R. (2003). A theory of entrepreneurial opportunity identification and development. *Journal of Business Venturing*, *18*(1), 105-123.

Audretsch, D.B. (1995). *Innovation and industry evolution*. Cambridge, MA: MIT Press.

Begley, T., & Boyd, D.P. (1987). The relationship of the Jenkins activity survey to type A behaviour among business executives. *Journal of Vocational Behavior*, *27*, 316-328.

Carter, S. (1999). Habitual entrepreneurs and business angels. *International Small Business Journal*, *17*(3), 89-91.

Cooper, A.C. (1985). The role of incubator organizations in the founding of growth-oriented firms. *Journal of Business Venturing, 1*(1), 75-86.

Covin, J.G., & Slevin, D.P. (1989). Strategic management of small firms in hostile and benign environments. *Strategic Management Journal, 10*, 75-87.

Davidsson, P., Low, M.B., & Wright, M. (2001). Editor's introduction: Low and MacMillan ten years on: Achievements and future directions for entrepreneurship research. *Entrepreneurship Theory and Practice*, *25*(4), 5-16.

Dees, J.G. (2001). The meaning of "social entrepreneurship". Center for the Advancement of Social Entrepreneurship. Retrieved April 28, 2007, from http://www.fuqua.duke.edu/centers/case/documents/Dees_SEdef.pdf

Drucker, P.F. (1998). The discipline of innovation. *Harvard Business Review, 76*(6), 149-156.

FON. (2006). Who is behind FON? Retrieved April 28, 2007, from http://en.fon.com/info/whos_behind.php

FON and roadrunner. (2006, February 21). Broadbands. Retrieved April 28, 2007, from http://www.dslreports.com/forum/remark,15526975?hilite=fon

FON, the largest WiFi community in the world, teams up with gigantic French ISP Neuf Cegetel. (2006, April 25). Martin Varsavsky. Blog of an entrepreneur. Retrieved April 28, 2007, from http://english.martinvarsavsky.net/fon/fon-the-largest-wifi-community-in-the-world-teams-up-with-gigantic-french-isp-neuf-cegetel.html

Ganitsky, J., & Sancho, A. (2002, July-September). Martin Varsavsky (A) (casos). *Revista de Empresa, 1,* 97-126.

Gartner, W.B. (1985). A conceptual framework for describing the phenomenon of new ventures creation. *Academy of Management Review, 10*(4), 696-706.

A global FON for all? (2006, March 9). *BusinessWeek Online*. Retrieved April 28, 2007, from http://www.businessweek.com/innovate/content/mar2006/id20060309_533258.htm?link position=linkxtra

Kakati, M. (2003). Success criteria in high-tech new ventures. *Technovation, 23*(5), 447-457.

Karagozoglu, N., & Brown, W.B. (1988). Adaptive responses by conservative and entrepreneurial firms. *Journal of Product Innovation Management, 5,* 269-281.

Lumpkin, D., & Dess, G.G. (1996). Clarifying the entrepreneurial orientation construct and linking it to performance. *Academy of Management Review, 21*(1), 135-172.

Lumpkin, D., & Dess, G.G. (1997). Proactiveness versus competitive aggressiveness: Teasing apart key dimensions of and entrepreneurial orientation. *Frontiers for Entrepreneurship Research*. Retrieved April 28, 2007, from http://www.babson.edu/entre/fer

Mackin, B. (2006, June). Worldwide online access: 2004-2010. Retrieved April 28, 2007, from http://www.emarketer.com/Report.aspx?bband_world_jun06

McClelland, D. (1961). *The achieving society.* Princeton, NJ: Van Nostrand.

Miller, D. (1983). The correlates of entrepreneurship in three types of firms. *Management Science, 29,* 770-791.

Miller, D., & Friesen, P. (1982). Innovation in conservative and entrepreneurial firms: Two models of strategic momentum. *Strategic Management Journal, 3,* 1-25.

Mueller, K. (2006, March). World broadband statistics: Q4 2005. Retrieved April 28, 2007, from http://www.point-topic.com

Oakey, R. (2003). Technical entrepreneurship in high technology small firms: Some observations on the implications for management. *Technovation*, *23*(8), 679-688.

Observatorio de las Telecomunicaciones y la Sociedad de la Información. (2006a, January). Indicadores: e-Europe. A1 Indicator: Percentage of people with access to the Internet at home. Retrieved April 28, 2007, from http://observatorio.red.es/indicadores/europe/Internet_jul2005/ indicador_a1.html

Observatorio de las Telecomunicaciones y la Sociedad de la Información. (2006b, January). Indicadores: e-Europe. J3 Indicator: Percentage of broadband households. Retrieved April 28, 2007, from http://observatorio.red.es/indicadores/europe/Internet_jul2005/indicador_j3.html

Observatorio de las Telecomunicaciones y la Sociedad de la Información. (2006, April 6). Indicadores: Por áreas. Ciudadanos. Encuesta sobre equipamiento y uso de Tecnologías de Información y Comunicación en las viviendas. Retrieved April 28, 2007, from http://observatorio.red.es/indicadores/areas/ciudadanos/banda_ancha

Panda Software. (2006, March 14). Las redes Wifi carecen de protección. *Press Room*. Retrieved April 28, 2007, from http://www.pandasoftware.es/sobre_panda/sala_de_prensa/Las+redes+WiFi+carecen+de+protecci%C3%B3n.htm

Park, J.S. (2005). Opportunity recognition and product innovation in entrepreneurial hi-tech start-ups: A new perspective and supporting case study. *Technovation*, *25*(7), 739-752.

Roberts, E.B. (1972). Influences upon performance of new technical enterprises. In A. Cooper & J. Komives (Eds.), *Technical entrepreneurship: A symposium*. Milwaukee, WI: Center for Venture Management.

Schumpeter, J.A. (1911). *Theorie der wirtschaftlichen entwicklung*. Leipzig: Duncker & Humblot.

Schumpeter, J.A. (1934). *The theory of economic development*. Cambridge, MA: Harvard University Press.

Shane, S. (2000). Prior knowledge and the discovery of entrepreneurial opportunities. *Organizational Science*, *11*(4), 448-469.

Skype invests in FON to increase WiFi availability. (2006, February 5). Skype Blogs. Retrieved April 28, 2007, from http://share.skype.com/sites/en/2006/02/skype_invests_in_fon_to_increa.html

Ucbasaran, D., Wright, M., Westhead, P., & Busenitz, L.W. (2003). The impact of entrepreneurial experience on opportunity identification and exploitation: Habitual and novice entrepreneurs. *Cognitive Approaches to Entrepreneur-*

ship Research. Advances in Entrepreneurship, Firm Emergence and Growth, 6, 231-263.

Westhead, P., Ucbasaran, D., & Wright, M. (2003). Differences between private firms owned by novice, serial and portfolio entrepreneurs: Implications for policy makers and practitioners. *Regional Studies, 37*(2), 187-200.

Westhead, P., & Wright, M. (1999). Contributions of novice, portfolio and serial founders located in rural and urban areas. *Regional Studies, 33*(2), 157-173.

Wong. P.K., Ho, Y.P., & Autio, E. (2005). Entrepreneurship, innovation and economic growth: Evidence form GEM data. *Small Business Economics, 24*(3), 335-350.

Zahra, S.A., & Covin, J.G. (1995). Contextual influences on the corporate entrepreneurship-performance relationship: A longitudinal analysis. *Journal of Business Venturing, 10*(1), 43-58.

Zahra, S.A., Jennings, D.F., & Kuratko, D.F. (1999). The antecedents and consequences of firm-level entrepeneurship: The state of the field. *Entrepreneurship Theory and Practice, 24*(2), 45-65.

Appendix

FON's Team

FON. (2006, October 31). Retrieved April 28, 2007, from http://en.fon.com/info/whos_behind.php

Advisors

- Andrew Rasiej, NYC public advocate candidate, political and WiFi activist
- Ethan Zuckerman, Harvard Berkman Center, founder of Tripod, top U.S. blogger
- Dan Gillmor, journalist, author of *We the Media: Grassroots Journalism by the People, for the People*
- Esther Dyson, Release 1.0 and CNET, CNET editor and successful investor in emerging technologies
- Rebecca MacKinnon, Harvard Berkman Center, Global Leaders of Tomorrow, W.E.F. founder of Global Voices
- David Weinberger, technologist, co-author of *Cluetrain Manifesto*
- Wendy Seltzer, Harvard Berkman Center, formerly, Electronic Frontier Foundation
- Christiane zu Salm, Interactive 9Live, named one of the 25 Future Leaders of Tomorrow by the *Financial Times*
- Álvaro Ibañez, Microsiervos, Internality, MyStrands
- Juantomas García, president of Hispalinux, founder and CEO of Mono::Lab
- Jon Berrojalbiz, Trading Motion

Worldwide Team

- Antonio Saez, CEO of FON Spain, formerly COO Ya.com and co-founder of Terra
- Jean Bernard Magescas and Tariq Krim, FON leaders in France, Municipal WiFi movement
- Ola Ahlvarsson, FON leader in Sweden, Result.com, named one of Top 10 European Internet Entrepreneurs by the *Wall Street Journal*

- Marko Ahtisaari, FON leader in Finland, worked as director of Design Strategy at Nokia, built and led the mobile practice at startup design consultancy Satama Interactive and co-founded Aula, is part of the team behind Blyk, a pan-European free mobile operator

- Yat Siu, FON leader in China, founder and CEO, Outblaze Ltd., Global Leader of Tomorrow at the World Economic Forum

- Dr. Jin Ho Hur, FON leader in Korea, founder, president and CEO of Bluemine Media Corp., founder, Iworld Holdings Limited. Founder, Inet, Inc.

- Joichi Ito, FON leader in Japan, Six Apart, one of the founders of the blogging phenomenon

Endnotes

[1]   However, he collaborates as a professor at the Instituto de Empresa in Spain and participates as a speaker at many conferences throughout the world.

[2]   In the case of Ya.com, a group of 50 employees earned more than 60 million euros in a few years. Available at http://www.el-mundo.es/encuentros/invitados/2005/06/1597/

[3]   The purchase of Albura (June 2005) provides more than 7,500 Km. of fiber optic cable.

[4]   New operating systems, such as Tiger by Apple and Microsoft's Vista, are considered for broadband.

[5]   Observatorio de las Telecomunicaciones y la Sociedad de la Información (2006a, January).

[6]   Observatorio de las Telecomunicaciones y la Sociedad de la Información (2006, April 6).

[7]   Observatorio de las Telecomunicaciones y la Sociedad de la Información (2006b, January).

[8]   Comisión del Mercado de las Telecomunicaciones (2006). El Mercado de las Telecomunicaciones en España durante 2005. Retrieved April 28, 2007, from http://www.cmt.es/cmt/centro_info/publicaciones/pdf/ resumen_2005.pdf

[9]   La Fonera's technical specifications, for advanced users, are: uses a chipset Atheros 2315, Linux 2.4, and the firmware of FON based on OpenWRT, which has 4MB of Flash and 16MB of SDRAM. It is also 802.11b/g and the antenna may be removed and changed to one with greater range.

[10] It is an obvious reference to Linus Torvalds, known for initiating the development of Linux.

[11] Referenced to Microsoft co-founder Bill Gates.

[12] The expected fee is 2 euros for 24 hours of use at any network point buying a "5 days pass", or 3 euros a single day.

[13]   Data provided by FON on October 31, 2006.

[14]   Index Ventures (www.indexventures.com) is dedicated to working with entrepreneurs who have the drive and ability to build world-class technology companies that can become global players in their market. They focus on investing in information technology and life sciences. Sequoia Capital (http://www.sequoiacap.com) define themselves as the entrepreneurs behind the entrepreneurs. Their favorite investment candidates are businesses operating in the electronic segments of the economy including Components, Systems, Software, and Services companies. They like to invest in new, rapidly growing markets where customers have enthusiasm for the company's products.

[15]   http://en.fon.com/info/whos_behind.php

[16]   Data provided by FON on October 16, 2006.

[17]   Jazztel is the leader of alternative operators to Telefónica in the Spanish broadband market.

[18]   In the case of WEP it is sufficient to use a simple PDA with Linux and a program sniffer such as AirSnort or WEPcrack to monitor the network and obtain the password being used to encode the data.

Chapter II

Remote Internet-Based Supervision Systems, S.L.

Andrea Bikfalvi, Universitat de Girona, Spain

Christian Serarols, Universitat Autònoma de Barcelona, Spain

Abstract

The present case study explains the process of creation of Remote Internet-Based Supervision Systems, S.L. (RISS), a spin-off emerging from the University of Figueres, Spain. It describes all phases, from formation to the present day, and the problems and challenges faced by the entrepreneurial team composed of academics and industry professionals. Starting in a lab shared by two computer engineers finishing their PhDs, their friendship later converted into a science-based new venture. After having developed products and survived financial difficulty, the company stood at the threshold of a stage of growth and a decision regarding the commercial strategy had to be taken. But some problems have arisen between the academic entrepreneurs and the industrial partner regarding commercial strategy.

Remote Internet-Based Supervision Systems, S.L.[1]

Marc Torres, cofounder and general manager of Remote Internet-Based Supervision Systems, S.L. (RISS) sat in his office after a hard day. It was Tuesday evening, January 23, 2007. He was not only tired but also worried. In the afternoon, he had had another long and heated discussion with his colleague, Carles, about the future of the company: about the business model and growth strategy. The discussions with Carles had been frequent during the last few months and disagreement on a certain topic was the subject of daily debates. Marc and Carles had been working quite well during the first years of RISS but now the deep disagreement about the future of the company worried him greatly.

Marc felt that he was at a crossroads. On the one hand, he was happy and highly satisfied to have been successful in starting a high-tech company that had created a powerful technology and already gone through the knothole. After having developed products and survived financial difficulty, the company stood now at the threshold of a stage of growth. On the other hand, the different viewpoints regarding the commercial strategy they should follow worried him greatly.

There were two clearly opposite points of view among the shareholders of RISS regarding the commercial strategy. During a recent meeting, one of the shareholders in favor of having an experienced professional sales force external from RISS and coordinated by their industrial partner said:

I think we should opt for a salesman with different experiences in the field. We are all technicians; we don't have enough experience to sell our products! We should focus on our core competences, which are developing products not selling them! Definitely, we must create a professional and experienced sales team with our industrial partner.

He could not even finish his argument when another shareholder expressed a completely different point of view:

I do not agree with such an idea. I do not think we should leave the responsibility of commercializing our products to our industrial partner. We have to be independent from this partner; otherwise we have the risk to be completely tight to his demands. Besides, how can our partner sell products to its competitors? These potential customers will not rely on this supplier. I do not think that our sales department should be composed of experienced salesman coming from the industrial partner.

Both points of view had arguments in favor and against. But the time was passing by and Marc had begun to give serious consideration to what to do if an agreement with the rest of the shareholders on the commercial strategy could not be reached. Instinctively, he began to review the start-up process of RISS, the problems they had had until now and the development of his relationship with the rest of shareholders. Perhaps the present situation is the result of some errors of the past, he thought, and he did not want to make another wrong decision.

Setting the Case

The former head of the Department of Computer Engineering at the University of Figueres was a very ambitious and active man who wanted to promote technology transfer between university and industry. During a department meeting in 2003 he encouraged his team to create their own businesses from the results obtained in their research: "By the end of the year each of you could have your own company." The results of such a statement did not take long to surface; within a few months a research group dealing with robotics in the department created a company.

This company, named Remote Internet-Based Supervision Systems, S.L. (RISS), took advantage of the embedded technology developed in the robotic field by applying it to other common daily operations.

RISS was founded in Figueres (Spain) in April 2004 by a group of young computer engineers with PhDs in computer science at the University of Figueres and some professors from the research group in robotics. Since then, the company has developed two different products, embedded solutions for remote monitoring, controlling, and supervising equipment such as meters (electricity, water, etc.) and other additional products related to computer help desk.

Technology, Products and Services Developed by RISS

Technology

The core technology used by RISS is grounded in the know-how developed by the group in embedded computers and free software applications (Linux-uClinux) obtained during its years of research in robotics and computer vision.

An embedded system is a special-purpose system in which the computer is completely encapsulated by the device it controls. Unlike a general-purpose computer, such as a personal computer, an embedded system performs one or a few predefined tasks, usually with very specific requirements. Since the system is dedicated to specific tasks, design engineers can optimize it, reducing the size and cost of the product. Some also have real-time performance constraints that must be met, for reasons such as safety and usability; others may have low or no performance requirements, allowing the system hardware to be simplified to reduce costs.

Embedded systems are often mass-produced, so the cost savings may be multiplied by millions of items. The rise of the World Wide Web has given embedded designers another quite different option by providing a Web page interface over a network connection. This is useful for remote, permanently installed equipment and avoids the cost of a sophisticated display, providing complex input and display capabilities when needed, on another computer.

Specifically, RISS has adapted the know-how they have developed within the robotics research group in embedded solutions to a commercially feasible application: remote Internet-based supervision systems for installed equipment like communal boilers (central heating), security, meters, and other applications.

The real innovation of RISS is the application of embedded technology to a field that did not employ this technology previously. The remote Internet-based supervision application is now a very promising market exhibiting exponential sales growth. The benefits of controlling and supervising remotely any application, such as cost reduction and efficiency, are obvious, according to Marc, "We are very innovative in our target market by adapting embedded technology to work with other applications."

The functioning of RISS' technology can be summarised into six different steps:

1. Gather information through meters (flow, temperature, electricity, etc.)
2. Detect any malfunction of the device (there are certain anomalies that can be solved without human intervention; thus, the system can correct it. For example, a low operating temperature of the boiler)
3. Solve the problem automatically by the system
4. Store all this information in the central memory
5. Send alerts and other information through an Internet connection (generally, through a ADSL line)
6. Human intervention in case it is needed

Products and Services

In the beginning, RISS focussed on offering embedded solutions into custom energy applications to control communal boilers to get hot water and central heating. Their first product, called K2Energy, was applied to a block of flats in Figueres, Spain.

K2Energy was designed for blocks of flats that had a communal boiler which met the heating and hot water requirements of each apartment. The system permits remote control supply of hot water and heating, thereby achieving significant energy saving. Moreover, K2Energy allows the measurement of each apartment's consumption. The final objective of such supervision is to improve the system's efficiency and to facilitate its maintenance. In addition, all the equipment is remotely supervised through online Internet-based technology.

Figure 1 shows the operation scheme of this product.

Figure 1. K2Energy operation scheme

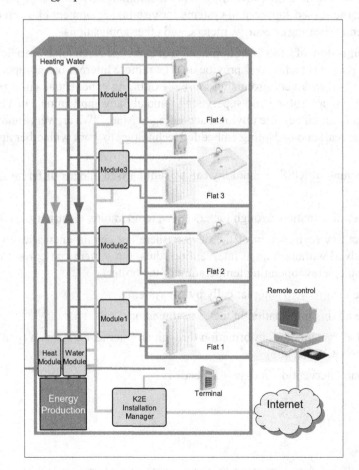

K2Energy is comprised of two main different devices: K2E electronic board and K2E installation manager. The K2E electronic board is installed in each apartment and it allows individual measures of the energy utilized. This device is also used to regulate the heating of each apartment by taking real-time meters through its two temperature meters (PT-1000), three flow meters (hot water, cold water, and heating), one valve, and a thermostat. K2E installation manager is in charge of processing data of each apartment to manage the whole building (communal boiler) and it also provides reports on daily consumption of energy, alerts, and so forth. It sends an alarm to the customer service of the boiler if it detects any malfunction of the device.

After their experience in this product, the founding team thought that these embedded solutions could also be applied to other fields, such as hotels. Therefore, they developed a product to manage all the services available in a hotel room. These services include the control of the air conditioning, minibar, emergencies, fire alarms, opening doors, blinds, and so forth. This product was named K2Hotel. Figure 2 shows the product's operation.

Figure 2. K2Hotel operation scheme

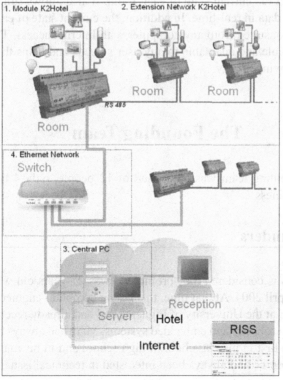

K2Hotel is a system that controls and monitors hotel rooms. It offers energy savings and better comfort and quality of services available in the room. The core of the system is managed by an electronic board named K2H. This is an intelligent device capable of simultaneously controlling different rooms. Located in different areas of the hotel, a communication bus board allows each module to manage the extensions placed in each room. Due to a modular hardware design, the system is easily adaptable to the needs and requirements of any hotel. The following services offered by K2Hotel can be highlighted:

- Air conditioning control of every room: an interval of temperature is established in order to avoid excessive energy consumption. The system can distinguish whether the rooms are occupied or not.
- Devices to save energy: for example, there are mechanisms that switch off the air conditioning when they detect that doors are open.
- The minibar can be monitored.
- Security warnings: intrusion, emergency, fire, and so forth.

A computer server monitors, collects, and stores the data provided by the electronic board (K2H) about the current state of each room. It also allows storing and analyzing of archival data in real-time. In addition, the current state of each room can be accessed and consulted from any computer with Internet access. This software application is flexible and adaptable to any user's needs and helps the generation of strategies for saving energy.

The Founding Team

Although the founding team was composed of 12 people, only 4 have actively worked in the business.

Working Founders

Marc Torres, who is considered the "promoter," was 27 years old when the firm was founded in April 2004. At that time, this young computer engineer was working as a researcher at the University of Figueres and had already received his PhD (February 2003) in robotics and embedded systems. Marc had always been a bright student, being the first in his class both in high school and in his master's degree program. Moreover, he had always been interested in technical issues and he was

Table 1. Products and services from 2004 to 2007

	K2Energy	K2Hotel
Installation*	25-125 flats	1 embedded controls up to 20 rooms at the same time
Monitoring	Hot water Cold water Heating	Air condition Heating Minibar Security
Technical specifications	Works on any energy source (gas, electricity, etc.) Any type of boiler	Simultaneous supervision of 20 rooms
Benefits (energy reduction vs. costs)	15-30% cost reduction in energy consumption 25% cheaper than individual flat heating 13% cost reduction in technical maintenance	Energy savings** Security control Better quality of the service Control
Development time	18 months	6 months
Target market	Spain	Spain
Price	Hardware: €250 per flat + €1,200 central installation manager Software:€1,800 euros (block of 25 flats) €7,000 euros (block of 125 flats)	Hardware: €500 per 20 rooms + €1,200 central installation manager Software:€3,500 euros

* There is no installation number limit
** Cost savings have not been evaluated yet

thinking of his future because the department could not offer him a stable position at university. During his doctoral courses he met Robert, who was also working on his dissertation in the field of robotics and embedded systems.

Marc was born and raised in Girona and spent his childhood with his two older sisters, a brother, and his mother. His father, who had a business related to building materials, died when Marc was young. Other than his father, there was no entrepreneurial tradition in his family. Furthermore, Marc did not have any professional experience except for some jobs (not related to embedded technology) that he took during several summers while he was finishing his master's degree. He had not even thought of creating a company before RISS due to his lack of experience in real business.

The idea to create his own company was motivated by a mix of different "trigger" events. However, the main two were: the need to find a job that combined research and a decent salary and an encounter with a local business man. This business man, Carles, had a company dedicated to remote control devices and went to the University of Figueres to look for new embedded technology to more efficiently control his systems. This was the embryo that later become RISS. With the aim of addressing his lack of professional experience, in September 2003 Marc decided to take postgraduate studies in "new knowledge-based venture creation and management" organized by the Technological Trampoline at the University of Figueres, a unit specializing in supporting spin-off creation from public research institutions. The following paragraph is the transcript of Marc's answer as to why he took this postgraduate course:

For me this course was very important. I am a technician and come from the academic domain. I had no idea about business management. The main drawback was that I took it too late. I was attending the lessons when the company was already operating. The day to day of the firm was going faster than the lessons I was receiving. In any case, this course was critical for my professional training.

In addition, he received a lot of support from his family. For example, one of his sisters helped him to identify all economic and non-economic support mechanisms existing in Spain for such a business.

Robert Llach was also a 27 year old computer engineer when he created RISS. He was born in Palamos, a tourist resort located in the northern part of the Catalan Mediterranean coast. While he was earning his master's degree in computer engineering at the University of Figueres, he shared an apartment in Figueres with other students. In 2000 he joined the same doctoral program as Marc Torres, where they met for the first time. Neither Robert nor his family had any entrepreneurial background or experience. Robert only had experience in academic research.

After several joint research projects, department life, long coffee breaks, discussions on how to keep going in their research, Robert and Marc became close friends. Shared interests and hobbies in addition to long hours of work in the same lab for four years strengthened their relationship.

At that time, his possibilities to pursue an academic career in the department were limited, because there were few stable positions and too many PhD candidates in the department. Thus, he was looking for other alternatives. Marc wanted to involve Robert in the business because he had a solid technical knowledge in the field achieved during his PhD and they were also close friends and colleagues. The following paragraph is the transcript of Marc's justification for Robert's involvement:

It was because Robert had learned a lot during his PhD and he knew much more about this technology than I do because his research was closer to the topic than mine. He was a specialist in embedded systems while I was a specialist in Artificial Intelligence.

Robert's initial role in RISS was exclusively being in charge of the technical development of the products and services offered by RISS. On the other hand, Marc took the responsibilities of managing the company. According to Marc, *"My functions in the company? Everything that is non-technical! I am in charge of human resources, grants and scholarships, and lately I am also in charge of the commercialisation of the products."*

The third co-founder who also works in the company is Marcel Proust (36). He is a professor in the Department of Computer Engineering at the University of Figueres. He already knew Marc because he had been his PhD supervisor. Although Marcel was a full-time professor and very focused on research, he had some practical experience in the computer industry because he had worked for a couple of years in a software development company. He also had some experience in managing research projects after 10 years being responsible for several research projects in the department. He was a very active and dynamic person. Marcel's involvement in RISS has radically changed over time. Initially, he was responsible for the relationship between RISS, the University of Figueres (especially with the Technological Trampoline), and CIDEM (a regional development agency for promoting entrepreneurship and innovation). In fact, he was the "public face" of the business, its public relations. At present, his involvement is much lower than it used to be, mainly due to the difficulty in combining a professional job at a business with his professorial duties.

The last co-founder who also works in the company is Carles Blanch. He is a 58 year old business man who acted like a business angel/industrial partner and encouraged the creation of RISS since the beginning. His background is clearly different from the rest of the founding team. This industrial engineer had no academic experience and contributed to the idea of combining remote supervision systems with embedded technology. He also contributed with the commercialization of the products as he directed a remote supervision company in Figueres. His professional and entrepreneurial experience in the field was very broad. He had worked for several years in a high-technology machinery firm and he had also created several firms. His main task in RISS was strategic planning and he also bought all the products that RISS was assembling.

Nonworking Founders

As the technology employed by RISS was first developed within the research group through three prototype robots, it was decided to incorporate other members of the group in the equity of the company. This practice of sharing equity in companies spun-off from the Department has been common practice. For example, Marcel had some shares in two previous spin-offs created within the group.

These non-working founders from the research group numbered 12 and represented 17.5% of the equity. However, within a year their equity was reduced to just 5%. In Marc's words:

We were too many. There are a lot of members of the department that have very few shares in the company. Although they were founders of RISS, they hardly worked in the company nor did they participate in the Board of Directors. They only represented 5% of the company.

Marc and Robert never worked again in the department after the company was created. Still, they keep a relationship with their former colleagues. In order to allow some professors and other research group members to work together with the founders in the initial phase of the company, RISS had to sign contract research agreements with them. This was a way to pay Marcel and some other counsellors for their work at RISS. Marc explains it as follows: "We had to sign a contract to collaborate with them. In fact, the main reason for doing so was to pay them for their contribution." At present, RISS does not maintain any technological collaboration. The relationship is now more personal than professional.

Origins and Development of RISS

Gestation Stage

After finishing his dissertation in February 2003, Marc Torres was unwilling to believe that he would spend all his life stuck between journals, papers, prototypes, books, and disinterested students attending his lessons. In addition, his department could not offer him a stable position at university. However, applied research was one of his main interests. He had spent four years working as a researcher at university and teaching lessons to undergraduate students. Although he was happy with research, he was not that satisfied with his salary and wanted to find a way to combine research and earn a decent salary.

At that time, emerging trends and policies at a regional and university level were promoting entrepreneurship and new venture creation. The technology transfer officers kept visiting the best performance departments to look for quality research to be transferred into a spin-off company. Suddenly, he remembered the words of the former director of the department: "each of you … could have a company."

Although it was challenging and risky, a light went on in Marc's mind. It was the alternative he was looking for; he felt that he could apply his extensive research developed within the last years into a practical application.

Marcel, who was Marc's dissertation supervisor, encouraged him to create something related to the knowledge they had both developed during his thesis: computer vision and artificial intelligence. After conducting some market research and visiting some potential clients to explain what their technology was capable of, they both realized that without a product they would not succeed in their business.

In the meantime, Carles, who already knew Marc, was looking for a technology provider in computer engineering applied to remote supervision systems. He had already visited Marc and Marcel's Department to initiate contract research to develop specific remote supervision software. Thus, when Marc heard about this, he contacted Carles and organized a meeting with some other members of the group. Carles' initial idea was to improve the efficiency and facilities of remote systems by applying embedded technology. In fact, Carles was very dissatisfied with his previous hardware and software providers. The microprocessors he used to employ for remote controlling devices were costly and it was difficult to enlarge their functionality, which limited Internet-based supervision and data storage.

The following paragraph is the transcript of Marc's answer to what extent the initial idea was innovative:

What we really did was to use an up-to-date technology developed for robotics' applications in a university setting and to apply it to a sector where its technology was developed years before. That is why we do not think we were very innovative. In fact, our technology depends on how you evaluate it. From a robotic point of view, it is nothing new. But when it comes to remote supervision, then, we have a very innovative product.

In fact, the products that RISS has later launched to the market were based on the technology developed for three prototype robots in Marc's research group:

- SERVET1, the first submarine robot developed jointly with colleagues from another university (Polytechnic University of Catalonia). In this case, the embedded solution used was an Intel 486 CPU platform with QNX, which is in charge of control tasks, while a Pentium III CPU platform is responsible for the vision applications such as generating visual maps (mosaics) of a seabed.
- SERVET2 was the second prototype of a submarine robot, small and spherical in shape, that uses an embedded computer for control tasks. At present, the research of this group is focused on the development of simple tasks related to computer vision, such as following an object into the sea.

- SERVET3 is a robot in charge of surveillance tasks. It uses a commercial robot (Pionner 2), an endoscope system composed by two cameras, and an embedded Pentium III CPU platform responsible for image capturing and processing. This vision system allows the positioning and the construction of a 3D map of the robot's environment in real-time. The communication with the remote computer responsible for the monitoring of the robot is conducted through an Ethernet wireless connection.

Overall, it can be considered that the detection of Marc's business opportunity lasted approximately four months and was a combination of different triggers: (1) to combine his research interests with a job that would increase his earnings; (2) to find himself a job position because it was difficult to achieve a stable research position at university; (3) to create something of his own; and (4) Carles's experience in the sector of remote supervision.

Planning Stage

The founding team did not invest much effort in planning, especially in determining the needs of different potential customers for the products they were planning to offer. This phase lasted approximately three months, from June 2003 to September 2003 and followed four main stages: definition of the business idea; extensive competitor and market analysis; preparation of a preliminary business plan which included an investment proposal; and the first prototype (this last stage kept going and ended in February 2005).

Definition of the Business Idea

Marc had been an active member of the Computer Vision and Robotics research group for four years. However, he did not have the experience or the knowledge to apply this know-how to a commercially feasible product. With Marcel, they both unsuccessfully tried to put their knowledge in the market. But the situation changed when Marc and Marcel organized a meeting with Carles, the owner of one of the most well-known technological groups in the region, TIC Group.

Carles and Marc had a previous relationship; Carles' son was one of Marc's closest friends. In addition, Carles had always tried to recruit Marc in his remote supervision firm. He knew of his good academic record and he thought that Marc could have helped a lot in the business.

The main issue to deal with in the meeting was to look for a solution to the problems in the field of remote control that Carles was facing and, thus, to better define his business idea. At this meeting officers from the Technological Trampoline were also in attendance. Actually, this meeting can be considered the starting point from converting the initial idea to a business opportunity. The following paragraph is the transcript of Marc's answer to what the business idea was:

On one hand I had finished my PhD in a research group specializd in embedded technologies. On the other hand there is the experience of TIC Group [Carles' firm in remote controlling]. We put the "embedded technology" and Carles put the "remote controlling." Carles' exact words were: If you are capable of creating a product with certain characteristics that fulfil my needs, then we have a clear business and market opportunity here! We had no clue about the market and Carles knew little about embedded technology. So, we complemented each other perfectly!

Based on the definition of the business idea, the entrepreneurs investigated the main needs this product should meet. According to Marc, they wanted to provide a product that served the following needs:

- Energy savings
- Real-time control of the building
- The possibility to exactly determine the individual consumption of each apartment
- To have a record that permits the analysis of historical data
- Analysis of global profitability of the installation/equipment
- Real-time alerts and warnings
- And all of these through embedded systems that are cheaper than using microprocessors technology

The main benefits of these technologies are easy and efficient management and time and costs saving and improvement, as well as online continuous remote control. RISS also provides product related software services, development, and maintenance.

At that time, TIC Group was the only exclusive distributor of RIBS products (one of the biggest remote supervision manufacturers in the world). So, TIC Group knew in-depth all related products and their advantages and disadvantages. The main pitfall was the technology used in these products: microprocessors, which can be considered a step behind embedded technology. Microprocessor technology was expensive and had several limitations: it was difficult to adapt to work with new information and communication technologies such as the Internet; it was not flexible and scalable; it did not have enough data storage capacity; and it lacked process capacity (number of actions to be conducted simultaneously).

Extensive Competitor and Market Analysis

The next step our team took was to roughly analyze the market, basically in two directions: was there any company offering similar or substitute services? And, what were the main characteristics that made this product useful for users?

We have to take into account that the founders were "action-oriented" more than "planning-oriented," especially because of the involvement of Carles in the team. Carles knew exactly what requirements the product should fulfil and who the main competitors were. In addition, Carles would buy all the products produced by RISS. However, the team was somehow encouraged to conduct a formal extensive competitor analysis and write a business plan if they wanted to receive the support from the Technological Trampoline.

Taking part in the Technological Trampoline is very beneficial for any technology-based company created by university researchers and professors. First, they provide an officer/consultant to help in the process of writing the business plan. Second, through an initiative called "Capital Concepte" they can provide up to €100,000 funding. Third, they help to apply to any existing venture creation or technology/innovation development programmes. Fourth, they offer courses on business management. Finally, they also offer office spaces under the market rate. For all those reasons, the team decided to join the Technological Trampoline program.

Their approach to the competitor and market analysis took different forms. First, they looked for similar initiatives all over the world. The result was a very accurate comparative table between the different competitors in this market, including those selling substitute products. All this information was based on a content analysis of their Web sites. The variables analyzed in each case were: date of founding, brief description of the firm, technology (proprietary vs. non-proprietary), product portfolio (characteristics, prices, promotion, etc.), clients, sales volume, financial ratios, and founders. According to Marc:

The sector we wanted to enter was quite complicated in more developed countries than Spain. There were several consolidated competitors and big companies with experience and brand awareness in the sector. This was a barrier to operate internationally; however, the sector was still undeveloped in Spain at that time.

They then roughly analyzed the supply-side focusing on hardware providers. The team thought that this would be one of the key issues for their business. The bargaining power of a small firm is limited initially because the minimum units needed to obtain scale-costs are rather high. Consequently, this issue could limit a future entry in another market.

The demand-side, the potential clients, was not extensively investigated because the requirements and characteristics for such products were specified by Carles according to his needs and experience in the sector. However, according to Marc this was a handicap for the future development of the company. Although it was a big advantage to have your production sold beforehand, not all customers had the same needs. In Marc's words:

We should have dedicated more time to investigate other potential clients' needs because later we experienced difficulty in selling technological products to customers that are not used to them. How can you expect them to trust a product developed by a small and unknown company? In addition, relying too much on a single customer is not a very intelligent strategy for the business.

Finally, they also attended several fairs, demonstrations, and conferences which provided them with insights on how the sector would evolve.

All the information gathered in this step helped them to detect a gap in the market and to gain knowledge of the sector they were planning to enter. Nonetheless, the outcome of this stage did not satisfy the team because it was too quickly executed and later they had to revisit this area.

Preparation of the Preliminary Business Plan, Including an Investment Proposal

Although the whole process of preparing the business plan was complex, interactive, and time consuming, this preliminary phase was done too quickly without an in depth and accurate analysis. The main objective of the team in this phase was to join the Technological Trampoline (TT) support program, and the condition for that was to have a preliminary business plan to be evaluated by TT officers.

This preliminary business plan was written by Marc and Robert only, with Robert contributing technical content. At this time, the team also decided how to share out the equity among them. Interestingly, this part did not take long and they all quickly came to an agreement. The decision was not based on the contribution of each partner in terms of money and labor—rather that the academic founders wanted to maintain the majority of the business, resulting in the following percentage distribution of shares: Marc 17.5%, Robert 17.5%, Marcel 17.5%, the rest of scholars 17.5% and Carles 30%. With this distribution, the academic founders of the business held 70% of the equity.

Initially, Marc, Robert, Marcel, and the rest of scholars would contribute with little money to the equity (only 5% of the total, €60,000) since they provided technical expertise working for some months with wages below market, but after this time, they would begin to earn a wage according to their responsibilities and capabilities. This was the agreement reached with the rest of the founding team.

At this point (end of September 2003) the team started to review the business plan draft and after four brainstorming sessions, the first business plan was finished. However, they all agreed that a more accurate market analysis was needed to successfully define their products and implement the business idea.

This draft was enough to obtain the support from the TT and a spin-off creation officer was assigned to help them write the business plan. In the beginning, the founding team was dubious about the contribution that the officer could provide. Obviously, the officer knew nothing about this technology, embedded systems, or the remote supervision sector. His working methodology was based on continuous questions and discussions with the founders. The following paragraph is the transcript of Marc's answer to what his impression of the officer's work was:

Actually, it is only now that I can clearly see the officer's contribution. While he was working here we thought he was very annoying because he kept asking picky questions the whole time. We could hardly work in peace! We wanted him to leave us alone .... However, I have realized that the questions he had asked us were essential for the development of our business. We are very satisfied with his work. He was highly involved in the project; thus, at the end, we even established a personal relationship.

This second stage of the development of the business plan with the help of the officer lasted until June 2004, after RISS was legally constituted. The involvement and support of the officer was essential to successfully write the final business plan. According to Marc, "We could not have done it without this his help. He even conducted the market analysis for us because he needed it in order to finish his Master's Degree and decided to use RISS as a case study."

Interestingly, the academic founders were expecting more support and involvement from the industrial partner (TIC Group) regarding commercial issues. In fact, TIC Group hardly got involved in this planning stage. They only facilitated some contacts and a list of competitors but without any further data.

First Prototype

Before legally constituting the venture, the team began to work on its first prototype. A prototype was essential to convince both potential customers and investors. In addition, the development of the first prototype was a condition put by the Technological Trampoline to fund the venture. This development phase lasted from September 2003 to February 2005.

Although the firm was not legally constituted, the team detected the need to incorporate a computer engineer specialist in embedded systems to help Robert (responsible for technical development) produce the first prototype. Hence, in April 2004, Roger joined the development team.

In the meantime, the founding team maintained sporadic meetings with members of the computer engineering research group to discuss some technical details of the prototype. Within this prototype phase Marc, Robert, Marcel, and Roger were occupying a small lab within the department while waiting for the TT to offer them proprietary spaces. This physical proximity helped the interaction of the team with members of the research group. In May 2004, RISS moved to a 15 square-meter office offered by the TT, which in few months enlarged to a 40 square-meter office.

In the following paragraph, Marc explains the difficulties they had to face when applying the embedded technology developed for robotics to a different sector:

We had the experience in developing these devices but they all used to operate in an academic environment. Then, when you move to the real world things change. The requirements are more specific and clients are more demanding. We could not afford a single failure in the product .... The testing in the lab was almost useless; we did learn a lot when we tested it in a real setting, but it took us triple more than planned.

Implementation Stage

The implementation stage lasted from April 2004 until the end of July 2005 when the first product was installed in a real setting.

Legal Constitution

Marc went to different public administrations to look for aid in the creation of the new firm. Finally, he decided to follow the support process established by the Technological Trampoline (TT) instead of other institutions. The main reason was that legal advice and other services were offered by the Trampoline free of charge. In addition, the TT's officers knew the project since the beginning and were very interested in spinning-off other new ventures from the University of Figueres.

This help meant that the TT paid for consultants, lawyers, and agencies helping the team in the administrative task of legally constituting the firm. The next step was to register the name of the firm and the trademark at the central registry office. A lawyer wrote down the company's bylaws.

The company was officially constituted on the 9th of April 2004 by the public notary. The process of legally constituting the firm had taken two months and had cost approximately €1,750. According to Marc, there was too much bureaucracy in the process:

It was incredible the number of forms we had to fill in and the time it took to constitute the firm. We could hardly believe spending two months in the process and paying almost €2,000 just to have nothing at all, except the right to begin our operations.

Then, they had to decide upon the location of the company. They opted for remaining at campus in a reasonably priced 15 square-meter office offered by the TT. Marc justifies this decision as follows:

Renting costs were very expensive in the city, so we had to stay in campus, in an office space below market rates offered by the Technological Trampoline. We started in an office that had no more than 15 square-meters. There were three of us but we were supposed to double within few months…In my opinion it was very important to stay on-campus because: it created brand awareness and it is a sort of quality distinction for a start-up. Besides it is easier to attract talented graduates, a guy studying at university will always be happier to work in a company located in the campus where he can combine studies with work.

Working Team Creation

From the beginning, only Marc, Robert, and Marcel were working in RISS. However, only Marc and Robert were involved full-time in the venture and earned a wage for their work. Marcel was working part-time and he was paid through a formal contract research project between RISS and the University of Figueres. Carles also worked part-time in the business but without getting any salary from the company. The rest of the members of the founding team did not work in RISS, though they were taking part in the board of directors and coordinated and developed certain tasks.

Marc's tasks included managing the business jointly with Carles; they were both acting as the CEO's of the company. This was very important for Marc because he lacked professional experience in the sector and in managing a business and Carles solved this problem.

The initial equity of €60,000 and a grant obtained from the Ministry of Science and Technology with the objective of facilitating the incorporation of PhDs in new technology-based firms was enough to create the initial working team, and to assure a minimal salary at least until the launching of the product.

Initially, RISS was very similar to a garage start-up. The funding was just enough to develop the first prototype but everyone knew that more funding would be needed in the near future. According to Marc:

Our initial idea was to demonstrate that we could do what we had planned. It was risky, a challenge, but we were convinced of our capabilities. Furthermore, our business plan was structured in two phases: the prototype phase where the main objective was to develop the product without the need of big investments and the launching phase where we would need much more investment and support to make the business grow.

Complementing the Team: First Equity Increase

The first prototype was ready by October 2004. By that time, RISS was given financial support from a regional development agency (CIDEM) through an initiative called "Capital Concepte" managed by the Technological Trampoline. Nevertheless, this financial funding was tied to the condition of an increase of the equity by 40%, that is, €75,000.

In order to carry out this equity increase, the team focussed on negotiating RISS's first round of investment with a business angel. Thanks to Carles, the team was able to find a business angel, Micky. He was a very experienced financial manager in the field of electrical and energy installations and appliances. He had earned a lot of money in a previous investment and was looking for new investment opportunities in the field. In addition, he was planning to leave his job through early retirement; thus, RISS could also be an employment opportunity for the future. His main task in RISS was to supervise the budget and other financial activities of the venture.

The incorporation of this business angel created some discussions and disagreements among the founding team because he got 30% of the equity for only €30,000. But it was necessary to incorporate this angel if the team wanted to obtain the €75,000 in funding from the TT. Furthermore, the distribution of shares between the academics and industrialists of the founding team changed radically. At that time, the academics only controlled the 40% of the equity while the industrialists controlled 60%.

The distribution of shares before and after this round of investment is shown in Table 2.

The whole situation created serious problems among the founding team members, particularly between the industrialists and academic founders. The situation almost

Table 2. Distribution of shares before and after RISS's second round of invest-ment

	% April 2004	% May 2004	% December 2005
Marc	17.5	10	25.5
Robert	17.5	10	25.5
Marcel	17.5	10	4
Carles	30	30	30
Micky	-	30	10
Other scholars	17.5	10	5
Total	**100**	**100**	**100**

led to closing the company. Marc had to put his foot down and convinced Carles to change this situation. In December 2005, Marc and Robert bought at nominal price part of the equity from Micky, Marcel, and the rest of the scholars. With this new situation, the academic founders again controlled the majority of the equity (60%).

Product Development and New Source of Revenues

In February 2005, everything was ready and the working team started to adapt their first prototype to have a marketable product. For five months, the team worked very hard to develop the first embedded system for remote supervision purposes in Spain and launched RISS's Web site in the first week of February 2005. During this period, Robert focused on the technical problems and on coordinating the development team of two members. Marc also helped in this task, but he mainly focussed on commercial and management issues. He visited many potential customers to show them the developments that had been made on the platform and to gather suggestions that would help to improve the service. He also compiled marketing databases Web sites to advertise their service and scanned the environment for new competitors, leads, and opportunities.

In summary, Marc focussed on every aspect related to the marketing plan, although his experience was not in marketing. Carles also gave support in this task but less than expected. Micky mainly focussed on administrative and financing matters. Finally, Marcel helped Marc in commercial tasks but he mainly focussed on public relations.

Unexpectedly, while they were developing their products, an established venture from the region got in touch with RISS. This company was seeking an enterprise resource planning (ERP) software provider and contacted the University of Figueres who gave the RISS contact. Although RISS did not want to be distracted from its core competences, this company offered a lot of money and a research contract for two and a half years to develop a customized ERP solution.

At this time, cash was running out quickly and RISS was not expecting many sales within the following months. The founding team agreed that this new source of revenue would be beneficial to solve cash tensions. However, the industrial partner highlighted the risks for RISS of not focusing on its core business: to be behind on development schedule, to dedicate too many resources to this new line, risk of competitors catching-up, and so forth.

In order to develop this ERP software, two more people were recruited from the University. They were still finishing their degrees and they both needed to do an internship in a company, so it was quite easy to involve them in the project at a very low cost.

This phase lasted until July 2005 when the first product was installed in a block of 15 flats in Figueres, Spain. This first customer was RISS' industrial partner, TIC Group.

Commercial Strategy and Rethinking of the Business Model

First Sales Strategy

Once RISS' first product was successfully installed in Figueres, the team directed its efforts to two different activities: the development of K2Hotel, due to a purchasing order that came from a local hotel via TIC Group and creation of a sales department and marketing actions to launch RISS' K2Energy.

At this point, several discussions among the founding team on how to organize RISS' sales department occurred. There were two clearly opposite points of view among the shareholders of RISS regarding the commercial strategy. First, the view shared by the industrialists' partner was in favor of having an experienced professional sales force external from RISS and coordinated by their industrial partner. Second, the academic founders preferred a wholly internal sales department independent from the TIC Group.

Marc was really worried about the possibility of having an external sales department. He thought that it could limit RISS' revenues because he considered that TIC Group's competitors would never buy a product from one of its competitors. In addition, he thought that TIC would not provide more revenues than the ones it was able to provide as a shareholder of RISS. In the meantime, Carles' shareholders from TIC Group were upset with Carles' involvement in RISS. They thought that

Carles spent too much time working for RISS and was neglecting his responsibilities in TIC Group.

A consensus was eventually reached. The team decided to create their own sales department, independent from TIC Group but incorporating Carles as a sales manager and another salesman that used to work in TIC Group, Josep. This agreement seemed to satisfy both groups of shareholders but not completely. On one hand they had a very professional and experienced sales force, extremely committed and with a deep knowledge of the product. On the other hand, it was composed of TIC Group's former workers who would probably provide the same sales as if they were working in TIC.

Furthermore, another problem occurred: wage policy. Carles and Josep, as experienced salesmen, were paid market salaries which were further exceeding what the rest of the team was earning. In the beginning, this fact was not a problem because the team believed that the money was well-invested and they relied on the salesmen's capacity of generating revenues. But after half a year, the situation changed dramatically.

In December 2005, Carles and Josep had not succeeded in their sales strategy and the result was that no single sale was made. Although having a limited sales budget, Carles and Josep had managed to take part in several specialized trading fairs, wrote several articles in energy related journals, and sent brochures to numerous TIC Group customers' mailing lists. In addition, new competitors from abroad were appearing on the scene. The environment was changing for remote supervision companies. This change in the environment significantly affected RISS; their competitors caught up with RISS' embedded technology by using better microprocessors and embedded systems capable of offering the same benefits at a low cost.

Nevertheless, RISS' main problem was probably the long maturation time before sale conversion. In the building industry, it takes at least one or two years from the planning stage until the building is constructed. Only now is RISS receiving purchasing orders from the offers made in 2005.

Rethinking RISS' Commercial Strategy and Business Model

Given previous arguments, the team realized that the business opportunity they were planning to exploit would not provide enough revenues to survive in the short time. Therefore, they organized a meeting with the rest of the founding team to analyze their business model. This change of orientation was forced by the necessity to generate revenues in the short time and took place six months after the first sales were made.

At this point, RISS was in a very delicate situation: costs were greatly exceeding its revenues; sales forecasts had been too optimistic; marketing actions had not succeeded; and new competitors were appearing on the scene. Therefore, a different marketing strategy was needed.

The team decided to cut down costs by firing the RISS sales force. Obviously, this affected the rest of the marketing actions conducted by the firm. Furthermore, the team decided to increase its customized software development activities until they would reach the break even point or they would find more funding to conduct a new sales strategy. This reorganization coincided with a change in the majority of the equity as explained before.

The future was not clear for RISS, but, luckily, in early 2006 the situation began to get better. Although they had not taken a decision on how to reorganize their sales department, purchasing orders began to materialize. Overall, the actions conducted by Carles and Josep were beginning to materialize into sales. In addition, one of the distributors developed by the former sales force began to send purchasing orders.

Cautiously, the founding team decided to put off the decision to rethink its sales strategy until the break even point was reached. Meanwhile, Marc was in charge of sales and marketing actions. The break even point was reached at the end of 2006. Table 3 gives information from the profit and loss account and balance sheet 2004-2006.

At this point, the product had achieved good quality standards and the company was ready to grow. The development of an effective commercial strategy is now the issue.

In general terms, RISS' clients can be segmented into four main groups:

Table 3. Information from the profit and loss account and balance sheet

	2004 (€)	2005 (€)	2006 (€)	2007 forecast (€)
Sales	52.150	214.000	305.000	512.000
Operating costs	75.150	275.000	280.000	482.000
Profit	-23.000	-61.000	25.000	30.000
Personnel	2-3	5-9	10-7	10
% Sales from products	0%	35%	63%	67%
% Sales from ERP and other software solutions	100%	65%	37%	33%
Yearly growth rate	-	310%	43%	68%

- **Project engineering firms:** They develop technical studies for the implementation of remote supervision systems
- **Industrial equipment firms:** They manufacture, install, locate, test, and maintain remote supervision systems
- **Technical maintenance firms:** They maintain remote supervision systems
- **Construction companies:** They build blocks of flats and negotiate with industrial equipment firms to allocate boilers and other installations

Although the firm has already reached its break even, the discussion on the different viewpoints regarding the commercial strategy has re-surfaced.

Carles' idea was that RISS should focus on its core technology and complement it with AI technology and sub-contract the commercialization of its products. In addition, there was also an acquisition offer made by one of RISS' biggest distributors that would guarantee its survival and would enable it to apply its technology to other services (i.e., electricity consumption supervision).

Marc, on the other hand, wanted to be completely independent from any other firm and maintain, even enlarge, the marketing department by contracting both a senior and a junior salesman. Hence, their main disagreement was on the very different and fundamental alternatives: whether RISS should in the future be a technological or a service company.

Appendix 1: Terms and Definitions

Artificial Intelligence or AI: Study of methods by which a computer can simulate aspects of human intelligence. In computer science this the branch that deals with writing computer programs that can solve problems creatively.

ERP: Short for enterprise resource planning, a business management system that integrates all facets of the business, including planning, manufacturing, sales, and marketing.

Embedded systems: Special-purpose systems in which the computer is completely encapsulated by the device it controls. Unlike a general-purpose computer, such as a personal computer, an embedded system performs one or a few predefined tasks, usually with very specific requirements. Since the system is dedicated to specific tasks, design engineers can optimize it, reducing the size and cost of the product.

Linux: A prominent example of free software and of open source development. Its underlying source code is available for anyone to use, modify, and redistribute freely, and in some instances the entire operating system consists of free/open source software.

Microprocessor: An integrated circuit that contains the entire central processing unit of a computer on a single chip. A microprocessor (sometimes abbreviated μP) is a programmable digital electronic component that incorporates the functions of a central processing unit (CPU) on a single semiconducting integrated circuit (IC). The microprocessor was born by reducing the word size of the CPU from 32 bits to 4 bits, so that the transistors of its logic circuits would fit onto a single part. One or more microprocessors typically serve as the CPU in a computer system, embedded system, or handheld device.

Remote supervision: Control of the operation or performance of an apparatus from a distance. In computer environments, remote supervision refers to any method of controlling a computer from a remote location. Software that allows remote administration is becoming increasingly common and is often used when it is difficult or impractical to be physically near a system in order to use it.

Spin-off: A new organization or entity formed by a split from a larger one.

University/research spin-off: A new company based on the findings of a member or by members of a research group at a university.

uClinux: Stands for MicroControllerLinux and is pronounced as *you-see-Linux* is a fork of the Linux kernel for microcontrollers (μCs, embedded systems) without a memory management unit (MMU).

Endnote

[1]   Name of the company and all names are disguised

Chapter III

BookingFax:
A New Concept of Tourism Intermediation

Salustiano Martínez-Fierro, University of Cádiz, Spain

Abstract

In this case we analyze the creation process of a firm from the tourism sector that has exploited a business opportunity opened up by new technologies. BookingFax acts as an intermediary between wholesalers of tourism offers and retailers, travel agencies, and even the final consumers themselves. The main objective of this case is to analyze how information technology in the tourism sector has constituted the basis of an idea to create a firm, and the role the firm plays in the tourism market. In addition, as the case develops it will become clear that information technology provides the competitive basis of BookingFax. The firm has used this key tool to enter the market, be competitive, and become the number-one firm in its sector in Spain.

Background

The firm of interest in this case was founded in July 2002, a transformation of the firm Avantur, created one year earlier. The earlier firm's mission was to inform just a few hotels of the existing offers. BookingFax was born out of "the need to improve the quality and speed of the communications between wholesalers and travel agencies" (Antonio Mariscal, CEO). Thus, the firm needed to go deeper into the world of technology and tourism to use, apart from the fax, the media the Internet provides to communicate offers. Tourism-sector firms did not sufficiently exploit these media at that time. BookingFax is a new formula for the communication and management of travel in Spain, and in a short space of time the new firm has gone international, entering the Portuguese market.

The company's name, BookingFax, is an amalgam of two terms relating to its activity: booking, a word that is well known and widely used in the tourism sector in Spain, and fax, which was the method firms once used to transmit information.

In July 2002, the firm's founders constituted a Sociedad Limitada (private limited company) with the name of BookingFax, S.L. Despite the high level of activity and business that the firm has attained in its short life to date, its three partners currently employ just six employees. From the day the firm started operating to the present, the following key milestones stand out in the expansion of the company:

- After one year, in August 2003, BookingFax earns its first profit.
- In November 2003, the firm introduces a new technology and begins to work on networks.
- After less than two years, in March 2004, BookingFax enters the Portuguese market.

Nevertheless, in order to get a better idea of the rapid growth and evolution of the company, we now offer a timeline of the main activities during the firm's first three years of life:

- **July 2002:** BookingFax S.L. is founded, introducing a new form of communication between the agents in the tourism sector.
- **August 2002:** The firm launches the first system for consulting travel offers on to the market, exclusively for the agents.
- **September 2002:** The system passes 3,000 registered travel agencies.
- **November 2002:** The firm introduces a new version of the system, which improves and speeds up communications between all the players.

- **December 2002**: The Association of Young Entrepreneurs of Cadiz[1] awards BookingFax its first Young Entrepreneur Prize.

- **January 2003:** The one millionth offer is consulted.

- **May 2003:** The multi-channel stage begins, with the launch of the consultation portal for consumers, TravelOfertas.

- **July 2003:** The abovementioned portal boosts the number of consultations substantially, and the system reaches 3 million offers consulted.

- **August 2003:** BookingFax earns its first profit.

- **September 2003:** The system continues to add channels, in this case with the launch of BookingFax Micro, BookingFax Corporativo, and BookingFax Travel in the market.

- **November 2003:** The firm presents a new telecommunications technology based on networks—NetBooking.

- **December 2003:** The firm launches its Virtual Room for product presentations and seminars.

- **January 2004:** The system reaches 7 million offers consulted.

- **February 2004:** The system adds more channels, with the publication of offers in more than 260 Web sites for consumers.

- **March 2004:** BookingFax goes international and enters neighboring Portugal.

- **April 2004:** The firm receives a special mention in the Andalusian Prizes for Entrepreneurial Success on the Internet.

- **June 2004:** The travel offer projector is up and running.

- **July 2004:** For the first time, users consult more than 100,000 firms in a single day.

- **August 2004:** 16,000 registered agents now use the system.

- **September 2004:** The number of offers consulted in the system now exceeds 15 million.

- **October 2004:** BookingFax wins the Special Ciudad de Jerez Prize 2004.

- **November 2004:** The firm launches the collection of portals Travel Temáticos on to the market.

- **December 2004:** The Boletín Diario de Novedades (Daily News Bulletin) now includes news and press releases inserted in BookingFax through the specific section "Canal BookingFax."

- **January 2005:** The system received 11 million consultations of travel offers during 2004, 95% more than in 2003.

As is evident from the timeline, in only three years the founders have won various prizes recognizing both their entrepreneurial initiative and the results they have achieved. The firm has entered the market strongly, soon achieving a high market share and earning a profit. Also of note is the high number of consultations that the system receives from potential customers daily, a reflection of the interest the firm has generated in the tourism sector.

We now briefly describe how the system works in order to shed light on the firm's activities: the emitters, who are the wholesalers or tour operators, insert information about their offers into the system, and BookingFax classifies and orders the information for its subsequent storage in its database. The firm makes this information available to those travel agencies that have previously obtained a license to access the database on the Internet. The final customers or users ask these agencies for products and the agencies look for suitable ones in BookingFax. In short, Booking-Fax acts as an information intermediary.

One point that does concern the owners of the firm considerably is the personnel. Although the firm's operations are fundamentally based on technology, a team of people must handle the information to make the database available for all groups of users. To allocate the personnel, the firm distinguishes between two broad groups of activities. On one hand, the production section, which is responsible for maintaining the system with regard to the day-to-day activities, and on the other, development, which is responsible for maintaining and developing new applications.

Currently, the firm has three partners. One of these, Antonio Mariscal, is the firm's CEO, and so he works in the firm. The other two partners do not work directly in BookingFax; one is responsible for technology, and the other for marketing. In turn, and reporting to the CEO, the firm has a sales manager, two people responsible for development, three in production, and one responsible for the firm's operations in Portugal. BookingFax has a total of six employees in Spain, not including the partners.

Economic-Financial Information

Table 1 offers economic and financial data that describe the evolution of the firm during its first three years of life.

In general terms, the data show that the firm has evolved positively in its first three years. Specifically, BookingFax's total assets were initially negligible, but by the end of 2004, its assets had risen to more than €134,000. The turnover increased markedly between 2002 and 2004, reaching almost €225,000 by late 2004. The firm consequently earned a profit of over €53,000 in 2004. The profitability and liquidity values have also evolved favorably. Moreover, the firm's maximum level

Table 1. BookingFax economic-financial data

	Dec. 31, 2004	Dec. 31, 2003	Dec. 31, 2002
Total assets (€)	134,500	67,129	3,998
Sales (€)	223,511	103,118	2,703
Profit for year (€)	53,451	15,973	523
Economic profitability (%)	39.74	23.79	13.08
Financial profitability (%)	73.27	81.90	14.82
General liquidity (%)	2.13	1.38	8.42
Indebtedness (%)	45.76	70.95	11.73
Number of employees	5	3	1

Source: The author, from SABI database

of indebtedness was in 2003, and this fell to 45.76% in 2004. Remarkably, the firm has achieved all this activity and level of business with only six employees.

Before continuing with the case, the next section discusses technology and the tourism sector in order to give some idea of the situation that BookingFax encountered when it started operating in the sector.

Tourism and Information Technology

The Internet realizes all its potential as a new communication channel and growing business opportunity in the tourism sector. Moreover, this sector is one of the most loyal users of e-commerce. For example, buying a plane ticket, organizing summer vacations, or choosing a hotel close to the convention center we have to visit because of our work are all now possible on the Internet.

The Internet is now undoubtedly one of the most important marketing and communication channels for tourism-sector firms, particularly as a complement to their traditional channels. Thus, according to data from the Center for Regional and Tourism Research, the online travel industry is the main engine of B2C (business-to-consumer) around the world, representing between 30% and 40% of total sales to final consumers. Specifically, in 2002, the industry confirmed the growth trend of the previous years: in Europe, the online tourism sector grew by 53% and reached a turnover of €7.3 billion, while the corresponding figure for the United States was around €30 billion.

The same sources are optimistic for the future, predicting that online tourism sales will continue to grow, reaching 7% of the total turnover in the sector in 2006.

The tourism sector has always shown a clear interest in innovation and the intensive use of information technology and advanced communications services. The new business environment of recent years, characterized by a strong concentration and increasing competition, is forcing the industry to confide in the new technologies as an essential support for its activity.

Very broadly, the tourism sector currently has the following technological challenges with regard to the relationships between customers, suppliers, and employees:

- To create global information systems, supported by common and unified processes in all countries.

- To maximize the opportunities for selling more products and expanding the service offered, optimizing the information flows.

- To reduce costs.

- To use its network, which includes an extremely high number of branches, as a channel to advise, train, encourage, and educate customers to use the new channels, thereby freeing the branches of non-value-added work. The branches can then dedicate their time and resources to serving and advising specific customer segments.

Thus, practically all the services and tools that the IT industry puts into the market nowadays are likely to be of use to tourism-sector firms in their activities.

Aspects such as connectivity, the creation of intranets, extranets, and VPNs (Virtual Private Networks), with special attention to their security and quality, are particularly important in this sector, in which real-time interconnection is critical. Connectivity is fundamental for the exchange of data between customers, wholesalers, travel agencies, hotels, and so forth, which are all actors and links in the tourist activity chain. But, in addition, as the reservation systems incorporate more functionality and multimedia elements—which will happen very soon—the agencies will need greater bandwidth and total availability.

In the current information society, the "network of networks"—the Internet—is proving to be a revolutionary tool for the future of the tourism sector, particularly in the area of distribution and sales, as well as in everything surrounding this: search for information, and combination, reservation, and purchase of tourism products and services.

The new information and communication technologies (ICT) have contributed decisively to the massive growth of tourism and the increase in the value of the supply and demand. In tourism, like in any other perishable, heterogeneous, and intangible product, information forms part of the product itself, as one of its factors of production.

Tourism firms already used new technologies from as early as the 1950s. First, this involved CRSs (computer reservation systems), which allowed airline companies to handle reservations automatically. Various mutually incompatible CRSs sprang up in subsequent years, and in the 1980s global distribution systems (GDS) were created to stick the different airline companies together. Now, these systems instantly supply information about the different consortia of tourism service providers, made up of airline companies and hotel chains. The travel agencies make their reservations and purchases of the services on offer using the terminals of these systems, which are located in their branches.

Thus, the new concept of electronic tourism ("e-tourism" or "online tourism") emerges. E-tourism involves the virtualization of all the processes and of the value chain in the tourism sector: accommodation, transport, leisure, travel, restaurant services, intermediation, and complementary services. This concept includes each of the functions of the tourism business, such as marketing, finance, accounting, production, strategy, planning, or management.

The new information and telecommunications technologies allow tourism firms:

a.   To have a global presence in the international market

b.   To research and develop new tourism products that satisfy the needs of particular market niches

c.   To reduce costs by integrating operating systems and increasing the internal efficacy of the firm (through intranet and extranet networks)

d.   To make prices more flexible, improving competitiveness and profitability.

e.   To save time

Nevertheless, using the new technologies does not guarantee success. Only those firms that, apart from having a clear idea of market needs, create real value for their customers will be able to survive in the long run. Tourism firms that adopt ICT often fail because of their inability to achieve sufficient market share or income quickly enough or their failure to increase the capital available to make the necessary investments in technology. Moreover, low levels of use often mean that companies cannot earn a sufficient return on their investment in the new technologies. Other reasons why many tourism firms fail include their inability to form alliances, re-orient their business model appropriately, or control their costs rigorously. Some of the many new challenges facing the tourism sector include the increasing complexity of the technological products and systems, consumers' growing demands, and the existence of specialist Web sites that compare tourism products.

Threats from New Technologies

The new information and communication technologies in use in the tourism sector will generate a series of threats and opportunities. Among the threats is the fact that the information society is a value added to the product being sold, so that the intermediation agencies' task should be to provide the information consumers need to decide which tourism services provider they wish to select. Direct contact between tourism services providers and customers will increase, which may have negative repercussions for the tourism intermediation firms, in other words, the travel agencies. This phenomenon is known as "disintermediation". Other threats lie in the lowering of entry barriers to new competitors due to the fact that having a large network of branches is now no longer an advantage and in the deregulation processes affecting the tourism industry in general.

ICT will also affect the management of the human resources, particularly because of the emergence of new forms of work, such as "teleworking", or because of the continuing need to re-train workers. Companies will also need to invest heavily in technology at the beginning to be able to offer quality services to the consumer, as well as an adequate and on-going maintenance. Firms will need to specialize to be able to provide a quality service quickly, and they will also need a considerable degree of flexibility to be able to adapt to the changes that occur in the tourism market.

Firms will also need to take into account the internal barriers in different countries, such as the language, culture, or the high level of taxes, as well as the fact that having an adequate technological structure in place is insufficient. The absence of physical contact between seller and buyer may reduce the value of online purchases, since sellers may not be able to convince consumers to purchase more expensive versions or additional products in this medium.

Information is transparent with ICT, and this will lead to an easier and quicker assimilation of the new practices that the sector leaders implement. This fact, as well as the fact that new competitors do not need to make big investments in property to enter the different markets, will reduce profit margins for a large number of tourism products, both in the online and the traditional markets.

In addition, the high costs of acquiring new customers will encourage tourism firms to perfect their loyalty-building systems. Finally, tourism services firms should not underestimate the suspicion and insecurity that e-commerce generates in a sizable proportion of consumers. Transactions on the Internet pose a series of legal problems, such as the question of their tax treatment, the legal validity of electronic commercial documents, copyright and intellectual property, and proving the identity of the parties in online transactions.

Opportunities of New Technologies

In contrast, the new technologies offer a number of opportunities to tourism firms, since merely entering the Internet produces an expansion in the business that many firms would find difficult to achieve in the traditional way. The new technologies are becoming progressively cheaper, and the marginal cost of providing the service to one new customer is lower on the Internet than it would be through traditional channels. If the firm manages to attract a large enough portfolio of customers, it will be able to achieve a return on its initial investment. Another opportunity opened up by the new technologies is the possibility of turning relationships with customers into something much more personal, individualizing the tourism product to extremes that would be practically impossible to achieve in the real world.

The new technologies will also allow already-established firms to use their mass of traditional customers as a starting point for their move into the Internet. These firms undoubtedly have a competitive advantage in this respect over the new firms starting up directly as dotcoms. ICT also eliminates geographic barriers, allowing firms to attract potential customers who would otherwise be unable to use their services because of the distance.

Finally, the new technologies will allow firms to combine their offer of tourism products with non-tourism products. The tourism firm can use portals to become a means of accessing other e-commerce products that would be difficult to commercialize in more traditional ways.

Consequently, the new technologies will also provide many benefits for consumers of tourism products, such as: greater price transparency, the possibility of a personalized offer, improved visual and graphical information (video, photos, maps, street plans, interactive products, etc.), absence of geographic and temporal barriers, greater power of decision, and more information, ability to compare different products, time savings, less need to reserve in advance, and cheaper products, thanks to lower production costs.

Recommendations for Tourism-Sector Firms

Pioneers in adapting themselves to these technologies normally become more competitive and increase their market share, so their global position in the tourism market improves. Firms that prove unable to adjust to the new technologies, in contrast, will lose weight in the tourism market, becoming increasingly left behind until their very survival is threatened. In this respect, tourism firms will need to develop multi-channel strategies that include all the intermediaries of the new e-tourism (Internet, fixed-line and mobile telephone, and digital television) to be able to respond adequately to market demands. Firms that continue to work exclusively with the traditional intermediaries (such as the GDS systems, or videotext) will see their customer portfolio progressively decline over time, along with their value.

There are arguments against the disintermediation phenomenon. These include: travel agencies are professional advisers, and they offer valuable services; travel agencies use their experience to save consumers time; the technology is difficult to use and costly for individual consumers; many consumers are not very computer literate, and, over time, the increasing complexity of these systems will demand even more such knowledge from the users; travel agencies offer free advice, and their advice adds value; the electronic intermediaries mainly serve the business market, and are more expensive; traditional agencies may be able to get more competitive prices through the right channels and agreements; the agencies provide consumers with human contact with the tourism industry; travel agencies limit the insecurity of travel if they take responsibility for all the agreements; and online transactions are not yet secure enough, and this is a concern for potential customers (as shown by the fact that consumers often use the Internet to look for information and consult availability, but close their transactions and pay in more traditional ways).

The traditional intermediaries will not disappear en masse. Only those that prove unable to adapt to the new situation, to consider e-commerce as another channel among their marketing strategies, to exploit the opportunities e-commerce opens up, or to provide the consumer of tourism products and services with value will inevitably disappear.

Thus, the new information and communication technologies will not end all tourism intermediation, but they will lead to important adjustments. The distribution channel will tend to shrink, new types of intermediaries will emerge, and firms that are not able to adapt to the new situation generated by the newcomers will disappear. This is the context in which BookingFax, a firm of recent creation, has proved able to adapt to the changes in the sector by using the new information technologies.

Setting the Stage

Before BookingFax entered the market, firms distributed information by fax. This is a very quick and reliable tool, but it did have its limitations, such as the loss of some faxes and the problem of data storage. The founders of the firm thought that they could solve these problems by using the Internet, as well as improve the speed of the system and increase its capacity of communication. What they conceived was a way to combine two well-known and highly related concepts that had rarely been able to exploit each other before—tourism and technology.

BookingFax stores information from the wholesalers, and makes it available to the travel agencies easily, comfortably, and directly, thanks to computer programs specifically created for information storage. In the past, when, for example, a cruise wholesaler offered something, it had to send faxes to all the travel agencies to communicate the offer. With BookingFax's arrival in the market, the wholesaler can now send the information to BookingFax by Internet, and BookingFax stores the information and distributes it to the travel agencies that are licensed to access the system. BookingFax thereby acts as an intermediary.

The main advantage that the entrepreneurs found was that practically all the retail firms – the travel agencies – had Internet-connected computers in their offices, which BookingFax would use to communicate with them. Thanks to this tool, communication is much quicker, and the agencies can put wholesalers' offers immediately to the final customers. This connection between one link in the value chain and the other is what was missing in the tourism sector before the advent of BookingFax. The function that BookingFax assumes soon found widespread acceptance in the sector.

Initially, the tour operators, agencies, and consumers were largely unaware of the existence of BookingFax in the market, so the firm needed to launch a strong advertising campaign. After its first six months of life, the firm already controlled 50% of the information in the Spanish tourism sector.

Case Description

BookingFax's system for communicating travel offers electronically is a platform of electronic supports designed to disseminate travel offers on the Internet. Each support in the system facilitates the processes of distribution between tourism services providers, travel agencies, corporate customers, and consumers, as can be seen in Figure 1.

This system gathers together the products offered by travel wholesalers, tour operators, reservations centers, airline companies, hotel chains, independent hotels, and tourist apartments. The system can then classify the offers by category and distribute them to the appropriate support depending on the user.

The system fundamentally has two advantages. On one hand, BookingFax's method significantly reduces the providers' communications costs, and, at the same time, it simplifies the retail agencies' work in terms of information and management. On the other hand, the firm's absolute independence with respect to the intermediaries and producers in the tourism sector, the number of users who consult the system, the continuing innovation of the process of communicating via the network, and

Figure 1. Diagram of BookingFax system

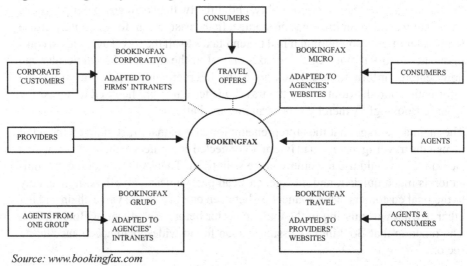

Source: www.bookingfax.com

the proven efficacy of the electronic system compared to the use of fax or e-mail, have converted BookingFax into the leading electronic communications medium of travel offers in the Spanish retail sector.

The supports that form part of the BookingFax platform were designed to facilitate information flows between all the actors in the tourism market; each of these actors has a dedicated tool suited to its needs. In this way, the core BookingFax system functions as a tool that is free to access and designed to help the travel agent manage the offers coming in from the service providers and make all types of technical information available. The following services complement this core system:

• **TravelOfertas:** This is a portal for the consultation of offers directed at the consumers. Travelofertas (Traveloffers) helps final consumers to plan their trips, and excludes offers that consumers can purchase directly from the provider in order to force the user to visit the agency. The mission of this medium is to raise awareness of travel wholesalers' products among consumers, allowing free access to the offers at the same time as they enter the exclusive market of the travel agencies. This portal has important advantages both for the agencies and for the consumers. For the former, the figure of the travel agency is stressed in the Internet, encouraging the user to visit any sales point in the country after choosing a particular offer, and the system can place search engines in the travel agency's own Web site. With regard to the final consumer, the advantages are that the system provides real-time access to all the offers available in the market, provides users with information before visiting a travel agency, and combines the widest variety of product offers in the market.

- **Travel Temáticos:** This is a collection of portals of themed offers. In total, 17 portals for consulting offers oriented at consumers segmented by product type. Travel Temáticos (Thematic Travel) allows consumers to access and locate products by subject matter. These portals are a response to how the demand for travel in the Internet is behaving. The demand is increasingly specialized and needs channels containing information about travel offers adapted to their particular travel interests. Among the advantages of this medium for the agencies are that it allows search engines of offers to be incorporated into vertical information portals, ranging from cruises or tours to offers of particular destinations such as Africa or the Balearic Islands. In addition, for the consumers, the portal provides real-time access to the offers available in the segment of interest in the market, provides them with information before visiting a travel agency, and offers products from the same or a similar subject category. Travel Temáticos can offer specific contents of travel offers to vertical information portals with high value added for their visitors. The offers appearing in these portals are on sale exclusively in travel agencies. An example is travelactivo.com, which includes travel offers relating to active and adventure tourism; ofertasdegolf.com, a portal for those wishing to practice golf on their vacation; or travelnieve.com, where consumers can find information about offers for Spanish or European ski stations.

- **BookingFax Micro:** Adapted to the travel agency's Web site, this medium allows the agencies to manage the destinations and offers, maintain a statistical control of the consultations consumers make, and make reservations by Internet. BookingFax Micro is the offer search application developed to be implemented in the travel agency's Web site, enabling the total management of all its contents and contact with the consumer through their reservation request. This service is a personalized application that automates the process of loading travel offers into the user-travel agency's Web site. The public can then consult, on the Internet, the latest offers that have arrived in their travel agency. In function of each agency's sales policy, BookingFax Micro automates authorized loadings and excludes other offers. The application also allows the user-agency to redefine destinations and group or ungroup products. In this case, the advantages for the agency are that its corporate image on the Internet is maintained, the agency has an administration program with exclusive accesses, and the system facilitates the management of the offers and of the travel providers, allows the tourist destinations to be personalized, and provides forms for requesting information and making reservations directly.

- **BookingFax Corporativo:** This service is designed to serve the corporate segment. It integrates into the corporate customer's intranet, enabling its managers and employees to look for and reserve offers managed by travel agencies. This electronic application allows travel agencies to place a medium for consulting offers in the intranet of its corporate customers, providing an important amount of value added to its service. BookingFax Corporativo (BookingFax Corporate) is oriented to travel agencies specializing in business travel. The application, which was tested by Carlson Wagonlit Travel, is designed to be installed in the intranets of corporate customers. The travel managers or employees of the firm can use this service to consult travel offers in the market in real time, and they can reserve through the travel agency. The service allows firms to adapt the interface to suit their corporate identity, provides information to corporate customers instantly and without them needing to do anything, improves the agency's chances of capturing corporate customers, allows the agency to keep a statistical control of the consultations by firms, provides an administration program with exclusive accesses, and allows the agency to manage the offers and the travel providers, as well as to personalize the tourism destinations.

- **BookingFax Grupo:** Adapted to the intranet of a group of agencies, this service enables the administration of users with access and the establishment of the group's sales policy by organizing the offers according to their priority. BookingFax Grupo (BookingFax Group) was developed to allow various travel agencies grouped under the same brand to maintain the same orientation with respect to the commercialization of the offers they publish in the system. The advantages for the agency are that the corporate identity of the group of agencies is maintained, the service provides an administration program with exclusive accesses, enables the management of the users accessing the medium, allows the group to establish the sale orientation of offers, and facilitates personalized communications with final consumers.

- **BookingFax Travel:** Integrated in the provider's Web site, this service allows providers to make all their travel offers published in BookingFax available on their Web site without actually having to do this task themselves. This medium is designed to be included in the travel wholesaler's Web site, which means that all tourist operators can have a platform for communicating the offers they are launching in the market. BookingFax Travel manages the provider's corporate Web site with regards to the offers. The main advantages are for the tourist operator, since the service distributes the firm's own offers in its Web site, has an automatic system for loading and publishing the offers, and allows the tourism provider to maintain its corporate image, as well as to personalize the tourism destinations in which it operates.

Special Services to Promote Communication

BookingFax's continuing analysis of the information processes in the tourism sector allows travel wholesalers and travel agencies to communicate more effectively by means of the different technologies and special services introduced by the firm. These include:

NetBooking

The technology incorporated in the BookingFax system allows travel agencies to contact the wholesaler's call center by Internet, eliminating the waits associated with telephone calls. NetBooking is a network-based telecommunications service that agencies can use to communicate, in real time, with the wholesaler's reservation center, and a single operator can take more than one call at the same time. This reduces the travel agencies' costs in telephone calls to the tourist operators, and means they do not waste time waiting on the phone. The system also allows real-time communication from the publication of the offer to the reservation, without needing any additional software. In addition, the operator receives fewer calls, the system informs the operator which travel agency is calling and identifies the offer that is being consulted, a single operator can take various calls at the same time, numerous operators can connect to the system simultaneously, and the system can record the conversations between the agents and operators.

Virtual Room

The videoconference platform integrated in BookingFax allows service providers to present their products to travel agencies from anywhere around the world, and allows up to 5,000 agencies to attend each presentation. The Sala Virtual (Virtual Room) is a videoconference service that provides a multimedia platform for tourist operators to present their products, as well as an Internet classroom to train travel agents. Among the advantages of this service for travel agencies is the fact that its eliminates the cost of attending seminars and presentations, allows the participants to interact in real time, allows travel agents to attend from their desk, offers continuous training on tourism products and services, and allows travel agencies to attend pre-recorded presentations or seminars. The system is easy to use and requires only an Internet connection and speakers. This service offers operators greater geographic reach and segmentation of publics, reduces the cost of commercial communication and training, enables immediate interaction with the travel agencies, the participants can provide instant feedback, approximately 5,000 participants can attend each presentation, firms can transfer any promotional media to a virtual space, and the system facilitates training about reservation systems using shared desktops.

Feeding Systems Using XML

The contents published in BookingFax can feed other types of consultation system thanks to the XML language. This allows third parties to display offers in applications they have developed themselves. This feeding through the XML language lets content published in BookingFax be transferred to other applications, such as the systems of information about offers developed by groups of agencies to be consulted by their own agencies or consumers. This allows agents to integrate BookingFax content into already existing systems, and allows them to develop new applications of their own to distribute the offers. At the same time, the destinations most on offer can be analyzed, as well as the providers appearing must often in the system, and the seasons can be compared.

Online Advertising

BookingFax is an advertising medium with significant impact among travel agencies, having exclusive spaces dedicated to covering particular product or tourism services categories. The high penetration rate of the system in the retail sector makes BookingFax the ideal advertising medium for creating brand awareness, communicating market positioning, advertising new products or services, and recalling reservation telephone numbers or e-mails. The advertising spaces can include banners ads of 486 X 60 pixels in TravelOfertas and the Daily News Bulletin. In addition, BookingFax disseminates the message depending on the product or service category in exclusive advertising spaces: the Canaries, tours, fairs, exhibitions, and so forth.

BookingFax is currently an essential channel for the distribution of travel offers, and, indeed, some travel wholesalers now depend entirely on this electronic channel to distribute their product offers. More than 190 providers use BookingFax, including wholesalers, tour operators, reservations centers, airline companies, and hotel chains.

BookingFax has become an essential tool for travel agencies, thanks to the large number of technological innovations it provides to travel agents in their daily work and the wide range of services the firm offers from a position of absolute independence with respect to the other tourism producers and intermediaries. Its most important advantages and uses are as follows:

- **Free access:** After travel agents register with the system, they have cost-free access to all the information published in BookingFax.

- **Rapid search:** The system speeds up search, efficiently classifying offers by category, provider, and destination.

- **Up-to-date information:** BookingFax avoids information errors, automatically deleting out-of-date offers.

- **Reduction in costs:** BookingFax increases productivity, and so cuts costs, by eliminating the need to receive faxes and classify offers. On average, these tasks previously cost around €6,000 per sales outlet per year.

- **News Bulletin:** The system sends the offers introduced by the providers on the previous day to the travel agencies from Monday to Friday in an e-mail.

- **Manual sending to third parties:** Travel agents can send the selected offer on to the customer by e-mail from the consultation system itself.

- **Automatic sending to third parties:** The travel agent can program the automatic sending of offers in function of customers' demand for destinations.

- **Storage of offers:** Both offers of interest and the offers sent can be stored in a personal folder for subsequent consultation.

- **Printing of offers:** Travel agents can selectively print offers depending on their interest.

- **Reservation telephones:** Each offer contains the provider's telephone number so that the travel agent can make the reservation.

- **Online reservation:** The offers also contain direct links to the provider's sales channel on the Internet.

- **Posters of offers:** The travel agents can visualize and print the offer with an improved quality. In some cases, the agency can insert its logo into such posters.

- **NetBooking:** Contact with the wholesaler's call-center is immediate with a telecommunications application allowing operators to attend travel agents live.

- **Mini-guides:** One-page tourist information guides about international destinations that the travel agent can print out and offer to the customer.

- **Offer projector:** The travel agent can visualize all the offers and check the latest offers, classified by destination and operator.

In turn, by registering, the travel agents can be identified by the system and so be handled personally. The system can also send the travel agency daily e-mails with the latest offers published. Each travel agent must register individually by filling in a free registration form.

Service providers can publish offers in the BookingFax system by obtaining a personal license that gives direct access to a user-friendly program. In the insertion platform, the provider introduces the title of the offer and its period of validity, selects territories and the groups of agencies that will be able to consult it, classifies the offer in the corresponding category, and includes the document to display. Before publishing the offer definitively, BookingFax staff thoroughly check the data sent by the provider, thereby avoiding any errors in the offers that might confuse the system's users.

The system's high penetration rate in the retail sector makes BookingFax an ideal advertising medium for creating brand awareness, communicating market positioning, advertising new products or services, and recalling reservation telephone numbers or e-mails.

Current Challenges/Problems Facing the Organization

BookingFax has become the most effective independent medium for the immediate dissemination of travel offers in the Spanish and Portuguese markets, considerably speeding up the process of marketing tourism products and services in travel agencies. The firm's current position in the market offers it the following advantages:

- BookingFax is the leading electronic system for communicating travel offers.
- BookingFax is absolutely independent with respect to the other actors in the tourism market.
- The system cuts communication costs effectively by substituting for the fax.
- Users can insert their offers directly into the consultation system.
- Users can classify their offers themselves, as well as segment them.
- The system sends information immediately to the travel agencies.
- The system provides ample statistical information about each offer.
- Producers can include accesses to sales channels to distribute their products among consumers.
- The system has an up-to-date database of the travel agencies, which is unaffected by changes in their address, telephone number, or e-mail address.
- BookingFax has agreements with the main retail groups to include its offers in their Web sites.

By December 2006, the firm had achieved the following levels of activity:

- Total number of travel agents registered: 26,664
- Total number of offers visualized: 24,511,514
- Total number of consultations: 49,979,052
- Number of offers currently active: 4,220
- Total number of providers with agreements: more than 300

One of the main problems facing the firm has been the competition. After BookingFax was founded, as many as 40 other firms appeared in the market, all aiming to do the same thing. All but one of these competitors, however, have since disappeared.

BookingFax's CEO and owner classifies these new competitors into two types:

1. Those who just wanted to make money in the same way as BookingFax, attracted by the minimum costs and high margins
2. Those who wanted to prevent the pioneer from controlling all the information in the sector, with all the market power that would entail

The only other firm currently operating in the market uses its own offers to supply its system, since it is both a provider and a distributor. Consequently, the competition is not very strong.

BookingFax is currently the number one firm in the sector in Spain and Portugal, with a market share of 95% in the former and 90% in the latter.

The firm's CEO believes that the firm's challenges in the future are to offer more services to the travel agencies, to integrate the firm completely into the Spanish tourism information system, and to expand beyond the Iberian peninsular.

In conclusion, BookingFax, the leading platform in the distribution of travel offers, distributed almost 17 million travel offers in 2006. The exact number of consultations was 16,759,604 offers, which is up 12% from 2005. BookingFax has not stopped growing since its creation in July 2002. Currently, the firm distributes the offers of more than 300 providers to 26,000 user-travel agents in Spain. In Portugal during the same period, the system has obtained 650,000 offers, distributed to 1,300 user-travel agents.

BookingFax is currently preparing to launch its system in the German market during the first three months of 2007. The firm is modifying the Spanish model to adapt it to the needs of German travel agencies. The headquarters of BookingFax Germany are in Lichtenfels (Bavaria), thanks to BookingFax's agreements with an important German producer of back office software widely used in German travel agencies.

Endnote

[1]   This association brings together young entrepreneurs from the province of Cadiz (southern Spain).

Chapter IV

Opportunities and Challenges in the Health Care IT Sector:
The ShiftMarket[1] Case Study

Andrew N. Garman, Rush University, USA

Mayur Patel, Rush University, USA

Rod Hart, Advantage Health LLC, USA

Abstract

The health care sector represents one of the largest and most rapidly growing IT markets in the world. Health care lends itself readily to IT entrepreneurship in a number of ways, but also poses some unique challenges. Many of these facets are illustrated through the experiences of ShiftMarket, a startup company developing and promoting technology-driven solutions for staffing hard-to-fill hospital shifts. Started without any external funding, ShiftMarket negotiated a strong beginning by pursuing technology transfer in collaboration with a U.S. hospital rather than building from scratch. At the time of this case study, ShiftMarket is facing some unexpected challenges and must re-evaluate its strategy moving forward.

Background

The health services delivery market can be described as encompassing all aspects of professional services aimed at improving health, including the infrastructure that facilitates its delivery and makes it more efficient. Health care is an enormous market, particularly in the United States, where it currently represents 16% of GDP, with over 6,000 hospitals delivering care.

In the privatized health care system of the United States, hospitals compete locally with each other for patients. Using traditional measures of market competition, health care would be considered extremely competitive—75% or more of the nation's hospital markets are considered "highly concentrated" (Welton, 2004).

Focus on efficiency. In these markets, operational efficiency has become a key driver of competitive advantage, and information technology is often viewed as the cornerstone for innovations in operational efficiency. Although currently the most visible attention is being paid to electronic medical records, information technology solutions are permeating throughout health care systems, optimizing everything from quality monitoring and telemedicine to patient and staff scheduling.

Collaborative innovation. Although hospitals may compete with each other within geographic regions, they are often highly collaborative with hospitals in other markets. Administrators frequently look to other hospitals to identify practices they might adopt to improve health care and hospital operations.

Dissemination of innovations is supported through a variety of activities. Two in particular are highly relevant to entrepreneurship: professional associations and operational benchmarking. In terms of professional associations, the health services industry has spawned dozens of them, many claiming membership rosters in the thousands or tens of thousands. Most of these associations sponsor annual conferences, typically involving members presenting on "best practices" from their hospitals.

Operational benchmarking involves identifying similar services across hospitals and comparing process and outcomes data to identify highly efficient and/or effective practices. Leaders in hospitals joining such organizations will encourage their administrators to access the data and contact peer organizations to learn new approaches. There is a normative expectation of collaboration within such organizations; if a member receives a call, they are expected to provide what they know to the person calling, in exchange for the opportunity to contact others in the network as needed.

Taken together, the operational benchmarking and professional associations create a climate conducive to disseminating innovations. However the climate itself is not sufficient to facilitate technology transfer on its own, and the chasm between innovation and dissemination represents a healthy breeding ground for entrepreneurial ventures.

The ShiftMarket Innovation

ShiftMarket Inc. was founded in the fall of 2003, with a focus on addressing one of the major problems facing providers of health care services: optimizing hospital clinical staffing. Hospital staffing processes often represent a source of significant inefficiency for several reasons. Like the retail sector, hospital staffing needs change daily, even throughout the day, based on patient volumes. However, unlike retail, the match between patient flow and staff availability has much less room for variability; in fact some regions dictate a specific staff-to-patient ratio for some professional positions.

Also unlike retail, the clinical staff of hospitals typically have extensive educational preparation requirements. Due in part to the length of time it takes to prepare these professionals, the health care market is in a near-constant state of shortage in one or more of the professions. (At the time of this case study, there were significant shortages in several of the nursing professions as well as radiology/ultrasound technologists and pharmacists.)

Employing more professionals than the organization needs creates a cost inefficiency—salaries are paid for professional skills in excess of what is needed. However, employing too few is even more cost inefficient. If a hospital does not have the professionals it needs to staff a service, it has two choices: (1) turn away patients and the associated revenue; or (2) seek additional professionals from a staffing agency. These agencies provide last-minute staffing needs to hospitals, but at a premium of two to three times the cost that staff employed by the hospital would cost. For example, a registered nurse might cost the hospital $20 to $25 per hour as a full-time employee; that same registered nurse would command $50 to $60 per hour if sourced through agencies.

A portion of that premium is paid to the health care professional filling the position, so working for agencies is a more lucrative career choice for professionals who have the flexibility for their schedules and work locations to change periodically. However, the professional's portion is typically small (25% or less). The remainder of the premium goes towards the agency's administrative costs, marketing costs, recruiting costs, and "carrying costs" (unutilized hours of employed agency nurses). Since the evidence to date is that most agencies are not making huge margins then the agency "middle man" represents a source of significant inefficiency in the staffing process. At the time of this case study, it was not uncommon for larger medical centers to be spending premiums in the millions of dollars for agency help.

In examining these staffing challenges, two former health care consultants, John Carvey and Paul Smith, concluded that the problem hospitals were facing was not one of staff shortage ("resource gap"), but rather of liquidity shortage ("liquidity gap"), as shown in Figure 1 from one of ShiftMarket's presentation. In other words, in many markets there were enough health care staff to go around, but the flow

Figure 1. Nursing shortage as a function of resource vs. liquidity gaps

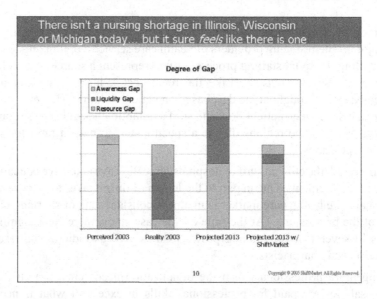

of information about areas of need was highly inefficient. Agencies were able to capitalize on this inefficiency by centralizing the need identification process and matching qualified personnel to them. John and Paul recognized that if hospital staffing managers were able to talk to the labor pool directly, they could cut out the middleman, staff the shifts themselves, and save a substantial amount of money in the process. Given the magnitude of potential savings—in the millions of U.S. dollars for some hospitals—it seemed there would be ample opportunity to recoup software development costs.

Setting the Stage

The Founders

John Carvey and Paul Smith worked together as health care consultants for a major U.S. consulting firm. Both had entered into consulting with backgrounds in health administration; John held a Master of Science in Health Systems Management from Rush University in Chicago; Paul held a Master of Health Services Administration and Business Administration from the University of Michigan. In their work together in the early 1990s, they found a kinship in their interest in entrepreneurship. John had left the firm to help start a new consulting firm, which was subsequently sold, and began work with a strategy firm. Paul had stayed on at the firm and gained extensive experience leading large health care IT and performance improvement engagements.

In the early 2000s the use of online auctioning sites had grown explosively, due in large part to the success of the consumer site eBay. Even before eBay's widespread success, numerous companies had begun experimenting with the use of auctioning as a tool for enhancing both process and market efficiency related to procurement (Jap, 2000). Auctioning was beginning to see application in any area where there were multiple suppliers of goods and services that could be standardized. From their work experience, Paul and John recognized that shift work had these characteristics—standardizability as well as multiple potential suppliers—and thus could theoretically be procured through a similar, but slightly different, reverse auction process. The idea seemed to have enough promise and enough entry barriers that it was worth investing the time to investigate in greater depth.

Estimating the Size of the Opportunity

At the time the founders began investigating this opportunity, there was a considerable volume of international press on the increasing reliance on agency nursing in Europe and Australia. While the founders recognized these as opportunities for expansion, they believed they would need to begin by developing a firm foundation within the U.S. health care market and so based their initial estimates there. There are several suppliers of health care market data, including the U.S. government and the American Hospital Association, as well as other trade associations and private groups. From these sources they modeled the size of the opportunity based on a "universe" of 5,764 hospitals, as well as a potential secondary market of 16,491 long-term care facilities. Recent surveys indicated that 72% of this hospital base (roughly 4,150 potential hospital clients). According to the U.S. Bureau of Labor Statistics, there are 2.4 million registered nurse positions in the United States; 3 in 5 of these (1.44 million) are in hospitals.

The difference in cost between agency and staff nursing could be estimated at $220 per eight-hour shift, or $57,200 per year per full-time vacancy. In 2002, the American Hospital Association reported that the average nurse vacancy rate in U.S. hospitals was 13% (in other words, 187,200 positions in total), suggesting that the total premium being paid out to agencies was approximately $10.7 billion per year.

Assuming current staff could be enticed to work hard-to-fill shifts at a greater premium to their base, the savings to the hospital would be $110/shift—that is, half the premium paid out to agencies for temporary nursing assistance. Conversations with contacts within major medical centers confirmed that many were spending in the millions of dollars apiece on agency nurse utilization, and it was an area many were targeting for improvement.

Because health care is a data-intensive business, most U.S. hospitals have internal IT resources capable of developing applications of this type. So for an externally-developed application to be competitive, it must clearly cost less than one might estimate internal development to cost. Taking $150,000 as a rule-of-thumb for development of an application of this complexity, an annual subscription rate in the $48,000 range was estimated as safely competitive with internal development. Based on a sales model involving annual subscriptions in the $48,000 range, the estimated total market size for U.S. hospitals was $200m per year in recurring revenues.

Factoring in penetration and market share potential, this estimate suggested that the market would be healthy for a "bootstrapped" approach, but would be very difficult to attract venture backing; the market share would need to be very substantial very quickly, and there would be little opportunity to correct course along the way. The founders thus concluded that they would need to pursue the opportunity through strategic partnerships and with as little outside funding as they could manage to move forward with, allowing them to maintain tight control over their products and customer relationships as they evolved.

Environmental Scan

Given both the emerging popularity of bidding technology as well as the pervasiveness of the staffing challenges, John and Paul knew it was possible, perhaps even likely, that other companies were working on products of a similar nature. Thus one of their first steps was to research emerging technologies in this area, using a multifaceted approach. Health care administration is replete with magazines and trade journals describing innovations, so electronic searching of databases containing these sources was an important early step. They also identified companies for whom market entry would be easiest—in particular, companies selling scheduling products—to determine who was working on these technologies, how far along they were in their developmental cycles, and what barriers to entry might exist. Additionally, they used their professional networks to scan for other entrepreneurial ventures that might be on the horizon in this space.

Through the processes described above they identified three other systems that either were developed or were being developed that were highly similar to their planned application. Two of these systems were developed in-house by hospitals; the third was being developed by a commercial start-up.

John and Paul contacted the hospitals to ask if they would be willing to demonstrate their applications, and, if the demonstrations suggested commercial viability, whether they would be interested in licensing their applications out.

One of the hospitals they contacted told them they had already worked out a business relationship with another company interested in commercializing their application.

The other hospital, Somerville Hospital, did not have any relationship. John and Paul previewed their application and found it to be particularly well designed and developed. Although it did not have all of the features John and Paul knew would be needed for commercial viability, it was very close. They also recognized that competitors were going to be entering the market soon, so the window of opportunity was not likely to be open for long. Thus John and Paul decided that a licensing agreement would make more sense to them than building from scratch, and worked out an arrangement with Somerville to make that happen.

The agreement with Somerville Hospital specified the creation of a new company, ShiftMarket, which would pay royalties to Somerville in exchange for access to their source code. Over time, ShiftMarket would modify the code to enhance its commercial potential for a broader base of hospitals. Over the course of several years, the royalty rate would decrease in planned phases, reflecting the upgrading ShiftMarket would be making to the application. Additionally, after a predetermined number of hospitals had signed on as clients, ShiftMarket would own the source code.

At the same time the deal was being arranged with Somerville Hospital, John and Paul were making inquiries to other hospitals they thought would be interested in an application of this type. Through these efforts, they were able to line up their first client (a previous consulting client of one of the founders) simultaneous to the finalization of the licensing arrangement. They were thus ready to pursue their first implementation immediately. John and Paul were also advantaged because they had an immediate source of revenue and did not need to float the company nor seek outside investors at that time.

Initial Product Development

Although Somerville Hospital's application worked well for its original purpose, it had not been designed with multiple-site use in mind. Its relatively small scale did not require highly structured coding; as end-users increased, however, the limits of the system would quickly become apparent. There was also a need to partition the databases by client for improved security. To these ends, John and Paul needed to enlist the help of dedicated programming resources.

Given the trends toward globalization at the time, John and Paul faced a decision about whether to subcontract the work overseas or to recruit a programming team domestically. The overseas outsourcing promised a significant cost-savings; however John and Paul were concerned about whether an offshore team would have the contextual knowledge necessary to redesign the application with sufficient sensitivity to end user needs. Ultimately they decided to recruit locally, focusing on contacts they knew who had previously developed applications for health care clients.

Product Sales

ShiftMarket decided to use an ASP model for providing its applications, which would allow them greater control and accessibility for troubleshooting purposes as well as the opportunity to create a use-based licensing fee structure. ShiftMarket would charge a one-time setup fee to cover onsite staff training on implementation and use; additional fees would be charged based either on a flat rate or on the number of shifts successfully filled by the application. This model allowed hospitals the flexibility of starting to use the application at a lower relative cost and pay for ongoing use through realized savings that the application delivered.

Serving as the initial sales force, the founders developed a pitch presentation that would allow them to efficiently explain their application to a nontechnical audience, so they could spend the balance of prospective client meetings describing the substantial value their product could bring to the client's hospital, as well as answering questions about the application. An example from this presentation is provided in Figure 2.

The months following the start of ShiftMarket saw a lot of early successes. The same media coverage that had brought Somerville Hospital to John and Paul's attention was also capturing the attention of other hospitals with similar staffing challenges. Thus ShiftMarket's early marketing efforts involved far lower costs than would have been the case otherwise. Somerville Hospital also had a number of strong nurse

Figure 2. ShiftMarket product description slide

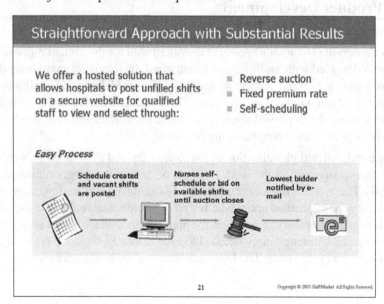

advocates who were well-networked nationally, who could advocate for the application as users. Between the nurse contacts and the media attention, ShiftMarket found they had a comfortable volume of inbound inquiries during these early months.

However, after the first six months, as the population of early adopters started to wane, the sales cycle—the time between an initial contact and a signed agreement—began to increase. Over time, the mix of more conservative hospitals in the customer base was growing larger, bringing with it greater front-end resource demands to close sales, as shown in Figure 3.

Paul and John were also beginning to recognize that the skills needed to sell, with limited support resources, a new evolving technology to early adopters were very different than the skills needed to sell established technologies that were supported by vast marketing resources to mainstream adopters. Several types of channel distribution arrangements/alliances were tried and evaluated with mixed results. Alliances with consulting firms, group purchasing organizations (GPOs), and other technology vendors were developed, but proved to add limited direct value in terms of generating new sales. As the sales cycle grew longer and more complex, these partners grew distracted by more immediate issues and more traditional activities for their businesses.

ShiftMarket hired a consultant with extensive experience in health care IT sales to help develop a sales strategy. The consultant had experience with start-up companies and so was sensitive to their budgetary constraints. After evaluating several options, and seeing that their main competitor was winning new business before ShiftMarket was able to get a foot in the door, it was determined that a direct sales force, supported by an effective telemarketing effort, was deemed the most effective approach for this stage of the business. It was also going to prove the most costly. ShiftMarket hired the sales consultant as their vice president of sales to implement the sales strategy.

Health care in general is a very challenging industry to sell into; salespeople need to have a solid understanding of the industry to begin with, plus the ability to quickly establish credibility with a breadth of clinicians and health care executives. While John and Paul were able to find good candidates through their professional networks and through the network of their new sales executive, they were finding that if a salesperson was good at getting initial sales meetings scheduled, they would not be nearly as good at following-through on the leads to close the sale. Conversely, they worked with some professionals who had proven track records but were far less adept at establishing and developing the initial leads. In addition, these sales people were used to being supported by application specialists who often did the actual demonstrations. This meant that ShiftMarket would need specialized direct sales and support resources, which required an even bigger upfront investment and at least 6 months before realizing tangible results—a significant concern for cash flow.

Figure 3. Increasing average sales cycle time over the course of the company's development

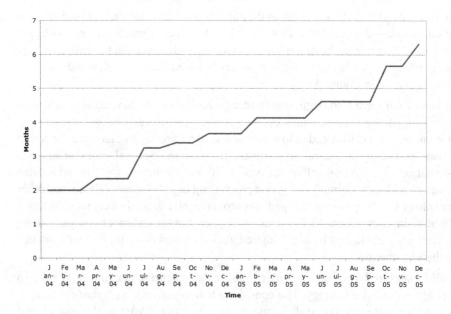

On the lead-generation side, John and Paul struggled to find salespeople who were the right mix of aggressiveness and integrity. Very early in the process they had brought on some salespeople based on their strong records of success, only to find that they were far too comfortable "telling the client what they wanted to hear" in order to move the sales process along. Sales tactics of this type were of considerable concern to John and Paul, who viewed the integrity of their company's reputation as critical to their long-term success. They addressed these concerns by hiring the sales executive to add more structure to the process, by developing and maintaining regular communications about the importance of integrity in the sales process, and by ending relationships with salespeople whose values didn't match their own.

On the closing side, it was becoming apparent that ShiftMarket needed to have salespeople who could establish instant credibility with potential buyers. They would eventually recognize that in addition to experienced sales staff they would also need experienced nurse executives, people who had lived the challenges of staffing in a shortage environment and who could speak directly and credibly to the key decision-makers within hospitals who were directly involved in the sales process. They were very excited when they found a highly qualified nursing executive willing to assist in both sales and implementation of the application. This nursing executive provided flexibility for ShiftMarket and continuity for clients who would work with this person pre and post sales.

While they were growing their U.S. business, John and Paul also were exploring opportunities in other countries that they had identified as facing nursing shortages. For these sales, they began with a strategy of finding partner firms in these other countries based on their network from previous international experiences. In addition, from their considerable press (both domestic and international) they received unsolicited requests from foreign companies interested in being value added resellers (VARs) for their application. Unfortunately, international sales proved a far more complex and challenging environment. In particular, although buyers on the administrative side of health care could see the potential value, the highly unionized health care environments in other countries often viewed ShiftMarket with considerable suspicion. Ultimately, no amount of U.S.-based data and testimonials could dissuade their concerns that ShiftMarket was some kind of backdoor approach to disempowering the health care unions, and many potential buyers backed down in the face of mounting union pressures.

Culture and Organization Development

Once John and Paul had added their initial sales force, they held a planning retreat in March 2005 to discuss the company's mission, vision, and core values. This is depicted in the slide shown in Figure 4, adapted from the retreat slides. They recognized that as a small, entrepreneurial firm, there would be dangers associated with having too short-term a focus. The retreat was held to help build a sense of long-term goals as well as commitment to those goals.

The vision and values mirrored those of the founders, who wanted to take a conservative approach with the venture, rather than a "do or die" or "bet-the-farm" strategy. If the venture did not move forward as anticipated, they wanted to ensure that their clients' needs and best interests were well safeguarded, as well as those of their employees.

Competition and Competitive Advantage

For many IT products, companies can create competitive advantage by focusing on continuous technical innovation. Given ShiftMarket's core market—hospitals and health care systems—a focus on continuous technical innovation would be less advantageous, and could even be self-defeating. Hospitals tend to care much more about stability and reliability than about innovation; they want products that work

Figure 4. ShiftMarket mission and vision

very well, and a customer support infrastructure that is accessible and sensitive to the importance of the work of hospitals. In this market, a reliable and user-friendly application was the entry ticket; sustainable competitive advantage in this context would ultimately come from evolving the applications to continuously streamline the steps it takes to use them while continuously safeguarding their reliability.

In the early days, ShiftMarket's principal competition was from Shift Genie. Like ShiftMarket, Shift Genie had developed their core application as a technology transfer from an existing hospital system's application. Unlike ShiftMarket, the management team at Shift Genie began with substantial venture backing, and the aggressive growth expectations that are typically commensurate with that backing. To justify these growth expectations, Shift Genie's plan of necessity involved dominating the staffing solutions space.

To pursue this plan, Shift Genie leveraged their capital into a sizeable direct sales effort. Shift Genie had an established alliance with the largest health care staff scheduling vendor, a company with over 1,000 hospital clients, which provided them with a strong base to start with. Together these forces provided Shift Genie with significant advantages; they often had first contact with prospective clients and were able to shape their perceptions. Many of their sales were closed without the client being aware of or seeing a demonstration of ShiftMarket's products.

In addition to aggressively marketing their own products, Shift Genie also focused attention on undermining the marketing of their competitors. When the early success of ShiftMarket came to their attention, Shift Genie developed a new Web site with the appearance of a neutral third-party information site. On this site they created hundreds of subpages, with content and meta-tags containing the ShiftMarket branding as well as Somerville Hospital's, which would point to the home page of the new site. The home page ostensibly listed vendors of shift bidding solutions, but in reality redirected browsers to the Shift Genie site. The effect was to push the ShiftMarket Web site far enough down into the search engine rankings that it would be very difficult to reach for anyone but a very dedicated searcher, with everyone else being driven into the Shift Genie site.

The strategy was both ethically and legally questionable, and ShiftMarket successfully challenged the practice on legal grounds. However the strategy was symptomatic of the more general, highly aggressive approach Shift Genie was taking in the marketplace, something that would prove to be an ongoing challenge for ShiftMarket.

As more and more hospitals began investigating shift bidding technologies, ShiftMarket was increasingly finding themselves competing against Shift Genie head-to-head for clients. Shift Genie would position themselves as a well-funded company that was "in it for the long haul," in turn depicting ShiftMarket as an undercapitalized start-up that could go out of business at any time. (This positioning was particularly ironic, given that ShiftMarket had been profitable since its first year in business, yet Shift Genie was running at a $1m / year loss.) These tactics led ShiftMarket back to legal involvement multiple times. In each case Shift Genie agreed to back down, but ShiftMarket saw there would be a need for constant vigilance.

Over time, the vendor "shootouts" were providing both Shift Genie and ShiftMarket with competitive intelligence regarding each company's perceived strengths and weaknesses and led to an on-going convergence of development priorities. In the meantime, as challenging as Shift Genie and ShiftMarket were finding the sales process, many of the other companies that had entered the market were finding it impossible to find a strong enough foothold to continue.

Competition also extended to the sales force. The skill set the sales force needed was so specialized that ShiftMarket found that its competitors were regularly trying to lure away their salespeople. This created additional challenges, as well as expense, as ShiftMarket struggled to keep their sales force from leaving for competitors with deeper pockets.

Current Challenges Facing the Organization

At the time of this case, ShiftMarket faces three principal challenges: competition from Shift Genie, the lengthening of the sales cycle, and barriers to systems integration. Each had implications for the cost of acquiring new clients, and was beginning to challenge the assumptions regarding profitability within the sector.

Competition. Although ShiftMarket had successfully headed off several of the most egregious of Shift Genie's challenges, the ongoing cost of involving legal representation to protect ShiftMarket's reputation was becoming a considerable expense and distraction.

Sales cycle. A closer analysis of the sales cycle was suggesting that new prospective client hospitals were qualitatively different from the hospitals who had adopted ShiftMarket's technology earlier on. The early adopters were characterized as more innovative generally, and, as such, had more streamlined and responsive approaches to technology adoption. These early adopters were also the hospitals experiencing the most acute and severe cases of staffing challenge; they were highly motivated to implement solutions quickly and stood the most to gain from their success.

The current mix of prospective clients included hospitals with significantly higher barriers to innovation. In contrast to early-adopter sites, in which decisions may have involved relatively few points of contact, many of these hospitals had multiple-hurdle approval processes with initial decision-making pushed much lower into the organizations but with far less straightforward pathways to ultimate approval.

Also, while all stood to gain from implementing the technology, for many the staffing challenges were not creating the same levels of institutional "pain" as was seen in the early-adopter sites. Some larger organizations would bring in multiple vendors for meetings before they had decided whether to invest in the technology in the first place; on some occasions prospective clients would abandon the process mid-stream, deciding it was not a high enough priority or that they might be able to cobble a similar application together in-house.

Systems integration. Increasing numbers of potential clients were asking for guarantees around systems integration—in particular, they wanted data to flow freely between their bidding software and their staff scheduling systems. ShiftMarket tried to be very responsive to these requests, but most scheduling system providers had no strong incentive to work collaboratively with ShiftMarket to facilitate systems integration. Indeed, some had told clients they planned to introduce similar products at some indefinite point in the future, so in some cases there was a clear disincentive. This lack of systems integration was emerging as an important barrier in some sales meetings, causing some hospitals to take more of a "wait and see" approach.

Strategic Options

ShiftMarket's growth has begun to slow and they are at a time where re-examination of their strategy is warranted. If they continue with their current stand-alone approach, the challenges described in the previous section may become more of a threat.

To address these current challenges, ShiftMarket has several options it can pursue. Because of their low start-up costs, margins on their product sales remain healthy, so one option is to compete more aggressively on cost. Historically, ShiftMarket had been offering their products at rates that were cost-competitive with Shift Genie's, forcing Shift Genie to lower their costs over time to meet ShiftMarket's. With more aggressive cost-cutting, ShiftMarket might weaken Shift Genie's position to a point where their forecasts would no longer yield their originally anticipated returns, making it more likely that Shift Genie would seek an early exit from the market. The principal disadvantage of this strategy, of course, was that it would quickly make ShiftMarket's own business less profitable.

Another potential approach is to meet the competition with a more aggressive growth strategy. This strategy would be particularly appropriate if the founders thought the window of opportunity for these applications was beginning to close. Such a strategy would almost certainly involve the need for outside investment, and thus a loss of equity on the part of the founders.

A third option would be to expedite the exit strategy and begin seeking a buyer for ShiftMarket. The company was neither as large nor as profitable as the founders had wanted it to become before selling or merging, so if they pursued a sale they were unlikely to see the kind of payoff they had initially hoped for. The most likely potential buyers would be one of the more established providers of related software applications (scheduling, time, and attendance, etc.), a large staffing agency looking to hedge against this potentially threatening technology, or one of their competitors.

Of course, other creative options may also be possible.

References

Jap, S. (2000, Nov/Dec). Going, going, gone. *Harvard Business Review, 78*(6), 30.

Welton, W.W. (2004). Managing today's complex health care business enterprise: Reflections on distinctive requirements of health care management education. *Journal of Health Administration Education, 23,* 391-418.

Endnote

[1]   Fictitious name

Chapter V

Breaking Through Barriers in New Technological Initiatives:
Entrepreneurs in the Context of Free Software

José Antonio Ariza Montes, University of Córdoba, Spain

Alfonso Carlos Morales Gutiérrez, University of Córdoba, Spain

Alfredo Romeo Molina, Blobject Founding Partner, Spain

Abstract

This work analyzes different factors in the entrepreneuring process in a company based in business opportunities advantages through the usage of free software in a technological context. Blobject connects opportunities for local development, usage of open source technologies, and new social trends in many consumers; tourists, in this case, as a example of respect for the environment and the desired "freedom and autonomy". This company offers different products and services using ecologic vehicles (electric energy), ease-to-use, such as GEM Cars -equipped with a touch screen computer- and Tours in Segways. The studied case shows the integration process from different technologies that connect through digital infrastructure. In this way, GEM cars use the GPS technology for location within a digital assistant, multimedia power (touch screen computer and audios and videos) to show the tourist opportunities in an specific place, and the needed adaptation for the language diversity.

An "Integral" Business Concept: Blobject

On April 28, 2005, the company known as Blobject, S.L. (www.blobject.es) was officially launched in the city of Córdoba (Spain). The initiative was the fruit of over 10 months of conceptualizing, designing, and developing on the part of three enthusiastic young entrepreneurs: Marco Antonio, Alfredo, and Laura, who, despite their youth and due to their wide spread experience, were already well versed in such varied fields as information and communication technologies and business consultation.

In its main business sector that competes with the traditional tourism sector, Blobject Tours offers a most original, practical, and fun way to visit a city of such monumental attractions as Córdoba, declared Heritage of Humanity by the UNESCO in 1984. This is achieved through its organization of various tourist routes visited in one of two different types of rented electrical vehicles (B1-Car y Segway). Furthermore, Blobject currently exploits two other business lines: consulting and distribution (as the distributor of electrical cars and Segways). Although this case focuses mainly on Blobject Tours, its connection and synergies for future development in other areas are evident, as will be seen in our final section.

From an entrepreneur's point of view, the Blobject project's foundations are based on three main organizational and contextual pillars (see Figure 1):

* First of all, the context has to be mentioned to explain two key elements that exploit opportunities at both macro and micro economic levels. On one hand, at a macro level, this initiative is part and parcel of emerging values in today's society, like the value placed on one's free time and the concern and respect for the environment in modern highly developed societies. On the other hand, at a microeconomic level, Blobject is an example of how to capitalize on the type of idiosyncratic opportunity associated with elements in space and time, where an unusual business model springs up and which, in this case, is closely related to the sightseeing potential of a city like Córdoba. In fact, social innovation can be just as important, or even more so, than actual technological innovation when it comes to uncovering business opportunities.[1]

Figure 1. Blobject's four pillars

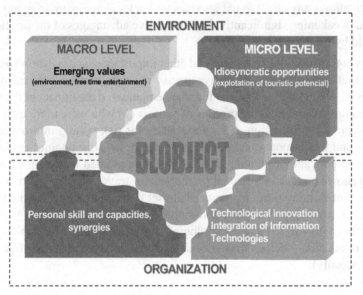

- The second pillar is made up of a fusion of individual talents produced by the association of the three founding partners of the company. As will be seen further on, the essentially complementary aspects of these young entrepreneurs are fundamental in the development of this initiative and contribute considerably to competitive advantages.
- Finally, and as the key differentiating element toward success, this integration of various sources with technological development has to be situated in a context linked to free software, an idea that will be enlarged upon throughout this chapter.

Global Changes and Local Opportunities

Social Changes and Tendencies in a Traditional Sector: Tourism

The impact of Internet use in the tourist sector has meant such radical changes at different levels that most travel agents involved feel they are again newcomers in what was their traditional activity. For example, the hermetically closed systems of distribution and mediating in tourist activity have burst wide open, since the Internet now allows any client to use services with a local company from any part of the world, weakening significantly the competitive advantages of the privileged position held by traditional agents.

Thus, the protagonists of this case identified other important changes in how tourism is regarded that also generated new ways to answer needs insufficiently catered to at a local level. When interviewed, the founders emphasized the impact of the great transformations undergone in the profiles of visitors (1) who were more qualified, (2) requested more information, (3) whose desire for risk-taking, improvisation, spontaneity, and much more autonomy compounded their disappointment in traditional tourist package deals with all activities programmed and planned ahead of time, (4) showed a lack of seasonal preference for travelling, thus reducing the concentration of holiday time in summer (shorter periods like long weekends or plain weekends are being used more and more to visit other cities), and (5) above all, whose ability to use the new technologies—more and more accessible to the bulk of the population—helped make decisions about what to do in their free time (Internet especially).

Local Opportunities as a Strategic Factor: "New Ways of Doing the City"

Córdoba's period of greatest splendor took place during the Califato of Abderraman III. Edmundo of Amicis relates that its fame reached all of the Far East and attracted the faithful from the most remote regions of Asia to its riverbanks where they fell to their knees to marvel at the mihrab in its Mosque. Doctors and poets were drawn to its flourishing schools, its huge libraries, and its magnificent court from all parts of the Muslim world. In addition to the city's undeniable charm, tourist attention must adapt to the times, since the trends and changes mentioned above demand an adequate response at a local level. Thus, Córdoba, like many other European cities graced with great monuments, is endowed with:

- An abundant and one of Europe's greatest[2] but relatively disperse cultural Heritage, which generates a great number of national as well as foreign visits.[3]

- An ever increasing tendency towards solely pedestrian streets around the historical areas of the city, which do not allow the entry of noisy and polluting vehicles, just as in many other cities (London, Malaga, etc.).

- An obsolete[4] offer to the visitor who would like, above all, to take full advantage of his time while also feeling free enough to follow his own inclinations.

The Business Concept: "New Ways to Visit the City"

These opportunities and the familiarity with the city (where, after all, the founders were born and have lived during most of their lives) are, to a great extent, behind this decision to situate a key company (Blobject Tours) in this city. Actually, it is a question of responding efficiently to the demands made by a certain type of tourist who would like to freely go sightseeing on his own, to get to know this varied though disperse monumental heritage. To do this, Blobject offers the use of rented alternative vehicles small enough to allow great mobility throughout the historical sector of the city and an extensive net of exclusive parking lots run by the company (some public, and others through agreements reached with private businesses such as restaurants, taverns, and souvenir shops). These are situated in strategic points of the city in order to facilitate and expedite a visit in the free time the tourist has to spend (see Figure 2). This idea is not totally original. On the Internet, the entrepreneurs also found this type of tourism in San Francisco (using, however, petrol-run cars that did not count on the advantage of information technology). Nonetheless, Blobject's initiative of a rental service for technological tourist cars really is a world wide first, its characteristics differing it from other business projects that might look similar at first, but actually lack the innovating factors incorporated by the Blobject backers,[5] as can be seen in Table 1.

Table 1. Innovating characteristics developed by Blobject

	Where the Idea for Blobject Originated	**Blobject Innovation (Gemcars)**
Basic Business Concept	Rental of Petrol-run Vehicles for Sightseeing	Rental of Electrical Vehicles for Sight-Seeing
Source of Energy	Polluting	Non-Polluting
Level of Noise Pollution	High	None
Interaction with the Environment	None; Closed Vehicle	High; Vehicle with Doors
Support for Tourist Attention and Integration of Information Technologies	Has None	It Does Exist
Parking Places Associated with the Initiative	None	Necessary

On the other hand, as far as the organization of SegWay-type tourist routes is concerned, there are similar projects in cities like Prague, Paris, and Barcelona that have proved to be totally satisfactory.

So the business idea of Blobject arises from the following coordinates: adjustment to the trends emerging in the tourism sector, especially those referring to the new profile of the city tourist, taking advantage of the opportunities that such a monumental city as Cordoba offers, and, finally, improving substantially and in a most innovative way the solutions available to respond to these needs. Once the decision had been taken to go ahead with this business proposition, the founders found four basic challenges ahead. These included making known what this totally new service was capable of, building commercial channels to sell these services, both locally and world-wide, improving the index of overnight stays in Cordoba, using the services of Blobject to visit places other than the Mezquita and the Alcazar of the Catholic Kings, and becoming recognized as an alternative for people with problems of mobility.

Personal Skills and Knowledge Management

A good idea incapable of being carried out is not much more than an illusion or dream whose difficulties seem to turn into insurmountable obstacles. The success of a business project depends on various factors, but undoubtedly one of the greatest is

Figure 2. Electrical cars and a look at one of the world's most famous monuments in Cordoba: The Mosque

the human factor. In this sense, Shalman (1998) identifies several aspects that have to be analysed to achieve the desired result: the human team, the opportunity, the risk and pay back and, finally, the work atmosphere. Of these, the most important is teamwork, and Shalman states, "when evaluating a business project I always begin with personal histories. Not because the human team of a new enterprise is the most important thing, but because without the right team, none of the other points are at all significant."

Researchers have studied this in depth trying to identify the characteristics that define the entrepreneur personality. Among the most frequently mentioned are ambition, self-confidence, optimism, impatience, creativity, intuition, and teamwork. An entrepreneur is not a superman or a superwoman, so it is practically impossible for anybody to possess this wide range of competencies. Precisely, a fundamental characteristic of the founders of Blobject is the complementary aspect of the capabilities and skills present, producing a synergetic effect that uplifts and contributes to the project.

Undoubtedly, one of the keys to the success of the Blobject project is the innovative technology its promoters have managed to develop—and apply—to a traditional sector like tourism. However, all this would not have been possible without its founders' inherent effort and personal capacity. Figure 3 shows a list of competencies the entrepreneurs have been able to catalogue thanks to their complementary formation and personal experience. As can be seen, the birth of Blobject has been possible due to the multidisciplinary characteristics of the founding partners, each contributing essential elements for the success of the venture and, especially, enough strong personal commitment to outweigh individual interests, sufficient enough to set aside professional stability in order to sail into a business adventure they firmly believed in.

Before setting up this business, Marco Antonio, Alfredo, and Laura had each traveled very different professional routes. Thus, Marco Antonio Castilla Gómez, age 33, had already accumulated a great deal of experience in creating and setting up companies, especially those related to the information technology sector. In 1995 he founded the McInformática Company, dedicated to the distribution of computer components, and the production center EOS Processor. In the year 2003, he was named "Young Entrepreneur" of the year for his business career achievements by the Córdoba Association of Young Business People. Marco Antonio is the partner whose experience in hardware has enabled him to create the interactive computer information stand.

Alfredo Romeo Molina, on the other hand, is specialized in free software and familiar with its technological possibilities as well as the technological business opportunities offered by this technology and, at the same time, people who can develop computer applications adapted to clients' needs. Alfredo got his degree in Finance from St. Louis University in the United States in 1997, a private university run by Jesuits,

Figure 3. Personal competencies (skills) of the entrepreneurs

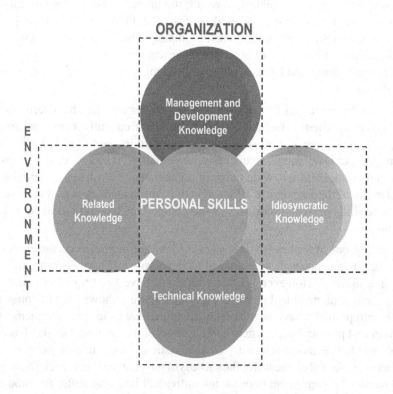

and worked for two years as a financial analyst in the Commerce Bank of St. Louis. Moreover, he is the developer of the Bichaco project, the only European company to get digital licences in order to use digital music in local entertainment establishments. Furthermore, he is the author of the book *The Red Pill, Free Software and the Digital Revolution,* the first book about free software written in Spanish.

Finally, Laura María Rodríguez Madrid has her Business Administration and Management degree from ETEA, a University Institution run by Jesuits in Córdoba. For the last eight years she has led a brilliant professional career in Deloitte Spain, specialized in the areas of strategic planning, administration, and human resources, and the re-engineering of processes in different sectors of activity. Laura is the person who contributes coherency, analysis, and methodology to management dealings in Blobject.

Tangible and Intangible Supports in the Innovation of Information Technologies

The Integration of Innovation Sources: Tangible and Intangible Elements

As can be seen in Figure 4, Blobject is a reality thanks to the integration of three sources of technological innovation. On one hand, the use of new hardware and software in a free software context has allowed a greater degree of adaptation for concrete business needs, though it has also meant less investment in research and development. As the entrepreneurs admit, this company would not have been viable in a software-owned context.[6] In the second place, Blobject is based on the use of alternative means of transport, due to the founders' business vision. These very easily managed vehicles, unavailable some years ago, are an ecological alternative to traditional cars, saving on fuel and maintenance costs (the cost to recharge the vehicle is $.50 a day and there are only minimum maintenance costs, since the electrical engine contains few pieces and components and needs no oil changes, no filters, no radiator belts, etc.) Finally the Blobject project would not have been possible without the current widespread use of geographical positioning technologies.

Intangible Element

The Opportunities Associated with the Use and Development of a Free Software Environment

Free software is the key to the project of Blobject, a company that takes full advantage of the business opportunities that have arisen around this technology. Free software (open-source software (OSS)) today is one of the most relevant resources for new undertakings based on information technologies, since it permits technological independence from third parties as well as the possibility for personalization according to individual needs. Software owners (closed-source software (CSS)), for whom commercial interests take precedence over technical needs, tend to create markets that present great obstacles for participation—monopolies or oligopolies in the best of cases—because of the exclusive rights that the manufacturer has on the software and which translates into an exclusive control over its improvement and distribution. On the other hand, freedom for modification, use, distribution, and copies are the drawing points of free software for some entrepreneurs who are opposed to a controlled and dependent technological context. In this sense, empirical evidence shows that the majority of horizontal markets in the software industry are

Figure 4. Blobject's technological innovation

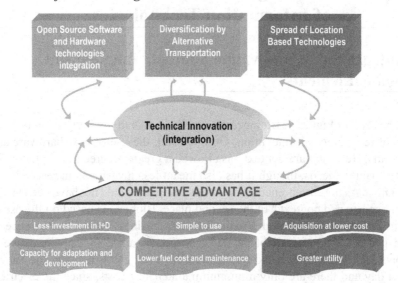

in the hands of a single or only a few companies, from operating systems and word processing packages, to graphic design applications or server applications.

Therefore, freedom, technical viability, and sustainability (Mas i Hernàndez, 2005) make software use rocket day by day, and, as Cearley, Fenn, and Plumier (2005) point out, this is one of the most relevant present day trends: as indicated in the Five Hottest IT Topics and Trends in 2005, the use of this technological context "is a catalyst that will restructure the industry, producing higher-quality software at a lower cost. It won't destroy industry giants such as IBM and Microsoft, but it will revolutionize software markets by moving revenue streams from license fees to services and support." So, by 2008, 95% of Global 2000 organizations will have formal open source acquisition and management strategies that address the challenges and opportunities that OSS introduces.

The technological context of free software allows the development of different business models, from direct ones (companies that sell software as a product, computer service companies, and hardware salesmen) (Hecker, 1998) to indirect ones (companies that use free software as a support for the exploitation of certain business opportunities). As indirect business models become successful experiences, they weaken the barriers set up by a "closed" technological context and the permanent dependence that direct ones imply.

Advantages of Free Software

The use of free software offers, by definition, various advantages in a project of this type. The execution time, personalization possibilities, and the reduction of costs were the most important reasons for Blobject's choice of free technologies in the founding of the company. Others include the following:

a.   Reduction in time-to-market. One of the fundamental keys for the success of technology-based companies is the correct planning of how to implant this technology. At the present time a company of these characteristics must begin to operate as soon as possible, since any technological innovation quickly becomes obsolete as newer technologies begin to appear on the scene. The Blobject project has been possible due to the use of a set of computer applications for free software—like operating systems, settings characterized by developments, data bases, and a geo-positioning application—which are available to any company, and that has greatly reduced the development time necessary for implanting a system of this type.

b.   Personalization according to need. Since both digital assistance and the center of control are totally new developments, Blobject can produce a made-to-measure application to fulfil any special company demands. This implies that previously carried out applications are the basis for the development of the technological assistant built into the company's vehicles.

c.   A significant saving in costs. One of the most important advantages in the use of free software is the savings in cost. The market has many applications and free tools that permit personalized adaptations for special company needs. Thanks to this, the development of the built-in digital assistant found in the vehicles has been achieved at a much lower cost, resulting in a shorter wait for the actual launching of the business.

d.   Free, but with some barriers. Free software is, in the end, a final license that is applied to a technological development. The difference is that certain free software technologies, like, for example, Linux, are not as well-known as ones developed on platforms of owned software as is the case of Microsoft. Therefore, the greatest barricade preventing the entrance of potential competitors lies in the demand for that specialized knowledge that until now has only been in the hands of the privileged few. Furthermore, a very deep familiarity with the community working in the area of free software is necessary to find the specific technological solutions needed to develop the company.

Access to the Use of "Free" Technologies in Geo-Positioning

One of the main problems found by promoters was the impossibly high cost involved in the ad-hoc development of necessary GPS geo-positioning applications, basically because businesses that have developed such technologies (like GPS traffic navigators in companies like TOMTOM or Garmin) have done so mainly for their own private use. That is why a set of free technologies was selected to turn out a version with the same range of possibilities offered by other GPS assistants but adapted to the specifications of Blobject.[7] So one of the technological corner stones of the company is based on the possible uses inherent in the geo-positioning of any object world-wide thanks to the system of satellites developed by the U.S. government. The general use of GPS technologies allows a company to offer its services in an open, independent way without any type of technological dependence.

Tangible Elements: "Alternative" Transportation Vehicles for Sightseeing in New Cities

Undoubtedly the heart of the Blobject company is found in its skills and shared knowledge, but these skills become tangible in the innovation developed, in the form of the two new alternative vehicles that Blobject offers to its visitors: electrical cars and Segway.

Electrical cars (B1-Car). These are electrical vehicles called GEMCAR manufactured by the Daimler-Chrysler Group. These cars are absolutely silent and ecological, as they emit no type of either gas or acoustic pollution and are propelled by a simple electrical motor capable of climbing the steepest inclines. In this way, the GEMCAR can cover the main part of urban transport needs at a much lower cost per kilometer than any vehicle with a combustion engine.

With two or four seats, the cars are equipped with a technological GPS assistant which permits the selection of different sightseeing routes throughout the whole city (we will make further reference to this later on). The tourist uses a USB key (Key Blobject), which is inserted into the technological assistant (AT Blobject). This shows the route and roads to be followed throughout the historical part of the city. Along this route, the visitor receives all types of information about the houses and palaces, churches and convents, fountains and gardens, ancient beautifully panelled doors, and feudal walls to be found scattered throughout the historical area of Córdoba, highlighting hundreds of interesting sights to be seen in the city. The vehicle's body work is made of a composite structure and thermoplastic panels, and a GE SHunt 72-volt electrical engine with front wheel traction. The car reaches a maximum speed of 40.2 kilometers and can do up to 50 kilometers depending on certain variables like temperature conditions, surface incline, and how the car is driven. It needs six gel batteries that are recharged with a 72-volt charger (similar to the type used by a laptop) that only needs a 220-volt charge. The recharging time is eight hours if the batteries are totally flat. Finally, the GEMCAR has a great potential for personalized adaptation due to the wide range of colors and accessories available, which allows a personal design to suit each client's taste.

Segway. The company offers another curious way to visit Cordoba. What at first looks like a simple skateboard, the Segway is the first personal transport gadget in its category, and is an agile, rapid, and sure way to move using slight and precise forward and backward body movements to glide forward. The vehicle can rotate 360 degrees on its own axis and is the first transport gadget on two wheels with an electrical momentum that maintains its own balance.[8] With smaller dimensions than an average adult's body and the ability to imitate human balance, the Segway permits a privileged view of the city. This ingenious vehicle is available in two different models: small (at 32 kilos it admits a maximum weight of 96 kilos and reaches a speed limit of 16 kilometefs per hour); and the bigger version (38 kilos heavy,  admits 118 kilo load, and a top velocity of 20 kilometers an hour) which adapts perfectly to different types of clients: personal mobility, mobility for security guard and armed forces personnel, off-road mobility, mobility for golf, and so forth. The lithium battery can do 40 kilometers in a charge. The recharge time is four hours when starting from empty.

When hiring the services, the clients are given a brief run-down on the functioning of the vehicle with a video demonstration on the company premises. The route begins, always accompanied by a monitor who acts as a guide through the narrow streets of the historical sector, explaining the most important architectural treasures that make up the historical splendour of Córdoba to the occupants (at least two people are necessary to begin the run). The company offers three passes daily (morning, afternoon, and night) for a maximum of six people, accompanied by a monitor around the Guadalquivir River area or through the more modern part of the city (charming nooks and crannies outside the traditionally more frequented runs). Normally, these routes are established ahead of time, although an itinerary could be arranged to accommodate a client who would like to visit some particular place in the city.

Integrating Elements in Technologically-Based Innovation: The Digital Assistant and the Center of Control

The Design and Development of Technological Tools

The business idea conceived by Blobject is such a novelty that it has demanded ad-hoc action from the very beginning, since no forerunners existed in the market that could serve as an example to orient the company.[9] Due to this, a great effort had to be made to design this service according to the needs that could be anticipated a priori. Thus the founders of the company found themselves dealing with the creation of two different technological tools to reach their goals. On one hand, the project required a digital assistant built into the vehicle, that is, a computer on board that would allow the client access to detailed information about the surroundings of the tourist routes. On the other hand, Blobject had to develop a control center that could actually oversee the service being rendered from back in the office.

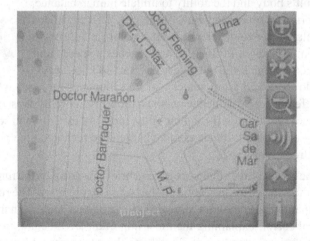

In both cases, the company has decided not to patent its technological innovations, since it firmly believes in a society of patent-free knowledge that encourages the creation of technologically based companies, thus contributing to the research and development of innovative products and services.

Digital Assistant

The electrical Blobject vehicle incorporates a digital assistant that offers tourist information based on geographical position. This tool is what allows the client access to detailed information on any point of interest found in the city. The system includes three languages to start out with (Spanish, English, and French). The design of the application itself allows audio files to be heard, videos to be seen and even reconstructions of other historical eras to be consulted. The principal functions of the assistant are the following:

- **Service based on position:** As the vehicle rides through the city's historical area, the assistant tells the clients about the different points of interest situated in a radius of less than one hundred meters. If the clients wish, they can touch the tactile screen to find all the information available on the database about the point of interest in question.

- **Features illustrating the points of interest:** Features include a textual description of each point of interest as well as a slide show with some up-to-date images, others from the past, and even virtual reconstructions, reproductions of audios, and videos and viewings of presentations. In this respect, Blobject is making a real contribution to the creation of content to make the cultural and historical heritage of the city of Córdoba better known. In order to go about this, agreements have been signed in collaboration with the Archaeological Seminar of Córdoba to create a database of cultural information about the city as a whole.[10]

Center of Control

The center of control of Blobject 1.0 is the application that manages and geographically references the many points of interest in the city, using various technological applications like the electrical vehicle or the digital assistant. This tool was designed with the several functions.

- **City management:** The center of control has not been exclusively designed for the city of Córdoba, but can also be applied to other municipal areas, which would allow for the geographical expansion of the company with a single centralized point of control.

- **Map management:** The map administrator allows any type of geographically referenced map to be included, thus complementing the strategy of business expansion.

- **Sightseeing management:** This application allows new tourist sites to be added to the program at any time in a geographically referenced way and to be placed into specific categories including cultural (monuments, museums, mansions and palaces, churches and convents, etc.), gastronomy (restaurants, taverns, bars, etc.), parking lots, and other local points of interest.

- **Creation of routes:** The center of control facilitates the creation of new routes depending on client needs in an intuitive, fast, and simple way.

- **Creation of presentations:** These presentations are especially oriented for those with some type of visual and/or hearing handicap, adapting the information to special needs through presentations integrating voice, text, and images.

- **Language use:** From the center of control any language that permits translation of the content into other languages can be chosen through a single interface.

- **Sponsor management:** This tool allows the incorporation of all types of sponsoring into the rest of the applications. For example, logos belonging to different sponsors (businesses, institutions, etc.) can be integrated into any or all of the points of interest.

Organization Structure, Resource Acquisition, Problems, and Results

From the very beginning, one of the principal competitive advantages of Blobject was the combination of human resources and the business idea. In the words of one of the three promoters:

In the composition of the team of promoters, what was fundamental was the fact that we all have known each other for a long time having lived in the same area, and we were all perfectly sure about what each could contribute, and what our strong and weak points are.

Figure 5. Organization structure of Blobject

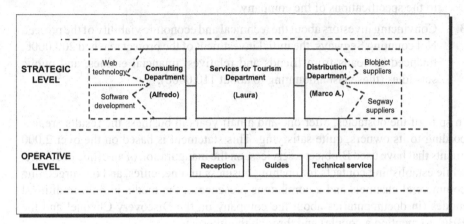

Thanks to the complementary facets of the founders, the organizational structure of the company today is a reality that revolves around three main strategical points: Tourism services (Laura), Consulting (Alfredo), and Distribution (Marco Antonio), which can be seen in Figure 5. At this same strategical level, Blobject is supported, on one hand, by companies specialized in Web technologies and the development of software (information technologies) and, on the other, by suppliers of both Blobject and Segway vehicles (automotion technologies). Finally, at an operative level, the company has hired various employees for reception, guide, and technical services duties.

At first, the acquisition of the "non-human" resources also posed some difficulties, since the investment needed to open shop required an initial fleet of vehicles, a site to keep them and recharge the batteries, another establishment for the actual rendering of the service and, among other things, city licenses for obtaining our own parking places and the government licenses required to open a car-rental business.

The main difficulties found by the founders in this initial phase were the following:

1. Implanting a radically new concept for sight-seeing in the city. In the words of Alfredo Romeo, "Both the introduction of the innovative model to visit the city as well as the creation of commercial channels took much longer than anticipated, which affected the predictions for income and expenses laid out in the financial planning." This difficulty was accentuated by the decision to include Segways in the company's fleet of vehicles.

2.   The development, almost from scratch, of an individualized technology adapted to the specifications of the company.

3.   Convincing investors about the technical and economic viability of the project. Not counting Segways, the initial investment of the project reached 200,000€, financed by loans from friends and relatives, financial entities, and public subsidies (these last amounting to about 110,000€).

In spite of the obstacles, after one and a half years in business the results are, according to its owners, quite satisfying. This statement is based on the over 2,000 clients that have used Blobject's services, on the inauguration of an office in Seville, while establishing contacts for opening business in other cities, and on burgeoning commercial channels and a continuous presence in the media in both traditional modes (in documentaries about the company on the Discovery Channel and the BBC, to mention a couple) and through the Internet.

A Marketing Plan for an Innovative Project

Given the innovative and original characteristics of Blobject's services, the marketing and commercial plan of the company has to differ greatly from any other in the tourist sector. Among other things, today nobody actually goes sightseeing asking specifically for an electrical car to visit the city or for a Segway tour to be organized. This circumstance gives rise to the need for a much more direct and aggressive commercial plan of action compared to other traditional tourist types of services.

The main advertising channels used by Blobject are the following:

•   **Shop:** The Blobject image, that of a company offering tourist services on a sustainable technological basis, is from the outset a guarantee in itself for clients because business is done on the company premises itself. At the present time there is a fleet of vehicles parked at the very doorway of the shop, as well as an interactive stand where information on Blobject services is available to tourists.

•   **Direct advertising:** In heavily visited tourist areas, members of the Blobject team hand out fliers directly with an original flair while riding by on the Segways and, thus, naturally attract the attention and curiosity of visitors.

•   **Tourist office:** The company has come to an agreement with the local tourist offices for the exposition and distribution of publicity leaflets.

- **Hotels:** In the reception area of the majority of the hotels established in Córdoba, information about the services offered by the company is readily available to clients.

- **Web:** Using an innovative company image, the business Web page (www. blobject.es), advertises the company's services and all necessary information for hiring any of the services available, from the electrical cars to the Segways.

A Dynamic Concept for Development

The Seeds of a Franchising System

From the outset, Marco Antonio, Alfredo, and Laura conceived of Blobject from the point of view of expanding the company to other places with similar characteristics to those found in Córdoba (a wide though dispersed spectrum of cultural heritage, historical areas limited to pedestrians, etc.) Their next project is to open a branch in Seville, another city of unquestionable historical attraction for tourists.

At the present time, the entrepreneurs are analysing two alternative formulas for growth: internal development using their own resources and the franchise model. As opposed to internal expansion, the franchise system is an alternative strategy for business growth that has enjoyed a boom in recent years. According to the specialized consultant Tormo and Asociados (2006), in Spain there are almost 1,000 franchise chains that embark over 60,000 establishments, which means a turnover of 17,500 million euros. In relative terms, franchises represent 15% of sales turnover and 10% of Spanish retail establishments.

The Blobject company model falls into the category of service franchises (the most original and authentic application of the principles behind the franchise since there is no product to sell) granting to the franchisee the novel and original working methods developed by the founders themselves. Blobject would offer the potential franchisee a business image, technical or commercial assistance, and, especially, their know-how and set of operational techniques which have been duly tried and tested and derived from their own experience as entrepreneurs. Even so, service franchisees undertake a greater risk as they are more vulnerable to imitation. To avoid this threat, Blobject must develop a policy of ongoing innovation and marketing and show a great capacity for growth that will let them attract the greatest possible market share in the shortest possible time.

With this strategy, Blobject would expand faster and in a more controlled way with lower growth costs than in the direct development of their own branches, thus limiting the risk that the business would have to assume. Furthermore, the technological development of the project itself permits the centralized management of a net of franchisees wherever they might be located.

Objects that will Dominate the 21ˢᵗ Century: Other Blobjects ...

The word is a contraction or portmanteau of "blobby" and "object" coined by design critic and educator Steven Skov Holt in the early 1990s. It was intended to refer to a whole series of objects based on curving and flowing designs created through CAD programs. In the year 2002, Bruce Sterling, a famous American science fiction writer, published Tomorrow Next, a book about the evolution of society as a whole. Sterling felt that blobjects would be the objects dominating the 21ˢᵗ century because of their design and the ease with which they could be reproduced, as well as their low cost. Two years later, the author himself gave a conference in the SIGGRAPH explaining why Blobjects would predominate in the 21ˢᵗ century.

Since then, the founding team of Blobject has latched onto the term and selected it to create their own firm, born in the 21ˢᵗ century and based on the technologies that dominate this century: free and sustainable technologies. This is why they contemplate this concept in their mission statement as well as in their vision of the company.

> **MISSION**
>
> To be promoters in the conception, establishment and growth of a knowledge based society.
>
> **VISION**
>
> To be an international reference point for the establishment of the "Blobject" ideal, understood as all innovation that flows out to society through the transfer of free and emerging technologies.

Despite this mission statement and open perspective, Blobject has been basically focused on Blobject Tours, the main theme dealt with here. Nonetheless, other blobjects are being developed. Some related business initiatives would include the following:

a.   **Blobject Distribution.** This area includes the establishment and growth of a knowledgeable society through the commercializing of three different products: (1) the company has the exclusive rights in all of Spain for the electrical vehicles used on the tourist sightseeing routes; (2) it has the distribution of the Segway electrical skateboards for Córdoba and Seville, thanks to the distribution agreement signed with the Magic Llums company, the exclusive importer in Spain for these gadgets; and (3) it also has the distribution of interactive tourist information stands.

The business area of Blobject Distribution is oriented towards commercializing technologically-based solutions focused mainly on sustained movement as well as on the sightseeing sector. The additional value derived from this distribution is the contribution of technological solutions developed by the consulting department. In this way, Blobject partakes in distribution agreements with different manufacturers that allow it to sell not only electrical cars but also Segways.

b. **Blobject Consulting.** The consulting department of Blobject S.L is the area that comes up with the products and services that the other areas will market. This business line focuses on the establishment of Blobject's association with world wide development in free software. The technological assessment offered by the company is aimed primarily at the tourism and entertainment sectors, as well as local government associations, always offering information solutions based on emerging, free, and sustainable technologies. Finally, the promoters' most immediate future challenges revolve around three. These include reinforcing advertising campaigns to familiarize society with this new concept of tourist visits to cities, perfecting the company's commercial channels, on the Internet as well as in the local market, and generating enough financial capacity to establish the company in other cities.

References

Boyd, C. (2005). Petite green cars tempt tourist. *BBC News,* August 29.

Cearley, D.W., Fenn, J., & Plumier, D.C. (2005). Gartner's positions on the five hottest IT topics and trends in 2005. Retrieved May 1, 2007, from http://www. gartner.com/DisplayDocument?doc_cd=125868

García, J., & Romeo, A. (2003). *La pastilla roja. Software libre y revolución digital.* Madrid: EditLin.

Hecker, F. (1998). Setting up shop: The business of open-source software. Retrieved May 1, 2007, from http://www.hecker.org/writings/setting-up-shop.html

Mas i Hernández, J. (2005). *Software libre: Técnicamente viable, económicamente sostenible y socialmente justo* (1st ed.). Barcelona: Cargraphics. Retrieved May 1, 2007, from http://www.infonomia.com/img/pdf/llibrejmas.pdf

Ollé, M., & Ludevid, M. (1986). *Como crear su propia empresa.* Barcelona: Marcombo Boixareu.

Shalman, W.A. (1998). Cómo preparar un plan de empresa brillante. *Iniciativa emprendedora y empresa familiar, 12,* 21-8.

Tormo & Asociados (2006). *Guía de franquicias y oportunidades de negocio.* Ed. Tormo & Asociados.

Endnotes

[1]   Ollé and Ludevid (1986) affirm that it is not absolutely necessary to be an inventor to create a company. The majority of the ideas that give rise to new companies are not due to technological discoveries, but are instead the result of careful observation of the changes and new necessities produced in the economy and society around us.

[2]   Córdoba aspires to be the European Cultural Capital in 2016, competing against other Spanish cities (like Malaga, Zaragoza, and Caceres) and such foreign ones as Paris, Florence, Lisbon, and Stockholm.

[3]   Spain is second in world ranking in the tourist sector. In the year 2003, Córdoba was seventh in the national ranking of cities in number of tourist stays in hotel establishments, with a total number of 630,818 visitors, only preceded by Madrid, Barcelona, Seville, Granada, Valencia, and Zaragoza.

[4]   Since the beginning of time, Córdoba has been characterized by its horse carriage rides, which have offered a customary tourist service (the horse carriage drivers, more or less prepared in local lore, serve as improvised tourist guides). At first, this sector felt threatened by the creation of Blobject, to the point where their protests were aired by the media.

[5]   Furthermore, the Blobject business model has since been imitated in such different locations as, for example, San Francisco (January 2006, http://www.etcars.com) or Amsterdam (June 2006, http://www.getaqiq.com).

[6]   Free technologies are those that can be copied, modified, and distributed freely thanks to access to the source code, that is, to the lines of program code developed. Among the most well known of these free technologies we find the GNU/Linux operating system, which makes up the main application engine developed in Blobject.

[7]   The main applications to be personalized for the company are GpsDrive, Python, wxPython, MySQL, SQLite, Eclipse, and Debian GNU/Linux.

[8]   It uses redundant systems (high-Torque systems), that are controlled by an independent switch board, built with independent sets of coils. When all runs well, both sets of coils share the load equally. If one of them fails, the Segway instantly disables the defective side and only uses the other coil to get momentum until coming to a sure and controlled stop.

[9]   A tangible proof of the originality of this project is the great number of national and international news media who have covered this news. For an example, see Boyd (2005).

10   Another of the projects coming from this initiative is the development of the Web page cordobapedia.org. This initiative means a transposal of the successful experiment that is the generic Wikipedia to a local setting: the generating of a virtual knowledge community in the context of historical and monumental heritage in the city of Córdoba, built on the free and voluntary contributions of all those who want to contribute to an ever wider knowledge of the city. As of May, 2006, cordobapedia has 1,474 articles available.

Chapter VI

NTC Co.:
Seeking and Screening Technological Venture Opportunities in Entrepreneurial Start-Ups

Antonia Mercedes García Cabrera,
Universidad de Las Palmas de Gran Canaria, Spain

María Gracia García Soto,
Universidad de Las Palmas de Gran Canaria, Spain

Abstract

This case illustrates in a holistic way the different components that affect the recognition of the technological venture opportunity environment, attributes that characterize technology-based entrepreneurs, type of organization created and of technology for the construction of a venture-and the interactions that occur among those components, and which ultimately result in the market innovation. These factors linked to the successful creation of technology-based ventures justify that cases contributed by emerging firms are more revealing and illustrative than those of already consolidated firms, that is, intrapreneurship. In large corporations, variables such as previously accumulated organizational knowledge and the corporate culture itself may have a negative impact upon their ability to recognize the future value of these ventures. For those reasons, NTC, an emerging business, offers a clear example of how the interaction of the entrepreneur, technology, and the accumulation of experience and knowledge interact to give rise to a technology-based venture.

Theoretical Basis for the Study

There is broad consensus, both in the literature and in the practice followed by entrepreneurs, on the sequence of the process of venture creation. The process begins with the search for an idea, followed by a rigorous screening of the idea, which gives rise to a venture plan that is implemented once the business has been started up. However, that agreement on the phases of the process does not extend to the norms and standards that the entrepreneur uses in each of those phases (Morse & Mitchell, 2006). In effect, the entrepreneur's experience in the venture creation, culture, and socio-cultural background, as well as the entrepreneur's personality traits, all determine the ways in which the entrepreneur carries out the process (Sarasvathy, 2001). In the particular case that concerns us, we can add the specificities of technological businesses, which include some special and significant circumstances due to the complexity and dynamism of this sector that is defined as a truly entrepreneurial environment (Park, 2005).

The proposed case is in the initial phase of the previously mentioned formal venture creation process: in other words, in the stage of seeking the idea for the venture. This stage, which is closely linked to opportunity recognition, has been the object of great interest in the classic entrepreneurship literature. Kizner (1973) was the first to use the term "alertness" to explain entrepreneurial recognition of opportunities. In that respect, and irrespective of whether recognition of opportunity is preceded by a systematic search for available opportunities or is due to an accidental discovery, recognition will depend on the entrepreneur's previous knowledge. More specifically, an entrepreneurial alert signal is activated when the entrepreneur notices information that is related to information that is already known (Ardichvili, Cardozo, & Rays, 2003).

However, according to Park (2005), the literature's interest in deciphering the aspects that determine the recognition of a successful idea has focused on the key components of that process and the later development of an innovation in the market; for example, the entrepreneur, the organization, the environment, or the actual process of firm creation (Arenius & De Clercq, 2005; Brockhaus, 1982; Gartner, 1985; Lee & Tsang, 2001; Robinson, Stimpson, Huefner, & Hunt, 1991; Shapero &

Sokol, 1982; Shaver & Scott, 1982, 1991). However, it is difficult for those partial approaches to explain technology-based start-ups since they ignore the nature and dynamism of the interrelations that take place between those previously mentioned components.

With our approach, the case is intended to illustrate in a holistic way the different components that affect the phase of recognition of the technological venture opportunity as well as the interactions that occur among those components, and which ultimately result in the market innovation that takes place in the process.

Background

The economic dependence of a geographical region on a single sector, as is the case in the Canary Islands (Spain), justifies the need to develop new sectors of activity that guarantee the medium and long term economic development of the territory. Furthermore, if that dependence is on the tourism sector and is based on natural advantages, such as climate, geographical location, or orography, with limited development of other differentiating factors that generate sustainable competitive advantages in the region (i.e., offer of quality accommodation, complementary services, etc.), the economic risk is accentuated.

However, the population of the Canary Islands has always been characterized by its constant and dynamic vocation for commerce. This traditional orientation has generated numerous initiatives of self employment and small and micro firms that have formed the basis of the region's economic drive and that operate alongside subsidiaries and branches of national and international firms, giving rise to the business structure shown in Table 1. Within that framework, local authorities, business associations, and some others institutions support the reorientation of that entrepreneurial spirit towards the creation of new, innovating firms based on knowledge and high technology. The creation of such firms would enable the territory not only to overcome its current single sector dependence, but also to avoid the traditional handicaps associated with the development of other industrial sectors where the disadvantages of the geographical remoteness of the Canary Islands (access to raw materials, transport costs, etc.) make it impossible for local firms to develop competitive advantages. To that end, public administrations as well as social agents (i.e., local universities, chambers of commerce, and business foundations) are making great efforts to favor the recognition of new business opportunities as well as to orientate and boost their later development. More specifically, those agents aim to promote a diversified, innovative, and consolidated business fabric by offering the following support: (1) training programs in new technologies and their possible uses, (2) training programs in technology-based entrepreneurship, (3) the promotion of

Table 1. Company strata by number of employees in the Canary Islands (2004)

Workforce	Firms	Total %	Accumulated %
0 employees	56,739	47.17	47.17
Between 1 & 2 employees	35,597	29.59	76.76
Between 3 & 5 employees	13,663	11.36	88.12
Between 6 & 9 employees	6,713	5.58	93.70
Between 10 & 19 employees	4,034	3.35	97.05
Between 20 & 49 employees	2,390	1.99	99.04
Between 50 & 99 employees	592	0.49	99.53
Between 100 & 199 employees	348	0.29	99.82
Between 200 & 499 employees	172	0.14	99.96
Between 500 & 999 employees	36	0.03	99.99
Between 1,000 & 4,999 employees	10	0.01	100.00
More than 5,000 employees	0	0.00	100.00
Total	**120,294**	**100.00**	**100.00**

technology workshops, (4) programs for university-business links, (5) a reduction in the bureaucratic procedures for starting up new businesses, and (6) the granting of fiscal and economic aid and subsidies, among others.

In 1995 the Canarian Chambers of Commerce, Industry and Navigation, and the Canarian Employment Service established a framework of cooperation that favored the founding of the Enterprise Creation Service, a project in which the Canarian Government participates and which is cofinanced by the European Social Fund. Within the framework of this program, newly created enterprises and already consolidated firms with new business projects are offered expert advice on the materialization of the business idea in a viable business plan, guidelines on the procedures necessary to set up and open a firm, training in fiscal and accounting obligations, and access to fiscal incentives, aid, and subsidies. With regard to subsidies, the following aspects stand out: (1) generic subsidies, which may or may not have to be repaid, (2) soft loans of an ICO type (unsecured loans) or for groups that are more difficult to integrate (e.g., women, immigrants, the disabled, long-term unemployed, the over-45s, single parents, etc.), (3) payment of a one-off lump sum of unemployment benefit for the creation of firms or self-employment initiatives, and so forth. This aid package is offered via virtual channels (Web sites) and in the physical premises of the One-Stop Enterprise Creation Office. This Office is a place that enables the entrepreneur to handle all the processes and procedures necessary to start up the enterprise and so avoid the complexities stemming from the distribution of competences among the different administrative levels throughout the territory. To be more specific, the One-Stop Office is authorized to accept and process the different administrative documents that the entrepreneur has to present to the various public institutions.

However, the successful development of technology-based business innovations is closely linked to the entrepreneur's recognition of the business opportunity, which forms the nucleus of the formulation of the business idea. Given that technological activities are subject to the complexity and dynamism typical of the sector, defined as wholly entrepreneurial (Park, 2005), in many cases emerging business initiatives are more creative and feasible than the development of new projects within the framework of already consolidated firms, that is, intrapreneurship. Individual and small scale entrepreneurs have a greater ability to recognize emerging business opportunities and a greater freedom to commit themselves to developing them since they are not subject to the influence of a consolidated organizational context, that is, previously accumulated knowledge, corporate culture, hierarchical structures, organizational complexity, formalized decision making processes, and so forth, that can inhibit the recognition of the future value of these new businesses (Christensen, 1997). The option of entrepreneurship also gives the population the responsibility for sector reorientation of the economy of a territory by creating spaces for those individuals with an entrepreneurial profile and vocation who find a suitable framework within the institutional environment on which to base new, technology-based projects.

Setting the Stage

Within the framework of training activities promoted by the Canarian public administrations, the Canarian Institute for Training and Employment has been organizing 500-hour "Microinformatics Systems Technician" courses since March 2003. Alejandro Melián, a telecommunications technical engineer specializing in image and sound, participated in that course as a teacher. At that time 31-year-old Alejandro was studying for a second university degree that would expand and complement his telecommunications training. More specifically, he was studying computer science, specializing in computer systems. Between 2002 and 2004 he was working as studies and systems coordinator in the Centro Superior de Estudios ICSE S.A. (ICSE Higher Center for Studies). As studies coordinator, he programmed courses in basic and advanced computer science and also taught on the courses. As the company's systems coordinator, he was supervisor and administrator responsible for the maintenance of hardware and software, both local and on the Web, and was the Web page designer and administrator of the remote connections (Internet/DSL) among the branches on the different Canary Islands.

Alejandro's professional orientation to information technologies and telecommunications began in the Image and Sound Laboratories of the University School of Telecommunications Engineering. In 1997, he received a University assistant's grant to maintain equipment and provide technical support to users. Two years later, in 1999, the University awarded him another grant, this time as a research intern, under which he took the role of network administrator in the University Library. In that role he assumed important responsibilities in the following areas: (1) the design, creation, publication, and maintenance of the University Library Web page; (2) the programming of routines in Delphi for the computerization of tasks specific to a library, such as archives, documentation, and so forth; (3) the administration of the Oracle-based integrated program Absys 5.0; and (4) the maintenance and renewal of computer equipment in the University Library. To complete this professional experience, between 2000 and 2002 he was an executive in the high-technology multinational Wasser Inc., where he undertook tasks for the Canaries related to the control of projects for the certification of Canarias Telecom's HFC (Hybrid Fiber Coaxial) Network, the development and control of projects for quality measures for Canarias Telecom's network, and the development of computer-based projects for screening Canarias Telecom's SQL databases.

With that experience behind him, Alejandro taught the previously mentioned Microinformatics Systems Technician courses, on which Felipe Ramos and Osvaldo Chaparro were students. Alejandro and Felipe had the chance to get to know each other in the breaks between sessions, and over cups of coffee they found that they were both on the same wavelength with shared professional and vocational concerns and related economic interests. This affinity appeared in spite of the big differences in their training and professional profiles. Later, Alejandro's friendship with Osvaldo and his trust and professional respect for him lead him to propose to Felipe that Osvaldo join the project because of his qualifications. Alejandro's recommendation was enough for Felipe, who accepted the proposal even though he did not know much about Osvaldo's personal characteristics and professional competence.

Felipe Ramos is 38 years old and holds a degree in business administration and management and a degree in tourism businesses and activities. His professional experience is in the airline sector and he began his career in 1987 when he joined IBERIA LAE S.A. as a flight operations assistant while also studying at the University. With his formal education completed, he started to work for EUROHANDLING UTE, where he was coresponsible for the accounting and fiscal management as well as administrative reorganization. In 1998, that company promoted him to head of the Passenger Department and head of commercial actions and customer relations. He took on the management of the Check-in and Boarding Department of Gran Canaria Airport with some 160 employees in his charge. After 2 years, his work in that area earned him a new job offer. Felipe decided to accept it and joined GRUPECAN, S.L., a goods transport and customs agency company, as manager. In that position Felipe placed special emphasis on and devoted considerable effort to the administrative and functional reorganization of the firm and to sales growth.

Osvaldo Chaparro is also a telecommunications technical engineer, having specialized in telephony and data transmission. At age 29, he is the youngest of the three but has accumulated wide academic training and professional experience that reveals his interests, his will to overcome difficulties, and his capacity for work. Osvaldo complemented his university education with other studies related to information technologies, including courses in digital transmission hierarchies, Internet telephony, computer and Internet networks, Nokia-GSM, microinformatics systems, and programming in various computer languages and Web environments with HTML, Flash, ActionScript, Javascript, PHP and other digital editing programs. With regard to Osvaldo's professional experience, he has a grant from the University Thermodynamics Laboratory for the connection of measuring equipment to the PC for monitoring, and for the design and programming of monitoring applications, among other tasks. He also has wide experience both in teaching and in the design and programming of software for business management, online teaching platforms, Web sites, and so forth, all aimed at local firms and institutions. Finally, he participates in the AMENA project as a technical engineer for Nokia Spain. His specific contribution is related to measuring coverage with TEMS, implementing help utilities for planning in Mapinfo and Access, choice of radio parameters, and network problem analysis and resolution.

As Alejandro, Felipe, and Osvaldo interacted, they perceived the value of two contrasting qualities that characterized them as a team: the common and the different. On one hand, they were three mature, experienced young men, tenacious fighters with a strong need for achievement; they all had university degrees, an interest in new technologies, and, most important of all, a desire to start their own business. On the other hand, there were significant differences in their professional backgrounds, experiences in the job market, and academic qualifications: two of them are telecommunications technical engineers with high technological capabilities and the third a graduate in business administration and management with wide ranging knowledge and business experience. However, those differences, rather than constituting an obstacle, provide an underlying value with the ability to generate important synergies on which to base an innovative, differentiated, technology-based business project, a project based on what is common from a social point of view and economically developed on the basis of the differences. At the same time, and from a relational point of view, they perceive that the personal profiles are perfect for the Alejandro-Felipe and Alejandro-Osvaldo pairings. However, the Osvaldo-Felipe pairing does not function so well since each detects in the other certain barriers to an easier personal relationship, which puts the smooth running of the business project at risk and could, in the end, affect its very survival.

Alejandro, Osvaldo, and Felipe reflected on the dynamism of the sector of new technologies applied to business management and sales and on the amount of available public funds and programs. The result was that they detected significant barriers to accessing those funds because the newly created enterprise had few merits and had not yet acquired a reputation and because of the lack of knowledge about the effects of ICTs for the independent professionals and small and micro enterprises that mostly comprise the local business fabric. For that large group of businesses, technological development constitutes an important motor for its growth and expansion. However, the rapid obsolescence of acquired software and hardware represents a handicap to the in-house development of information technology-related activities. In the context of Micro and SMEs, the search for maximum efficiency with the lowest possible consumption of resources is a prerequisite for success. In that respect, the hiring of human resources specialized in ICTs and the updating of such technologies generate high costs that those enterprises can not assume, which leads to high inefficiencies that justify the outsourcing of the activity. In fact, only 14% of Canarian firms employ specialized technicians to develop those activities while 74.9% opt for outsourcing (Canarian Statistical Institute, ISTAC, 2004). However, the sector has a very bad image in the local context because the customer is over dependent due to technological ignorance, and because of the frequent breakdowns, system failures, and the limitations and restrictions imposed on the functions of the jobs, which limit personal development. Apart from that, the practices of some firms include surcharges for repairs, excessively high monthly standing charges for maintenance, and so forth.

With those arguments in mind, the three young entrepreneurs conceived the idea of creating a technology-based venture to respond to the needs of Canarian businesses for assistance, communication, and technological innovation and training. Consequently, the general concept of the business was clear but the group had significant doubts about how to bring it about. There were significant problems and uncertainties:

1. **Existence of demand:** Their initial business idea was, in their opinions, a winning combination of a service that they were able to offer and a market with a clear need for that service. However, there were two key questions: "To what degree was that market need not met?" and "What were the new venture's chances of capturing that market?" To a great extent, that would depend on their ability to differentiate their offer from others that might exist in the market.

2. **What activities should the new venture initially offer?:** Felipe thought that hardware repair and maintenance would be a good way to attract customers and develop a trusting relationship with them. This would facilitate cross-selling (i.e., the strategy of offering new products to current customers based on their past purchases), making the later sale of other ICTs services feasible. However, Alejandro was totally opposed to the idea. In his opinion, the origins of the new venture had to be linked to information management, training, computer science, and telecommunications in SMEs and any activity that contributed to projecting the image of the company as a hardware workshop should be avoided.

3. **The need to guarantee short-term economic and financial viability:** The idea was that Osvaldo, Felipe, and Alejandro would work full-time from the

outset of the project. Therefore, the new enterprise's activity had to provide an immediate source of income for personal and family livelihoods.

With a clear will to undertake the project and aware of the potential value of their idea but reluctant to devote time and effort to a badly designed business initiative, they decided to mature their project and go into the development in depth and analyze the conditions under which it would be viable. Thus, two ideas occurred to them: (1) to enroll in an entrepreneurship program, choosing the one organized and taught by their local university, with the aim of having access to innovation workshops and establishing relations with accredited professionals in the field of new technologies; (2) to create a real estate Web site and to intermediate in the sector in order to know the technical and commercial capability of the team. Thus, www.viviendacanaria.com was born in September 2003 (Figure 1).

Figure 1. Web site of the real estate agency

Case Description

The close links between the social and business agents in the Canarian Archipelago led to the creation of Las Palmas University-Business Foundation (FULP) to promote, boost, and spread all types of activity related to education, research, and culture in the Canaries, especially at a university level. That foundation recognized the key role of technology in the creation of innovative ventures and, aware of the institutional support for entrepreneurship in the Canarian Community, instigated a program of university support for the creation of businesses. More specifically, the FULP designed the ICEI (Initiative for the Creation of Innovative Enterprises) Canarian program. The objective of ICEI was to promote and orientate initiatives to create technology-based enterprises. To that end, it offered information and guidance to future entrepreneurs to help them start up their activities in that field. The ICEI program was based on two basic structures:

1. **The ICEI Web site:** This serves as the motor of the project by being a tool that the entrepreneur can turn to in any of the phases of the venture creation process. It provides a series of services that include the identification and confirmation of entrepreneurial values, enrollment in a program of university support for the creation of ventures, specific information on the fiscal and economic advantages of the Canaries, access to a network of local, national and international experts, and so forth.

2. **The Continuous Training Center:** Constituted within the FULP, and jointly supported and managed by the local university, it offers a wide range of training that meets the different needs of the local context. More specifically, The Continuous Training Center offers the Program of University Support for Venture Creation, which contains such aspects as an innovation workshop for the initial orientation of entrepreneurs and a business start-up workshop, as well as a training schedule (e.g., skills for drawing up a business plan, market research methods for start-ups, marketing of innovative products, etc.).

As part of that training program, Alejandro, Felipe, and Osvaldo attended innovation workshops organized by the ICEI. Within the framework of entrepreneurship, innovation is understood as the combination of technology and market needs to create a profitable business opportunity (Trott, 2002). Therefore, innovation can take place only when the entrepreneur is capable of identifying market and customer needs and including those needs in the design of a new product or service defined with a suitable technology developed by an organization with the necessary resources and capabilities. With that understanding of innovation, the ICEI workshops are based on those key components that explain the recognition of the opportunity and the later development of an innovation in the market, that is, the entrepreneur, the environment, and the actual process of venture creation (Gartner, 1985).

Entrepreneur

As far as the entrepreneur is concerned, the purpose of the innovation workshop is to identify the particular cognitive features of the entrepreneur in the participants. Those features, according to Mitchell, Smith, Morse, Seawright, Peredo, and McKenzie (2002) and Mitchell, Smith, Seawright, and Morse, (2000), include: (1) knowledge and access to contacts, relations, the necessary resources, and assets to develop the business idea, (2) the will, understood as commitment to their entrepreneurial project, and (3) the capacity, in terms of knowledge and skills, to create a venture. Another objective of the workshop is to confirm the entrepreneurs' maturity in terms of their conviction of the values underlying entrepreneurial behavior, for example, the acceptance of risk, a spirit of hard work, the wish to assume responsibilities, set goals, and achieve them through one's own efforts, the desire to feel free to take one's own decisions, and so forth (McClelland, 1961; Mueller & Thomas, 2000). The three young entrepreneurs easily passed that test. Furthermore, the previously mentioned professional complementarity of the founding partners suggested the suitability of combining technological and commercial capabilities and basing the business project on two cornerstones: (1) constant technological alertness, and (2) organizational management capability, and knowledge of the typologies and characteristics of the firms in the sector and market dynamics.

Environment

Within the program, Felipe had weekly meetings with José Cárdenes, the director of the innovation workshop, with the aim of screening the possible viability of that initial business project. José Cárdenes was invited by ICEI program to participate in these workshops not only because of his professional experience in innovation but also because he is a renowned expert in legal and fiscal issues, types of company constitution, and property rights and patent registration. He is currently manager of the multinational **Delphi Institute of Management in the Canaries**. José orientated the work in the innovation workshops to the analysis of market trends, the real needs of the local market, and the competitors' offer in response to those needs since our young entrepreneurs only had an intuitive idea based on their own experience.

Trends in the ITC Market

The analyses conducted by the Spanish Association of Electronics and Information and Telecommunications Technology Enterprises (AETIC) clearly show that the different world regions included in the 2004 study have seen greater growth in the information technology markets than in the telecommunications markets. The results highlight the stability of the European Union and the United States markets, which have been boosted by the emerging economies of Eastern Europe and Asia and increased by more than 7%, compared to the 4.6% growth of the world market. However, only Japan has seen a slowdown in the ITC market growth (2.6%). Regarding the behavior of software as opposed to hardware markets, the software area displays particular dynamism with a 5.5% growth in Europe and 6.8% in the USA.

The Spanish information technology market is expanding at a slower rate than the Spanish economy as a whole. Its growth rate (4.7%) continues to be above the European average but the long standing gap between Spain and Europe remains. In Spain, as in the worldwide context, the services segment is growing much faster than the products segment, with software and computer services standing out. With regard to the latter services, their contribution to job creation is notable and is based on the continuous advance of both one-off and recurring exploitation (definition and application of exploitation norms and standards, standard work station design hardware/software configuration, management of technical infrastructure and security copies, establishment of computer-based security policies, etc.) such as program development, implementation, and maintenance.

The *Information Technologies* report prepared by the AETIC and the Ministry of Industry, Tourism, and Trade makes it clear that this market progress is due to the overall growth in purchases by households, businesses, and public administrations. These results differ from those of the previous year, when purchases were mainly made by households, which indicates changing trends in the public and private sectors. In fact, the best data for Spanish firms is in their level of use of ICTs in terms of PCs, Internet, and online shopping, which is above the European Union average, although that is not the case with online sales. More specifically, there is significant progress in the development and implementation of new technologies in all the Autonomous Communities of Spain. There is particularly high penetration of ICTs in firms based in Madrid, Catalonia, Navarra, and Cantabria, while Extremadura, Murcia, Canarias, Baleares, and La Rioja have the lowest level of penetration (N-Economía, 2005). In the case of public administrations, seven out of the sixteen communities enjoy growth in ICTs penetration above the national average, the Canaries being one of those seven. The Canarian public administration also has the third highest budget for ICTs, behind the Basque Country and Asturias, although the percentage of firms that use the Internet to interact with the administration is still low, which justifies the larger budget.

Trends in the Application of ICT as a Source of Business Competitiveness

The important role of ICTs in the economy is, to a great extent, due to their effect on the improved competitiveness of firms. The incorporation of ICTs in the business management processes has led to an increase in firm performance. This is due to the wide range of applications of ICTs and the fact that they reduce the cost of production, internal communication, and human resources. The incorporation of ICTs has been accompanied by increased investment in technology and in consulting and collaboration services, thus creating business opportunities for firms that decide to offer technological services.

To be more precise, the implementation of ICTs in firms leads to changes in the ways of performing valuable activities related both to the firm's general processes (e.g., accounting, human resources, budgets) and to supplies, production, and sales, thus affecting the entry and exit of inputs and outputs, respectively. With regard to management tools, firms can make use of standard integrated solutions such as that provided by enterprise resource planning (ERP), and the appropriate accounting or human resources tools developed to meet the needs of the firm. Other management tools are e-procurement, e-learning, and intranet for employees.

In reference to interaction with the customer, ICTs offer software to manage customer relations (CRM), as well as new ways to communicate with the customer (e-mail, company Web site, online catalog, automatic telephone handling, automatic interactive voice, pop-ups, etc.) that are replacing traditional communications such as the telephone and postal service. In that respect, online advertising is based on advertisements/links on other Web sites, electronic magazines, Web banners, pop-ups, and Web seminars. Online communications with the customer is also reinforced by automated processes to accept, follow up, and deliver orders for supply chain management (SCM), Helpdesk, virtual customer complaints management, and automated sales calls. The information that firms gather about their customers constitutes a new factor of customer segmentation that can be used to design more effective marketing programs depending on ICTs. In that respect, the firm can classify its customers according to their access to Web pages, to online technologies, to user communities, and so forth, and build customized Web pages with automated crossed sales programs and dynamic, personalized pricing policies. The technologies used for the data analysis in that last task include data marts and data warehouse or statistical data mining, among others. The use of ICTs in the process of interaction with the customer reaches its maximum in the establishment of wholly virtual shops, which may or may not be parallel to the off-line business.

The contribution of ICTs to improved business competitiveness also lies in the use of software in the supply process. The most widely used software includes: Electronic Data Interchange (EDI); networks of communication with the supplier; demand

and restocking planning programs; supply management; provisioning, payment and electronic approval; XML (extensible markup language) based communication; and provider relations management (PRM). Finally, purchases from suppliers can be conducted via electronic mechanisms for inter-firm trade, for example, B2B (business to business). B2B has basically been driven by the creation of Web sites to form groups of purchasers. The firms form groups to create those Web sites and so join forces to be able to enjoy a better negotiating position.

Potential Local Demand

The workshop addressed the quantification of the overall potential market as well as the specific demand for the technological service that the new venture would offer. The initial idea was based on attending to professionals and micro and small enterprises. However, discussion in the innovation workshops and the gathering of information permitted a clearer view of Canarian demand. More specifically, the study of the impact of ICTs in the outermost regions of the European Union (2001) revealed three different customer segments in the Canary Islands: public administrations, small and micro enterprises and large enterprises (banking, insurance, tour operators, etc.). The firms in that last group either have their own ICTs procurement departments outside Canarian territory or belong to multinationals that cover their ICTs needs from the county of origin. Therefore, the principal customers of Canarian ICTs firms are found in the other two market segments. That information led the group to extend the viability analysis to a second, growing market segment: public administrations. The most important aspects of those segments are now discussed.

According to data for 2004 provided by the Spanish National Institute of Statistics (INE), there were 120,294 companies in the Canaries, 99% of which had fewer than 50 employees and 88% with fewer than 5. This means that 105,999 firms could be considered the general potential market. A more precise quantification can be made from the data provided by ISTAC (2004), which indicates that in the previous year 63.8% of those firms have contracted services from some ICTs development firm. It is also necessary to analyze the current level of technological development of those micro and small Canarian enterprises, as well as to investigate their future technological, telecommunications, and innovation needs. The INE's 2003 Survey of the use of ICTs and electronic commerce revealed that 96% of Canarian firms used the computer as a work tool. Moreover, it estimated a 2% growth as a result of market development and the actions of the public administration to promote the full implementation of the information society.

In spite of the widespread use of computers, there was a low level of computer integration in the firms, fewer than half of which had their computers installed in a local network. This inhibited the development of team work, made it difficult to manage technological resources, provided low storage capacities, and entailed greater risk of information loss. That low level of integration was even more accentuated in the implementation of Wi-Fi or wireless networks, with fewer than 5% of Canarian firms having installed them despite the clear advantages, which include: lower installation costs, no installation or cable laying works, redistribution of physical space without architectural or installation works, greater ease of internal mobility, promotion of "brainstorming" policies and cost reduction since in the case of relocating, the wireless network is a movable asset while the cable network is automatically amortized. In addition, fewer than 20% of the firms had Intranet since they were either unaware of what Intranet is or thought that Intranet could not meet the organizational and management needs. However, experts state that there are clear advantages of having networks like Intranet, not only in the business field but also in the corporate, educational and institutional fields although the characteristics of the organization itself will justify its implementation. In practical terms, Intranet can generate efficiencies in firms when it is used in the different functional areas.

INE studies also confirmed the widespread use of Internet in Canarian firms. In effect, firms considered it important to access and exploit the advantages offered by the Net and 88.42% of them had Internet connection. However, the acceptance of the advantages of Internet did not extend to the use of extranet, since fewer than 14% of Canarian firms allowed their customers or suppliers to access the organization to conduct sales transactions, exchange information or integrate customers and suppliers into the production chain.

Therefore, use of the computer in the micro and small Canarian enterprises was, to a great extent, limited to its use as a tool for document processing, accounting, human resources management and other routine aspects of management. Furthermore, the purpose of the firm's connection to Internet seems to be to serve as an element to transmit and receive data by e-mail and, occasionally, to develop the firm's own Web page (30.12% of Canarian firms). This contrasts with the population's growing use of the Internet in general and of electronic commerce B2C in particular. Electronic transactions in Spain involved a total of 143.6 million euros in 2003. The expansion of Internet use in banking and the provision of online financial services had also consolidated over the previous three years. This trend led to the inference that micro and small enterprises would also soon have to accept the challenge of fully incorporating the use of ICTs in their management. To that end, the Spanish Public Administration announced, on the one hand, the Plan Avanza for the incorporation of SMEs into the Information Society at three levels with interest free loans of up to 30,000 euros, and on the other, the Plan Moderniza for the management of the change and integration of the public administration itself into the IS. The question of security is also worth mentioning since fewer than 50% of firms used secure servers and backed up their data, which shows that there was considerable ignorance of the risks that new technology use entailed as well as bad handling of the technological elements that could significantly reduce those risks.

After that analysis of the use of ICTs in firms, Alejandro, Osvaldo, and Felipe concluded that, in the Canaries, there was a growing market with sufficient technological means since Canarian firms' computer equipment and ability to access Internet were similar to those of firms in other Spanish regions. However, the market was not highly evolved, and there was little use of those basic technological infrastructures in more advanced programs (networks, intranet, and extranet) that provide substantial technical, managerial, and communications improvements and are able to generate competitive advantages. Furthermore, they became aware that SMEs were not informed about the public programs of funding and support for those activities and training. Those analyses and discussions among the group led them to conclude that this imbalance between infrastructures and application was due to the Canarian businesses' lack of knowledge regarding the potential usefulness of those technologies and institutional support. Thus, their predictions were confirmed about the existence of technological needs yet to be met in this market segment and the need for public aid programs for that purpose, to overcome the barriers stemming from the bad image of the sector.

The other segment of potential market to be analyzed was public administrations. The interest in this segment stemmed from the need for those institutions to channel structural funds received from the European Union to investments that maximize the expansion of the information society in the Canaries. The Auna Foundation's IV Annual Report on the Development of the Information Society in Spain (eEspaña, 2004) provides the keys to the importance of this segment. The report recognized the increase in actions promoted by public administrations to spread the use of new technologies among the population, with the consequent notable rise in the number of Internauts, cable-modem lines, B2C transactions, and so forth. However, the recognition of those substantial improvements did not exclude the need for public administrations to continue in their efforts to achieve the generalization and consolidation of the Information Society.

In that respect, the World Summit on the Information Society (Geneva 2003-Tunis 2005) laid the foundations for the promotion of ICTs as a tool to promote the economic and social development of every region and so reduce the digital gap. The most important contributions included those related to e-inclusion (universal access to ICTs) and e-learning (learning from the use of ICTs and other educational content by means of ICTs). The Spanish Administration tackled that task both through direct action and through grants for the development of ICT ventures. In effect at the time there were approximately 300 open lines of subsidy and aid programs, both at a national and a local Canarian level, that aimed to promote the use of ICTs, improve training, and, more specifically, promote the development of the Canary Islands.

The business idea proposed by Alejandro, Osvaldo, and Felipe could make significant contributions in those fields. With regard to e-learning, they could offer telematic teaching platforms, either free of content or including training offers developed to that end and based on the partners' own training and experience. Their contribution to e-inclusion would be linked to the use of ICTs to strengthen SMEs and the more disadvantaged groups (i.e., women, immigrants, the over 45 age group, the disabled, etc.). Finally, their contribution to micro and small enterprises could help improve the Canarian business fabric and consequently the development of the region.

The Competitors

The data offered by INE show that the principal activity of only 1.10% of the 120,294 companies operating in the Canaries was related to new technologies. This indicates an underdeveloped sector of activity with low levels of competition, with a ratio of 91 companies per new technology firm (see Table 2). 69.58% of the new technology firms were dedicated to computer activities, and one third of those specialized in the repair and maintenance of computer equipment. The remaining 30.42% (403 firms) performed activities related to R+D+I. In order to learn more about the competitors, there was an exhaustive analysis of the activities that they offered, with the conclusion that only 84 of the 922 companies provided services related to software, EPI sales, Rep and Net services, wholesale, retail, company and/or public administration consulting, training, and Web page design. Moreover, these companies provided two or three of those services and none offered each and every one of them. Therefore, the number of real competitors in the Canary Islands was only 21 and comprised small and medium enterprises that at least offered ICTs consulting services and had employees with high technical and business qualifications.

The proposed business idea was basically related to the provision of an overall service to firms that included ICT assistance, consulting, and implementation, and was understood not as an activity to maintain the current computer system, but as a support for system migration over time by evolving the applications that improve the efficiency, management, and competitiveness of firms. Meanwhile, the activities aimed at the institutional market would include ICT training and the establishment of e-learning and e-inclusion activities, which could only be carried out with the collaboration of administrations, associations, and trade unions since their implementation required aid from European Social Fund. At that moment, the group of young entrepreneurs studied the idea of cooperating with a business association that was either important or linked to public institutions, in order to have access to that market.

Table 2. Potential competitors in the Canary Islands (2004)

Activity	Number	Percentage
Computer Activities	**922**	**69.58**
Maintenance and repair of office and accounting machinery and computer equipment	432	32.60
Consulting for softwares and supply of computer programs	325	24.53
Data processing	85	6.42
Other computing related activities	52	3.92
Consulting for computer equipment	17	1.28
Data base related activities	11	0.83
Research and Development	**403**	**30.42**
Research and development in social sciences and humanities	304	22.94
Research and development in natural and technical sciences	99	7.47
Total	**1,325**	**100.00**

In sum, we can say that there were competitors for the proposed activity in the micro and small enterprise sector, although there was no predomination of firms offering these integrated services; therefore, there was a considerable margin for action. With regard to competition in the institutional market, the situation was even more favorable since there were hardly any companies that could provide those services.

Venture Project

After Felipe, Alejandro, and Osvaldo had spent many hours working and gathering information under the supervision of José Cárdenes, and after long, heated debates among the group members, there was a contagious effect that aroused enthusiasm for the project among all of them. That enthusiasm would be further kindled by the small successes that the Web site, www.viviendacanaria.com, was enjoying and that enabled them to obtain some finance to cover the start-up and running costs of the new firm. Those shared illusions gave rise to close personal relationships between the members, which eventually led to José's direct involvement in the project. While the business idea was becoming a specific project that could be undertaken by the future partners, preliminary agreements for collaboration with José, from which everyone would benefit, were being forged. Let's look at their achievements.

Carrying out the project required defining the service-market area that would support the venture's activity, as well as designing the management structures and systems and identifying the internal resources and capabilities necessary to make the venture start-up feasible. In that respect, the joint experience and knowledge of the entrepreneurs, the decisions taken regarding the construction of production capacity, and the development of a management team that combined technical and management capabilities at a single level all contributed to the viability and efficiency associated with the business initiative.

The group clearly committed itself to differentiation as the competitive strategy. To that end, they decided to offer a wide range of technology-based consulting services that included management, virtual marketing, training, quality, corporate image, and communication, always taking the needs of their customers into account. The services to be marketed would be "made-to-measure," with products and services adapted to what the customer wanted and really needed and channeling it as far as possible through some line of aid or subsidy from public funds.

More specifically, the offer to the market segment of micro and small enterprises combined two complementary programs. The first was a project to adapt those enterprises to new technologies, which permitted the implementation of internal functioning tools (phases I and II of Plan Avanza), on one hand, and opened the business to Internet (phase III of Plan Avanza), on the other. This project would include a diagnosis that detected inefficiencies and the possibilities of technological development while also identifying the training needs of the staff. On the basis of that diagnosis, a proposal adapted to the client firm would be designed. That proposal included the technological supports necessary to increase competitiveness and efficiency: software services (development of intranets, extranet that connected the firm with customers and suppliers, and corporate webs, digital signature, electronic invoicing, telematic communications with the administrations, and electronic transactions with third parties), hardware services (network installation, equipment installations, etc.), infoware services (control of the use of computer-based resources by employees, generation of internal statistics, data bases, etc.), and humanware services (human resource training for computing management, implementation of virtual training platforms in the firm, etc.). Finally, the program included the management and maintenance of hardware and software to ensure that it operated correctly and to incorporate innovations that supported a better functioning of that infrastructure and the management of documents for application for public aid (see Figure 2 and Figure 3).

The second program aimed to facilitate and motivate the segment's investment in ICTs. To that end, the new venture would conduct a search for details of the aid and subsidies available under the current legislation and the fiscal treatment of investments in ICTs. That information would be given and explained to the client-company to facilitate access to the aid, subsidies, and advantages offered by the different public programs to promote the use of ICTs in businesses. Therefore, at the instigation of José Cárdenes, they and other entrepreneurs would create the Canarian Association of Graduate Entrepreneurs (ACEU) to access that market.

With regard to the institutional segment, the importance of directing marketing actions at associations, professional and business organizations, trade unions, and institutions became evident in the workshop. Apart from the software, hardware, infoware, and humanware services that improve internal functioning, the Technological Transfer Centers program would also be offered. This program consisted of designing joint technological innovations, such as the creation of common data bases, from which all the stakeholders in each institution would benefit. The program also included the transfer of model experiences in the application of ICTs in each sector (e.g., trade, hotel and catering, tourism), in order to provide references that encourage the stragglers in each sector to adopt ICTs. As a result, the new venture would be able to access potential new customers.

However, since the high technology market differs from the consumables market, commercial success is associated to the brand in a different way. The value of a brand is associated with a constant level of security and quality rather than to positioning the brand among an elite or prestigious community. The achievement of a high market share creates the brand itself since market leadership is valued as a synonym for security. Once that position is achieved, a firm can enjoy higher margins and generate greater profitability. However, that is a slow process and the capture of customers is gradual and not without difficulties, to which one can add the fact that the subsidy process requires and average of between 9 and 11 months (if it is approved). All that, together with the need to embark on a business project that was self-financed from the very start, slowed down the start-up of the new venture. Faced with that situation, the group proposed business diversification as a mechanism to generate financial synergies that would make the business viable. In that respect, Alejandro considered that they could offer the market a teletraining platform under the Moodle environment while opting for different subsidies and

Figure 2. Technological services

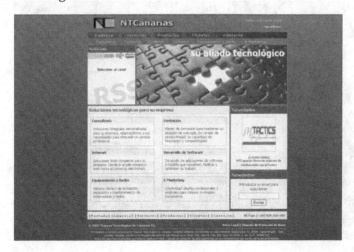

projects or public tenders related to their activity. His idea was well received by his colleagues, who quickly suggested parallel actions. Thus, a new line of business linked to the opening of various virtual shops (for example, self-tests and products for prevention of occupational hazards, etc.) was proposed.

With regard to the legal form of the new enterprise, the company, which would be called NTC Co., would become a Limited Liability Company with three partners. The group had rejected the idea of constituting the company with a venture capital firm that would provide funding since their priority was to retain full control of all business decisions in their project. The organizational structure would have a linear and coordinated design. Thus, the administration area would develop the coordination tasks necessary for the correct functioning of the firm, including the operational management of the virtual shops. In effect, the administration manager would be responsible for the accounting and financial control of the firm as well as for developing its marketing plan. He would be its top outside representative, undertaking any necessary marketing and public relations tasks, including making financial-economic assessments for the projects negotiated with customers.

The functions of the computing and telecommunications technical engineers would be related to the production process. They would be responsible for design and programming for the effective functioning of the virtual shops. In addition, and based on the diagnosis of customer needs, they would design and implement the most efficient solutions to those needs and monitor their optimum functioning and make the adjustments required in each case, under the project management system. In the execution of projects aimed at institutions, they would ensure strict compli-

Figure 3. Technological products

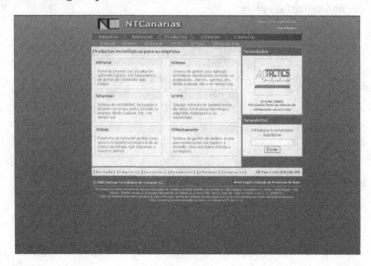

ance with the deadlines and contents established for the proper development of the technical and training aspects of each project. Furthermore, the structure would enable decisions about each project to be taken in a coordinated way between the commercial partner, who would have the capacity to propose actions, and the technical partner, who would confirm the technological ability to develop the project within the established period and within budget. Finally, the tasks related to planning, organization of the activity, control, and decisions to contract outside services would be undertaken jointly by the three partners.

The productive process is human capital intensive and, therefore, it is extremely important for technological knowledge to be continuously updated. In that respect, the three entrepreneurs would participate in technological forums, continuous training programs, and post-graduate courses in management and technological specialization in order to ensure that the customers' needs would be met. The permanent staff would comprise the partners, with technologists, PhDs, and other specialized human resources incorporated when required by a project. Moderate investment would be needed to conduct the activity since it only entailed the acquisition of modest tools and equipment, and the equipping of the offices.

Regarding the available technology, the idea consisted of making use of the standard software and hardware existing in the market and NTC would adapt and adjust them to meet the particular needs of each customer. In that respect, NTC signed an agreement with three suppliers to guarantee access to the supply of basic materials. As a result of those agreements, NTC become a *product partner* of ServeisWeb and mTactics, as well as of PCTelecos. PCTelecos is a computer assembler with nationwide franchises that wishes to expand in the Canaries and allows NTC to operate within the system but without franchise or image costs. ServeisWeb is a provider of Web storage, domain registration and transfer, and advanced Internet services and products while mTactics is a reference company in the corporate mobile applications market. NTC also made use of the Moodle training platform. In relation to hardware, NTC signed cooperation agreements with Binary System and Sycom, under which NTC received a 20% discount on purchases from those two firms.

It stands out that the efforts made in the workshops led to the efficient combination of the specific attributes of the three entrepreneurs, market conditions and the technology available to achieve a business innovation in which the following characteristics coincide: (1) the offer of a service in an emerging market, (2) a local context of action, and (3) a role of technological follower. According to Park and Bae (2004), those characteristics correspond to entrepreneurial initiatives features as 'proactive location": entry into a local market with technologies developed by other firms.

A personal and professional relationship between Felipe, Osvaldo, Alejandro, and José Cárdenes developed in the meetings held within the framework of the workshops and led to the establishment of various draft collaboration agreements. There were several aspects that made that alliance attractive. First of all, the main activity of Delphi Institute of Management, the firm headed by José Cárdenes in the Canaries, was as a consultancy for firms and public institutions. As a result, that firm could take the products and services offered by NTC to the target market segments. Second, NTC possessed important technological assets in terms of the experience and training of the partners. Therefore, for Delphi Institute of Management, the alliance meant a window to new technologies and products emerging in the local market. Consequently, there was a strategic complementarity between the two parties since technology and market constitute two key factors in the success of a consultancy business. That synergic effect was originally sought through an initial project proposal that contemplated a joint training program aimed at the institutional market and, more particularly, at the Foundation linked to the local university.

The draft collaboration agreements, in which other entrepreneurs on the University Program to Support Venture Creation also participated, included the creation of the Canarian Association of Graduate Entrepreneurs (ACEU). That association would comprise the entrepreneurs participating in the course, with the FULP (university-business foundation) as an honorary member. The association would be created with the aim of bringing together the graduate entrepreneurs from the various courses of the program to find mutual support and obtain synergies. José Cárdenes also played a leading role in the association by offering free advisory services at the end of the course. José Cárdenes and the ACEU reached an agreement under which the latter would rent several offices and infrastructures to Delphi, who would later sublet individual offices to each of the interested entrepreneurs. This enabled fixed costs to be shared and facilitated the economic viability of the projects.

The corollary of the ICEI training program was that the entrepreneurs attended several finance workshops. Some finance workshops were organized in which the entrepreneurs had the opportunity to present their innovation projects to private investors, financial institutions, and public bodies. Eleven of the sixty projects participating in the 2004-2005 course obtained funding that supported their working launch. NTC was received with great expectations in those workshops due to the high quality of the presentation by the project promoters. As a result of those finance workshops, the firms emerging from this program obtained subsidies from the Canarian Government and the Canarian Employment Service. They also accessed collateral-free private funding, but subject to supervision of the project by ICEI (FULP).

The entrepreneurs in this case gave a very high evaluation of their experience in the University Program to Support Venture Creation, organized by ICEI. The program enabled them to establish relations with institutions and business associations in the field of new technologies, and to contact consolidated private firms in the field of integrated business consultancy. Additionally, it provided a guide for the materialization of the initial business idea in a viable business project and the necessary initial financial support. The development of those contacts and aid played a significant role in the materialization of the idea and its later start-up.

Current Challenges and Problems
Facing the Organization

The most important challenge facing NTC is to consolidate the business project in the local market so that the venture becomes a leader in the provision of high added value services in the field of new technologies. However, the group will take care that this growth does not outstrip capacity, since their maxim is "rapid response to customer demand." To be able to do that, it is essential to monitor the balance between growth and capacity, understood as the available work hours and the bundle of different knowledge that is precise, available, and tested by the team. More specifically, the founding partners state that their main responsibility and greatest challenge is to meet and exceed customer expectations in that field. In that respect, the path that NTC must follow in order to achieve leadership includes the long-term development and maintenance of its competitive bases, namely: (1) constant, efficient technological alertness that provides feedback on technological trends and directions, and (2) optimum strategic and operational management of the enterprise.

Technological alertness first requires the partners to be permanently updated, as well as the implementation of an information system open to the outside (forums, specialist journals, conferences, seminars, etc.) that enables the group to be in the vanguard of new technological advances. Osvaldo, Felipe, and Alejandro also believe it is necessary to create an association to complement ACEU, but in the context of new technologies (ACEPTA). This association would permit the combination of already existing business initiatives and entrepreneurial initiatives based on new technologies, irrespective of the level of formal qualification of the members. Thus, in addition to university graduates in engineering and computer science, the association would also include entrepreneurs with technological studies (vocational training), and counselors for self-employment initiatives organized by local public bodies (town and island councils). The ACEPTA association would be constituted with the purpose of offering associates access to lines of investment and funding, a task in which NTC is expert, providing shared infrastructures, partners (members make use of and spread the products and services generated by the entrepreneurs) and general mutual support. The benefits that NTC would obtain from its participation would be related to the window to new technologies, access to technological suppliers, and access to potential customers, as well as being ACEPTA's principal supplier in the handling of subsidies aimed at non-profit organizations such as the public administration segment.

The technological observatory established in the firm would be able to identify opportunities and threats appearing in the area of action, providing the basis on which the firm would adopt offensive or defensive strategies. In that respect, the information that is gathered would form the basis for decisions about the growth and/or diversification of the business in a way that would stimulate other innovations that revolve around the firm's core technological capabilities.

Moreover, NTC must achieve optimum strategic and operational management. In that respect, the main challenges are linked to the development of corporate values that prioritize teamwork, flexibility, autonomy, the right to make mistakes, creativity, efficiency, and the satisfaction of customers and the other stakeholders, as key aspects on which to base constant innovation. The firm must also find the best ways to control and contain expenses because the quality and customized attention would decline if it does not do so. To that end, the partners must become involved in a process of continuous improvement in which the operating processes are reviewed and redefined in ways that guarantee their optimization. Another key aspect related to improved management is linked to obtaining certification of quality. On one hand, that certification would contribute to the efficient management of the firm and, on the other, it would offer the market unmistakable signs of the firm's good business practices.

Finally, it should be stressed that from the moment when Alejandro, Felipe, and Osvaldo met and conceived the idea of developing a joint project until the project began to function, they were full-time dedicated to the project and often worked until daybreak. However, although they still have many complex challenges to face, their conviction and confidence, together with their growing commitment to the venture, leave no doubt about the enthusiasm and passion with which these three young entrepreneurs will accept those challenges.

References •

Ardichvili, A., Cardozo, R., & Ray, S. (2003). A theory of entrepreneurial opportunity identification and development. *Journal of Business Venturing, 18*, 105-123.

Arenius, P., & De Clercq, D. (2005). A network-based approach on opportunity. *Small Business Economics, 24*(3), 249-265.

Brockhaus, R.H. (1982). The psychology of entrepreneur. In C. Kent, D.L. Sexton, & K.H. Vesper (Eds.), *Encyclopedia of entrepreneurship* (pp. 39-56). Englewood Cliffs, NJ: Prentice Hall.

Christensen, C.M. (1997). *The innovator dilemma: When technologies cause great firms to fail*. Boston: Harvard Business School Press.

Deeds, D.L., DeCarolis, D., & Coombs, J. (2000). Dynamic capabilities and new product development in high technology ventures: An empirical analysis of new biotechnology firms. *Journal of Business Venturing, 15*, 211-229.

Gartner, W.B. (1985). A conceptual framework for describing the phenomenon of new venture creation. *Academy of Management Review, 10*(4), 696-706.

Kirzner, I.M. (1973). *Competition and entrepreneurship*. Chicago: University of Chicago Press.

Lee, D.Y., & Tsang, E.W.K. (2001). The effects of entrepreneurial personality, background and network activities on venture growth. *Journal of Management Studies, 38*(4), 583-602.

McClelland, D.C. (1961). *The achieving society*. Princeton, NJ: Van Nostrand Reinhold.

Mitchell, R.K., Smith, J.B., Morse, E.A., Seawright, K.W., Peredo, A.M., & McKenzie, B. (2002). Are entrepreneurial cognition universal? Assessing entrepreneurial cognition across cultures. *Entrepreneurship Theory and Practice, 26*(4), 9-32.

Mitchell, R.K., Smith, B., Sewright, K.W., & Morse, E.A. (2000). Cross-cultural cognitions and the venture creation decision. *Academy of Management Journal, 43*(5), 974-993.

Morse, E.A., & Mitchell, R.K. (2006). *Case in entrepreneurship*. London: Sage Publications, Inc.

Mueller, S.L., & Thomas, A.S. (2000). Culture and entrepreneurial potential: A nine country study of locus of control and innovativeness. *Journal of Business Venturing, 16*, 51-75.

Park, J.S. (2005). Opportunity recognition and product innovation in entrepreneurial hi-tech start-ups: A new perspective and supporting case study. *Technovation, 25*, 739-752.

Park, S., & Bae, Z.T. (2004). New venture strategies in a developing country: Identifying a typology and examining growth patterns through case studies. *Journal of Business Venturing, 19*, 81-105.

Robinson, P.B., Stimpson, D.V., Huefner, J.C., & Hunt, H.K. (1991). An attitude approach to the prediction of entrepreneurship. *Entrepreneurship: Theory and Practice, 16*(4), 13-30.

Sarasvathy, S.D. (2001). Causation and effectuation: Toward a theoretical shift from economic inevitability to entrepreneurial contingency. *Academy of Management Review, 26*(2), 243-264.

Shapero, A., & Sokol, L. (1982). The social dimensions of entrepreneur. In C.A. Kent, D.L. Sexton & K.H. Vesper (Eds.), *Encyclopaedia of entrepreneurship* (pp. 72-90). Englewood Cliffs, NJ: Prentice Hall.

Shaver, K.G., & Scott, L.R. (1991). Person, process, choice: The psychology of new venture creation. *Entrepreneurship Theory and Practice, 16*(2), 23-45.

Chapter VII

Waleli:
Bringing Wireless
Opportunities to Life

Paul Kirwan, Nikos, University of Twente, The Netherlands

Peter Van der Sijde, Nikos, University of Twente, The Netherlands

Aard Groen, Nikos, University of Twente, The Netherlands

Abstract

This chapter tells the development story of Waleli, a high-tech company utilizing the latest proven developments in wireless communications to bring innovations to the market. It presents the journey of the firm through the entrepreneurial process, from initial idea right through to value creation. Furthermore, it looks at the roles and origins of network contacts and how these impact the entrepreneur's effort to accumulate the necessary resources to establish and subsequently develop the firm. This chapter adds to our understanding of network activity in the entrepreneurial process and as a real life case has relevance to both potential and practicing entrepreneurs in that it details the trials and tribulations of the process, and academics, as it provides in depth data on the role of the network in the entrepreneurial process.

Background

History of the Organization

Waleli[1] is a high tech company which utilizes the latest proven technological developments in wireless communication to bring innovations to the market. It aims to develop wireless communications to solve needs, both between people (mobile applications) and between machines and apparatuses (machine-to-machine, or M2M, communication), in a simple way.

Siete Hamminga, the founding entrepreneur, graduated with a master's degree in industrial engineering and management from the University of Twente in 2001. During his time as a student he ran a one man business, Well-Suited, selling suits to students. He also completed an internship with Unilever in Switzerland and while enjoying the work, this experience reinforced his desire to start his own business. He completed his Master's thesis in Silicon Valley studying the business models of Internet service providers (ISPs). His study period coincided with the collapse of the Internet bubble and his thesis was accordingly entitled "Back to Basics." Inspired by his stay in Silicon Valley, he, along with Roel Pieper (former vice president of Philips, current professor of e-business at the University of Twente and chairman of Favonius Ventures, a venture capital firm specializing in funding software start-ups), and Vincent Kouwenhoven wrote the book *Beyond the Hype* (see Figure 1). In this book, top Dutch executives give their vision on e-business now that the hype is over. Based on these experiences, Siete Hamminga founded Waleli in February 2002.

Armed with the knowledge he obtained in Silicon Valley, Hamminga recognized that current mobile technology ideas were far ahead of consumer needs. The practical idea for the business came from his brother, who posed the question "Why can't a mobile phone be used to answer the doorbell?" To answer this he conducted some formal research, borrowed some money, built the prototype, and launched the "GSM-doorbell." While developing this product he continued to come up with ideas to bring practical solutions to meet needs in a simple way using wireless communication; this became the mission of his company.

Type of Business

Recognizing that current mobile technology ideas were far ahead of consumer needs, Siete founded Waleli on the premise of developing applications for wireless communication which meet needs in a simple way. Siete recognizes the great potential of wireless communication and Waleli has capitalized on this with its first product: the "GSM doorbell." Subsequently, Waleli has extended the market for this product

Figure 1. Beyond the hype

by identifying its usefulness in an alternative industry, that is, health care. Waleli has further increased its product and service offerings to include among others the "Basiqphone" and "MMS-witness" (see Products/Services Provided).

To meet the needs of its customers Waleli engaged with them to transform innovation into concrete products and/or services. Waleli's products have two things in common: they are wireless and they meet needs in a simple way. Further, these applications are thought of and evaluated based on their market potential. Waleli's client portfolio ranges from large corporations through to SMEs; most of these companies have established names and market positions, for example, KPN, Siemens, and JohnsonDiversey.

Waleli views the key to being successful in this market as being able to bridge the technology market gap. Critical within this process is the role of participation, as it allows everyone to excel at what they do best. Also integral to this process is the "art of limitation," defining what a product should not do. To this end, Waleli is a networking organization; it works with specialized development teams and partners to meet the needs of specific project assignments. The innovative nature of the venture's process of turning ideas into applications has been recognized through participation in several innovation competitions where Waleli has won prizes including the LiveWIRE Business Award (www.shell-livewire.com), the Top Three Business Boost, and the Innovation Trophy. Further to their successes with product innovation and building a customer base, Waleli completed a share issue in August 2004 allowing continuing professionalization of the company and in-house innovations. Waleli lists Shell and Roel Pieper among their shareholders.

Siete believes that the IT opportunity based company of the future is small, maneuvers professionally, and has access to efficient resources all over the world. Waleli's international orientation is to grow and remain small at the same time through having a small presence in major international cities, for example, Amsterdam, Berlin, Shanghai, and San Francisco. Currently, Waleli has some products being produced in China, its leaders work with MBA students in Cambridge and have distributors in Belgium and clients in Switzerland, and it is developing new businesses in Germany and Sweden.

Products/Services Provided

As previously mentioned, products of Waleli have two things in common: they are wireless and they meet needs in a simple way. Highlighted in Table 1 is a summary of the major products and services offered by Waleli.

Management Structure

The management structure of Waleli (see Figure 2) is hierarchical; it is led by Siete Hamminga, the founding entrepreneur. The management team consists of Allard van de Rhee as technical director and Hans Joosten, marketing director. Allard van de Rhee started his working career in 1988. Following the fall of the Berlin Wall in 1989, he moved to Eastern Europe to exploit the opportunities within the semipermanent and prefabricated construction market. By 1992 he was in a managerial position and he gained further international experience pursuing business opportunities in Albania when its boarders were opened the following year. In 1995, he returned to the Netherlands and became project leader in a film-set construction firm, which, in 1998, led to him setting up his own enterprise, WharfProductions. In 2003, having sold his share of WharfProductions, he joined Waleli.

Hans Joosten studied business economics at the Catholic University of Brabant. After graduating in 1994, he started working at Nashuatec, a market leader in copier and prints systems. Five years later he introduced a business-to-business formula under the flag of BelCompany, a component of the stock exchange quoted Macintosh. From the middle of 2002 until joining Waleli in the beginning of 2004, he was responsible for the strategic new business team within Nashuatec. Both Allard and Hans are current shareholders in Waleli. There are currently nine operational staff within Waleli, some of whom are focusing on industrial design for multiple projects. On the individual project level, Waleli has one person responsible for each of these. Overall, there are 45 people working on Waleli projects.

Siete views his shareholders as external to the organizational unit; they provide advice and guidance but as the majority shareholder the final decision is his. In addition to the organizational unit there is an external network of firms, including

Table 1. Waleli's major product and service offerings

Products			Services		
Product	**What it is/does**	**Industries**	**Service**	**What they do**	**Industries**
GSM-Doorbell	A system that connects a visitor who is ringing the doorbell to the mobile phone of the homeowner	Construction Health Care	Innovation Fource	Using four representatives from the client and four representatives of Waleli, four product ideas are conceived and visualized related to the wireless opportunities of the client's field	All industries with the potential to exploit opportunities in wireless technologies
Switch 21	Product that simplifies the forwarding of telephone calls from fixed lines to mobile telephones	Telecoms	MMS-Witness	Collaboration with the Dutch police force to stimulate the use of digital camera phones for recording criminal activity and also implementing a management system for recording such images	Security Telecoms
Basiqphone	Mobile telephone which only makes and receives calls, features large reading display and touch buttons	Telecoms			

Figure 2. Organizational structure

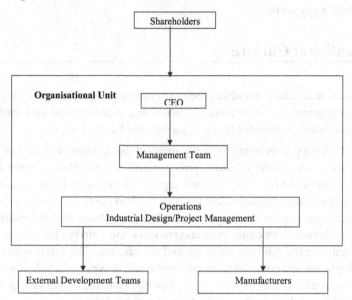

software development teams and foreign manufactures with whom Waleli partner to meet various product requirements.

Siete concedes that this structure would not have been recognizable in daily operation up until recently. In the early development phases, the group was so small and roles were not so well defined that there was no formal organizational structure. However, Siete feels that such a structure is a prerequisite to achieving Waleli's current growth plans.

Financial Status

At foundation, Waleli was valued at one million euros. At the second round of financing in June 2006, the value of the company had almost doubled. Revenues for 2006 are forecast to be over 1.2 million Euro but may be significantly higher (100%) depending on the go ahead of some larger projects. The current challenge is to create cash cows and recurring revenues instead of hourly based project revenues.

Strategic Planning

Waleli has recently begun implementing a growth plan to the year 2009. In this plan Waleli's leaders outline their intentions to develop their organizational structure, international activities, and M2M markets. These events are covered in detail in the Current Challenges section.

Organizational Culture

The organizational culture has always been very entrepreneurial but with the growth plan some organizational structures are becoming more defined and formalized. Nevertheless, Waleli continues to portray a hip and trendy image.

Siete identifies people as being Waleli's greatest asset. However, he has learned some lessons in his human relations policy which has resulted in some changes over the lifetime of the firm. Initially, to keep costs low Waleli hired a lot of graduates and interns. It later became clear that this method cost a lot of time and energy bringing these employees up to speed; therefore, the focus shifted toward young people with relevant work experience and contacts. Siete strives for a results driven culture based on personal responsibility and enthusiasm. The effort is paying off. Waleli's employees do not need to be entrepreneurs; however, they do need to have an entrepreneurial attitude. In some cases, this is stimulated by allocating shares in spin-offs which result from the work effort of employees.

Given the relative size of the company, Waleli spends quite some effort on professionalizing processes like project registration, bookkeeping, public relations, and human relations. This is based on the ambitions and awareness that processes have to be in place before growth absorbs all operational attention.

Setting the Stage

Problem Setting

Entrepreneurs developing new ventures based on IT opportunities are faced with the traditional problems of starting a venture, namely, gathering scarce resources, acquiring knowledge, establishing a reputation, and attracting suppliers, customers, and partners (Autio, Yli-Renko, & Salonen, 1997; Birley & Cromie, 1988; Brush, Greene, & Hart, 2001; O'Farrell & Hitchens, 1988). In many cases, because of the nature of the opportunity, these new ventures are more often operating in international markets. This creates further problems for the starting entrepreneur, as the resources which have to be gathered are sometimes internationally dispersed and they must also prepare both domestic and international sales channels. Further, significant investments must be made to create internationally acceptable goods and services and the pursuit of international trade requires knowledge of international markets and establishing international networks. The resources involved in these activities are significant (Diamantopoulos & Inglis, 1988) and given that high tech new ventures are especially resource poor, lacking the required time, capital, and capabilities to sufficiently prepare international markets (Doutriaux, 1991), investing in international activities may come at the expense of other activities.

Objective

As all starting new ventures are faced with such problems, we describe the entrepreneurial process of Waleli and illustrate how new ventures based on IT opportunities can overcome this paucity of resources through effective networking activities. The entrepreneurial process is a process driven by the entrepreneur, wherein ideas are recognized, prepared, and exploited leading to value creation (Van der Veen & Wakkee, 2006). Waleli, similar to many other IT ventures, is operating in an internationally competitive market. Specifically, this chapter tells the story of the roles and origins of various network contacts and how these impact the entrepreneur's efforts to accumulate the necessary resources to establish and subsequently grow the firm.

Case Description

Small Beginnings

Siete's ambitions when starting the company were to develop applications for wireless communication which meet needs in a simple way. As previously mentioned, the initial product idea was the GMS-doorbell, a system allowing the occupant of a house to communicate with and open their door through their mobile telephone. Having just graduated from university, Siete Hamminga did not have sufficient resources to launch the business of his dreams. On February 15, 2002, he registered as a "sole trader" at the Chamber of Commerce. Right from the beginning, Siete had a five point strategy for what he had to develop in the coming period: (1) patent, (2) proof of concept, (3) business plan, (4) professional delivery, and (5) cost price analysis. He created a budget estimating the costs of achieving each item on his five point plan. To meet this budget he entered into an arrangement with three private investors, who would lend him €5000 each. In this arrangement, Siete offered three scenarios depending on the development of the company over a 12 month period:

1.   If the product idea is sold after a year, then the investors would receive an additional €1,500 on top of their original investment

2.   If the company attracted external investment leading to a share issue, then the investor's loans would translate to a 2% stake in the company

3.   In the event of the first two scenarios failing, then the investors would forfeit their investment and Siete would not be liable

Siete also registered for a temporary entrepreneurship position[2] (TOP program), which entitled him to an interest-free loan of €12,000 as well as access to a mentor. Part of this program also involved writing a professional business plan.

Siete also set about finding a company that could produce the proof of concept. His modus operandi is that when he is in contact with one party and they inform him that they are not interested, he asks them to suggest a party who might be. Through this method he came in contact with Chess. Chess provides services, products, and solutions in the field of automation for electronic products, development of micro-electronics, embedded software, and business-critical applications. Given his resource constraints, Siete struck a deal with Chess to defer 40% of the development costs for one year, with the stipulation that he would have to pay this 40% if the company ceased to exist. Siete summed up this approach by saying "these were the kinds of deals I made; I made deals everywhere to gather the resources, since I had no money."

Siete also joined several networking organizations to give him some support, both morally and "hopefully" professionally, in the process of starting his own firm. It was at one of these, the De Industrieele Groote Club (IGC), a chic business club in the heart of Amsterdam, that he met with Alexander Berger. During conversation over a beer, it emerged that Alexander ran a graphic design company, G2K. At this time Siete was relying on students from the University of Twente to design his logo, but he was unhappy with their efforts as he felt that it was of a comparable level to what he could produce himself.

Siete explained to Alex the origins of the Waleli brand and his aims for the company. Waleli is the Cherokee Indian name for the humming bird; a bird that characterizes itself by its compactness, velocity, and beauty. It is no larger than a finger bone, it has a velocity of 80 kilometers per hour, yet, despite this, is capable of hovering perfectly still in the air, the wings moving so quickly that not even in slow motion can they be captured with a normal camera. Siete's ambition for Waleli was to be similar to the humming bird, that is, a compact yet mobile company.

Alex said that his firm created and designed corporate identities and he offered to undertake this work for Waleli at cost price (see Figure 3). G2K still does this work for Siete today, and, further, he and Alex have become good friends. Reflecting on this scenario, Siete remarked, "At that time it was a really good decision to go for

Figure 3. Waleli's corporate logo

the professional branding and image. Alex pointed out the essence (of this) to me. This was all window dressing to me." Siete didn't want to expend too much energy into these activities, but he changed that strategy within 10 minutes (of talking to Alex) because he realized that "if you start communicating with a hotmail account and a cell phone and print your own business cards you position yourself at the lower end of the market."

The €12,000 from TOP coupled with the investments from the private investors allowed him to build the prototype, buy the patent, create a professional appearance, and fund his own basic costs for the year. In addition to this, Siete realized that he would need an office to work form. He asked Roel Pieper if he could use the attic space in his office premises in Bloemendaal, Amsterdam, free of charge. Roel Pieper agreed to this request, giving Siete not only office space and facilities free of change but also providing him with a professional appearance from the start. This is best illustrated by early visitors complementing the offices and enquiring "Mr. Hamminga how many people are working here?" To which Siete's standard reply was "Around 20 people." This was in fact the truth, however, these people were not employees of Waleli.

During this time, Siete also initiated contacts with Heijmans and Bouwfonds, two of the leading housing construction firms in the Netherlands, with a view to them using the GSM-doorbell in their new building projects. Siete had a friend, who had a friend who worked in Bouwfonds and he used this contact to first pitch the idea. Siete expresses the importance of having a contact name within the company, "You need to have a name within the company and you need to have the name of the person who referred you to them." He also expressed the importance of reusing the contacts you have established when in conversation with other potential customers, for example, when in conversation with Heijmans he told them that Bouwfonds were interested.

At the end of the first year he had produced his "umpteenth" business plan, the prototype had been built, and several project developers were particularly enthusiastic. However, no revenues had been earned. Siete had to go back to the investors and painfully reveal that their money was lost. Despite this setback he remained undeterred; in fact, these experiences increased his belief in the product and he decided to carry on, having learned his first lesson, "It is a challenge to bridge the gap between enthusiasm and commitment… and that takes time."

The Search for External Financing

To move the business forward Siete realized that he needed external financing and decided to conduct a share issue. Roel Pieper had previously indicated that he would invest but Siete did not want to solely rely on this contact and instead he made a list and contacted several leading Dutch entrepreneurs who he thought might be interested in investing. Unfortunately, with these solicitations he failed to find any investment; however, he did receive a copy of one of the entrepreneur's motivational books and the owner of a chain of record stores sent the following amusing response: "Dear Siete, I have made an arrangement with the bank that they don't diversify into selling compact disks and I don't issue any loans."

At the IGC business club Siete also encountered an experienced businessman who expressed an interest in investing in start-up companies. Siete went to the businessman's house to present his business plan; however, this was to yield further disappointment as the businessman commented with a compassionate sigh "opening your door with your mobile is never going to meet a market need. You seem like a likeable guy to me…I'd recommend you look for a decent job as soon as possible."

At a later stage, Siete was able to generate some enthusiasm among four financers. They were even willing to give him an advance payment so that he was able to maintain his livelihood and commitment to the venture. On request, Siete arranged meetings with the management of Nemef and some project-developers so that the potential investors would be able to assess the general opinion about Waleli, that is, to get an idea about his reputation and his chances for success. These meetings were positive, but before the first deposit was made, the investors suddenly pulled out. *"We got carried away by your enthusiasm. We're sorry but Waleli is still only in a development phase and this is too early for us to invest. We think you'll be successful and that we're going to read about you on the front-page of the newspapers,"* remarked one of the potential investors.

Shortly afterwards, Siemens, through their director Kees Smaling, expressed an interest in a plug and play variant of the GSM-doorbell. The importance of being a product developer for a multinational company such as Siemens was not lost on Siete, who remarked "Wouldn't it be fantastic for Waleli as a one man business to acquire Siemens as a client for product development." In June 2003 an offer was eventually tabled but two months later owing to deliberation from their legal department an agreement had yet to be finalized.

Siete then received some encouraging news. He had entered his business plan in the New Venture Business Plan Contest, an initiative of McKinsey & Company organized by "de Baak Management Centre VNO-NCW." The organization called Siete with the specific request to be present during the prize-giving ceremony and not to sit on the balcony. Siete enquired as to whether they ask that of all the participants, and they replied, "Well yes, but you are among the candidates short-listed

Figure 4. De Telegraaf article

for the prize." Waleli was among the short-listed candidates; however, it did not win the prize and while the initial good fortune of being nominated was a boost, the experience left Siete despondent.

The situation reached a crisis point. Siete had managed to stretch the restricted starting budget to cover the first 18 months. However, following this, his business and personal finances could not be separated and the demands for payment were piling up to the point where he couldn't take it anymore. Together with his girlfriend he decided to go on vacation to reflect on whether or not he would continue with the business. While on vacation, on the morning of the July 30, Siete received a telephone call from his good friend Daan Westdijk to inform him that there was an article about Waleli's "GSM-doorbell" on the front page of one of the leading Dutch national newspapers, *de Telegraaf* (see Figure 4).

The Tide Turns

Siete decided that he was only willing to stop the enterprise if he had the feeling that he had tried everything. He formulated a list of five things to do before allowing himself to quit and he set about these on his return, but not before sending a copy of the newspaper article to one of the potential investors who had previously backed out.

Siete also sent a candid e-mail to Siebren de Vries, the founder and owner of Chess telling him he was considering his options for the business (see Table 2). Siebren was at that time on a sailing holiday with his family but recognizing Siete's cry for help he answered, "If you drive to the harbor in Hindelopen, I'll meet you there." Siebren encouraged him and said that he should not stop now after coming so far. He offered him a short tem contract to investigate the M2M market possibilities for Chess. This helped relieve the immediate pressure.

In the meantime Siete realized that Waleli could not continue as a one-man band. On September 16, 2003, Siete received a job application letter from an enthusiastic young man, Daan van Kampen, who had read the article in the Telegraaf and was enquiring about the employment vacancies on the Waleli Web site. In reality, finances were not available to recruit new employees; Siete had only put the vacancies on the Web site to create a more professional profile for those looking. Siete reacted honestly to Daan (see Table 3), who still chose to come for an interview. A short time later, Daan started an internship with Waleli earning €350 per month and with the intention of applying to other companies while gaining some experience.

At the same time Allard van de Rhee and Siete got to know each other through a mutual acquaintance. Siete had mentioned in conversation with this acquaintance that he was looking for someone like minded who understood the fundamentals of entrepreneurship, and she recommended Allard. Allard had just sold his holding interest in WharfProductions and was considering something totally new. They met on the 29th of September and decided to begin working together gradually, with Allard eventually becoming a shareholder and taking on the position of technical director.

Three days before beginning the cooperation with Allard, Siete had brought the situation with Siemens to a head. Siete felt that the uncertainty had to come to an end, in essence, "it was now or never." He organized a meeting with Kees Smaling during which he said, "Kees, you want to pay me to think of opportunities but at the same time you are paying your lawyers to think in problems. I think we need to put a bomb under them to push the situation forward. The following week the contract was finally signed. With the contract secured Siete had the courage to ask the question that had been on his mind for a long time: "why did you choose Waleli when you have your own research and development department?" The answer was simple: "if we do it ourselves it takes four times longer, it costs five times as much and just before it is ready the project gets killed." Through this experience Siete learned the justification for Waleli's existence.

The following month Waleli won the regional final of the LiveWIRE Young Business Award and with it an invitation to compete in the national final, taking place at the head office of Shell, in the Hague. LiveWIRE is an international Shell-program that has been running in the Netherlands, in conjunction with Syntens, the innovation network for entrepreneurs, since 1997. The competition helps technically innovative entrepreneurs with the development of their company, offering personal advice and a professional network. LiveWIRE aims to increase the entrepreneur's chances

Table 2. Siete's cry for help

Mail to Siebren de Vries (founder and owner of Chess). Date: July 1, 2003. Time: 10.22 a.m.

Dear Siebren,

I would gladly appreciate if, in the coming period, we could organize a private and confidential meeting to discuss the progress of my initiatives and your possible role in this. Your possible role could be from one of the following options: (1) to invest a small quantity of risk capital as an informal investor, (2) to employ us as a client working to make your Bluetooth-vision concrete

Current Status
- There are seven developers who are interested in implementing the system as standard in new building projects
- "Het Bouwfonds" (market leader) wants to use the application of the system in a press campaign this Summer
- Siemens have requested and received a tender for the development of a plug and play version on the basis of DECT
- The Executive Board of Isolectra have written to inform us that they want to incorporate the product in their portfolio
- The market leaders in door (Krego) and lock (Nemef) manufacturing are interested in the product concept and want to market it as a total concept also incorporating their electronic lock
- The LTO expressed an interest in marketing the product to their 90,000 farmers and market gardeners
- The current patent is too broad and will have to be adopted to new insights
- Products which bear technological resemblance are being developed at this time
- Within Waleli two new product concepts (concerning Wifi and Bluetooth) have originated which are being developed with others

Despite these developments all is not well with Waleli. In spite of the enthusiasm from the market and from some major players, a serious problem exists bridging the gap between generating "interest" and actual cash flow. My gut feeling tells me that Siemens will not pursue the offer. Also, discussions with external financiers have yielded positive feedback with respect to belief and trust in the entrepreneur but not commitment to actual deals. At the moment my business and personal finances have been stretched to the limit, forcing me to consider changing direction.

Following Steps
There are four possible solutions:

1. To raise some limited bridging capital from one or two informal investors at short notice
2. To undertake part-time consultancy/project management activities to generate cash flow for Waleli
3. To generate direct cash flow by taking a part-time job
4. To leave Waleli dormant and look for a full-time job

Best regards,
Siete Hamminga

of success, while adding to the knowledge base of individual companies. Winning the regional final gave Waleli some prestige and helped raise the company's profile among potential investors. Besides Roel Pieper, who always expressed an interest in investing, now Menno Witteveen van Haagveste and André Smit from Shell were also enthusiastic about investing. In early December 2003 Siete met with two further potential investors, this meeting went particularly well and the men were expressing an interest. Siete asked them if they wanted to see the business plan, to which they replied "there would want to be something seriously wrong with it for us not to come on board."

The New Start

On December 9, 2003, the rental contract for the office premises at Keizersgracht 203, the former business premises of Adam Curry (media and podcasting entrepreneur), was signed. Waleli acquired the photo copier machine belonging to Adam Curry in exchange for a GSM-doorbell. They further acquired free desks and chairs through contacts of Daan and Allard and these were immediately resold to acquire capital for new modern office furniture. Waleli were fortunate in that Aquadia, the former ground floor tenants at Keizersgracht had recently gone bankrupt, allowing Siete to cheaply purchase flash desks, chairs, and shelving from this company. The office space was thus brought into the style of Waleli; later this was to become known as "waleli-ization." The office premises were rented allowing for the potential growth of Waleli but in the meantime this left them with more space than was required. Waleli again saw an opportunity in this situation and decided to sublet the office space to other starting entrepreneurs. This action not only allowed Waleli to have their own office space rent free but it also increased the presence within the premises, giving clients the impression that Waleli was a larger company than it actually was. There was now a successful aura surrounding Waleli.

On January 21, 2004, Waleli also won the national final of the LiveWIRE Young Business Award, beating off competition from over 300 other starting entrepreneurs. In the same period, Hans Joosten contacted the company about potential job op-portunities. Hans had many years of sales experience working within Nashuatec, a global leader in the field of document management solutions, services, supplies, and consultancy, but he wanted to be an entrepreneur. However, he didn't want to "start from scratch," rather, he wanted to partner with a starting enterprise. Allard, Hans, Siete, the five "informals" (informal investors) had a meeting to discuss the relevant inputs and division of shares.

All in all these affairs were concluded on May 27, 2004, and at the same time it was decided to set up a limited company; thus Waleli B.V. (limited) was born. In the period that followed, Siete went to meet Gert and Bart, two of the original informal investors, for coffee. On behalf of Waleli he returned their investment, including

Table 3. Siete's correspondence with Daan van Kampen

Mail from Daan Kampen. Date: September 16, 2003. Time: 3:49 p.m.

Dear Mr. Hamminga,
 	
Some time ago I read an article in the *Telegraaf* about the GSM doorbell, which I read with great interest. I tracked down your Web site and have read about your business. Your vision and also the connection between machines and mobile telephones offering many opportunities appeals to me.
 	
I have recently graduated from the University of Leiden, where I completed the Master program on Media Technology. At the moment I am looking for a job that is related to my studies. After reading your Web site I thought that is where I want to work. It would fit perfectly to my training to work in a small company with such an innovative atmosphere and I think it would be fantastic to work in such a team. I have a great affinity for technology. I have even persuaded my parents to purchase a home automation system. Although this system does not work at present with the mobile telephone its use in this system is possible. And the GSM door bell is course a beautiful supplement to such a system.
 	
On your Web site it stated that in January you were looking for:
   -    Marketing & sales manager
   -    Financial manager
   -    Management assistant/secretary
 	
I take it that these functions have been filled in the meanwhile. Therefore, I wonder if there are other job openings within your company.
 	
With Kind Regards,
 	
Daan van Kampen

Mail to Daan Kampen. Date: September 16, 2003. Time: 2.11 p.m.
Dear Daan, Firstly, thank you for your interest in Waleli. I have received your mail and CV and it looks good. I shall be honest and frank in my reply. Waleli is still in the starting phase, it is not more than a one man business with a passionate and ambitious entrepreneur behind it. The appointments were never filled as there were merely "window-dressing." BUT, … A lot has happened since then. The GSM doorbell is set to fly, we have signed a partnership with Chess and this week I am getting things started with Siemens. Things are beginning to really happen and I am beginning to think about hiring people. From this perspective I would like to meet you with a view to a possible working relationship. If you are still interested given of the new information which I have outlined above, then with this mail I invite you to visit me at Bloemendaal. In the coming time this is possible on Monday the 23rd, Thursday 25th or Friday 26th of September. Kind regards, Siete Hamminga

the bonus. They reacted with both astonishment and delight and promised to be available for business support in the future if the need would arise.

Waleli had morphed from a one man business to an entrepreneurial team and the next challenge was to broaden the scope of the company from that of a single product to having a developed product portfolio. The existence of the venture would no longer be dependent on the success of the GSM-doorbell. The search then began to develop further applications for wireless communication which meet customer needs in a simple way.

Broadening the Scope/In Search of Opportunities

Waleli always had the intention and ambition of serving both the consumer and M2M markets. Their first M2M project, which was also their first international activity, was with JohnsonDiversy in Switzerland. Siete contacted an old colleague of his at JohnsonDiversy, which had previously been a subsidiary of Unilever. Soon they found a M2M opportunity to work on. JohnsonDiversy have large cleaning machines, the activities of which were logged twice a year onto a laptop. By implementing an M2M solution, the data is now collected daily, allowing the client to lease the machines per hour while also charging per hour used, thus increasing revenues and efficiencies.

To generate short-term cash flow, Waleli began operating their consultancy services and the "Innovation Fource" (see the section on Products\Services Provided). The Innovation Fource is a clever strategy,as it is not only beneficial to the client but it also provides further opportunities for Waleli. At the end of each session the client has four concrete and visualized product ideas, the ownership of which is retained by the client for a 12 month period; after this time has elapsed, ownership reverts to Waleli. Further, Waleli offers their clients the opportunity to work together in the product development and bringing the product to market and in these instances the client company retains ownership of the ideas.

In the summer of 2004, Waleli developed the "21Switch" (see Table 1 for more information). This switch allows forwarding of telephone calls from fixed telephone lines to any other phone. The system was previously available but uptake was low because it was a pay service and it required a series of actions to activate it. Waleli simplified this process so that it can be done at the flick of a switch. Waleli pitched this idea at KPN and by Christmas they had initiated a trial run with some 3,000 households. Depending on the outcome of the trial, Waleli might need to supply KPN with some 4.2 million switches to be distributed free to KPN's customers.

Fortunately for Siete, he had already begun a relationship with a manufacturer who is capable of meeting such demand. When carrying out his original search for someone who could produce the "21 Switch," another starting entrepreneur mentioned a Dutch manufacturer in China. Siete coincidently met the daughter of the company's owner, having already received the quote for the initial production. Siete used this opportunity to find out more information about the father and it transpired that he has seven factories, employing some 5,000 people, in China. Siete concluded, "Our relationship with this production company is becoming a very interesting asset for Waleli."

Waleli continued to churn out ideas through the Innovation Force and also through the new product development team throughout the course of the following year, including, among others, the Basiqphone and the MMS-Witness Collaboration with the Dutch police force. Waleli continued pursuing leads in the M2M market but unfortunately these can have a long time delay before projects are realized, and this was especially true for Waleli, as they have insufficient resources to devote to these activities. By this time Waleli had grown to a business with 13 employees, many external development teams, some of which are located at Keizersgracht, and a valuable association with the Chinese based manufacturer. Despite this growth, Siete's ambitions for the company have not yet been realized and for this to happen, some challenges must first be overcome.

Current Challenges

Organizational Challenge

Through its Innovation Fource and internal innovation activities, Waleli has a new business idea funnel which creates multiple opportunities for the firm. However, this also creates the challenge of managing the process of going through the funnel so that they are not focusing on 20 projects at the same time and spending too much time on particular projects. To this end Waleli leaders developed a business model to evaluate their product portfolio, that is, to stop, kill, or recycle projects, and also to see if the resource allocation matches the potential projects revenues (see the project assessment model below). An important issue here is creating recurring revenues because Siete recognizes that Waleli will never reach its growth potential by only doing development projects and sending invoices for the hours worked, as Siete remarked "Then it is a capacity company and you won't ever get big." For Waleli to grow, it needs intellectual property, so it can do royalty agreements or margins on its own products *or* they get shares in exploitation companies, for example, an inventor comes to them and says "I have this great product idea and it fits well with the vision and competencies of Waleli. Can you help me to develop the product and put it to the market?" Waleli says "Yes, we can" and instead of charging €200,000, they charge €100,000 and take a percentage stake in the idea. Only through these

Figure 5. Waleli's project assessment model

Runners (70%)	**Applicants** (25%)
Receptionists (5%)	**Mummies** (0%)

mechanisms will Waleli ever grow to meet the growth expectations of the share-holders. It is a daring strategy in the sense that it has a relatively high-risk profile but given the criteria for stopping and starting projects the outlook on recurring revenues is a very important one.

The rationale behind the project evaluation model is to match resource allocation with the potential of the project. To do this Siete defined criteria to judge their current project portfolio; projects with greater potential and that have a greater synergy with Waleli's image and mission should get a greater resource allocation than those that have less potential. Siete commented "This is logical and makes good business sense; however, in practice, it was not always the case." The model (see Figure 5 has four quadrants, which are explained as follows:

1. **Runners:** Are those projects that have a paying client behind them, that is, they are currently cash generators. 70% of Waleli's resources will be allocated to such projects.

2. **Applicants:** Are those projects which might become a runner. Contacts have been established but final contracts have yet to be finalized. These projects will absorb 25% of the resource allocation.

3. **Receptionists:** Are those projects that might go live but Waleli is not going to put too much further energy into them. Waleli will remain by and large passive, as Siete feel that they have done everything to acquire the project and now it is up to the client. Waleli's only action will be to phone the client once a month to see if there is any progress on their part. These projects are allocated 5% of Waleli's resources.

4. **Mummies:** Are those remaining projects in Waleli's portfolio, they are used as examples but are inactive. These projects include projects that were both successful or unsuccessful and no resources are allocated to these projects.

Siete has presented a growth plan (2005-2009) to the shareholders in which the project appraisal scheme and the growth paths are important elements. In order for Siete to act on a high level and have less time spent on operational requirements, he needs to have people around him who are able to work independently and see the necessity of creating revenue streams from all available opportunities. Up until now Waleli has been very reactive with its recruiting policies. In essence, its leaders have never actively recruited for a particular position; rather, potential employees have approached them. Siete remarked "People have always approached us and when they are enthusiastic, we say great, come on board. We don't pay too much but you are more than welcome."

On a positive note, this has resulted in Waleli having a very enthusiastic and young team. Conversely, this has also resulted in poor role definition because it has not been defining roles and then hiring the people to fill them; rather Waleli has been taking on staff and then examining what the staff could do. Another drawback of having such a young, albeit enthusiastic, team is that these employees lack a prior reference point for what it is like to work in an actual company. To illustrate this point Siete recounted a recent conflict with respect to the use of Microsoft's MSN™ in the office. Siete was aware that MSN™ was been used by the office staff to chat with friends during work hours; however, he saw too many windows open at one time and felt it was being over used, so he asked his employees to curtail their use of the program. This did not happen, which lead to Siete uninstalling MSN™ from all the computers. The employees responded saying "We are a hip company, we are a cool company in the heart of Amsterdam, we should be allowed to use MSN™." In return Siete asked them to name one company that takes itself seriously that allows their employees to use MSN™ during office hours. Siete concluded, "They understood my position but they have a lot to learn."

From the MSN™ experience, Siete established new criteria for the hiring of future employees. First, new employees will have to have prior work experience. "Very basically, they will need to know what it is like to work, especially in a professional environment." Second, Siete wants future new employees to bring in a relevant network of their own. Siete explained the benefits of this policy as follows, "If you have been a product manager at Philips you know how certain things work, you probably bring in your own network, so it gives Waleli a flying start." Thus, Waleli is changing its recruitment policy from a very responsive or reactive approach to a more focused approach. That is also one of the main reasons it has written the growth plan: to establish where Waleli wants to be in 2009. Part of this process entails evaluating who it already has employed and what tasks they perform, establishing what job openings need to be filled and then evaluating what kind of people they need.

Internationalization Challenge

The current challenges include going international with the 21Switch product. Waleli has already made contact with, among others, Deutsche Telecom, British Telecom, and Telia (Sweden), and these contacts are close to fruition. To help with international efforts, Waleli has entered into an arrangement with Lawrence Masle. Lawrence Masle is an American with a very strong corporate track record; he was vice president of Corporate Communication and Business Development with Ericsson in Sweden. He then went to London to set up an Ericsson office there and following this he went to work for Philips in the Netherlands. Lawrence is currently self employed and teaches MBA classes at a university in Belgium.

Lawrence Masle had read several articles on Waleli and on reading the third one he thought it would be interesting to meet the founder. Siete and Lawrence had several lunch meetings and they decided to start working together. Siete told him on their first meeting that given his curriculum vitae he couldn't afford to employ him, but Lawrence said he was not looking for a job. They settled on an agreement where Siete pays Lawrence a fixed amount every month to cover general expenses. Lawrence recognizes the potential in Waleli and he wants to be involved so much so that he also wants to invest in the company and Waleli is planning a new share issue in the coming time in which Lawrence will participate. Their first project together was to jointly go to Stockholm, where Lawrence introduced Siete to his network, that is, the people who used to work for him there. While there they also met the former CEO of Ericsson, Mr. Sven Christian Nielsen, who is currently on the board of Telia, and through him Waleli began discussions for introducing the 21Switch to the Swedish market.

In a previous shareholders' meeting, Siete informed the shareholders that he wanted to expand the company to give it more of an international orientation. To do this Siete planned to focus on getting smaller offices operational in other countries. The shareholders agreed that it was a great idea but they had their reservations, saying "Let's work on Waleli in the Netherlands first" and also questioning "Who is going to do that, when your time is required here?" So Siete changed this strategy and said "Tickets rather than offices." Let us first focus on developing markets in North Western Europe and finding the right person for this task. Those things collided: the right person, someone who had experience at the highest corporate levels and was internationally orientated, came along at the right time and Lawrence is now conducting the international business development.

Market Challenge

Waleli's ambition is to have a strong presence in both the consumer products market and the industrial applications for the M2M market. Currently, Waleli's activities in developing its market for M2M applications is constrained by a lack of resources, especially in relation to the time available to dedicate to these activities. It only has one live project, namely JohnsonDiversy, dealing with the M2M market. Siete's aim is to embark on the acquisition of M2M projects creating a luxury problem, whereby when they acquire projects they can employ staff to work on these activities.

To develop his M2M aspirations, Siete attended a networking meeting where he hoped to find small development companies with whom he could jointly develop M2M opportunities and possibly take-over, or at least bring under the flag of Waleli. To his surprise, however, he found that the participants at this meeting were all actually potential clients, so Siete took the opportunity to discuss potential business opportunities and made a good head start. The event itself was organized in part by a competitor of Waleli but as a paying guest Siete had no scruples about using this opportunity to pursue acquisitions. In fact, all the companies were responding so positively that Siete took the list of all the companies, including those who did not attend but had expressed an interest in doing so, and called these companies, saying how they missed each other but that he was curious as to what they were doing in this area.

Waleli currently has a list of some 10 projects, half of which arose from the M2M networking event, which have already been discussed with various firms. Siete realizes that they won't acquire all of these projects but hopes to be successful with between one third and one half of these. In the growth plan he outlined plans to hire a senior M2M person. The ideal candidate would be a seasoned business person with the relevant experience and, of course, the relevant network for developing this market. This position will be the top earning position in the firm and there will be a dedicated budget for undertaking these activities. Siete hopes to have acquired some projects so that the day the new employee takes the position Siete can say "Well, I've already acquired three projects, the management of these and the relevant extended development teams will take 60% of your time, while the other 40% will be for acquisitions."

All the projects on the M2M list have also been evaluated using their new business model and there are three projects there Waleli is actively pursuing. These are all projects with larger firms, as the potential upswing from conducting business with such firms is higher. Also, through his experiences of dealing with potential M2M projects, Siete has learned a valuable business lesson, namely, when you put so much time and effort into a project and it doesn't work out, you should look and see who else could use it, that is, offer it to the competitor. Siete remarked that this is an obvious business practice in which they did not previously engage but they are going to more actively pursue this strategy in the future.

References

Autio, E., Yli-Renko, H., & Salonen, A. (1997). International growth of young technology-based firms: A resource-based network model. *Journal of Enterprising Culture, 5*(1), 57-73.

Birley, S., & Cromie, S. (1988, September). *Social networks and entrepreneurship in Northern Ireland.* Paper presented at the Enterprise in Action Conference, Belfast, Northern Ireland.

Brush, C.G., Greene, P.G., & Hart, M.M. (2001). From initial idea to unique advantage: The entrepreneurial challenge of constructing a resource base. *Academy of Management Executive, 15*(1), 64-80.

Diamantopoulos, A., & Inglis, K. (1988). Identifying differences between high- and low-involvement exporters. *International Marketing Review 5,* 52-60.

Doutriaux, J. (1991). High-tech start-ups, better off with government contracts than with subsidies: New evidence in Canada. *IEEE Transactions on Engineering Management, 38,* 127-135.

O'Farrell, P.N., & Hitchens, D.M. (1988). Alternative theories of small-firm growth: A critical review. *Environment and Planning, 20*(2), 1365-1383.

Van der Veen, M., & Wakkee, I. (2006). Understanding the entrepreneurial process. In P. Davidsson (Ed), *New firm startups* (pp. 27-65). Cheltenham, UK: Edward Elgar Publishing Ltd.

http://www.shell-livewire.com

http://www.utwente.nl/top

http://www.waleli.com

Endnotes

[1]   For information on Waleli, see www.waleli.com The information is the present tells the story of development until May 2006.

[2]   For information on the TOP program, see www.utwente.nl/top/.

Chapter VIII

Workcenter SGD:
A Technology-Based Revolution in the Retail Reprography Sector

Cristina Cruz, Instituto de Empresa, Spain

Guillermo de Haro, Instituto de Empresa, Spain

Ignacio de la Vega, Instituto de Empresa, Spain

Abstract

In 1999 Alfonso de Senillosa, Spanish entrepreneur, after finishing his studies in the United States, decided to create Workcenter SGD. The company was born on the basis of following the same idea and services that Kinko's® created successfully in the United States, with nearly 1,300 retail stores devoted to reprographic services. Nevertheless, in four years the company went far ahead of the original idea, developing new technologies that helped manage the growth, control operations, and reduce costs. By 2005 the company had grown up to 20 stores all over Spain and Senillosa was celebrating his 38th birthday while deciding his next step in the company's future leveraging on the technology and operations already designed.

The Birth of Workcenter

In the early 1990s, while a student at the University of California (Los Angeles), Alfonso was surprised to discover centers that not only provided reprography and office services based on the latest technology for use by both professionals and students but that were open round the clock. They caught his interest because at the time such technologies were not widely available in Spain.

Once he had completed his studies and had achieved a curriculum vitae that he described as "a headache, even for staff at the employment office," he decided to take this idea to Spain to see if he could make a living out of it. He understood that it was a risk but, as he stated, he was "at the age when you don't mind taking risks."[1]

Together with two friends who had a more technical background and greater professional experience, Alfonso drew up a business plan, which was essential for making the project credible and obtaining the 60,000 euros needed to open a small reprography business on Guzmán el Bueno Street in Madrid. Senillosa stated:

The market study we based the business plan on is probably the most complex one we've ever done. We interviewed all sorts of people, visiting universities, offices, and so forth, to find out exactly what the demand was for this sort of service. Since then, with the growth of the company, the process has become simpler because we've learned a lot about the concept and we now know much better what sort of products and services we should offer.

Alfonso and his friends provided 30,000 euros (5 million of the former pesetas) and the rest came from a bank loan. Senillosa was quick to understand the hardships involved in being an entrepreneur because his contribution came partly from the sale of his motorbike and his car, his most important belongings at the time. But the sacrifice was worthwhile. In January 1998, after two years running the small establishment on Guzmán el Bueno Street, they sold it and used the funds, in combination with financing from some Business Angels, to open the first Workcenter in Madrid on San Bernardo Street.

Alfonso was clear about it from the outset. "I always thought that if a business is to be successful, it's not so much a question of having a completely new idea as of creating sound foundations. The concept worked wonderfully in the U.S., and all we did was to adapt that business model to the specific needs of Spain." This was why by the end of February in the year it was created, the center was already offering its services 24 hours a day. The result was a total of 200,000 customers the first year and break-even in the fourth month.

At that time, the reprography sector in Spain was comprised of family-run companies with very limited potential for growth and management. Most of them worked for a few, very specific customers. Workcenter introduced much more professional management so it was able to offer new technologies to other groups, such as students and professionals who also needed these services. Since this business model was unknown not only in Spain but throughout Europe, the opening of Workcenter led to the creation of a new demand that was one step ahead of customers' needs. Customers could draw up an idea, design it, lay it down in a document, and send it, all from the same place and with advice on the use of the latest technologies available on the market.

The fact that the stores were open 24 hours a day was another differentiating element in the Workcenter business model. As the founder explains:

There can be no doubt that our nonstop opening hours made an impact because there was a latent demand. What we did was to eliminate the time limits within which many professionals were working. Previously, they had to complete their work by a specific time so that they could give it in to the customer the next day. Also, the opening hours turned into an essential marketing tool, giving the business great visibility. With very limited resources and a very small investment in advertising, we were able to transmit our business idea because, when the whole of Madrid turned off its lights, the Workcenter was the only place with its lights still on!

This was one of the reasons why the location of the stores was of great strategic importance. The policy was that all Workcenters should be in very busy, central streets, with large storefronts so that people could see in, and that they should be very well-lit. As stated by Purificación Peña, Financial Manager of Workcenter:

Unlike other growing companies that could adapt to any sort of premises, initially we insisted on a specific type of store in a specific location so that they could serve as real "shop-windows." We do not invest in advertising. Our main advertisements are our stores so they have to be very visible in all the cities we work in. The idea is that when someone needs to produce a document they should recollect the image of Workcenter. And the fact is that we became so well-known that, later on, we were able to open less visible establishments in the same cities.

The Reprography Sector

In 2005, the world market for reprography could be estimated at about 850,000 million euros, with several different sectors. The first was corporate services, with 500,000 million euros. This segment included large volumes of printed documents, as well as consultancy, software, and facilities management. This market was mainly served by the equipment manufacturers, although outsourced services were gradually finding a niche. The retail segment comprised students, SOHO (small office-home office) customers and SMEs (small and medium enterprises). Their demand had traditionally been for photocopies and printing but, with the widespread use of the new digital formats for documents, the range of possibilities had expanded (color, paper size, etc.) and the demand for services with a greater added value was rising sharply.

Moreover, this was a very fragmented sector. According to the Spanish Reprography Association,[2] in 2003 Spain had 2,256 reprography companies, with total sales valued at 1,550 million euros. Most of them were small photocopying businesses that were unable to invest in new equipment and mostly used analogue technologies. Less than 7% of them employed more than 20 people and none of them worked beyond their local area. In fact, in early 2005, Workcenter, with 16 centers, was by far the competitor with the largest number of centres specializing in printing and services, to the extent that, in the words of the company's founder, "We really have no direct competition because there are no other companies in Spain with a similar business model to ours."

In 2005, the market was in a rather strange situation. The sector had undergone great changes during the last decade with the arrival of the "digital revolution." Many companies had had to invest heavily to replace their analogue equipment with digital equipment and to find staff capable of using the new technologies. Another new feature was the creation of printing networks which made it possible to do the design in one location, send it to another, and then print it, maintaining the quality of the end product. Therefore, from being just a producer of paper for printing, the sector now embodied the art of processing and dealing with computer files and converting them into documents which were seen as valuable tools for communication.

Also the sector was growing significantly. The increasingly widespread use of color printing and different formats was leading companies and professionals to request more document services. Demand wanted more quality services based on the new technologies, needing sophisticated equipment and know-how. Also, standard customers were increasingly better-informed, demanding, and expected more personalized service.

Finally, the trend in the large corporations in Spain was approaching the average figures for Europe where, according to a study by IDG,[3] at the end of 2003, more than 60% of corporations were outsourcing their reprography requirements and the remainder who were not yet outsourcing nevertheless were considering it for this type of service. In order to compete in this new market, the large manufacturers such as Xerox, Ricoh, and Canon had started to include printing and reprography services for large corporations in their product portfolios but their conditions were strict, with contracts implying minimum times of guarantied service and volumes of photocopies that had to be made as a minimum, and in case the company could not reach those figures it would have to pay them. This was one of the reasons why these large manufacturers were not as successful with the SME segment as they were with the large corporations.

The Growth of Workcenter

According to Alfonso de Senillosa. Founder of Workcenter:

Growth in our business model has always been based on "exploring." First we found out if the first store worked, then we considered the challenge of the second one, then the idea of opening in a different city. Once these three steps work, you can say you have a model with potential for growth as a chain. From then on, we accepted the challenge of growing and reaching new markets.

Purificación Peña, Financial Manager of Workcenter, states:

For me, the process of growth has been like "building a house." In the companies I had worked in before, the foundations and structure already existed and all you could do was adapt things. But in Workcenter there was no house, not even founda-tions, so it was clear where we had to start. And I feel that everything we have now is a bit mine, because we've all helped to lay the bricks. Alfonso says it's like his child, but it's like a child with many godparents!

According to Belén Huidobro, Cofounder of WorkCenter:

Everything was chaotic at the start—the working method, closing the tills. There had been no analysis of the different tasks involved—everyone did everything. Over time, responsibilities were segmented, new processes were set up, and lower job profiles were taken on. Gradually we saw that things were working better and now we wonder how it was ever possible to work like we did at the start.

Implementation of a business model for round-the-clock reprography and office services required the coordination of shifts to guarantee timing and quality in any job, however complex. The company met this challenge by creating a digital order tracking system (DOTS), so that every job could be planned and organized, opti-mizing costs and time, knowing who was involved, controlling quality, and dealing with alerts regarding timing. The DOTS system showed the status of jobs online and sent out an SMS system when the job was ready, thus improving on the delivery period promise. This system, in turn, was run by a department called the Workcenter Operations Management and Administration Control (WOMAC), described by Alfonso de Senillosa as "the control tower of Workcenter operations."

Process management went together with a human resources policy that aimed above all to create a very strong team on which growth could be based. The founder was aware that the sector mainly comprised family-run businesses and he determined from the start that employees should be offered a career, in order to both professionalize the business as much as possible and to boost job satisfaction, which was, in his opinion, "at least as important, if not more so, than customers."

The company's staff was characterized by a very high level of turnover at the lower levels (the shift work was very suitable for students), but with little turnover at middle management level and among center managers. Staff recruitment was carried out at store level and selection processes for managers was rare. All store managers participated in the final decision. Evaluation processes were adopted for all positions to try to correct any mistakes made in the selection process and to detect any potential candidates for promotion.

The remuneration policy changed with changes in the company. Initially, a system of performance-related incentives was adopted, at the discretion of the store manager. This proved to be not very transparent so, in 2003, the company decided to introduce a radical change, after first formalizing all the processes and acquiring all the necessary information. The new policy, still in force in early 2005, was that 100% of the staff should share in the profits. So, depending on the profits obtained by each store at the end of each month, incentives were distributed among all the staff, on the basis of their category. "This meant that all staff, absolutely everyone, was very much concerned that the store should work efficiently. They understood that this was the key to profits and therefore to their incentives."

The problem of transparency was resolved by communication. Every month, each manager received the calculation of profits, which was presented and explained to the staff, so that everyone knew how the month had gone, how the cost structure worked, how much had been sold and, above all, how all this would affect his or her pay-packet at the end of the month. "When we were told of the change in the payment policy," says a Workcenter employee, "we felt a new stage was beginning which would offer great possibilities because the variable part of the wage was unlimited. It really represented a great motivation for all of us."

With its efficient process and personnel management, the business model turned out to be easy to replicate and the company was able to open new stores without having to substantially increase the head office structure. The managers became responsible for business units that were structured like small companies, with everything they needed to work efficiently available in store and almost complete independence.

The Arrival of Financial Partners

Another feature was that growth in the business model always went together with the incorporation of quality partners. In the words of the founder:

From the outset, both I and the other partners who had joined me at the start of the adventure were aware that, from a financial point of view, we would not be able to achieve the growth that the company deserved without calling on outside resources.

Therefore, in 2000, the company's founder offered two large banks—Banco Santander and BBVA—an interest in the company. "They both accepted," says Senillosa, "provided they would both be subject to the same conditions." They valued the company at 24 million euros and each provided 3 million, a 12.5% stake in the company. "I think what convinced them was our daring and, above all, our potential for growth." Later on, the banks increased their investment to 15.6% each, and BBVA transferred its interests to the IBV Corporation.[4]

The Board of Directors was one of the keys in this new stage of the company. Chaired by Alfonso de Senillosa, it included some of the company's initial partners as well as senior representatives of the Grupo Santander and the Corporación IBV. Others were invited to boost the company's value, such as Alfonso Martínez, the cofounder of Telepizza, who had great experience in the retail sector, as well as other successful entrepreneurs. In this way, the knowledge already gained by Workcenter was enhanced with the necessary information for creating a chain of stores. The company's professional management ensured financial and operational control, as well as the necessary long-term vision for reaching cruise speed.

Consolidation of the Business Model

The first store in Madrid was followed in 2001 and, after the entry of the banks into the share capital, another six were opened, including two in Barcelona. The company then continued to expand geographically, opening a new store in Valencia in 2002 and another two in Seville.

Each of the company's stores was a different world but they all had a similar structure. They all offered digital printing, office services, packaging, and despatch to both corporate and retail customers. But the weight of the different services varied from center to center. The services were divided into two main lines: store services relating mostly to printing (just in time and by order), and office services. The former involved above all printing in black and white and color, large formats (posters and drawings), and finishes. The latter involved the renting of computers with Internet access, "self-service" photocopying, office equipment, printing, fax, and videoconferencing. As a result of an agreement with DHL, packaging and despatch services were also offered in 2002. Success with this product led them to increase their services in 2004, including four new package formats, as well as documents and an increase in the number of destinations, both national and international.

Felipe Corcuera, General Manager of DHL Ibérica, states:

The idea was to draw up an agreement for collaboration so that Work-center would become the first center specializing in the packaging and despatch of documents, exploring all the logistics possibilities that were offered by the Workcenter's "capillarity" and long opening hours.

Documents could be received in centers either directly (from customers seeking assistance at the counters or from the stores' corporate assistants) or by e-mail or telephone, by phoning the WOMAC. Just-in-time jobs were requests made at the counter when the customer expected to leave the store with the finished document so work had to be done on the spot. Other jobs were introduced into the DOTS system. This initiated quality controls and production by the center's production team, under the leadership of the shift's Head of Production. At all times, there had to be one person responsible for production and work in process in the store at all times. With each change of shift, this person changed but the information was in the system and in just a few minutes the new shift took control of the store and of any jobs without affecting the key factors of quality and time.

Once the work was complete, it was stored until it could be delivered either in the store or by Workcenter's own logistics service (motorbikes, vans, and other services) to the customer. If completed in advance of the deadline, the customer was notified by SMS with the aim of both improving the service and freeing storage space.

Gradually, the number of loyal customers grew. They knew and appreciated the company's services. This led it to increase the "self-service" products, thus freeing the counter and offering benefits to customers (such as lower prices). New technologies, such as the Express card for using the computers and for printing and copying, improved customer satisfaction and led to a great improvement in the efficiency of the centers' operations.

The Birth of WBS

The increase in outsourcing of reprography services on the part of large corporations (Facilities Management) represented a growth opportunity for Workcenter and in mid-2004, it launched its WBS division (Workcenter Business Solutions). The birth of this division was partly made possible by the signature of the largest contract for reprography signed in Spain in 2004, between Workcenter and the Grupo Santander.

The origin of this agreement can be traced to early 2000, when Grupo Santander announced its decision to move to a new head office 27 kilometers from Madrid, with the aim of centralizing all its services and achieving savings of over 50 million euros a year thanks to centralized services and new working methods. The world's largest business campus was to cover 395 acres (about 160 football fields) and start functioning in the middle of 2004, with a staff of 7,000.

This project posed rather unusual reprography needs. First, the move was to be done gradually so any contract had to be flexible over time. This made it difficult to estimate the volume of copies, which was the figure usually used as a basis for drawing up contracts. Also, scalability was necessary, with an integrated solution in which it was possible to control expenditure and achieve constant improvements in production, logistics, and administrative processes for documents.

Previously, Grupo Santander had had its own reprography center in-house, which used equipment rented directly from the manufacturer for 5-year periods. This limited production to the maximum capacity of the machines (assuming there were no breakdowns) and to the center's working hours (normal office hours). At peak periods, the machines proved insufficient, so delivery periods had to be extended.

The solution proposed by Workcenter in the bid presented in response to the Grupo Santander's tender was a mixed model, with a small reprography center in the "Financial City" for jobs that were especially urgent or confidential, and an Industrial Production Centre (IPC) close by which would deal with the rest of the ever-growing production. The Grupo Santander work was to receive priority in the Workcenter's DOTS. The model adapted in real time to varying volumes of printing work because peaks could be sorted out during the night-time hours of the 24-hour centers, increasing the capacity of all the machines in the Workcenter network, producing in parallel if necessary. At off-peak times, the Group only used the Internal Center and, if necessary, the IPC in Alcobendas, without having to pay for machines that were not being used at the time. Scalability was guaranteed by Workcenter's logistics system. By adapting its delivery processes, the WOMAC could serve the Financial City from the nearest Production Center using any of the other IPCs during peak periods, constantly controlling workloads and delivery times. Regular shuttle services delivered orders, in order of priority, inside and outside the Grupo Santander premises.

All this meant that it was possible to substitute fixed costs by variable costs, eliminating the need for office space for machinery and supplies as well as energy costs. Unlike normal practice in the sector, the contract was signed for 2 years, so that prices could be updated every so often instead of reviewing them at the end of a 5-year contract. Also, the Workcenter network allowed documents to be produced at the destination, saving time, expenditure, and handling, and reducing uncertainty about delivery and quality by, for example, providing services to the territorial units in Barcelona and Valencia.

Workcenter's bid was the cheapest of all those received and, because of the wide range of services and the flexibility it offered, the Grupo Santander decided to adopt this new model, involving a radical change in its working method. After several months of successful functioning and several thousand operations, Workcenter began to draw up an important campaign to promote its WBS area. In view of the experience gained and the reference of such a demanding customer as Grupo Santander, the WBS was considered to be one of the company's most promising areas. At the end of 2005, corporate business amounted to 27% of the company's total sales, and WBS was providing services to a large number of companies in different sectors, including banking, telecommunications, and advertising.

The Technology in Workcenter

The technology was one of the key success factors in the development of the chain of stores, helping the growth and helping control of the business from a financial point of view. Alfonso de Senillosa was not an expert in technology. He had never studied a degree with any relation to technology, computer sciences, or anything similar. Nevertheless he was able to develop a system like DOTS that was admired by his admired Kinko's®.

One of the first points to be taken into account related to technology is that it was totally devoted to the operations. Whatever could help improve operations was always welcomed by the founder. Given the fact that everybody in the company had a variable retribution related to the results of the company not only the IT department was thinking about new ways to improve the business, everybody was. It is very common to hear that any new implementation of IT in a company must have top management support. In the case of Workcenter this was clear. Even not being an IT person, Alfonso was always fond of looking for new ways to do the things, and also to do them internally.

That is another of the curious points about the company. Except for the enterprise resource planning (ERP), all of the rest of developments were made internally. The IT Manager, Sergio Sierra, was responsible for most of the developments, dedicating half of their time to maintenance and infrastructures and the other half to improving operations.

The core of the business was the ERP and the DOTS system, but other technology was playing an important role in the company. First of all, the Internet, being Workcenter one of the first businesses to offer Internet access for professionals in Spain, not to talk about the 24 hours system. To implement a professional billing system, Alfonso analyzed various providers until he made the decision of going to Canada and the United States to find the perfect partner. The magnetic cards that could be bought and recharged in the so-designer-expenditure machine at any store were a success. With this system the customers could self-serve without going to the counter, and the control of the usage of the computers via Pharos software was perfect. Pharos software was also used to connect internally in the stores some of the photocopying machines.

In fact, that was the other important technology supporting the business: photocopying machines, printing machines, and other technologies related to the world of printing and processing documents. To improve results and better serve customers the company had made the decision to not attach to only one provider, and if the best color machine was from Xerox, that was the one at Workcenter, just in front of the black and white machine from Ricoh. Managing this equipment was difficult and critical for the business, not only from a technological point of view, but also from an investment stand point. To make decisions and bet on a technology or a machine bigger or smaller was a competitive advantage or a fail for a store. The know-how about providers and stores acquired with the years helped improve a process to design the technology needed to run operations in any given store. The investment could range from some thousand euros in the smallest machine, to some hundred thousand euros for a good color printer and copier from Xerox.

The interconnection of the machines inside each store was another challenge that, once solved, improved a lot of operations. When a customer arrived at the front counter he could ask for his account, being identified in the system. If the job he wanted was in a digital support (CD, DVD, or any other storage system), a work order was created in the DOTS with the information about the customer, the kind of job, and the delivery time. At this moment the production manager at the store was also including an estimate of the production time. The DOTS had a centralized control system where the delivery time was tracked comparing it with the estimate. For example, if the estimated time of production was four hours, and the delivery time was today at 1400, at 1000 the tracking system at DOTS changed the color of the work order on the screen to red. The black color indicated that a delay was going to happen. This DOTS software was developed internally, integrated with the ERP, Acqua, and with the Pharos system. This way the company could control almost in real time the daily operations. Everyday the managers could see via the Web, the sales from the day before in each store, the jobs produced, the jobs under production, the jobs made in each machine, and also detail the revenues coming from each product or service.

At the end of the process was the implementation of a system to send short messages to the customer when a job was finished in advance of the expected delivery time. This initiative was seen as a way to improve customer experience.

The ERP was Aqua. This software was not created internally, dedicating development time to create tools that were not in the market, were adapted to the idiosyncrasy of the company, and could be customized easily. Aqua was an ERP from a small Spanish firm with a good track record in ERPs for retail stores, even with an implementation in the reprographic sector.

The training was critical. We have seen that the smallest store has Internet connection for customers, the operators had to manage information from the ERP, the production machines are interconnected, and the DOTS system must be tracked every day several times. From the newcomer to the Manager of a store, all where trained in some basic maintenance and understanding of those technologies (from a technical but also business point of view, making them know the importance of it in their P&L and in their variable retribution).

Workcenter improved its Web page in 2005. The new site was mainly devoted to communication. There was a platform for e-commerce developed in the year 2000, but the experience has showed that the kind of customer who was loyal to the concept of the company preferred the direct contact with a store, or the development of a B2B solution customized like the one made at Grupo Santander. The integration with the DHL tracking system was an important point, as it enabled the company to be able to leverage on their technology to improve the experience for the shipping services.

At the end of 2005 the technologies of the company where more than proved. New developments were beginning; for example, an internal CRM system to help follow a project since the quotation was made, also integrating it with the DOTS and the ERP. With many years of good performance and a clear culture of developing, managing, and buying technology thinking about integration and interoperability, Workcenter was prepared for the next steps: having a clear vision of how technology was able to help them improve operations and acquire competitive advantages.

The Future of Workcenter

Everything looked promising at the close of 2005. Prospects were excellent; sales exceeded 12 million euros, with EBITDA of 3 million euros from the centers. The successes of the business model and brand recognition were beginning to bear fruit. But some small clouds were appearing on the horizon.

On one hand, it was essential to determine which path to follow in the future. The nuclei of the company's business were small and medium companies, professionals, and private persons. The remainder came from large companies and professional organizations and the percentage was growing. But the WBS business, on which the company had placed its bets, was completely new and was a very different business to that of the stores themselves. The resources earmarked for the WBS could not be used to increase the number of new stores. As one of the company's shareholders stated, "The main challenge was to organize Workcenter as a services company that could provide a broader personalized service than can be given by a small entrepreneur but offering greater flexibility than the large corporations."

Opening new stores was another of the main issues. Organic growth was showing its potential for ensuring the chain would grow in a profitable, controlled way. And experience showed that the existence of several centers in the same city was beneficial in that it enhanced brand recognition and generated large economies of scale. But there was a limit. Was it better to increase the number of centers in the cities where they were already working, with the consequent risk of cannibalization and internal competition? Or should they focus on capillarity, opening new centers in new cities so that the 24-hour Workcenter model could make itself known in places where it would face no competition?

This led to another important factor for growth. All the Workcenters were owned by the company. The possibility of franchising to increase the number of centers fast while maintaining profits was rejected. The business model was based on the company culture and on its staff. Looking after the staff so that they would look after the business and maintain the company's quality standards was critical but could be complicated in a franchise system. Also, rapid growth in the number of centers required faster promotions, and it was necessary to respect the time needed to find a store manager through internal promotion. The option of finding managers from outside the business would go against the company's policy of promotion from within and of supporting the staff so that they would support the company. On the other hand the technology developed was easy to implement to control and help grow via franchises, giving an added value to those new members of the Workcenter family.

In addition, maturity of the business model and growing knowledge of the market were encouraging Alfonso to consider new risks. Workcenter was not just the leading chain in Spain. No other reprography company had created a similar network of centers anywhere in Europe. The potential of the company's 24-hour working method in other European locations was not to be underestimated.

While he analyzed all the details in the San Bernardo center, following the checklist with which he checked everything in the stores (quality, personnel, processes, service, marketing, cleanliness, etc.), Alfonso was considering all these subjects. It was essential that they should continue innovating in products and services, because they had to continue leading their sector and also because demanding customers insisted on this from the only reprography company that was competing by offering differentiation. And it was also essential to make the right decisions about the direction and the speed at which the company should move.

By June 2006 the company had increased the number of stores up to more than 21, and was opening stores at a rate of 4 each 6 months without increasing the internal resources (head count, for example). A new more powerful ERP was beginning to be a must, and the development of new managers was a critical issue. New WBS customers had joined the Workcenter Production Network for Key Account Customers, and the company was increasing operations in all the cities where they had presence. Those achievements were again thanks to the smart implementation of technology to support growth and operations, and the appropriate management of equipment.

Conclusion

When thinking about technology and entrepreneurship, our first idea is software or technology development. In this case we have been analyzing a business in a traditional sector where the digital technologies had implied a revolution. That revolution has been led by a young entrepreneur who was able to manage all those concepts in a very simple way: thinking about the best for the business, risking and implementing technology regularly, trusting in a young but smart team for IT and operations working together, aligning all the important elements perfectly (retribution, operations, quality, technology development, customer satisfaction, and the P&L), and creating a culture of innovation.

Endnotes

[1]   All the quotations given are taken from transcriptions of interviews carried out by the authors with the company's founder, employees, and investors during the first few months of 2005, as part of the Workcenter case study.

[2]   http://www.aer-repro.com/

[3]   International Data Group (http://www.idc.com/)

[4]   The IBV Corporation was created in 1991 by IBERDROLA BBVA as a tool for applying its investment strategies in the field of industrial promotion and development, with each partner maintaining a 50% stake in the group.

Chapter IX

ThePCBShop.com:
Taking the Commodity Bull
by the Horns

Steve Muylle, Vlerick Leuven Gent Management School, Belgium

Veerle De Schryver, Tools for Growth, Belgium

Abstract

This case describes the entrepreneurial process as it happened for Europrint, a manufacturer of Printed Circuit Boards (PCBs), from 1991 until 2006. It offers an entrepreneurial perspective on the European PCB landscape, highlights the successful launch by the manufacturer of a dot.com in this highly competitive B2B environment, and illustrates the transition by the manufacturer to electronic business to break the product commodity cycle. As a final point, the case also reveals how the manufacturer's off-line and online business activities were consolidated and leveraged for maximum impact across Belgium, Hungary, and India.

Introduction

Monday, February 2, 2004, was a memorable day for Europrint, a manufacturer of printed circuit boards (PCBs), headquartered in Mechelen, Belgium. Luc Smets and Dirk Stans cut the ribbons that launched ThePCBShop.com, culminating their entrepreneurial efforts of the past 13 years. Since Europrint's foray into e-business at the end of 2000, the medium-sized enterprise has not only managed to fight off commodity pressure in its traditional sector, but it has also taken the vanguard in the online market. As Luc Smets commented:

ThePCBShop.com is the next step in our continuing effort to match our product and service offerings to customer needs. While our competitors are just whistling in the dark, we have been able to turn a corner and build a successful business on the platform of Internet technology.

As it had scored a series of victories, Europrint was looking into franchising ThePCBShop.com concept to downstream intermediaries—small businesses that could tap into the benefits of e-business without incurring hefty set-up costs. Even though Smets and Stans were entering unknown territory, they were confident that small dealers would appreciate this dynamic, modular platform for its extensive content, registration, administration, and payment support functionalities. By hooking into this platform, small dealers would be able to cope effectively with commoditization, an area in which Europrint had clearly led the way.

The Stadium: The European Landscape

A printed circuit board is a thin board made of insulating epoxy to which electronic components such as resistors, capacitors, and integrated circuits are fixed by solder (see Exhibit 1 for a depiction).

The simplest kind of PCB has components and wires on one side and usually metal (mostly copper) interconnections (the printed circuit) on the other. PCBs may have components mounted on both sides and may also have many internal layers, allowing more connections to fit in the same board area. PCBs are used in a variety of fields for everything from communications and medical and industrial equipment to home electronics, airplanes, and automobiles.

Industry categorizes PCBs as either bare boards or populated boards. While populated boards are end products that can be installed directly into another product with little or no additional processing, bare boards undergo further processing before becoming

Exhibit 1. Printed circuit board production panel (Source: Company information)

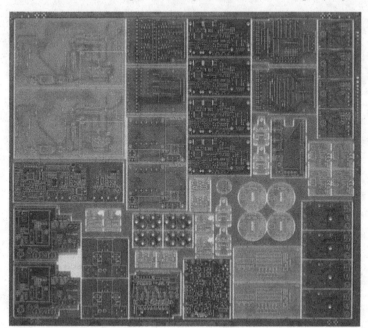

part of the finished product. The production of bare boards involves a fairly wide range of activities and players, as shown in Exhibits 2A, 2B, and 2C.

It all starts with design. Either an in-house design department or a subcontractor translates customer requirements into design specifications through the use of computer-aided design (CAD). Subsequently, the design is turned into a physical board by virtue of computer-aided manufacturing (CAM). These bare boards are then sold directly to end customers or indirectly to traders and assemblers. Traders offer a wide assortment of specialized bare boards from various manufacturers for resale to either assemblers or end customers. Assemblers go beyond mere buying and selling of bare boards and add components to the board, turning it into a finished product for end customers without assembly capabilities. End customers are either original equipment manufacturers (OEMs) that incorporate boards into other products sold in the business or ultimate consumer market, or they are users that deploy PCBs in the set-up or support of manufacturing and business processes. While these end customers may well do their own design and assembly, they always turn to manufacturers for board construction because this is a highly specialized activity outside their core business. Besides OEMs and users, individual hobbyists (typically electronics professionals) occasionally buy bare boards.

Exhibit 2A. The PCB production process (Source: Company information)

The production process starts with a fiberglass sheet with a copper layer laminated on one or both sides. The first step is drilling holes for component mounting and interconnecting the layers.

After drilling, the holes are washed out and a thin chemical copper layer is precipitated into the holes, interconnecting both sides of the board.

A photosensitive film is applied to the board and the connection pattern is established using a photographic process.

In the wet processes, the copper in the holes and on the tracks is further built up using a galvanic process and the excess copper between the tracks is etched out.

To protect the copper image, a layer of lacquer (solder mask) is applied to the surface of the board.

A metallic coating is applied to the holes and on the solder islands to ensure solderability.

A legend with component markings or other information is printed on the board.

The finished board is inspected and the connections are tested.

PCBs come in two types and four orders of magnitude. PCBs that are highly complex technologically are set apart from low complexity PCBs, as their manufacture calls for special production machinery. In addition, customers may require various amounts of PCBs. For product development purposes, just a few prototypes do the job. Small series production is done either for end customers selling a limited number of big-ticket items (e.g., PCBs used in conveyer belts at airports) or for companies with a product in an early stage of its life cycle. As customer demand scales up, PCB manufacturing expands to medium-sized and large series. Consumer electronics companies, for instance, typically require large series for incorporation in their mass-marketed products. At the same time, PCB unit prices drop with increasing volume, as exemplified in Exhibit 3.

Exhibit 2B. Value system (Source: Case authors and company information)

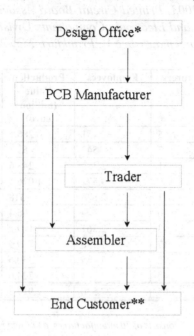

* In-house or Sub-contractors
* * Original Equipment Manufacturer / User / Consumer

Entering the Arena: The Launch of Europrint

At the beginning of the 1990s, prototypes and small and medium-sized series PCBs were typically marketed on a local scale, with domestic design offices, manufacturers, traders, and assemblers serving local end customers. Some cross-border activity took place, although it was geared primarily towards the highly industrial German Ruhr area. A direct consequence of the local nature of the PCB business was the difference in prices across different regions, especially between Eastern and Western Europe. To be more specific, the relationship between price and order size was much more pronounced in Western Europe than in Eastern Europe. While large series typically involved lower unit prices in Western Europe, this was not necessarily the case in Eastern Europe. But, prototypes and small series were available at lower unit prices in Eastern Europe. By the time the Berlin wall had come down almost completely,

Exhibit 2C. Overview of Western European PCB manufacturing market 2003 (Source: PCB Production Europe 2003, Printed Circuit Board Association, Verband der Leiterplattenindustrie e.V., and Electronic Components Division, Zentralverband Elektrotechnik- und Elektronikindustrie e.V., Frankfurt, May 2004)

Location	Manufacturers	Employees	Production Value (million euro)	% of Production Value
Austria	5	2,451	286.1	9.8
Belgium	7	543	53.3	1.8
France	51	2,383	243.6	8.4
Germany	109	9,572	1,026.5	35.2
Italy	71	2,875	318	10.9
Netherlands	6	-	66.4	2.3
Spain	23	2,361	199.2	6.8
Switzerland	17	1,196	159.9	4.7
UK	72	3,455	339.6	11.6
Rest	44	-	224.6	8.5
Western Europe	405	27,530	2,917.2	100

Note: The Central European market consists of 70 manufacturers, employing 1,500, with a production volume of 80 million euro.

Note: The world production value for rigid PCBs is estimated at $28.79 billion in 2003, with Japan accounting for 27%, China 19%, America 17%, Taiwan 12%, Europe 12%, Korea 8%, RoW 5%.

Figures are based on survey estimates including double counts across countries.

Exhibit 3. Example of a price calculation (Source: Company information)

A double-sided printed circuit board with dimensions 100 mm by 160 mm (size known as "euro card") with a standard delivery term of 2 weeks has the following price, depending on the number of ordered prints.

Amount	Price per Unit (euro)
1 unit	61.98
2 units	36.96
10 units	14.81
100 units	5.32

the Eastern European PCB market had opened its gates, revealing the price gaps. Enter Luc Smets and Dirk Stans.

In 1990, Stans, a sales manager at Disc—now Mania Technology, a large manufacturer of machines, systems, and software for the production of PCBs—was made responsible for developing the company's plotter business with PCB manufacturers in Northern and Eastern Europe. At that time, Smets, a general accounting manager at Baltimore Aircoil International (a large manufacturer of industrial cooling towers and condensers) was looking for a new professional challenge and joined Stans on several of his prospecting trips. Since potential customers could not easily afford Disc's plotters, the two former college buddies came up with the idea of selling the prospects' PCBs in the BeNeLux (Belgium, the Netherlands, Luxembourg), justifying the PCB manufacturers' outlays for new plotters. Thus, in 1991, Europrint was born. While Smets hit the ground running, Stans did not get into the operational side of things until 1998 (see Exhibit 4 for a company overview).

Europrint started out as a trader. Like most intermediaries in the PCB business, it set up shop with a personal computer and a telephone. Whereas traditional traders went bargain hunting for manufacturers that were suffering order shortages, Smets chose to focus on buying prototypes and small series PCBs from Eastern European manufacturers for resale in the BeNeLux. Besides the price differential, his decision to target customers of prototype and small series PCBs was motivated by the fact that the majority of local BeNeLux suppliers (manufacturers such as Alcatel, ATEA, ACS, BLE, Philips PMF, SEW, and Viscom; traders such as Belman, Cumatrix, E.P.S., Flatfield, and PCB Engineering) focused on the medium-sized series segment, while the large series segment was already in the hands of Asian bulk manufacturers.

Yet potential customers balked at PCBs fetched by Europrint because of their inferior quality. As a result, Smets and Stans turned to a single supplier to alleviate quality concerns. In 1993, they bought themselves into Vilati Circuits Kft, a Hungarian supplier, thus entering the PCB manufacturing business for prototypes and small series, offering both low and high complexity PCBs. In 1996, Europrint started a small preparation and production unit in Mechelen, Belgium, to serve local customers requiring instant delivery. In 1998, Europrint became the single shareholder of Vilati Circuits Kft and renamed the company Europrint Eger Kft. Two years later, Europrint decided to move its Belgian production unit to Ghandinagar, India, in a 60/40 joint venture with Circuit Systems India Ltd. (CSIL), a local PCB manufacturer. Since early 1999, CSIL had been a supplier of medium-sized volumes of standard technology boards for Europrint. The joint venture, Europrint India Ltd., took on two roles: (1) it targeted the local Indian market of prototypes and small quantities, and (2) it acted as an engineering unit for the Europrint and CSIL production units, preparing customer orders for manufacturing. Also in 2000, Europrint relocated the production of quick turn around jobs to Hungary, as its logistics service provider, TNT, changed its route from Budapest – Köln to Budapest – Bierget (Belgium).

Exhibit 4. Organizational structure (Source: Company information)

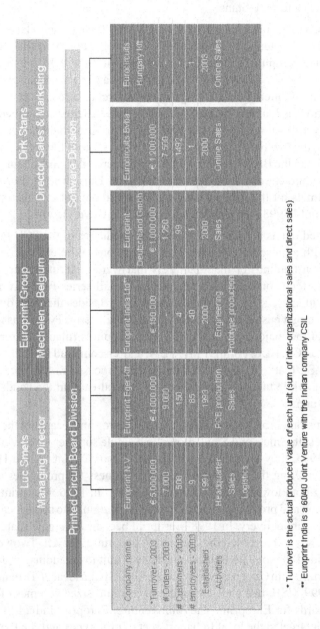

Exhibit 4. continued

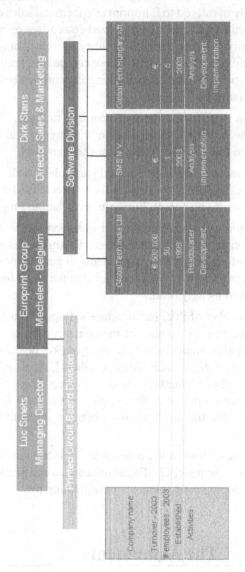

Europrint was going after market share and directed its efforts towards assemblers, traders, and end customers in the BeNeLux and the (West) German market. To become a local supplier in Germany, the Europrint Deutschland GmbH sales office was established on January 1, 2000. Assemblers, such as Alcatel division in Geel, Belgium, with hundreds of millions of euro in turnover and high material costs (typically 80% of turnover), constituted a major customer segment for Europrint. In contrast, traders were only of interest to Europrint as ephemeral sales opportunities. End customers were mostly small and medium-sized enterprises operating in various sectors such as security systems (e.g., 3SI Security Systems), automation (e.g., E.I.A.), and medical equipment (e.g., Kostal). These companies, unlike assemblers and traders, valued Europrint's technical consulting capabilities and exerted less pressure on prices and margins.

Market sizing was not an issue for Europrint. According to Stans, "To an ant that takes a bite out of an apple, it doesn't matter whether it's a whole, a half, or a quarter apple. The ant is bound to bite off more than it can chew anyway."

As the millennium approached, this logic seemed particularly valid. Demand for prototypes and small series PCBs sky-rocketed as the market moved in sync with the Internet and telecom boom. At one point, Europrint even had to turn down orders.

However, this boom period was short-lived, and it was soon followed by a market collapse in 2001. Excess capacity glutted the market and large series manufacturers entered the medium-sized and small orders segments to get the most out of their production runs. Almost overnight, prices plummeted in the small orders segment. The commodity bull reared its ugly head.

All over the world, the number of PCB manufacturers dropped drastically. In Belgium, the shakeout decimated the number of manufacturers from about 30 to 7. Irrespective of their size, all companies lacking clear market positioning and lean operations had left the scene (e.g., ACS, Alcatel [Ghent], Apec, ATEA, MBLE, Philips, and SEW). Ironically, the number of traders shot up. These traders exerted further downward pressure on prices as they exploited the manufacturers' order shortages and accommodated the needs of assemblers, a segment that switched suppliers easily.

Europrint was in dire straits. How would it forestall price erosion and establish a sustainable position as a key supplier of PCBs? Should Smets and Stans not leave this market altogether and redeploy their resources in something more promising?

The Armaments

Both men decided to bite the bullet. If commoditization posed a severe threat, Europrint was not taking it lying down. Smets and Stans set out to draw the battle lines for the next era of Europrint.

A first line of defense was a conversion of Europrint's product offering. While other manufacturers either supplied low complexity PCBs (e.g., CMK) or focused on customers with highly complex demands (e.g., ACB), Europrint served a broad range of the market, irrespective of product complexity. Rather than being a low vs. high complexity PCB manufacturer, Europrint wanted to stick to its knitting as a highly flexible, market-oriented solution provider. Thanks to its past investments in production machinery, Europrint was capable of serving all customers except the ones requiring exceedingly specialized PCBs.

As low complexity PCBs were dragged down to a commodity status, Europrint went to great lengths in product and production process standardization to beat the commodity bull at its own game. After carefully analyzing their customers' purchase order history for the previous 5 years, Europrint standardized various product attributes (e.g., board thickness of 1.55 mm, green mask, white text, and a minimum drill size of 0.35 mm) so that it would still be able to fill 80% of the orders. In addition, it reconfigured the way PCBs were placed on a standard production panel to maximize PCB output (see Exhibit 1). Rather than having one type of PCB per panel, several specimens required by several different customers could now be produced off the same panel (two to three different types in 1998 running up to an average of 11 types in 2004), significantly reducing waste. Both measures made it possible for Europrint to radically cut production set-up and film costs—shaving 50% off its production cost. Given sufficient volume, Europrint could now sell its products profitably at a price far below market level. In a similar vein, the company replaced the traditional process of price quoting with a newly developed price matrix, whereby customers now rented space on the master panel. Prices were fixed for three standard sizes with predefined quantities and delivery terms.

Yet, the commodity bull did not submit to this red flag. According to Smets:

Not only did we know how to standardize, we were also able to develop an innovative pricing mechanism for our new offering. Through direct mail, we pushed the new restricted offer into the market. However, the problem we faced was that the company pushing the new offering into the market was the same company that had a history of communicating flexibility, which was at odds with the standardized product offer.

While customers were swayed by the low prices, they still viewed Europrint as a full service provider rather than a no-frills low-cost supplier. Instead of abiding by Europrint's newly instituted product standardization policy, customers persuaded the sales representatives to continue to offer the customized products and personalized service they had grown used to.

As a consequence, Smets and Stans worked out a second line of defense: the launch of a new company with accompanying Web site as a standardized channel to sell standardized products.

Exhibit 5. Customer and Order Growth at Eurocircuits (Source: Company information)

Quarter	Customers ordering	Orders	Turnover (euro)	Average order value
Q3/2000	41	96	13.307,00	138,61
Q4/2000	89	241	30.916,00	128,28
Q1/2001	115	432	58.206,00	134,74
Q2/2001	136	482	74.416,00	154,39
Q3/2001	161	512	78.309,00	152,95
Q4/2001	189	716	99.948,00	139,59
Q1/2002	222	877	120.444,00	137,34
Q2/2002	252	914	138.407,00	151,43
Q3/2002	281	1024	164.137,00	160,29
Q4/2002	350	1352	224.359,00	165,95
Q1/2003	415	1750	283.659,00	162,09
Q2/2003	443	1678	287.770,00	171,50
Q3/2003	471	1739	283.568,00	163,06
Q4/2003	511	1989	323.723,00	162,76
Q1/2004	663	2686	421.153,00	156,80
Q2/2004	773	3086	519.921,00	168,48
Q3/2004	705	2327	342.122,00	147,02*
Q4/2004	822	2972	508.235,00	171,01
Q1/2005	967	4017	689.581,00	171,67
Q2/2005	1098	4370	747.858,00	171,13
Q3/2005	1102	4363	792.596,00	181,66
Q4/2005	1152	4715	831.990,00	176,46
Q1/2006	1328	5748	1.023.521,00	178,07**
Q2/2006	1338	5529	1.069.959,00	193,52
Q3/2006		5844	1.199.857,00	205,31

* Factory in Hungary closed from July 20-August 20, 2004 due to relocation to new building

** Introduction of A la carte service & removal of Plot&Go service for business users

The Toreador: The Launch of Eurocircuits

In October 2000, Eurocircuits bvba, a two-person online venture, was launched. Whereas Europrint would position itself as a full service provider for complex PCBs, Eurocircuits would become the reference in the standard technology segment. Recalls Stans:

Even an incredibly low price does not keep your installed base from demanding personalized service. At Eurocircuits we did it the other way around. We started from scratch, no expectations, and proposed a standardized offer in a standardized manner: take it or leave it.

Even though Europrint had already established an online presence back in 1993, Smets and Stans lacked expertise in developing a full-blown e-business venture. Indeed, Europrint's Web site merely provided information on the company's location and its activities in two languages (English and Hungarian). In 1998, technical content was added to the Web site, which was maintained until February 2, 2004.

An analysis of the competition revealed that virtually none of them engaged in online commerce. Only PCBpool, a German intermediary, had a Web site supporting price calculation (through e-mail quoting) and online order placement. A check across the Atlantic showed that manufacturers in the United States were some steps ahead. PCBexpress.com, for instance, also offered highly standardized PCBs and marketed these through various subsidiaries.

Notwithstanding their limited experience in the online market, Smets and Stans had a clear vision. Their objective was to develop a Web site capable of supporting the entire order-to-delivery process online, with the exception of the production process, which was handled by Europrint Eger's ERP system, a system developed in-house with the help of local Hungarian programmers. By virtue of process automation, there would be no impact on current employee workload nor a need for more hires (given the high cost of labor in Belgium).

Yet, after receiving proposals from three local Web site builders, Smets and Stans shelved their ambitious plans. The quoted prices were simply unaffordable. Fortunately, Smets and Stans had developed a friendship with Paresh Vasani, managing director of CSIL Ltd., who also had his own software company, Globaltech India Ltd. Smets remembers it this way:

The good man claimed he could realize our plans in 2 to 3 months time, for €20,000, which did not amount to much compared to the local proposals. So, we let him take the project. Needless to say, it did not work out quite the way we had envisioned it.

After 9 months, the first version of the Eurocircuits Web site was launched (ECv1), at the initial budget cost. Customers tempted by Eurocircuits' low prices could visit the Web site, get an instant quote, and place an order online. Order follow-up, however, was done manually. Smets elaborates:

We received a version that ran on ColdFusion, backed up by an MS Access database. Good enough for e-commerce. And that is how we started. The reason that we did not have an e-business Web site was that we were incompetent to write specs clear enough for a programmer to understand, because a programmer speaks a totally different language. As a matter of fact, we were a good example of how not to do it. So, at that point, our dream of a fully integrated online order-to-delivery cycle was just that, a dream.

At first, orders came in at about two a day. However, things picked up quickly, and soon employees were complaining about the heavy workload. As orders started coming in at eight per day, given that the average order throughput time was 10 days, employees were looking at 80 order follow-up actions. Moreover, delivery notes and invoices also needed to be handled manually. Consequently, Eurocircuits got back in touch with the Indian software developer to come up with a new version, capable of automated order processing. An analyst came over for brainstorming, process mapping, and working out the technical issues. After 6 months of development, ECv2 was launched off the ColdFusion and Access database. However, Version 3 was already being planned, as the Access database was bound to reach its limits. Indeed, orders were growing exponentially and the system could not handle more than 20,000 orders (limitations of the Access database). While ECv2 was up and running in April 2002, Version 3 was developed on Web services technology (ASP. Net), backed up by an SQL database, and run on a Web farm (multiple servers).

Given Eurocircuits Internet-only business model, it became clear rapidly that technology and software development were indispensable to the company and its future. Therefore, Smets and Stans became joint proprietors of the Indian software house, Globaltech India Ltd., in March 2002, shortly before the launch of ECv2. According to Smets:

We were now operating on two fronts in India. On the one hand, there was our software team that was mainly working for us and kept on growing, and on the other hand there was the preparation unit. As both companies had shared partners and proprietors, communication was prompt and the operation less risky. Everything was in-sourced as it involved the lifeblood of the company.

Version 2 was built based on agreed hourly costs and total number of hours. The total cost amounted to about €37,500. Unlike Versions 1 and 2, the development of Version 3 grossly exceeded the budget. An initial estimation of €100,000 quickly gave way to an actual cost of almost €300,000 to build a flexible platform, make it operational, and create Version 3 itself. With the launch of Version 3, Eurocircuits had become a company with one employee and lots of PCs.

The Cheering Crowds: Marketing Communication

Unlike Europrint, which relied solely on personal sales, Eurocircuits was exploring other promotional methods. At first, it contacted former Europrint customers by e-mail, as it wanted to regain lost orders by migrating these customers to its Web site. A customer survey was conducted after 6 months and showed positive feedback on Eurocircuits. From that moment onward, Eurocircuits was actively used to acquire new customers.

Eurocircuits Version 2 was officially announced in September 2002 at the STI^2 fair in Brussels, Belgium. At every subsequent trade fair—CeBIT in Hannover, Germany (March 2003), Electronics & Automation in Utrecht, The Netherlands (March 2003), Hannover Industrie Messe (April 2003), and Ineltec in Basel, Switzerland (September 2003)—Eurocircuits allowed visitors to place an order on a stand-alone Web server. This gave visitors the opportunity to experience first-hand how easy it was to use the online application.

Eurocircuits also started placing ads in Elektor, a respected publication for all professionals and hobbyists actively engaged in electronics and computer technology, available in four languages across Europe. After placing some small ads in Elektuur (the Dutch version of Elektor) in 2001, Eurocircuits started a full-scale Elektor campaign in the Summer of 2002. The campaign inaugurated the ThePCBshop, a shop that sold standardized PCBs, discussed in Elektor, online through Eurocircuits. According to Stans:

This was our smartest marketing move ever. We see it as "marketing through the backdoor," as half of the Elektor readers are involved in buying PCBs in their professional lives. You can do the math: about 100,000 subscribers, three readers per issue, and half of them are professional PCB users.

Not surprisingly, Eurocircuits' brand awareness burgeoned as it advertised its PCB business in the Dutch, English, French, and German issues of Elektor. However, fairs were by far the most effective tool for winning orders. While about 53% of the visitors that registered for trade fairs placed orders, only 35% of the Elektuur registered readers did so. The major barrier was that Web site visitors who set out to buy online had to sign and return a hard copy document outlining the general conditions before they could place an order. Yet, Elektor brought in a vast amount of prospects. Stans elaborated:

Ads and exhibitions added up to an average monthly cost of slightly over €6,500. For Q1 of 2004, this amounted to €30 per customer that placed an order with Eurocircuits—with an average turnover of €645 per customer. Turnover of 4.65% seems like a fair marketing cost to me.

Eurocircuits geared its efforts directly towards end customers and quickly established critical mass by offering user convenience, speedy service, and, above all, radically lower prices! See Exhibit 5 for an overview of customer, order, and turnover growth. Traders and assemblers were put off by the fact that Eurocircuits fixed an order number in the solder mask of each board for logistical tracking reasons, making it easy for buyers to trace back the initial price through Eurocircuits' online price calculator.

Taming the Commodity Bull

On February 2, 2004, ThePCBShop.com was launched to consolidate the Europrint, Eurocircuits, and Elektor segments. While hobbyists could turn to Elektor PCBs and the "plot and go" service—a tool for ordering single and double sided prototypes in very small series (maximum of nine pieces)—professional users could order prototypes and small series up to six layers and up to 1,000 pieces. For mature products, a stock order application was made available, allowing Europrint to manage customer inventory based on a yearly contract. Both Europrint and the customers benefited, as the customer could monitor inventory levels online, significantly reducing administration process costs.

ThePCBShop.com offered a broad range of functionality. Following online registration, customers could access a price calculation tool as well as information on order status, credit status, invoicing, and purchase order history. Furthermore, companies could register several users so that engineers could order prototypes directly online with the purchase department keeping an eye on spend. Company-specific pricing arrangements could be built into the system as well.

In terms of administration, the Internet now did a lot of the heavy lifting. While Europrint and Eurocircuits still ran parallel to each other for the most part (from order to billing and payment), they met during preparation, production, and logistics.

The moment a customer placed an order online, the PCB design was sent to Europrint India Ltd. The layout was screened and the panel data relayed to the Europrint plant in Hungary for production. Subsequently, the manufactured PCBs were shipped via courier to Europrint Mechelen, the logistics unit, where the individual orders were picked and packed. Finally, the order was sent to the customer by courier. According to Smets:

Initially, Eurocircuits could not survive without Europrint. Its production volume was simply too low so machines would be on hold most of the time. Yet, at this moment, Europrint would not be able to survive without Eurocircuits, which makes production runs more profitable and directs the electronic support of our business processes.

Eurocircuits had quickly amassed 2,500 registered users, including 250 of Europrint's 450 active customers. While online sales reached 16.37% of total sales in 2003, Eurocircuits expected that figure to jump to 37.65% in 2004 through ThePCBShop. com (see Exhibit 6 for an overview of online and off-line sales growth).

Competitors in the BeNeLux (like Flatfield and PC-Antwerpen) envied Eurocircuits being first to the online market and promptly followed by launching their own Web sites, announcing prices 5% to 10% below those of Eurocircuits, ECv2. Stans explains, "That was plain window dressing. They merely tried to enhance the attractiveness of their traditional business. Contrary to offering discounts wrapped up in a Web site, Eurocircuits' prices were based on a sound business model."

On the European market, there were only two other competitors who were able to ward off the commodity bull: PCBpool, the German market leader with over 10,000 customers, and Olimex, a Bulgarian manufacturer, primarily targeting the U.S. market. PCBexpress, the U.S. player, was not able to get a foot in the door, as its Web site was only available in English. Eurocircuits had learned the hard way and was quick to offer multiple languages beyond English (Dutch, French, German, and Hungarian) after having received complaints from French and German customers.

The Banderillo: Franchising ThePCBShop.com

While Smets and Stans were already planning Version 4, they considered TheP-CBShop.com a viable prototype ready to be put in the market. Intermediaries with

Exhibit 6. Overview of Turnover Growth and Consolidated Income Statement. Europrint Group (Source: Company information)

Europrint Group - Turnover Growth

Year	Offline Mechelen	Offline Eger (Direct sales)	Offline Total	% Offline	Online Eurocircuits*	% Online	Total Euro
1994	1.535.662	193.053	1.728.714	100,00%			1.728.714
1995	2.158.290	312.427	2.470.717	100,00%			2.470.717
1996	1.926.204	370.241	2.296.445	100,00%			2.296.445
1997	2.328.003	430.608	2.758.611	100,00%			2.758.611
1998	3.222.616	599.221	3.821.836	100,00%			3.821.836
1999	4.216.394	675.558	4.891.952	100,00%			4.891.952
2000	4.721.062	905.611	5.626.672	99,22%	44.223	0,78%	5.670.895
2001	5.236.269	911.075	6.147.344	95,19%	310.878	4,81%	6.458.222
2002	4.616.220	948.100	5.564.320	89,58%	647.347	10,42%	6.211.667
2003	5.072.994	1.154.308	6.227.302	83,50%	1.230.363	16,50%	7.457.665
2004	4.705.876	1.439.001	6.144.877	77,70%	1.763.811	22,30%	7.908.688
2005	4.395.017	1.568.951	5.963.968	66,08%	3.062.024	33,92%	9.025.992
2006*	3.850.000	1.750.000	5.600.000	53,85%	4.800.000	46,15%	10.400.000
2007**	3.000.000	2.000.000	5.000.000	45,45%	6.000.000	54,55%	11.000.000

* Estimated figures (as per 05/10/2006)

** Budget

Source: Company Information

a solid customer base could leverage the ThePCBShop.com concept under their own name. The franchisees would be responsible for marketing communication and customer follow-up, while the orders would be relayed to Eurocircuits' online system. Eurocircuits would thus be able to secure fast distribution of its products without incurring the full marketing costs, while the franchisees would be buying into a proven system enjoying low prices. Smets explains:

What we are trying to do is copy the P&G model: develop one kind of washing powder in different colors and put it in various boxes. If you have 11 competitors in the market, 6 are actually your own brands.

The entrepreneurs were also considering further leveraging their technology investments by selling the platform on which ThePCBShop.com runs to other small and medium-sized businesses outside the PCB industry. Companies selling "Internet-friendly" products would thus be able to enjoy process optimization benefits as they face the commodity bull in their own markets.

A Lap of Victory: Evaluating ThePCBShop.com

It was Friday, October 6, 2006, and Smets was preparing the budget for 2007. He budgeted €11 million total revenue for the Europrint Group for 2007, with 54.55% of that coming from Eurocircuits, a full €6 million! With close to 6,000 online orders in Q3 2006 at almost €1.2 million, Eurocircuits was about to surpass Europrint in significance. Also, Eurocircuits had amassed 4,000 customers while Europrint had a mere 350.

Early 2006, Smets had decided to position Eurocircuits at the heart of the business, and this was well received by the market. Eurocircuits now offered three services, in line with customer needs:

1. **Verified service:** A standardized offering, based on a configurator with limited options (e.g., board thickness of 1.6mm; green mask) and a public price calculator
2. **A la carte service:** A modular offering, based on an online price request tool that allows multiple combinations (e.g., 0.8mm-1.55mm-2.4mm board thickness; blue, green and black masks; etc.)
3. **On demand service:** A tailor-made offering which is handled online, supported through personal off-line commercial and front-end interactions

Exhibit 6. continued (Source: Company information)

Europrint group	2.001		2002		2003		2004		2005	
Net revenues	6.458	100,00%	6211,667	100,00%	7457,665	100,00%	7908,7	100,00%	9026	100,00%
Cost of net revenues	3.900	60,39%	3693,144	59,45%	4174,875	55,98%	4262,3	53,89%	5123	56,76%
Gross profit	2.558	39,61%	2518,523	40,55%	3282,79	44,02%	3646,4	46,11%	3903	43,24%
							0		0	
Staff expenses	1.100	17,03%	1146,198	18,45%	1253,502	16,81%	1572,9	19,89%	1730,6	19,17%
Other expenses	155	2,40%	170,478	2,74%	160,787	2,16%	278,23	3,52%	293,26	3,25%
Total Expenses	1.255	19,43%	1316,676	21,20%	1414,289	18,96%	1851,1	23,41%	2017,9	22,36%
							0		0	
EBITDA	1.303	20,18%	1201,847	19,35%	1868,501	25,05%	1795,3	22,70%	1885	20,88%
Depreciation	420	6,50%	525,006	8,45%	521,829	7,00%	709,31	8,97%	916,9	10,16%
EBIT	884	13,68%	676,841	10,90%	1346,672	18,06%	1086	13,73%	968,14	10,73%
Interest and other income, net	-67	-1,04%	-55,003	-0,89%	-117,168	-1,57%	-224,8	-2,84%	-245,7	-2,72%
Income before income taxes	817	12,64%	621,838	10,01%	1229,504	16,49%	861,21	10,89%	722,39	8,00%
Provision for income taxes	-76	-1,17%	-99,948	-1,61%	-232,251	-3,11%	-157,5	-1,99%	-105,3	-1,17%
Net income	741	11,47%	521,89	8,40%	997,253	13,37%	703,75	8,90%	617,13	6,84%

Eurocircuits became the name of the game, consolidating all previous initiatives and reconciling the off-line and online channels. Indeed, traditonal Europrint customers were now redirected to Eurocircuits' on demand service and the PCBShop.com umbrella brand name was kept for hobbyists only. The Europrint brand was bound to fade away. Smets clarified through his personal mantra: The only stability is change!

In order to be successful, the entrepreneur lived by this mantra, and identified the following as best practices:

First and foremost, focus on the market. Don't let your own resources and capabilities drive your business. If there is an online market, develop it! Second, don't spread yourself too thinly. Trials to leverage our technology investments, for instance, had consumed way too much time and cost and it had proven extremely difficult to turn the platform into a satisfying product for a specific customer. Third, be aware of cultural differences. While small is considered beautiful in Belgium, for instance, it is very hard for small enterprises to attract and retain the right people in the software industry in India. Indeed, while the number of employees in Mechelen, Belgium, had stayed at 9, the engineering division in India had grown to 150 people in Q3 2006 and is budgeted to grow to 250 in 2007.

Chapter X

Cember.net

Ayşegül Toker, Boğaziçi University, Turkey

Arzu İşeri-Say, Boğaziçi University, Turkey

Nihan Çolak-Erol, Euda LLC, Turkey

Abstract

Inception of the Internet leads to emergence of online communities in the virtual space where spatial proximity and time are no longer constraints in establishing and developing relationships. Online social networks are online communities basically providing a channel through which information about potential social and economic exchange opportunities can be presented, searched, and leveraged by the network members. The distinguishing features of a social networking site are the use of explicit representation of member-provided information and relationships between members, thus embedding trust and referral mechanisms into the network. Cember. net, a Turkey-based online business networking start-up provides a platform through which its members can locate potential economic exchange partners. However, Cember.net differentiates its business model from those of major online competitors by incorporating means to foster social interactions and exchanges. Cember. net, with its continually growing member base, presents networking opportunities to its members by not only advancing the quantity of relationships but the quality of the relationships as well.

Background

The number of Internet users increased from 16 million to 1,018 million between December 1995 and December 2005.[1] The rapid growth of the Internet created many new business opportunities for entrepreneurs. A new breed of innovative Internet business venture creators called "netrepreneurs" have influenced the way people live, learn, work, and do business. The most common Internet-related business models can be classified as development of software and hardware applications, selling products and services, customer service and support, public and investor relations, and providing information or advice. As online technologies proliferate and diversify, the influence of the Internet extends beyond mere economic exchanges to the social domain of interactions.

Creating social networks based on virtual communities is another attractive business model not only for entrepreneurs but also for existing companies seeking to enhance their business through the Internet. Likewise, non-profit organizations also start virtual communities in order to exploit the opportunities offered by Internet technology.

In traditional forms of social networks, the participants are friends, neighbors, people working together, and members of clubs or special organizations (Lea, Yu, Maguluru, & Nichols, 2006). Face-to-face relationships between such social network members are constrained by physical location and time. Different types of traditional networks provide benefits limited in scope to their members based on the members' common interests and shared goals.

The removal of physical boundaries through Internet technology both advances the relationships among members of a community and enables members of a network to contact members of other communities. In virtual social networks, time is no longer a constraining factor in developing new relationships. Therefore, the probability of reaching more people through the Internet is higher than that offered by traditional forms of interaction. Terveen and McDonald (2005) describe online communities as "social spaces built on technologies such as chat rooms, newsgroups, and bulletin boards where people go to discuss topics that interest them and to meet others" (p. 408). Online community platforms are indeed "exchange facilitators" promoting and structuring social and economic exchange opportunities between members. The member population of online communities tends to increase at unprecedented rates soon after a well-planned and managed community Web site is launched, as exemplified in the case of an online business networking venture, LinkedIn (Hoyt, 2004).

Cember.net[2, 3]

There is a new platform in the Internet for those who want to enlarge their business network. Cember.net, launched in September 2005, is the first business networking site in Turkey.

— Turkish BusinessWeek

History

The idea for Cember.net came up in January 2005 while the founders of the platform were employed as IT consultants in one of the world's largest business consulting firms in Germany. The founders, a married couple, were temporarily working abroad and in the long-term were planning to continue their careers in their home country, Turkey. Their long-term plans included a major decision to start their own business in the IT consulting sector, where their educational background (they both had computer engineering degrees and one of them also had an MBA) and work experience could give them a head start. Coinciding with their logistics and business plans, the business environment in Turkey was evaluated as lacking in the area of online business networking. The "market" did not have a "Turkish" online networking platform, although some business professionals were already using established channels, such as LinkedIn. Therefore, they took the first step to build up an efficient professional communication channel, namely, an online business networking platform, Cember. net, in Turkish. Cember.net (www.cember.net) went live on September 1, 2005, as a result of about 600 man-days of work by the founders. Unlike most start-ups in the virtual world, Cember.net was launched without venture capital.

The aim of the founders was to create an online business network platform for Turkish-speaking business professionals from all over the world and their venture was the first entrant to the market with a well-prepared platform with such a specific purpose. This platform was planned and designed to enable Turkish professionals to create valuable and efficient business partnerships and also to design their future careers. The targeted segments are mainly high-profile business professionals and/ or small and midsize entrepreneurs. Currently, 95% of members have university degrees. The founders believed that the positioning of Cember.net is very critical to differentiate it from existing social networking sites; therefore, both the design and the promotion of the Web site were carefully planned and implemented to maximize the visual and content differentiation.

Differentiation was also strengthened through the development of "forums" (160 forums operated by November 2006). This served two purposes. One of the purposes was to ensure customer bonding that was accepted as a crucial factor for online social and business networking by increasing the value offered to members and making them "part" of the community. This also helps to increase a sense of ownership and leads to self policing of the network. The second purpose was to provide members with opportunities to develop the "whole" picture of a member in the network and to meet socially sometimes as face-to-face interactions help to reinforce the relationships that have been established online. This was considered to be a differentiating factor for promoting the platform since social interactions tend to have a bonding effect and ease the formation of relationships.

The founders announced a fee-based membership subscription as of March 1, 2006, creating another additional type of membership category. The decision to have fee-based membership is not a common and accepted practice, especially for a professional and career-focused Web-based application in Turkey. Generally, Turkish Web applications try to survive with advertisement incomes. In fact, some Turkish Internet experts claimed that Cember.net would be a total failure if its membership became fee-based. In order to prevent customer loss against the introduction of a subscription fee, management decided to group customers into two categories. Free membership was kept as one of the categories, allowing for only a limited set of functions to be available for such members. On the other hand, members with fee-based subscriptions could benefit from a wider array of functions in the network. As a result of this decision, Cember.net management achieved its goal of introducing fee-based subscriptions, and at the same time kept advertisement income intact. The current distribution of income generating activities may provide a clue about the success of this decision; subscriptions provide the majority of income, and considerable revenue is still generated through forum sponsorships and advertisements.

With four members in the management structure, two of them being the founders of the network, along with voluntary but closely monitored forum moderators, and outsourced functional operations such as accounting, and so forth, the management of Cember.net has adopted a strictly followed and rule-oriented structure. Certain rules are demanded by members to be implemented without any exception, such as keeping forum discussions in their content boundaries. Other codes and conducts have been developed by the founders as part of their strategic plans and implemented strictly. A system of continuous checks and balances ensures that the profile of membership and participation is kept at a preset high standard, and the interactions in the network are realized within the context of the goals of the network. Thus, differentiation in the target segments can be sustained.

Today, Cember.net has more than 200,000 members and continues to grow rapidly although it only has a brief history of 22 months (see Table 1).

Table 1. Milestones in the development process

September 2005	Cember.net goes Beta version
November 2005	First official off-line Cember.net meeting
February 2005	Events package goes live
March 2006	End of Beta version
	Cember.net goes live
	Fee-based membership is introduced
May 2006	Career package goes Beta
July 2006	Profile and forum pages are opened for Google search
August 2006	Survey function goes live
October 2006	Cember.net reaches 100,000 members
July 2007	Cember.net reaches 200,000 members

Registration

Every person who wants to join Cember.net can easily become a member by filling out a member profile form through the Internet. In the member profile form, the current company, position, and title in the company, as well as the industry are mandatory fields. Educational background, previous business experience, and membership in other organizations are the fields that might be opted for if members want to provide more information about themselves. In other "to see" and "to be seen" easily, members may also enter some keywords in the "things I look for" and "things I offer" areas.

At the registration stage, members define their usernames and passwords and are granted a confirmation from network providers. When the registration process is complete, a member homepage with a unique URL address (e.g., www.cember. net/pr/aysegul_toker) is created in the network. Through this home page, members can update their personal information and see messages and new contact offers from other members. They can also customize other members' access to some fields in the profile information according to personal privacy concerns.

New members might be invited by existing members or they may engage in the network by themselves. There are no restrictions of any kind for becoming a member in the registration stage. However, Cember.net management holds the rights to end membership in cases of misuse of the network, like sending messages with inappropriate content or exploitation of the network for other than business purposes. Member complaints about misuse are carefully investigated by the managers and necessary actions are taken without delay to ensure the continuity of operational network procedures and rules.

Services

Individual home pages: Logging in to Cember.net means connecting to individual home pages where members can use all functions of the network such as searching, messaging, and participating in forums. At the individual home page application, a member first creates an identity in the network and then is provided with a subplatform to manage and customize network functionalities. These are discussed in detail:

1. **Searching:** A member may use the search function to find other members according to some search criteria. A search is executed by typing keywords on the search pages based on 12+ different criteria such as company name, city, country, industry, interest, and so forth. Searching can be used by members for purposes such as looking for business partners, advice, information, and knowledge.

2. **Messaging:** A member can directly send a message and reply to a message from other members of the network. The purpose of a message may be an invitation to another member to add that person as a contact, giving information or asking for help.

3. **Contact management:** This function enables members to enlarge their own personal networks. Cember.net's contact management system is comprehensive in terms of sharing business/personal data, and allowing messaging. A member can construct his own network by asking permission of the members he wants to add as a contact. This function also allows viewing "contacts of the contacts." Using this setting, a member is given the chance of reaching a lot of people and forming his own personal network.

4. **Forum contribution:** Forums are virtual platforms that enable members to share information/knowledge on specific business or interest/hobby related issues and satisfy some social needs in the network. In fact, such platforms providing social networking opportunities have always been a part of traditional business networks. Contacting or meeting with a business partner through such means is quite common in Turkish culture. Every member can initiate, participate in, and/or manage a forum easily.

5. **Recruitment:** Members of Cember.net can post job offerings and their "curriculum vitae" at the career platform. This is a feature that has been activated very recently as a free-of-charge service. However, in the near future, job offerings are planned to be a fee-based service.

6. **Announcement boards:** All members of Cember.net can post their personal or business-related announcements by using these boards.

Types of Membership

There are two types of membership in Cember.net: standard and gold. Standard membership with modest privileges is free, whereas gold membership with upgraded privileges requires a subscription fee.

1. **Standard members:** They can perform a basic search based on two criteria (name and city), join forums, receive messages from other members but reply to only five messages a day, use contact management, send "Join Cember.net" invitations, use the career platform, and join online and off-line activities announced in the network. These members can not send messages to other members. This kind of network presence is for members who are only interested in the "to be seen" functionality.

2. **Gold members:** In addition to the functions allowed for standard members, gold members are granted with all capabilities of the search function and can send messages to other members. They can also see and contact their home page visitors. A gold member can initiate a forum and announce an activity in the announcement board. In order to have the "to see" benefits, gold members should pay a subscription fee or bring 10 additional new members to the network every year.

In addition to standard and gold memberships, a third category, "platinum membership", is planned to be activated very soon. Platinum members will be privileged by an "invisible member" property. In particular, visits of platinum members to other members' home pages will be disguised. These "invisible members" pay a premium fee in order to enjoy platinum membership benefits.

Value Propositions: Exchange Opportunities at Cember.net

Cember.net is an individual-oriented medium rather than a company-oriented one. It offers a networking platform for high-profile professionals. In line with its mission—to help people be more successful and innovative in their business by presenting opportunities for creating efficient business networks through the Internet—Cember.net primarily facilitates searches for valuable exchange opportunities for its members:

•   Opportunity to make new business connections such as finding potential customers, partners, vendors, and suppliers. With the help of the search functionalities, members have the opportunity to locate the best choice among other Cember.

net members. After the search process, members can get in touch with potential business partners through Cember.net. Up until now, about a $100 million volume of business contracts has been reported to Cember.net management. This amount is likely to increase as the number of members increases.

- Opportunity to access field experts and acquire knowledge/experience. Experience and knowledge exchange is one of the major forms of exchange taking place at the platform. This kind of member-to-member knowledge exchange without an immediate economical return has the potential to yield prospective business partnerships, consulting opportunities, and contracts.

- Opportunity to join in interest groups. This is the social domain of Cember.net. Interest groups were "business only" at the beginning of the venture. However, there was a high demand to have interest groups in topics outside of the business arena such as sports, health and wellness, music, and several different kinds of hobbies. Today, there are 150+ different forums with more than 70,000 members. Cember.net management claims that every day there are 10-20 new forum requests received, but only a few of them can be operationalized due to a careful selection process.

- Opportunity to find jobs or engage in recruitment. Cember.net *Career*, which has been in beta-test phase since May 2006, now hosts more than 30,000 resumes. As the current members are high-profile professionals, the resume database of Cember.net *Career* is also highly selective. With an online recruiting service that is going to be launched soon, the job offers will be subject to a selection process and only high quality job offers will be posted in the career site.

- Opportunity to grow business networks through off-line events and workshops. In order to build strong and trustworthy business relationships, it is essential to know the person with whom you are doing business. Cember.net has initiated regional community meetings in several cities so as to create a basis for face-to-face member communication. When the number of Cember.net members reaches a critical mass, the organization of industry/sector-specific community meetings as well as business-related workshops will be feasible.

- Opportunity to enhance social networking through off-line events and activities. Some members are not using Cember.net solely for business purposes. There is a significant member population extending their Cember.net relationships to the social domain of life. Social events mostly take place in İstanbul where the majority of members are located. For example, recently a group of 120 members made an excursion to Büyükada—an island which is a popular destination for daily trips from İstanbul. Almost each week there is a movie or a bowling get-together. Most of these off-line activities take place around either interest groups (e.g., photography group, movie group) or regional communities (e.g., İstanbul– Marmara region community, İzmir– Ege region community).

The technical infrastructure attributes such as speed, reliability, service accessibility, ease of use, and personalization/customization capabilities (Szmigin, Canning, & Reppel, 2005) are the enablers by which Cember.net makes value exchanges among its members possible and effective. Finally, Cember.net as the service provider assumes responsibility both for designing and managing the processes that support member interactions.

The Cember.net Web site exhibits testimonials from its members acknowledging how the networking platform provided them valuable business networking opportunities (see Appendix for member testimonials).[4]

Competition and Critical Success Factors

Online social networking has been hot since the late 1990s. Founded in January 1997, sixdegrees.com was perhaps the earliest well-known social networking company adopting social network principles in the virtual world. Members joined by completing a profile and providing a list of connections to be invited to join. The service embraced both social and business networking by providing the means for finding friends, locating specialists, promoting a business and chatting with members sharing similar interests. By September 1998, there were one million members with nine million page views per month, which became a lucrative source for attracting a significant amount of advertising revenue for the company.[5] The founder sold the company in January 2000 for $125 million. A year later, there were 3.2 million members from 165 countries. However, sixdegrees.com shared the same fate with many other "initially successful" dotcom companies, and could not resist the burst of the Internet bubble.

A second generation of social- and business- networking companies began to resurface in the early 2000s with replicas of business models of their predecessors. With its member base of 8 million today, the U.S.-based business networking company LinkedIn (www.linkedin.com) that was founded by venture capital of $11 million in May 2003 still promotes the basic inspiration with its adage "Relationships Matter." LinkedIn, with is stringent business networking focus, differentiates itself from social networking and matchmaking companies which claim to connect people for fun, romance, and more.

Being players in the arena of online business networking and having similar business models, LinkedIn and Cember.net can be considered as major competitors. However, Cember.net positions itself as a network comprising a social networking domain, too, as long as it nurtures business networking. Besides, Cember.net with its Turkish content targets high-profile Turkish speaking business people from all over the world. Though this seems a very restrictive approach for an Internet company, one might safely argue that the present setting offers more value in terms of relevancy from the member-generated content. The founders of Cember.net are confident enough to declare that they judge LinkedIn as a key benchmark rather than a major competitor, as these two networks have different target markets and value offerings.

It is a fact that the number of members is a key success factor for online networking companies, whereas the strength of the relationships is a measure which is mostly unmentioned perhaps due to its immeasurability. Rothaermel and Sugiyama (2001) argue that "the relationship between a virtual Internet community's size and success is curvilinear, that is, it exhibits diminishing marginal returns and past some point diminishing total returns" (p. 306). Cember.net, by successfully incorporating social networking opportunities into its business model, seems to enjoy the benefits of close-knit and strong ties in its network, although it hardly acts globally for the time being. However, this "locality" contributes to its niche market success. Close-knit communities in fact exhibit a high level of trust, collectively held knowledge, and strong relationships (Rothaermel & Sugiyama, 2001). The speed and the focused targeting with which the platform operates comply with the demands of the members who are primarily motivated to use the network for finding simple, efficient, and fast solutions to their business related inquiries (which may also be a culture specific member expectation, as suggested by the founders in a personal interview, November 9, 2006).

Some other prominent online business networks are:

Ecademy.com (www.ecademy.com): Ecademy is a business-networking site of trusted business connections for people to share contacts and business opportunities. It provides a geographical list of networking regions globally, to be used for arranging meetings and events off-line.

Ryze.com (www.ryze.com): Originally was an online business networking site, but members use Ryze to communicate with other members for dating or social networking purposes through the use of photos in each member's profile. It organizes off-line events and also lists a section for classifieds to which members can post.

Spoke.com (www.spoke.com): A professional networking site that helps people to build their business network connections online. The value of the network increases as more professional members are added. Spoke uses e-mail details and other member-provided information to strengthen the relationships in the network. In helping to find a job, Spoke also enables members to obtain referrals through people they already know.

Although there are no Turkey-based individual-oriented online business networking sites, the following service provider Web sites in Turkey can be defined as competitors to Cember.net because of the similarity of their value propositions:

Kariyer.net (www.kariyer.net): Founded in 1999, it is the first online human resources and career site in Turkey providing services for job search and recruitment. With its large candidate database, it serves as a mediator to meet job and employee seekers. Additionally, it is a content provider presenting recent articles and interviews about career life. Interaction is not allowed between participants.

Yenibiris.com (www.yenibiris.com): Being part of one of the biggest media groups in Turkey, Yenibiris, as an online job market, provides exactly the same services as those of Kariyer.net.

Kobi.net (www.kobi.net): It provides communication opportunities to small- and mid-size businesses. That is, it is a business to business (B2B) communication and information/knowledge sharing platform. It was founded by KOSGEB (Small- and Medium-Sized Industry Development Organization – Turkey) to support small- and medium-sized enterprises (SMEs). Its aim is to enable SMEs to utilize information technologies and enhance business relations. It provides announcement boards, recruitment and job searching, a firm index, and useful information related to business, secondary, and spot sales. Current awareness is, however, weak among the targeted segment.

Online member-to-member exchange facilitators can be segmented with respect to their focus on the domain of exchanges: social exchanges such as finding spouses, dates and friends, and economic exchanges such as finding business partners, contacting qualified job candidates, and getting in touch with prospective clients. Regardless of their focus, exchange facilitators may further position themselves in the market by whether they allow member-to-member interactions, that is, social networking, or not. The main distinguishing features of a social networking site are the use of explicit representation of member information and relationships between members, thus embedding trust and referral mechanisms into the network.

In the social exchanges domain, perhaps the most well known match-making company is Match.com, with over 15 million members worldwide, which launched its Web site in 1995. The online dating and friendship service, Yonja.com—targeting young Turkish people—differentiates its "matching model" from that of Match.com by the ability to browse a "friend of a friend." Yonja.com proved to be a successful venture with its three million members and ranking as the 398[6] most traffic-generating site in the world.[6] Friendster.com, like Yonja.com, helps people to find dates and make new friends through connections of people they already know. Tribe.com, another

Figure 1. Positioning of Cember.net

	Social Exchanges	Economic Exchanges
Matching and vouching	• Friendster.com • Tribe.com • Yonja.com	Ecademy.com • • *Cember.net* • • Spoke.com Linkedin.com • Ryze.com •
Matching	• Match.com	Kariyer.net • Yenibiris.com • Kobi.net •

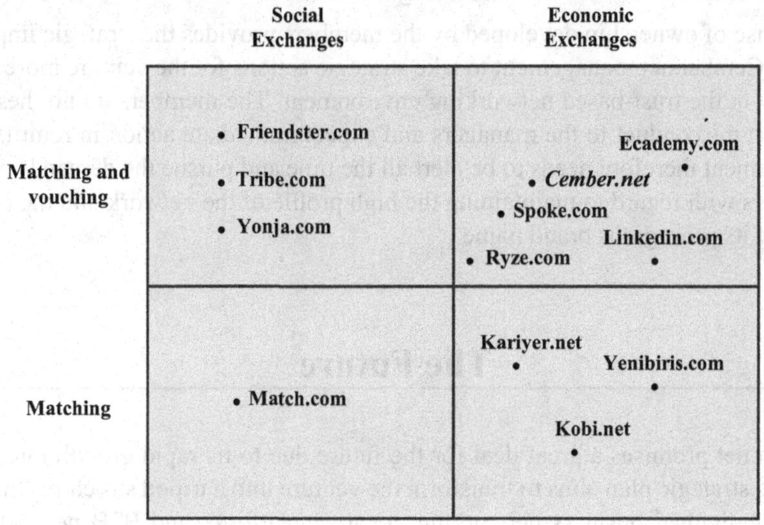

social networking site, offers the joining opportunity to countless "tribes" such as poker, underground hip hop, and so forth.

Figure 1 illustrates the positioning of Cember.net among the companies that have sought to exploit the Internet to facilitate exchanges between people—whether they are social or economic—by improving the matching and vouching processes.

Cember.net owes its success to both its hard-working management (the founders report that they have been "living in the office" since the launch of the venture), the strong entrepreneurial skills of the founders, and also to differentiating itself against other companies in its targeted market. The "spirit" of the company closely resembles the business approach of the founders. It has been designed to operate with a "no frills" understanding, only allowing for the development of precise functions with relevant values for the networking needs of its members. This sharp business approach can easily be seen in the way the founders talk about their business venture.[7] The enthusiasm, the joy, and the care they reflect to others is partly what ensures their business success.

The founders of the venture were strong-willed and creative in their business planning through their adaptation of a networking platform to the Turkish high-profile business culture which emphasizes trust in close-knit groups and acquaintances. Such an adaptation was facilitated by the social networking domain although the business networking was the strongest strategic goal of the venture. This is an indication that the awareness of different cultural values can be designed into a business system as positive contributions towards achieving a successful result.

The sense of ownership developed by the members provides the strategic impetus for the Cember.net management to take strategic actions for the venture more confidently in the trust-based networking environment. The members do not hesitate to report misconduct to the managers and expect immediate action in return. The management therefore needs to be alert all the time and pursue the demands of the members with regard to maintaining the high profile of the network and the continuity of its prestigious brand name.

The Future

Cember.net promises a great deal for the future due to its rapid growth rate. The existing strategic plan aims to transform the venture into a tripod structure consisting of individual business networking, a career platform, and B2B networking, with individual business networking as the strongest leg of this tripod structure. The founders of Cember.net manage the venture's strategic developments in the same strict way that they implement their business plans. The strategic plans for the venture were laid out very early in the venture in line with the vision and goals of the founders. The founders had a clear vision of what they wanted Cember.net to become when they first started the venture. This venture was planned as a stepping-stone for future developments as one in a series of projects which would provide strong network connections for the founders.

The strategic plans have been realized and implemented through detailed analysis and consideration at each step. Some of the strategic steps have been carried out with more confidence because they were also demand-driven. The members voiced their preferences and wishes in evaluations or forums, and if those were already present in the strategic plans it gave the founders the drive to implement the plans with more confidence.

The career package is one such progression. It is a major strategic step with regard to its content and development opportunities. The market already has similar product offers. However, the uniqueness and high-profile challenge provided by Cember.net need to be extended into such new developments. A study has revealed that as many as half of all jobs are found through networks, with as many as one-third found when the employee is not actively searching for a job or when the employer is not actively searching to fill a vacancy in a position (Granovetter, 1995). Headhunting consultants who use Cember.net's services confirm this finding. Professionals tend to look ahead in their career plans and consider better offers although they might already be employed by highly prestigious companies. The culture also plays a role in this process. "Personal referrals" and "friend of a friend" understanding tend to work better in some cultures, like the Turkish culture, where in-group collectivism is a pervasive cultural value (Papalexandris & Panayotopoulou, 2004). Therefore, the career package needs to be developed with these points in mind, incorporating a referral process to increase the performance of the package. The recruiting service which is part of the career package will be closely scrutinized and controlled in order to maintain the high-profile image of Cember.net's membership community, one of the strongest differentiating factors of the venture.

Another strategic path to follow is expansion into different regions and countries to attract high-profile professionals and to widen networking opportunities. In this expansion plan, the primary focus will be on countries with which Turkey has the highest level trade relations. Establishing new local "Cember.nets"and bridging these networks are expected to create additional value for members.

In the meantime, Cember.net continues to follow its strategic and business plans with utmost care, strictly implements its operational rules, and aims to provide its high-profile professional members a selective high speed-high value business networking platform.

References

Granovetter, M. (1995). *Getting a job: A study of contacts and careers*. Chicago: University of Chicago Press.

Hoyt, D. (2004). *LinkedIn (A)*. Stanford Graduate School of Business, Case: ON-3A, Harvard Business School Publishing.

Lea, B., Yu, W., Maguluru, N., & Nichols, M. (2006). Enhancing business networks using social network based virtual communities. *Industrial Management & Data Systems*, *106*(1), 121-138.

Papalexandris, N., & Panayotopoulou, L. (2004). Exploring the mutual interaction of societal culture and human resource management practices: Evidence from 19 countries. *Employee Relations*, *26*(5), 495-509.

Rothaermel, F.T., & Sugiyama, S. (2001). Virtual Internet communities and commercial success: Individual and community-level theory grounded in the atypical case of TimeZone.com. *Journal of Management*, *27*(3), 297-312.

Szmigin, I., Canning, L., & Reppel, A. E. (2005). Online community: Enhancing the relationship marketing concept through customer bonding. *International Journal of Service Industry Management*, *16*(5), 480-496.

Terveen, L., & McDonald, D. W. (2005). Social matching: A framework and research agenda. *ACM Transactions on Computer-Human Interaction*, *12*(3), 401-434.

Appendix: Member Testimonials

An extraordinary portal... Cember.net has increased the standards in the virtual world.

A network member, Philip Morris SA.

In addition to its growing success, I congratulate Cember.net for its contribution to employment and for providing an effective communication channel both to professionals and companies by its career package in the human resources area.

A network member, Fortune Career Training and Consultancy.

An excellent platform, I reached many people for reasons of business alliances and locating prospective coworkers and became friends with them. I acquired new clients, and became a customer of several companies. Thanks for everything.

A network member, Networx Information Technology and Communications.

Endnotes

1. Source: Internet World Stats – Usage and Population Statistics. Retrieved November 30, 2006, from http://www.internetworldstats.com/stats.htm

2. "Cember" means "circle" in English. "Cember" reads like "chember" which sounds like the word "chamber". This sound resemblance was an important factor for naming the venture Cember.net.

3. Cember.net was presented by Ms. Nihon Erol (together with Ms. Betül Sungurlu) as part of her class requirement under the supervision of Dr. Aysegül Toker in the Executive MBA Program – Boğaziçi University in 2006.

4. Retrieved May 8, 2007, from http://www.cember.net

5. Tim Jackson (1998, September 21). Inside track—six degrees from success—two online companies with a single shatteringly simple idea are prospering. *The Financial Times,* p. 16. Cited in Hoyt (2004), p. 11.

6. Special Report: Internet in Turkey. (2006). The Internet and Web Rating Association.

7. Personal Interview with Ms. Nihan Erol and Mr. Çağlar Erol, founders of Cember.net (2006, November 9).

Section II

Corporate Entrepreneurship (Intrapreneurship)

Chapter XI

Telemedicine in Practice:
Comitas Comunicaciones S. A.

Jose Aurelio Medina-Garrido, University of Cádiz, Spain

María José Crisóstomo-Acevedo, Jerez Hospital, Spain

Abstract

The case of Comitas Comunicaciones is a clear example of corporate entrepreneurship in the telecommunications sector. This firm was founded to offer telecommunications services in general and telecommunications services applied to telemedicine in particular. Comitas exploits business opportunities in the health care sector that no other firm is currently focusing on adequately. As the case develops, the technical and market difficulties that the firm has faced will become apparent. The role of the incubator firm is particularly important in this case, since it has provided Comitas with resources, capabilities, and technological knowledge that are complementary in the firm's new activity: information and communications technologies services (ICT) to support telemedicine.

Background

Comitas Comunicaciones S.A. is a Spanish firm that offers integrated communications products and services in three highly specialized areas: communications, systems engineering, and telemedicine.

Founded in 1995 under the name of Tecnobit Comunicaciones, S.A., in the Tecnobit group, it remained a part of this group until 1999. The firm relaunched in 1999 as a limited company. It increased its capital, took on its current name, and moved to its current headquarters in Tres Cantos, in the outskirts of Madrid. Now independent from the Tecnobit group, Comitas sells telecommunications equipment and Inmarsat traffic.

Comitas began to offer services in a new market in 1996: that of telemedicine. It positioned itself as one of the most advanced firms in the world in its sector. It subsequently established a dedicated broadband network to serve telemedicine customers and other customers requiring its services because of their decentralization in multiple locations, such as large firms.

Since 1998 Comitas has been the Spanish distributor for the Norwegian firm NERA Satcom AS, a leading firm in the manufacture and commercialization of terrestrial, maritime, and Inmarsat satellite communications terminals. Moreover, thanks to its contract with the Norwegian operator Telenor Satellite Services AS, the firm is Inmarsat Service Provider (ISP) and Point of Service Activation (PSA) for Inmarsat. With these operations, Comitas has become the leading firm in the sale of equipment and traffic flow for Inmarsat communications in Spain.

In 2002, Comitas started operating commercially in depth in the telemedicine field, developing its TM-64 network, also known as the Thematic Health Network, which soon incorporated Military Health. The TM-64 network currently interconnects 51 health centers from different organizations. Comitas has also exploited its network and provided other value-added services to other companies, some outside the health care sector.

In short, Comitas is an innovative firm with its origins in the telecommunications sector—mainly the sale of satellite communications services—that exploits its technological resources and capabilities to adapt them to the health care sector, specifically to telecommunications services for the practice of telemedicine.

Telemedicine is part of eHealth, which involves the use of information technologies in the health care sector. The World Health Organization defines eHealth as the combined use in the health sector of electronic information and communications technology (transmission, storage, and recuperation of digitalized data) for clinical, educational, research, and administrative purposes, both at the local site and at a distance.

This same organization defines the concept of telemedicine as the delivery of health care services, where distance is a critical factor, by health care professionals using information and communications technologies for the exchange of valid information for diagnosis, treatment, and prevention of disease and injuries, for the evaluation of research, and for the continuing education of health care providers, all in the interests of advancing the health of individuals and their communities.

Telemedicine is not an alternative medicine; it is a new way of providing conventional health care services made possible by the use of information and communications technologies (ICT). In many cases this can be done more efficiently, and in others, more fairly. The efficiency improves via an improved accessibility, speed in the attention, shorter response times, incorporation of alerts, cost savings, early diagnosis and treatment, quality of service, and so on.

Telemedicine allows doctors to communicate among themselves when carrying out and interpreting their diagnostic tests, and doctors to communicate with patients for their treatment and monitoring. These services can be provided either in real time or delayed. In delayed, or asynchronous services (store-and-forward), the information (clinical data and images) is collected, stored, and sent to the doctor without needing to coincide in time with the doctor. In real-time, or synchronous services, the information is exchanged in real time. This option poses logistical problems since the interlocutors must coincide in time.

Advances in the field of telemedicine are leading to the appearance of new services that were unthinkable in the past, such as remote consultations for a second opinion, remote monitoring of chronic patients in their homes, or of patients in emergency situations, virtual doctors' visits, among others.

The various specialties that doctors can support using telemedicine include eDermatology, eHomecare, eOpthalmology, eNeurology, eRehabilitation, eEmergencies, eICU, eOncology, eCardiology, eGastroenterology, ePathology, ePsychiatry, eLaboratory, and eRadiology.

In general, the clinical telemedicine services that can be offered using these technologies can be classified as follows:

- **Teleconsultation:** Doctors can consult with specialists remotely to obtain a second opinion. Teleconsultation can take place either in real time (synchronously) or delayed (asynchronously). When the consultation is in real time it is normally based on the Internet or other networks and it tends to involve videoconference. Both teleconsultation and telediagnosis, which is described next, can involve the digital or postal sending of all types of diagnostic tests (mainly images).

- **Telediagnosis:** Teleconsultation between doctor and patient, which can include the remote measurement of physiological parameters. Patients often make remote consultations using videoconference. During the videoconference, various medical apparatuses can be used enabling the doctor to make a more effective diagnosis. These peripheries include the electronic stethoscope, video-otoscope/laryngoscope, or the fixed-image camera, which takes images of the skin.

- **Tele-emergency services:** This basically consists of teleconsultation and telediagnosis in emergency situations.

- **Telescreening:** This involves the use of telediagnosis services in large-scale programs investigating the presence of diseases in the population (e.g., malignant melanomas), or complications of such diseases (e.g., diabetic retinopathy).

- **Telemonitoring:** The continuing or intermittent monitoring of physiological variables, activity, injuries, and so on, of patients with known illnesses to monitor their progress and consequently to adapt their treatment if necessary. It also includes monitoring progress in patients' postoperational rehabilitation processes, and the monitoring, for example, of elderly people liable to suffer falls. ICT can also be used to control patients with chronic illnesses such as diabetes, asthma, or allergies. Doctors can obtain constant information about their patients thanks to different systems such as Internet forms, or the transmission of data using cell phones or PDAs.

- **Telesurgery:** The surgeon remotely controls a robotic apparatus to assist in surgery. This can include virtual visualization of the area being operated on, and teleconsultation with other specialists during the operation.

- **Tele-education:** The provision of educational services and support for patients to be able to manage their own illnesses appropriately.

Apart from those telemedicine services, the broader eHealth includes the following applications of ICT to the needs of the health care industry, among others:

- **Hospital information systems (HIS):** These are software applications designed to computerize health care institutions' administrative and management processes. They include the interconnection and exchange of information between different departments or with suppliers.

- **Electronic health records (EHR) or patient electronic records (PER):** The information on patients' medical records is digitalized so it can be accessed and handled electronically.

- **Laboratory information systems (LIS):** Systems that computerize laboratory processes, digital handling of analyses, and so forth.

- **Tele-radiology and picture achieving and communication system (PACS):** Systems to digitalize X-ray photographs and handle digital images for further storage, capture, processing, transmission, and presentation, using ICT.
- **Telepharmacy:** Electronic handling of pharmaceutical services.
- **Tele-appointments:** Service of medical appointments by Internet or other networks. The system handles the doctors' agendas and patients can make appointments to see their doctors.

Telemedicine offers numerous benefits for patients, for health care in general, and for administrative processes in health care centers. With regard to the patients, the advantages include the following:

- Continuous remote attention
- Fewer hospitalizations
- Monitoring patients in their home
- Less time spent in hospital
- Availability of tools for educating patients and helping them to manage their illness themselves
- Possibility of conducting medical tests at the patient's home
- Remote assistance for careers
- Remote monitoring of elderly
- Rehabilitation at home
- Increase in doctor-patient contact using new technologies
- Improved quality of life and quality of service received

Doctors also benefit from telemedicine when delivering their health care services:

- Optimization of access to information (medical records, medical images, etc.)
- Possibility of consulting for a second opinion remotely and in real time
- Possibility of attending a larger number of patients, with an increased quality of service
- Possibility of remotely attending patients with mobility problems or in locations that are difficult to access
- Possibility of remote assisted surgery

Table 1. Comitas Comunicaciones financial data 1998-2003 (euros)

	2003	2002	2001	2000	1999	1998
Operating revenue/turnover	4,453,786	4,982,503	1,498,190	713,920	734,010	869,600
P/L before tax	-369,147	24,108	-552,780	-382,590	-37,260	61,660
Total assets	3,040,052	2,149,820	1,144,910	771,620	465,800	320,270
Shareholders' equity	1,094,789	746,840	391,010	427,060	219,980	135,100
Economic profitability (%)	-12.92	0.96	-48.10	-42.46	-7.58	12.30
Financial profitability (%)	-34.95	2.76	-140.83	-76.72	-16.06	29.16
General liquidity	1.23	1.18	1.04	1.68	1.83	1.63
Indebtedness (%)	63.04	65.26	65.85	44.65	52.77	57.82

- Possibility of conducting statistical analyses on a large amount of data
- Possibility of continuous education and training

The management and administration processes of health care centers can benefit in the following ways:

- Optimization of access to information
- Less time needed to locate and manage information, and for relations with suppliers, inventory, and so forth
- Improved communication between departments and with suppliers
- New ways of accessing data remotely
- Easy access to statistical data on use of material or resources, spending, and so forth

As can be seen, the development of telemedicine has been encouraged by a number of needs and opportunities. On one hand, the need to get around limitations in access to health care services, whether due to geographic, orographic, climatological, or socioeconomic barriers, because of a situation of isolation (military ships, state of war, prisons, etc.), to seek an expert opinion from a prominent doctor, or simply out of convenience. And on the other hand, telemedicine adoption has proved possible because of the availability of communications infrastructures and the readiness of health care organizations to accept the organizational changes that are inevitable when introducing new technologies.

Comitas meets the technology needs of health care service providers wishing to implement telemedicine. Apart from its TM-64 system, which supports communications, the firm also designs and commercializes highly reliable, comprehensive solutions with numerous added features in videoconferencing technology, and it has substantial experience in the field of telemedicine. In telemedicine, the firm has developed modular solutions for various medical specialties: radiology, ultrasound scanning, cardiology, intensive care, dermatology, and so on, with videoconference support and transmission of visual exploration images.

In its early days, Comitas Comunicaciones posted very poor financial results due to its significant investment in technology and the slow adoption process of the new standard in the market, the firm needing to win the confidence of health care institutions and other organizations. Table 1 shows the firm's performance up to the year 2003. The current data are unavailable, but what is known is that the firm has begun to earn profits.

Along with its growing turnover, this firm has also gradually increased its number of employees. Its payroll has grown from just 3 in 1998 to 20 currently.

Comitas stockholders at the present time mainly include members of its management team and other investors close to them. Comitas was relaunched as an independent firm outside its parent company in 1999 with an equity capital of approximately €60,000. The members of the management team are the main stockholders and they are mainly telecommunications engineers. After various increases in its capital with the managers and employees buying most of the stock, the company's equity capital now exceeds €3.6m. In fact, all Comitas employees are stockholders at the present time (each one investing as much as they have been able and willing to).

Setting the Stage

Comitas currently operates in three business lines that are mutually complementary: satellite communications, telemedicine, and the exploitation of a virtual private network (TM-64 network), which currently supports telemedicine services and other value-added services functioning in broadband. Nevertheless, initially the firm's main activity was selling satellite communications services.

Comitas acts as a satellite communications operator at the national and international levels. Currently, the company is a communications operator with license C and C2 from the Spanish Telecommunications Commission, as well as Inmarsat Service Provider (ISP) since 2000, and Point of Service Activation (PSA) for Inmarsat since 2001. This allows Comitas to offer all its customers the services of activation and invoicing of Inmarsat, Iridium, and Thuraya traffic. This activity has in a very short space of time brought Comitas a turnover of close to €3m in satellite traffic.

Comitas is a regional service center (RSC) offering the full range of Inmarsat terminals from the Norwegian company Nera Satcom and able to offer a comprehensive service to its customers. In fact, in Spain it is the biggest distributor of Inmarsat communications terminals from NERA Satcom, and at the same time it distributes EMS and Hughes R-BGAN equipment.

Comitas has a wide range of satellite communications terminals (see Table 2), giving it global coverage of voice and data in the terrestrial, maritime, and aerial sectors.

Comitas is also the official traffic distributor in Spain for the operator Telenor Satellite Services, the world's biggest Inmarsat operator. Comitas is by far the biggest distributor of Telenor satellite traffic in Spain. Meanwhile, Comitas sells approximately 1% of global Inmarsat communications traffic, and is now ranked the 10th largest distributor in the world. This allows the firm to enjoy the largest possible range of discounts from Telenor, providing it with solid margins from the sale of traffic flow.

Comitas offers a wide range of value-added services in the area of communications traffic:

Table 2. Satellite communications terminals offered by Comitas

	Voice	Fax	Data	GMDSS*	Terrestrial	Maritime	Aerial
Worldcommunicator	4.8 Kbps	14.4 Kbps	64 Kbps	No	X		
Worldphone family	4.8 Kbps	2.4 Kbps	2.4 Kbps	No	X	X	X
Rbgan	No	No	144 Kbps	No	X		
Thuraya	4 Kbps	4 Kbps	9.6 Kbps	No	X	X	
Iridium	4 Kbps	4 Kbps	10 Kbps	No	X	X	X
Fleet 33	4.8 Kbps	9.6 Kbps	9.6 Kbps	No		X	
Fleet 55	4.8 Kbps	14.4 Kbps	64 Kbps	No		X	
Fleet 77	4.8 Kbps	14.4 Kbps	128 Kbps	Yes		X	
Aero Swift	4.8 Kbps	4.8 Kbps	256 Kbps	No			X
Nera Bgan	4 Kbps	No	384 Kbps	No	X		
Hughes Bgan	4 Kbps	No	492 Kbps	No	X		

* *GMDSS: Global Maritime Distress Safety System*

- Invoicing and handling of any type of Inmarsat, Iridium, and Thuraya terminal

- Direct and permanent connection with Inmarsat and Telenor control center, which means that responses are immediate

- Support and customer service 24 hours a day, 7 days a week

- Direct handling of all aspects of communications services offered by Inmarsat

- Handling of registrations and cancellations of terminals and cards, as well as registrations and cancellations of services

- Reception and handling of requests for service activation of mobile earth stations (MES)

- Assignment of INMARSAT mobile numbers (IMNs)

Moreover, Comitas offers a number of other value-added services, as well as various IT solutions, including:

- A specific server for accessing the Internet designed for Inmarsat terminals, free of charge, which optimizes communication and connection times using this method.

- E-mail software called E-mail Advanced that optimizes the sending and reception of e-mails. Users can have as many e-mail accounts as they need, without extra cost.

- Personal calls service for ship crews (Crew Call), which discriminates between "official" calls and personal calls from crew members through a simple password system.

- Satellite Direct Service, which saves customers from paying surcharges on M2F calls (mobile to fixed, or boat to land), making them equivalent to F2M calls.

- Videoconference and multiconference, for which Comitas has a high-performance multiconference multipoint control unit (MCU) allowing up to 30 simultaneous points in a videoconference, with various forms of visualization that change dynamically.

- Videostreaming server available to all the users of Comitas' network. The server offers users high-quality multimedia content at all times. The service enables the sending of videos, live simultaneous transmissions, teletraining, and so forth.

With regard to the types of link used, Comitas designs private networks using the best performing and cheapest technology and operator in each particular location. These private networks perform better than the well known virtual private networks (VPNs), which the firm also installs. Security is totally guaranteed because the network is functionally independent from the Internet, the bandwidth is always 100% guaranteed, and the response times are lower.

The networks used are: Inmarsat (www.inmarsat.com), Integrated Service Digital Network (ISDN), Fiber Optics, Local Multipoint Distribution Service (LMDS[1]), and WiFi systems.[2] The Comitas brand is familiar in the Spanish market, particularly in the defense segment, which provides around 43% of its turnover in communications. Comitas is the Spanish army's main supplier of satellite communications via Inmarsat.

Comitas is currently Spanish State Contractor for ICT services (highest classification), which is awarded by the Ministry of Economics and Finance. This enables the firm to bid for government contracts worth at least €600,000.

With regard to the firm's organizational structure, apart from the top management team the firm has the following functional areas:

- Department of Business Development
- Department of Administration
- Department of Programs
- Department of Operations

The firm's marketing strategies include strengthening the loyalty of its current customer base. For this purpose, Comitas offers excellent after-sales service, and strengthens its relationships with its customers in order to evolve in accordance with their needs, detect any problems in its services, and add maximum value to its value chains, in which the firm intervenes to make some of its activities virtual. This customer orientation has helped it acquire other customers thanks to its excellent reputation.

Case Description

Like in many entrepreneurial projects, Comitas' telemedicine project is the result of a new opportunity that was detected and appropriately exploited.

Comitas had already provided satellite communications to the Spanish Ministry of Defense for several years. When Spain sent troops to participate in the UN blue beret contingent in Bosnia, the Ministry of Defense asked the firm to develop a system allowing its EMATS (army medical units) to communicate with the Ministry of Defense central hospital, Gómez Ulla, more interactively than would be possible by telephone.

What began with a single camera was Comitas' first step into the world of telemedicine systems. From this point on, Comitas began to develop its TM-64 telemedicine system. The system is named after the 64 Kbps that the system had initially. Now, the system's minimum speed is 128 Kbps providing telemedicine in remote and isolated locations. In Mauritania and Sierra Leone, the system is now offering telemedicine at 256 Kbps. In other areas with terrestrial lines, the system usually offers from 1 to 1.5 Mbps, reaching as high as 2 Mbps in some areas.

At present, the TM-64 system allows doctors to offer medical support to patients located anywhere in the world, with the same degree of precision and reliability as standard medical practice demands. The system allows doctors to communicate among themselves and send electronic data in real time.

To be able to develop its technology, Comitas had to make substantial investments in research and development. It has a staff of seven engineers and three technicians. The company started by installing the first node of its future telemedicine network. It was then able to begin negotiations with the main distributors and manufacturers of medical equipment to develop an adequate telemedicine system.

An initial problem was the lack of a sufficiently secure global standard that supported communications both on all types of terrestrial computer network and by satellite, and which was freely available. Thus, Comitas understood that it needed to develop its own software for health care communications, an obligation that at the same time proved to be an opportunity. Comitas began to work without following any previously established model. The telemedicine model that Comitas aimed to create was one in which the doctor in a reference center received the information in real time, wherever the remote center existed.

Telemedicine offers medical assistance in delayed time as well as in real time, but Comitas has focused on providing technical support for remote medicine in real time. The firm's technology allows primary-care professionals to transmit patients' medical data electronically from a remote location to a reference center. In the reference centers there are qualified professionals ready to attend patients in real time.

Comitas has integrated three elements that the firm considers fundamental for providing support to telemedicine:

- A system for capturing, transmitting, and receiving medical data
- Software to manage the system
- Its own communications network specifically designed for the health care sector (TM-64), to offer a secure and reliable communication of medical data

After a period of development, the firm began to commercialize its telemedicine solution TM-64 in 1996 with the Spanish Ministry of Defense. His Majesty King Juan Carlos I of Spain inaugurated the TM-64 telemedicine system in Gómez Ulla Hospital, the Ministry of Defense central hospital.

This first experience with the Ministry of Defense was a success, and subsequent improvements to the system have allowed the firm to commercialize and install the system with other public and private customers.

The TM-64 system consists of telemedicine equipment, the TM-64 software, and a communications channel. The telemedicine equipment meets basic medical needs for obtaining diagnostic tests, but adapted to enable the information obtained to be sent electronically (this normally involves images, videos, sounds, or simply data). The equipment satisfies characteristics that are common and indispensable in telemedicine: portability, robustness, ease of use, and reliability.

With regard to the TM-64 software, this integrates the medical information so that it can subsequently be sent, received, and visualized via a communications channel. The TM-64 network operates on dedicated circuits, which are not shared (unlike the Internet), and are protected by encryption systems to guarantee full confidentiality.

The minimum communications channel required to carry out a telemedicine session with voice and videoconference is 64 Kbps. The communication can use either satellite or dedicated terrestrial circuits.

All centers currently using the TM-64 system are integrated in a telemedicine network that effectively turns them into a virtual medical and scientific community. Apart from attending patients, users can share experiences, clinical sessions, conferences, and training courses simultaneously and interactively, thanks to a multiconference facility.

The organization of the medical services that Comitas offers its customers is also noteworthy. This organization consists of two types of center: remote centers and reference centers.

The remote centers, or help stations, can be, for example, local hospitals, field hospitals, health centers, rescue units, or ships. This is where medical personnel collect medical data from the patients, and send them, via telemedicine, to the reference centers.

Remote centers must have a basic telemedicine system consisting of a workstation, a router, a videoconference system, and the TM-64 software. For diagnoses, remote centers should ideally have certain modular equipment adapted for telemedicine. This may include visual exploration equipment (using mobile cameras with a powerful zoom), dermatoscopy, ophthalmoscopy, otoscopy, vital signs measurement (blood pressure, heart beat rate, temperature, and saturation of oxygen in blood), electrocardiograph, ultrasound scan, radiology (image scanner), hematology, microscopy, endoscopy, spirometry, or stethoscopy.

In the reference centers there are installations specially designed to provide medical support to the remote centers. Reference centers are normally located in large hospitals that have a wide range of medical specialists at their disposal, as well as the necessary equipment and communications.

Reference centers also have a workstation, router, videoconference system, and the TM-64 software. Optionally, they can also have a radiology monitor.

Comitas has been able to develop and continually improve its TM-64 telemedicine system by working closely with specialist doctors and customers who can give their impressions at any time. Customers are strongly involved in this process, so that the hospitals and centers in the TM-64 network feel they are an important part of it. In addition, thanks to the continual improvements to the system, Comitas can update the system already installed in customers' organizations, often without extra cost.

Comitas is fully aware that the success of its business depends on the creation of network externalities. In this respect, the TM-64 standard owned by the firm becomes more valuable the more centers that use it. Thus, the firm is observing a disproportionate growth in its customer base.

The firm now has an extremely varied customer base (see Table 3). Its customers are both private companies and public organizations (mainly in Spain), in its two main business areas.

Comitas also provides training courses for its customers in how to use its TM-64 application and its network. These courses take place in the firm's offices, as well as in some hospitals in the network. The users can also opt to study on their own with Comitas manuals, in which case they can clear up any doubts with the firm via a user-friendly interface and videoconference.

Moreover, aware that its users are health care professionals who are rarely experts in this technical area, Comitas can optionally manage their configurations remotely to make sure that the system is operating perfectly at all times.

Comitas fully guarantees the security of its network, since it is private, encrypted, has a limited number of users, and is isolated completely from the Internet. To prepare for any eventual problem, Comitas has organizational routines in which a team of professionals oversees the network on the look-out for possible security problems, configuring firewalls when necessary.

Among the TM-64 telemedicine system's most important benefits are the following:

Table 3. Comitas customer base

Communications	Telemedicine
• Construction companies • Electronics companies serving fishing, merchant, and recreational sectors • Companies belonging to Telefónica Group and Movistar Global • Fishing and merchant fleets • Health care institutions • Communications media (TV, radio, press, agencies) • Spanish Ministry of Agriculture, Fisheries and Food • Spanish Ministry of Foreign Affairs • Spanish Ministry of Defense (Spanish navy ships) • Spanish Ministry of Education and Science • Spanish Ministry of Labor • Spanish Ministry of Labor and Social Affairs (Social Institute of the Navy) • NGOs • Spanish Prime Minister's Office	• Company first-aid stations • Clinics and private health care organizations • Medical insurance companies and mutual occupational accident companies • Social Institute of the Navy • Spanish Ministry of Defense • Spanish Ministry of Education • Spanish Ministry of Health • Spanish Ministry of Labor • NGOs • Public Health care institutions (e.g., Madrid Regional Ministry of Health and Consumer Affairs)

- It allows doctors to attend to patients located anywhere in the world.

- Users can transmit a large number of diagnostic tests in real time (data and high-resolution images), which specialist doctors can then use.

- It supports the decision-making concerning the diagnosis, prescription of a treatment, stabilization or transfer of a patient, and monitoring of their evolution.

- The diagnosis is obtained more quickly, so treatment can follow more quickly.

- It minimizes the number of trips patients must make to distant health care centers.

- It reduces the demand for hospital beds when diagnosis and treatment are available in situ under the supervision of specialists.

- It improves the handling of patient discharges in real time when diagnoses are negative.

- The functioning of the system is easy, intuitive, user-friendly, and attractive.

- The system offers good interactive communication via high-quality videoconference.

- Data and medical images are transmitted and received in real time (videoconference, ultrasound scan, etc.), or with a few seconds' delay (X-ray images).

- It integrates with software satisfying international standards (e.g., DICOM v.3 or Windows).

- The transmission of the health care data is secure and reliable. The system guarantees the confidentiality of patients' data—to protect their privacy—and the integrity and authenticity of the information transmitted. This function is provided by SIMED,[3] a secure computer system that allows users to record, view, and manage certified telemedicine sessions.

- It supports the continuous training of specialists with sessions in real time (multiconference), online materials and content (high-resolution Web multimedia), highly realistic audiovisuals (videostreaming), and so forth.

Comitas' growth strategy is reflected in the great variety of customers that is evident in Table 3, as well as in the growth in the payroll to satisfy the expanding demand. Starting with just 3 employees, over time Comitas has grown to the 20 employees of today. Both employees' and managers' jobs are highly versatile, often spanning more than one department and involving general responsibilities such as handling the press, quality issues, or the Comitas Foundation.

The Comitas Foundation was created in 2003 to develop and promote telemedicine through practical projects with a social impact.

The Foundation is a nonprofit organization that aims to spread and promote the use of telemedicine for humanitarian purposes in third-world or developing countries, either in specific emergency situations or in projects involving nongovernmental organizations (NGOs) in such countries.

In humanitarian projects, Comitas can finance up to half the cost of a telemedicine project through its foundation. The company also works at zero profit in this type of project, in terms of equipment sales, employee hours, and communications traffic.

One of the Foundation's most important projects is the Chinguetti Project. Chinguetti is the seventh holy city of Islam, and it is located in the desert of Mauritania. It has a population that ranges from 3,000 to 6,000 inhabitants, depending on the time of year. There are no telephones and communication with the outside world depends on two radio sets, one in the mayor's office and the other in the health center. The water supply depends on a single well and the electricity from two generators, which work for only four hours a day. As in the rest of Mauritania, the average life expectancy is 53.8 years, and there is a high infant mortality (12%). There is only one doctor for every 10,000 inhabitants. Health care in Chinguetti depends on one small clinic and its single nurse. The town does not have the diagnostic resources required to treat diseases like tuberculosis, anemia, or infections. Its inhabitants often suffer pathologies caused by poor hygiene, contaminated drinking water, or malnutrition. Medical materials and medicines are in very short supply.

This dramatic health care situation led a group of Spanish doctors who had visited the town to create the Chinguetti Foundation in 2002. It had just one objective: to create a hospital offering decent medical care to the population. The hospital La Fraternidad was the result.

The Comitas Foundation installed telemedicine equipment in this hospital, allowing it to obtain specialized assistance from doctors in the 16 Spanish hospitals integrated in the TM-64 telemedicine network.

Thanks to telemedicine, La Fraternidad Hospital can request assistance from specialists in any of the reference centers in the TM-64 network for a wide range of specialties and pathologies. With the support of a satellite videoconference system, the hospital's doctors can carry out clinical sessions with the most difficult patients in collaboration with these specialists. This allows the hospital's doctors to decide on the diagnosis, select the most appropriate treatment in function of the available resources, and supervise monitoring of the patients. And the hospital can carry out electrocardiograms or dermatological explorations for these specialists in real time, and even monitor and stabilize patients that may require transference. Thus, Chinguetti's inhabitants now enjoy the potential support of the 2,500 doctors of all specialties who work in the hospitals of the TM-64 telemedicine network.

Thanks to its humanitarian telemedicine projects, Comitas has entered the African continent. At the present time the company is studying cheaper satellite solutions so that humanitarian telemedicine projects can be sustainable in Africa. At the same time, it continues to invest in research and development to improve its TM-64 telemedicine system and the Thematic Health Network.

Among Comitas' growth strategies, the firm has opted for forward vertical integration, creating the subsidiary Real Time Telemedicine Services[4] (RT2S) in 2006. Comitas owns 95% of the stock of this company, which delivers health care services via telemedicine. At present, RT2S has five doctors in its team who respond to the telemedicine consultations made to them. With the creation of RT2S, Comitas has gone from being a mere technology firm to also being a provider of medical services, using the group's own technology. RT2S is a reference center for other health care organizations, using the Thematic Health Network, TM-64, operated by Comitas.

As is evident from the above discussion, Comitas is a clear case of corporate entrepreneurship, which, inheriting the entrepreneurial spirit of the organization that incubated it, has in turn engaged in corporate entrepreneurship itself with RT2S.

After more than 10 years working in the field of telemedicine, Comitas is sure about the philosophy underpinning this activity:

- Patients should have fair access to health care services, regardless of their location

- It is necessary to reduce the time it takes to diagnose, prescribe treatment, stabilize, or operate on a patient

- Team-based medicine should be encouraged, enabling consultation between specialists

- Ethical principles and international regulations concerning the practice of telemedicine should be complied with

- And, perhaps the most important: telemedicine should move data, not patients

Current Challenges and Problems
Facing the Organization

Comitas Comunicaciones' star software, TM-64, has a common core that does not meet all customers' needs perfectly. These customers are very diverse, and they do not always have the same requirements. Thus, the firm has gradually adapted its telemedicine solutions to these needs as customers have expressed them. Consequently, the TM-64 system is now modular and segmentable, although all versions have a common core.

Another challenge facing Comitas has been to earn general acceptance for its standard so that network externalities can develop. This has been gradually achieved as the system has found more customers and the TM-64 network has grown. Now, the network is a virtual health care community where all the points are interconnected. This allows TM-64 customers to interact with each other and to offer medical services remotely to others in the network. Networks are more valuable the more members they contain, so Comitas decided to create its own reference center in the shape of the company RT2S.

One of the problems that Comitas has had to resolve was the problem of bandwidth. The services cannot all work efficiently with low bandwidth. In the early days, Comitas used a bandwidth of 64 Kbps. Now, its lowest bandwidth is in ships (128 Kbps) and its highest is 2 Mbps. The aim is to find a compromise between what is really necessary and what is feasible economically.

One of Comitas' biggest concerns is how to support telemedicine services at the global level and at a competitive price, but the terrestrial communications network does not reach everywhere. In this respect, the capabilities and the knowledge in the field of satellite communications that the firm inherited from its incubator have been an important weapon. Comitas is currently considering whether to buy a new space segment to offer satellite communications in Africa at competitive prices. The aim is to make humanitarian telemedicine models sustainable in that continent.

Apart from technical questions, telemedicine throws up all sorts of other potential problems that must be handled carefully. On the one hand, medical practice with inadequate equipment can lead to wrong diagnoses and, consequently, to inappropriate treatments. Health care is not like any other service—the patient's health is at stake. Thus, the firm has tried to put in place all the technological resources available, as well as develop those not offered by the market, in order to give doctors using Comitas systems the best technological infrastructures possible. But to arrive at the best possible system, it is not enough to have the best possible engineers and technicians. The firm has always taken doctors' opinions into account as well. The firm has consequently improved its system year after year, every so often adding new equipment for remote diagnosis.

Complex legal questions must also be considered in telemedicine projects. These include the fact that medical practice is governed by different legislations depending on the country, the protection of private patient data, and the need for informed consent before the system is used to prevent doctors being sued for medical negligence. Thus, Comitas works with a number of law firms whose legal experts (mainly in health law) advise it in this area.

On the other hand, Comitas wishes to inspire confidence among both doctors and patients, and is fully committed to seeking total quality. In this respect, in 2004 the company obtained UNE-EN-ISO 9001:2000 certification of its quality system for its activities in the marketing, distribution, installation, and after-sales service of communication systems (terminals via satellite), and in telemedicine, videoconference, and the management of communications traffic. Comitas ensures that its quality control system is maintained adequately with regular internal and external audits that guarantee the integrity of the system and compliance with the abovementioned standard.

The firm considers that its customers and the firms with which it works are the best source of information for improving quality. Thus, the firm pays particular attention to customer complaints and any criticisms from its collaborators, using them as the main source to improve its system.

Another difficulty that Comitas has faced is changing the mentality of the traditional health care system. People have been talking about telemedicine entirely naturally in the firm for over 10 years now. The evolution in the health care culture that telemedicine needs to find a space has been much more difficult. But, slowly, society seems to be becoming more receptive to telemedicine, to such an extent that a number of organizations are beginning to explore new uses for the technology. Comitas is finding that the market is opening up to it increasingly readily. Its turnover has increased exponentially in recent years, and the firm is beginning to turn a profit after many years of strong investment and losses.

One initial problem that the firm had was to be able to get software providers involved in the development of the telemedicine system. Eventually, instead of a problem, Comitas obtained real support from the suppliers. In fact, their collaboration has proved very valuable. In some cases they have supported Comitas by handing over their drivers to integrate their products into the TM-64 system. They realized that working with Comitas opened up new market opportunities that they had not previously foreseen.

Another potential problem that quickly disappeared was the possibility that the firm's communications infrastructure would be limited as a consequence of the lack of support from the communications operators. In fact, these operators have actively collaborated with the firm.

At the present time Comitas has no serious competitor in its real-time telemedicine business. But the firm is convinced that competitors will soon appear. Thus, it has attempted to find a desirable positioning in the market as quickly as possible. The firm's commitment to continuous improvement also leads it to value competition more as an incentive than as a threat. Under this perspective, when firms face competition they always try to improve their products, services, and management systems.

Another present and future challenge for the firm, which may also prove to be a technological challenge, is the portability of the communications equipment—which must operate in any location—and of the telemedicine diagnosis equipment. Comitas has made much progress in this area, but is always mindful of the fundamental philosophy behind telemedicine: the data, not the patients, should be moved.

Endnotes

[1]   LMDS is a broadband wireless access technology offering voice services, access to Internet, and communications on private networks.

[2]   WiFi means Wireless-Fidelity, which is a set of standards for wireless networks based on IEEE 802.11 specifications. WiFi is frequently used for accessing the Internet.

[3]   SIMED requires identification when connecting. The communications take place via secure connections between reference centers and remote centers using SSL3 on IPSEC. Access to the data is only possible through the reference center's server. To ensure the integrity of the information, each document in a session, and indeed the session itself receives a digital ID, preventing anyone from modifying any documents or substituting them for others in any particular telemedicine session.

[4]   http://www.rt2s.net/

Chapter XII

The Business Expansion Process of Applied Research Center (ARC):
Entrepreneurship, Interpreneurship, and Intrapreneurship

José Luis González, Institute of Kompetitiveness & Development,
Orkestra, Universidad de Deusto, Spain

Edurne Loyarte, Vicomtech, Spain

Iñaki Peña, Institute of Kompetitiveness & Development,
Orkestra, Universidad de Deusto, Spain

Abstract

The purpose of this chapter is to describe a real story where key subjects related to a business expansion process of a young IT-based applied research center (ARC) are discussed. More specifically, key theoretical notions will be examined linked to the day-to-day events occurred in ARC. This IT-based organization traced an original expansion trajectory based on the creation of two spin-offs during its infancy period. This chapter highlights general concerns associated with knowledge management and the capacity of innovation which emerged during the business expansion process. For purposes of this study, these concerns can be classified in three main theoretical areas: Entrepreneurship, Interpreneurship and Intrapreneurship.

Background

Information and Communication Technologies (ICT) Industry

International European Context

After the technology crisis in 1999, the ICT industry boosted during the early years of the current century. According to the European Information Technology Observatory's report (EITO, 2006), the overall European market of ICT industry reached a value of € 659 billion in 2005 (see Table 1). Europe has become the biggest ICT market, with one third of the total market value worldwide. European ICT firms represent approximately 34% of the world market value, compared to 28% of United States firms, 14% of Japanese firms, and 24% of firms from the rest of the world. Whereas the European ICT industry grew by 3.7% in 2005, the United States ICT sector increased by 3.9% and the Japanese sector by 2.1%.

In a recent report, the European Commission's Industrial R&D Investment Scoreboard 2006[1] shows that 18 of the top 50 biggest spenders on R&D and 5 of the 10 companies with fastest R&D growth are from Europe. Most of these companies belong to

Table 1. Worldwide ICT market by region: Percentage breakdown calculated on market values, 2004-2006, euro billion (Source: EITO, 2006)

Regions	2005 value	2004 %	2005 %	2006 %
Europe*	659.00	34.1	33.8	33.6
U.S.	545.00	28.2	28.0	28.0
Japan	287.00	15.1	14.7	14.3
Rest of the World	457.00	22,6	23.5	24.1
Total	**1,948.00**	**100.00**	**100.00**	**100.00**
Note: * Europe includes the European Union (EU), Norway, Switzerland, Romania, and Bulgaria				

Figure 1. European Information and Communication Technology (ICT) market by product, 2005 (Source: EITO, 2006)

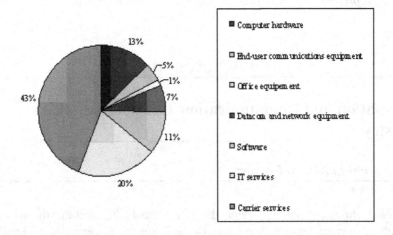

the ICT industry. The European ICT sector consists of seven sub-sectors (see Figure 1). The Services and Software industries are the most important sub-sectors, with a share of 74% of the European ICT market. Moreover, the number of ICT firms has increased substantially in the Services and Software subsectors, where companies lead the R&D spending in Europe. The European ICT market is expected to grow in the coming years, primarily due to the push effect of these subsectors.

National Context

In 2005, Spain was the most dynamic economy in the Euro-zone. According to the European Information Technology Observatory report (EITO, 2006), Spain was expected to achieve a 4.1% market value share of the European IT sector and a 8.2% market value share of the European Telecommunications sector in 2005. Overall, the country reached a 6.4% market value share of the ICT sector in Europe.

Spain reached the fastest growth rates in both IT and Telecommunication sectors in 2005, with a growth rate of approximately 7%. The Services and Software sub-sectors will also lead the ICT market growth in Spain according to the opinion of many experts. While the Software sector grew by over 10%, IT sectors grew by 8% (see Table 2).

Table 2. The Spanish ICT market: Market value, 2005, and growth rates, 2002-2005, euro billion (Source: ENTER, 2006)

ICT sectors	2005 value	2003/2002 %	2004/2003 %	2005/2004 %
Telecommunication services	27,055	11.1%	12.80%	7.90%
IT services	4,740	0.1%	5.40%	7.90%
Software	2,514	5.8%	7.10%	10.40%
Hardware computer	4,021	3.2%	1.60%	5.10%
Office equipment	508	1.4%	-1.80%	0.60%
Transfer and communication data	869	-6.0%	3.20%	3.60%
Network equipment	1,723	-12.2%	12.70%	6.10%
End-user electronic equipment	5,654	16.0%	10.20%	14.90%
Audiovisual sector	4,327	10.5%	16.90%	7.90%
Total ICT	**51,411**	**7.9%**	**10.50%**	**8.30%**

Description of ARC

Applied Research Center (ARC) is a computer graphics organization located in a medium-sized city in Spain (i.e., a city of approximately 200,000 inhabitants). The parent firms, AlphaGraph and the local firm BetaCom, founded the joint venture ARC at the end of December, 2000. The new research center was introduced to society during an official press event on February 26, 2001. ARC develops visual and interactive communication technologies in the field of computer-aided graphics and is located in the Omega Technology Park of the town. Since its inception, ARC has grown steadily and become a successful non-profit-making organization.

More than ever before, R&D activities are conducted in a global way among a complex myriad of worldwide institutions. In addition, we are witnessing an increasingly multimedia and multimodal-driven society. Computer graphic technologies are one of the main enablers of this current trend. ARC was born in this context as a result of a joint venture (i.e., 50/50 ownership) between a local (i.e., BetaCom) and a foreign institution (i.e., AlphaGraph). ARC is a member of the foundation led by one of its parent firms, AlphaGraph Foundation. AlphaGraph Foundation is a large German institution with members from several countries. Network members develop local research projects and cooperate with international partners simultaneously. On one hand, the market demand encourages firms to develop new products jointly through alliances, especially when the product is technology-based. On the other hand, collaboration among members allows synergies and efficiency gains in terms of economies of scale, "time-to-market" and "time-to-result" (Culpan, 1993).

After five years of research and business activity, today ARC is a well-known international center for research, development, and technology transfer, with about 50 researchers involved in more than 60 applied research projects (financed by private firms and public institutions), and an annual budget of about € 2.0 million.

The following items summarize ARC's mission as stated in its Annual Report:

- To come up with the needs of companies and institutions in our environment related to applied research, development, and technological innovation in the computer graphics field
- To develop visual interaction and communication technologies based upon the latest advances in computer graphics and its development in specific applications and products in conjunction with the industry
- To contribute to the general body of knowledge in the field through the training of new researchers and the publication of their results in internationally recognized journals and conferences
- To pursue quality and excellence in scientific, technical, customer service, and internal organizational aspects

The technologies developed by ARC are applied in different fields of research.[2] These include:

- Digital TV and interactive services
- 3D medical imaging processing and telemedicine
- Virtual reconstruction of archaeological-historical heritage, GIS, and tourism
- Edutainment and conversational user interfaces
- Multimedia and industrial applications

The knowledge and technologies that ARC masters, directly or indirectly via the research network, give added value to its clients. ARC offers the right answer to their specific needs, allows customers to take advantage of technological opportunities, and proposes improvements or developments for their products based on the latest advances in scientific and technological knowledge. ARC's goal is to serve as a bridge between both local and international environments. Furthermore, ARC has inherited from AlphaGraph the culture of being a technological bond between basic research, industry, and society (see Figure 2).

ARC follows a clear quality policy in all aspects of its activity. ARC is certified according to the ISO 9001:2000 standard for the whole scope of activities. This

Figure 2. ARC's international research network and its role as a catalyst of computer graphics technology (Source: ARC)

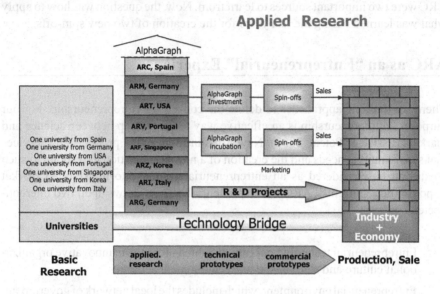

certification reflects the deep involvement of ARC with quality in all aspects. It reinforces the belief and the striving for excellence in applied research and the meeting of customer needs.

In 2005, as a result of the growing pattern of the organization, ARC created two new tech-based spin-off firms. *Entrepreneurship, interpreneurship,* and *intrapreneurship* were relevant issues the management team and board of directors of ARC had to deal with simultaneously.

Setting the Stage

ARC is currently able to develop interaction and visual communication-based technologies, which are mainly addressed to the media and computer graphics industry. After the founders and managers of ARC had acquired expertise and experience during the early life stage of ARC, they aimed at achieving business growth with the creation of two new firms. In other words, ARC was ready to go through an "intrapreneurial process" to achieve growth goals.

We should keep in mind that ARC itself was the result of a joint venture of two other firms, AlphaGraph and BetaCom. As an entrepreneurial project, ARC managers learned to build up a firm from its own venture experience. Certainly, the "entrepreneurial" and "interpreneurial" experiences acquired during the gestation process of ARC were two important sources to learn from. Now, the question was how to apply what was learned during the last years for the creation of two new spin-offs.

ARC as an "Entrepreneurial" Experience

There are multiple approaches to define the concept of entrepreneurship. For our purposes, entrepreneurship is an effective way to fill the gap between science and market (Hisrich & Peters, 2002). New firms introduce new products and services that satisfy market needs and the creation of a new organization to respond to such needs can be considered as an entrepreneurial response to unexploited market opportunities. Currently, ARC's entrepreneurial activity draws upon two interconnected contexts:

- Entrepreneurial technological capital, which includes an innovative organizational culture and state-of-the-art technological activities
- Entrepreneurial environment, which includes the local network of government, universities, technology parks, and private firms

Entrepreneurial Technological Capital of ARC

As an organization which develops most of its economic activities in the field of new technologies, ARC has made a considerable effort to embed an innovative culture internally and externally in the entire organization and to develop technological activities in an efficient manner.

Innovative Culture

Conventional wisdom suggests that innovation is fundamental in any entrepreneurial process (Drucker, 1985). ARC's innovative spirit is evinced by a diverse management team (i.e., three researchers from different disciplines in their early 40s). The CEO, Antonio Martínez,[3] is a PhD in engineering. He is currently a university professor and has strong ties with different agents of the local economy (i.e., other technology centers, private firms, and local government authorities). His associate director, Alberto Arias, a PhD in engineering, is from Latin America and worked in the past for AlphaGraph. The CFO, María Vargas, is a PhD in economics and she leads the managerial and administrative tasks of the center. An innovative company uses multidisciplinary teams with significant autonomy dedicated to carrying out the

Figure 3. ARC's staff disciplines (Source: ARC)

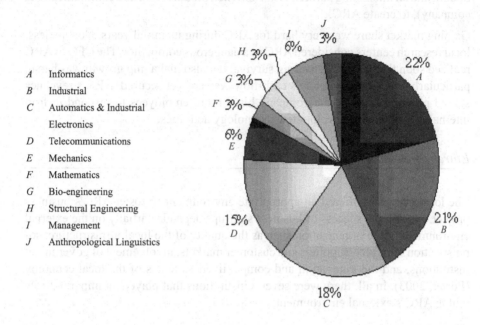

A	Informatics
B	Industrial
C	Automatics & Industrial Electronics
D	Telecommunications
E	Mechanics
F	Mathematics
G	Bio-engineering
H	Structural Engineering
I	Management
J	Anthropological Linguistics

projects. The management team of ARC believes that the formation of cross-functional teams is an effective manner to design and to develop innovative new products. In fact, several authors state that companies throughout the world are beginning now to realize the benefits of these cross-functional teams in product development activities (Wheelen & Hunger, 2004). ARC's staff includes graduate students and young PhD scholars in different disciplines (see Figure 3). Most staff comes from the following fields: electronic engineering (22%), industrial engineering (21%), automatics and industrial (18%), and telecommunications (15%).

Tech-Based Activities

The activity of ARC consists of meeting integral innovation needs of firms and institutions. The majority of ARC's activity is focused on five applied areas which were mentioned in the background. The parent firm AlphaGraph was to a large extent responsible for the technology orientation of ARC. Before the creation of ARC, AlphaGraph was looking for partners worldwide in order to strengthen its network. A network with a mixed membership base (i.e., members from several countries) would enable better access to EU projects and grants. After an exhaustive search for partners in Europe, AlphaGraph found an attractive business and technology-development environment (i.e., Omega Technology Park and its local economy in Spain), and an interesting partner, BetaCom (i.e., broadcasting and communications company), to create ARC.

Gaining market share was very hard for ARC during its initial years. Nonetheless, local research centers considered ARC as a dangerous competitor. The CFO of ARC realized soon that not only ensuring survival but also managing growth was harsh, particularly when the company's cash-flow was not yet secured. ARC's revenues started growing fast and the company hired more employees to respond to firm internal growth and to develop new technology activities.

Entrepreneurial Environment of ARC

The local economy offered an appropriate environment to foster ARC's business project. Indeed, the success of business start-ups depends partially on the external environment of the organization such as the quality of the local infrastructure, sophistication of rivalry, suppliers and customer markets, involvement of government institutions, and the innovation and competitiveness levels of the local economy (Porter, 2003). In all, there were several institutions that played an important role within ARC's external environment:

- Government
- University
- Technology parks and technology centers
- Private firms

Government

Local government authorities are aware of the significant impact that companies like ARC generate in the economy (i.e., job creation, emergence of new products, technologies, and exports). Undoubtedly, local government authorities can shape an environment to foster strategic industry sectors or economic activities. ARC was located in a place where the local government was very supportive of the creation of new tech-based firms.

Local government authorities had targeted 18 strategic research areas to implement their support programs. These research lines are described in the Strategic Research Program of the Regional Government's Plan of Science, Technology and Innovation (see Table 3), which sets up the procedures for integrating science, technology,

Table 3. Government's strategy research lines (Source: Regional Government's Plan of Science, Technology, and Innovation)

Area	Strategic research lines
1. Competitiveness Main Area	1. Nanotechnologies 2. Microtechnologies 3. High-performance manufacturing 4. Advanced transport of future 5. Intelligent materials
2. Environment and Energy	6. Micro-energies 7. Management of the quality of the air 8. Recovery of the ground
3. Information Society	9. Virtual reality 10. Wireless 11. Linguistics info-engineering 12. Extended digital firm
4. Quality of life	13. Higher education in the 21st Century 14. Rehabilitation and conservation of immovable property 15. Biomaterials and biomedical technologies
5. Living resources	16. Functional and proteomic genomic biopharmacology 17. Agricultural and fishing production 18. Alimentary security of agricultural and fishing products

ARC's performance

and industry. ARC fits into some of these strategic research lines such as virtual reality, advanced transport of future, high-performance manufacturing, linguistics info-engineering, and biomaterials and biomedical technologies.

Universities

There are four universities in the local region (see Figure 4). The most important is Delta University which provides approximately almost 57% of graduate students of the local economy. Lambda University, with 1% of graduate students, is the youngest university in the region.

ARC has agreements and recruits employees from all the local universities. Table 4 summarizes the enrollment and graduation figures in the local universities for the year 2005 in the main disciplines demanded by ARC.

Figure 4. Graduate students according to universities: All the branches (2000-2005) (Source: National Statistic Institute)

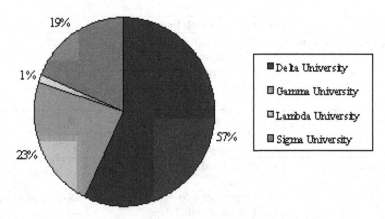

Table 4. Graduate students in the local area (2004/05) (Source: Regional Statistics Institute)

Engineering degrees	Enrolling students	%	Graduated students	%
Electronics	1,790	4%	382	5%
Industrial	3,356	8%	511	7%
Automatics and Industrial Electronics	431	1%	110	2%
Telecommunications	1,125	3%	147	2%
Number of students registered in all the degrees offered by the universities	**41,827**	**100%**	**7,077**	**100%**

Technology Parks and Technology Centers

While the creation of technology parks has become an important local government policy action to foster tech-based businesses formation, Spanish tech-based businesses find serious obstacles in transferring technology from research centers to private firms (Martínez Barea, 2003).

There are three technology parks in the region where ARC is located: Epsilon-park (with 146 firms which represent 16 industry sectors), Omega-park (with 28 firms which represent 12 industry sectors), and Zeta-park (with 86 firms which represent 13 industry sectors). They are strategically located within a radius of 100 km and all of them are focused on the development of state-of-the-art technologies (see Table 5).

Table 5. Tech-parks in the local area (Source: Epsilon-park, Omega-park, and Zeta-park)

Tech-parks	N° firms	N° industries	Industries	
Epsilon-park	146	16	• Aeronautics • Audiovisual • Automotive • Biosciences • Computer science • Consultancy • Documental management • Domotics	• Electronics • Energy and the environment • Engineering services • Company services • Mechanics • Neurosciences • Telecommunications • Telematics
Omega-park	28	12	• Audiovisual • Electronics • Energy and the environment • Documental management • Mechanics	• Molecular medicine • New materials • Telecommunications • Telematics • Transport and logistics
Zeta-park	86	13	• Aeronautics • Agrofeeding • Computer science • Electronics • Energy and the environment • Engineering services • Company services	• New materials • Opto-Electronics • Telecommunications • Telematics • Transport and logistics • Welfare and healthcare technologies

There were many advantages that contributed to the location of ARC at Omega Park: geographic location, facilities, services, and public image of being located in Omega Park. Besides, the parent firm BetaCom is also located in the same Omega Park area. Omega Park hosts company services, telecommunications, electronics, and audiovisual firms. In fact, 11% of its firms belong to ARC's industry sector, that is, to the audiovisual field (see Figure 5). This concentration of related high-tech firms in the Park would allow ARC to benefit eventually from spill-over effects across firms and across different industries.

Private Firms

The local economy is characterized by a dominant manufacturing industry which has undergone important changes in the last few years. On one hand, products and processes have been renewed and on the other hand, diversification and industrial

Figure 5. Industries of the firms located in Omega-park facilities (Source: Omega-park)

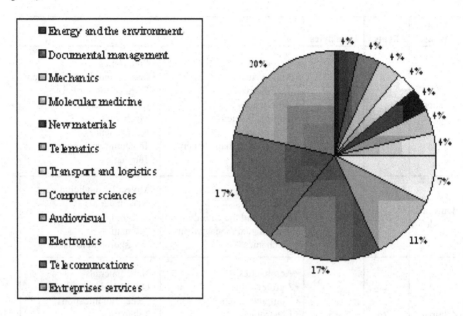

innovativeness is encouraged through the creation of new ventures specialized in state-of-the-art technologies.

Overall, R&D expenditure has doubled in the region in the last five years. While private firms' share of total R&D expenditures of the region is 65%, the share of the public sector is 30% (see Figure 6). ARC's financing has experienced a similar pattern. ARC's funds from private firms increased from 36% of total revenues in 2001 to 51% in 2004.

To summarize, ARC relies extensively on valuable human capital. As part of the entrepreneurial technological capital of ARC, its staff is capable of working on individual and group projects efficiently and effectively, which is important for generating an entrepreneurial spirit within the organization. ARC's human capital is a key asset in developing its tech-based activities and competing both in local and global markets. Furthermore, the environment where ARC is located fosters entre-preneurship and innovation activities. Agents of this environment provide tangible and intangible support to ARC, which is expected to contribute positively to ARC's business performance and to the development of key core competencies.

ARC as an "Interpreneurial" Experience

Following Richter and Teramoto (1995) and Richter (2000), we use the term *inter-preneurship* to refer to the process of connecting to cooperative and strategic networks. Organizations are no longer self-sufficient, and often rely on R&D alliances and collaborative agreements in order to lead market innovation and to preserve an advantageous competitive position in the marketplace (Lorange & Roos, 1994). Certainly, most of world's leading companies rely on collaborative agreements (Gugler & Dunning, 1993). Further, tech-based firms prefer to establish collaborative agreements through a joint venture form because it provides an equitable participation and facilitates coordination (Osland & Yaprak, 1993). As mentioned earlier, ARC was the result of a joint venture between AlphaGraph and BetaCom, two institutions from different countries. They went through an *interpreneurial* process to create a new venture with the aim of exploring new technologies and product applications.

According to transaction cost theory, interfirm partnerships allow organizations to face competitive challenges of rapid technological change by minimizing risk of leakage technology and financial exposure, and by expanding innovation through creativity and learning processes among alliance partners (Contractor, Kim, & Beldona, 2002; Culpan & Kostelac, 1993; Oxley, 1999). The internalization of learning experiences acquired from parent firms was a source of competitive advantage, which was not available to other competitors. Not all the firms are born as a consequence

Figure 6. Research and development financing in the local area (Source: Regional Statistics Institute)

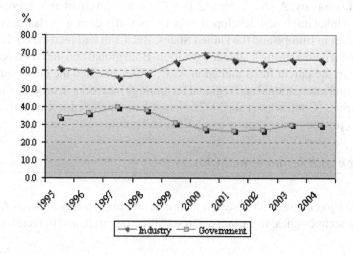

Figure 7. ARC's inception and favorable nurturing conditions during the interpreneurial phase

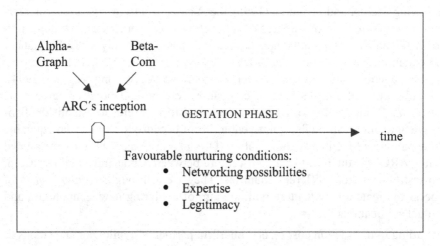

of an *interpreneurial* process. Currently, ARC has partners in seven countries that are actively carrying out local research projects and cooperating with each other internationally, which enables the process of time-to-market and time-to-result to be optimized. Since its inception, parent firms have provided ARC with at least the three following advantages during its gestation phase: networking possibilities, expertise, and legitimacy (see Figure 7).

Networking Possibilities

Each parent company, AlphaGraph and BetaCom, had a remarkable success history. While AlphaGraph had developed over 18 spin-offs during the last 5 years in different places in Europe and the United States, BetaCom had focused on the local market where it held a strong leadership position. Both global and local perspectives inherited from the parent firms melted in ARC, which enabled the new venture to establish strong international and regional technology networks in order to increase learning benefits (Contractor et al., 2002). Network ties included research institutes/ universities, private firms, venture capitalists, and public institutions.

Cooperation with Institutes and Universities

Cooperative agreements with research institutes and universities allowed ARC to explore new technologies, to participate in scientific research, and to recruit human resources from local and foreign universities. For instance, having access to research partners of the parent firm AlphaGraph brought substantial advantages to ARC, such as an efficient transfer of knowledge and the development of new technologies carried out jointly among network members from remote geographical locations and distinct research fields (i.e., cross-discipline approach). Table 6 illustrates the networking possibilities which arose for ARC due to the support received from AlphaGraph and BetaCom during the nurturing phase.

Cooperation with Firms

Not only universities and research institutes are relevant in bringing together these two spheres, but also private firms play a key role in linking science to market, or vice-versa.

Although local and regional private companies were mainly the manufacturers of ARC's innovative outcomes and helped to exploit the technology developed within the organization, ARC also benefited from cooperative contracts with foreign firms (i.e., firms from Italy and Germany). Again, some private firms that were partners or customers of the parent firms became collaborators of ARC. Briefly, the new venture went through a learning process of how to establish cooperative agreements with private firms under the know-how and supervision of the parent firms.

Table 6. Networking possibilities for ARC with research institutes and universities during firm gestation (Source: AlphaGraph)

Country of Origin	Number of Institutes	Number of Universities
Germany	3	2
Portugal	1	1
Italy	1	1
Spain	1	2
Singapore	2	1
Korea	1	1
USA	2	3
TOTAL	11	11

Cooperation with Venture Capitalists

A recent report suggests that the entrepreneurial capacity of the local economy where ARC is located is 5-6% of the adult population, that is, one of twenty people chooses to set up a firm in the local area (De la Vega, Coduras, Justo, Cruz, & Nogueira, 2005). Besides, some facts on business demography revealed that the mortality rate for young firms (i.e., age up to 5 years from inception) was 48%. Presumably, this rate was a bit higher for R&D-orientated firms (Morales & Peña, 2003).

ARC's survival was ensured due to the continuous support of the parent firms, but a growth strategy requires an injection of financial capital. Usually, financial institutions are reluctant to offer loans to entrepreneurial projects due to the lack of company history, especially when the entrepreneurial project deals with R&D activities where the technical viability of the project is often uncertain, and even if certain, the potential to yield returns is usually obscure. An important advantage of ARC was the access to venture capitalists through the parent firm AlphaGraph. AlphaGraph had a program congregating its young scientists with venture capitalists. This networking possibility allowed ARC to obtain seed capital and funds from foreign markets to finance its business expansion.

Cooperation with Public Institutions

During its initial years, ARC collaborated closely with local government authorities to launch many of its research projects. However, efforts to obtain grants have shifted from local institutions to foreign institutions as the venture has continued a growing business trend. In a sense, AlphaGraph had wide experience in obtaining funds from European institutions, so ARC benefited from the support and know-how provided by its parent firm in accessing EU grants. Figure 8 shows that the ability of ARC to collect funds from European Union and Spanish public institutions has increased substantially in recent years. While grants obtained from non-local institutions in the 2001-2004 period has increased from 8% to 19% of all the funds gathered by the venture, ARC's reliance on local grants has declined from 56% to 30%. Interestingly, grants from local government institutions represent currently only one third over all funds, whereas private investors represent more than half. At the time of the firm's inception, the situation was the opposite, that is, more than half of ARC's funds came from local institutions, whereas private firm funding represented a bit over a third of all funds. Clearly, the role played by private firms and local government institutions shifted during the gestation phase.

Figure 8. Networking possibilities for ARC with public institutions during firm gestation (Source: ARC)

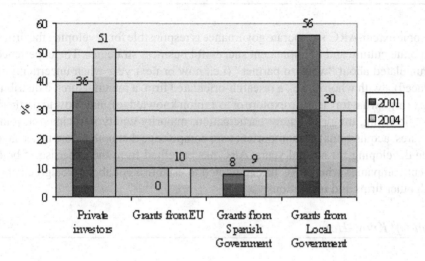

Funding and Grants from Private Firms and Public Institutions

Expertise

In addition to bringing new networking possibilities, parent firms provided ARC with valuable expertise. Parent firms were ready to share the knowledge and experience embedded in their respective organizations in order to build up a successful venture. Cross-transfer of human capital in corporate governance membership positions and research staff levels among AlphaGraph, BetaCom, and ARC facilitated the flow of knowledge and expertise from parent firms to the young venture. We could classify this expertise into three categories: operative know-how, business management know how, and spin-off know-how.

Operative Know-How

Although ARC's main business activity is to conduct applied research in the field of computer graphics and multimedia, its knowledge base is complemented by new wisdom coming from related technical fields (i.e., the areas of engineering, life sciences and e-business, developed by parent firms). The transfer of specific knowledge occurs through employee exchange programmes, by which researchers visit other institutes and universities located abroad. Researchers exchange knowledge via collaboration in research projects and via co-authoring in high-level scientific publications.

Business Management Know-How

To some extent, ARC's corporate governance is responsible for developing the firm's corporate culture and to implement successful business strategies. The experience accumulated about "when to partner" (i.e., now or next year when uncertainty is reduced), "with whom" (i.e., a research-orientated firm, a manufacturer, a distribution firm), "what for" (i.e., to explore or to exploit knowledge), and "how to partner" (i.e., licensing, minority equity participation, majority equity participation, joint ventures, acquisitions) is an important core competence that both parent firms have been developing for several years. ARC has benefited from the expertise of both parent companies when ARC has attempted to establish collaborative agreements with other firms and institutions.

Spin-Off Know-How

It seems that ARC is trying to replicate the same parents' *interpreneurial* experience in the local economy through the creation of two firm start-ups. The expertise of the parent firms considerably reduces the likelihood of business failure of the two spin-offs. It is expected that the new ventures will receive all the support from parent firms and will be nurtured in optimal incubation conditions (see Figure 9).

Figure 9. Replication of the nurturing process pursued by ARC

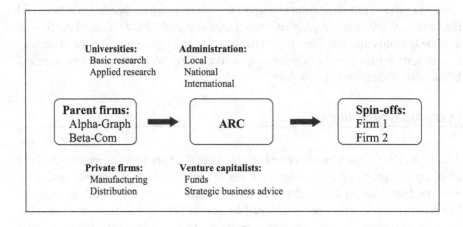

Legitimacy

A third advantage of ARC in being part of the *interpreneurial process* developed by AlphaGraph and BetaCom was legitimacy. ARC was supported by its parent firms and all the network structure and expertise embedded in their respective organizations. Being part of this "big family" added credibility to ARC and opened new windows of opportunities for collaborating with top research centers, for negotiating better conditions with financial institutions, and for awarding international grants (Elfring & Hulsink, 2001). Gaining the recognition that ARC has now would take decades if it had to start from scratch. The *interpreneurial process* granted outstanding legitimacy to ARC in an efficient and accelerated manner.

Additionally, ARC belonged to a local research alliance named Local Research Consortium (LRC). LRC was one of the two major local technological research alliances. The alliance consisted of a selected group of eight well-known technological centers and it was founded with the aim of concentrating the knowledge and experience of its members in order to reach a critical mass able to unleash innovative processes of considerable socio-economic significance. LRC gathered the strengths and skills of alliance members in order to generate synergies between complementary areas of specialization. LRC intended to delve deeper into a strategic process of specialization that placed a powerful technological infrastructure at the disposal of the marketplace and society in general. All members of the research alliance maintained their autonomy as independent organizations and represented the following research areas: mechatronic, microtechnologies, biotechnology, energy, environment, materials and processes, industrial management, and information technology. LRC had 900 research employees and annual revenues of approximately 49.2 million euros.

Being part of LRC also added legitimacy to ARC, since ARC was considered to be one of the major players on technological grounds in the local area. Furthermore, ARC managers thought that the organization could reach through LRC what ARC could not reach individually and that the technological development of their projects was going to advance faster at a lower cost.

In sum, we could outline ARC's advantages and disadvantages from cooperation for its business creation, consolidation, and growth process in Table 7.

Case Description

Despite its young age, ARC was involved in an important expansionary project with the creation of two spin-off ventures. Interestingly, rather than buying other existing firms, ARC preferred to grow internally via spin offs. An "intrapreneurial"

Table 7.

ADVANTAGES	DISADVANTAGES
• Interfirm cooperation allows the development of modern technologies while risk is reduced (i.e., cooperation with other research centers and universities). • ARC can absorb knowledge and expertise from business partners in order to shorten the bridge between science and marketplace. • Cooperation with venture capitalists brings not only funds, but also networks and managerial experience of capitalists. • Cooperation with local and European public institutions can enhance the creativity of ARC by developing international-multidisciplinary cross funded projects.	• ARC is a young organization to come up with multiple strategic alliances alone. • ARC's management team lacks experience in forming inter-firm collaborative agreements. • After a threshold level of alliance partners, an effective management of all the cooperative agreements can become a very complex task. • Alliances among local partners are difficult to deal with, but alliances with international alliance partners can be even more complicated.

process was in course. Why did this option of "intrapreneurship" or "corporate entrepreneurship" prevail?

ARC attempts to bridge the gap between science and market through its applied research activity for interactive computer graphics and multimedia technology. ARC follows not only a market-pull strategy, where market needs determine technological development, but it also undertakes a technology-push strategy by establishing new businesses when the market cannot find an outlet for promising technologies. By the time ARC reached the age of five years old, it created two new ventures in order to continue innovating and developing new technologies.

Innovation can be defined as "the setting up of a new production function" through "new combinations" of factors (Wickham, 2001; Young, Francis, & Young, 1993). A new business can be considered as the result of an innovation process where a combination of new factors is set up in order to create new products and services. To encourage innovation and creativity, an organization must design a structure that will provide autonomy to spin-off units while maintaining some degree of control at headquarters. Guth and Ginsberg (1990) define intrapreneurship as "the birth of new business within existing organizations through renewal of the key ideas on which they are built, that is, strategic renewal". To remain competitive, firms must continually innovate. Firms have responded by undertaking corporate entrepreneurship involving (1) creating new businesses within the existing business, and/or (2) transforming existing businesses through strategic renewal that alters business resource patterns. Internal or corporate venturing has received the majority of corporate entrepreneurship attention, both in academic research and in managerial actions. Yet new ventures may be more effective when started outside the firm than inside. Consolidated organizations often develop internal spin-offs, taking minority equity stakes in smaller, entrepreneurial companies that may identify opportunities, develop products, and implement new technologies more quickly than the parent firm. ARC is precisely a good example of this phenomenon.

ARC is a technological applied research center that develops its own technology in the top research lines of the Strategic Research Program of the Regional Government's Plan of Science, Technology and Innovation. When alliances are focussed on cooperating with local and foreign partners, these relationships allow partners to integrate technology developments in a global setting (Mourdoukoutas & Papadimitriou, 1998). ARC established strong international and regional networks since it could access cutting-edge technology through its global network.

ARC's business creation and consolidation process was influenced mainly by two driving forces: "entrepreneurship" (a technological capital, based on the implementation of an innovative culture and high-tech activities, embedded within an entrepreneurial environment where agents support technology-based firm start-ups), and "interpreneurship" (with networking, expertise, and legitimacy relationships among different institutions). As a result, ARC benefited from its entrepreurial and interpreneurial learning experiences at the moment of applying its technological knowledge and business management expertise to the current "intrapreneurial" expansionary project.

Spin-Offs Developed by ARC

ARC has developed two spin-offs in recent years, Spin1 and Spin2. One of the spin-offs is a replication of the *interpreneurial experience* that ARC has gone through. That is, an independent firm is created in the form of a joint venture with another partner. The second spin-off experience takes the form of an *intrapreneurship experience*. In this case, a new firm is created exclusively by ARC. It seems that high growth expectations of an internal business unit have led ARC to take away that unit by conferring complete autonomy. Nonetheless, the new spin-off belongs fully to ARC and its owner-entrepreneur.

On one hand, Spin1 S.L. was founded by ARC in May 2004. This spin-off firm offers services and products with an added value in information technologies applied to medicine. SPIN1 markets ARC's R&D projects and also identifies new projects to improve diagnosis and medical therapies, working in cooperation with hospitals, clinics, and health centers. The main fields of activity of SPIN1 are medical information systems, telemedicine, medical image treatment, computer assisted surgery, and radiotherapy. The applied technologies are: telecommunications, security, computer graphics, virtual and augmented reality, 3D medical image processing, data extraction, medical image analysis and manipulation, telemedicine, tracking and optical systems, and simulation.

On the other hand, Spin2, S.L. is a company founded in March 2005. Its core activity is software distribution and the implementation of turnkey projects. The main expertise areas of SPIN2 are knowledge about interactive TV, the implementation of new channels on the Internet, and new support from a communicational point of view including consulting, contents, communication pull, and corporate communication (Web sites, TDT, TV, and radio on the Internet).

These two examples show the embedded culture of intrapreneurship and innovation in ARC. Actually, ARC's aim is to meet the innovation needs of the companies and institutions. To meet these requirements, ARC:

- Works in applied research and development of multimedia technologies for visual interaction and communication
- Fosters the mobility and formation of researchers
- Collaborates closely with the industry, universities, and institutions, and complements other technology centers

Thus, the knowledge and technologies that ARC masters, directly or indirectly via the network, give added value to its customers. In addition, ARC supports the creation of technology-based new companies, especially in those sectors in which the lack of companies prevents the completion of the innovation circle. In theses cases, ARC is supported by the international network to which it belongs in order to identify spin-off potentials:

An important goal of ARC is to supply society with technology transfer from basic research to the industry. Its research activity is determined by market dynamics. Moreover, the technologies in which ARC works are of a horizontal nature and allow its application in different areas of research and markets. In the case that ARC develops a prototype or a technology which could be interesting for the end user but no distribution company for this technology or prototype exists, ARC managers start a strategic decision-making process for a new spin-off (see Figure 10). This decision-making is generated by the interest detected in demo sessions and experts meetings and by the lack of companies on the market which could support the technology developed.

The Intrapreneurial Process

The strategic decision-making process pursued by ARC during business expansion can be summarized by the following steps.

Figure 10. Screening to identify spin-off potentials (Source: AlphaGraph)

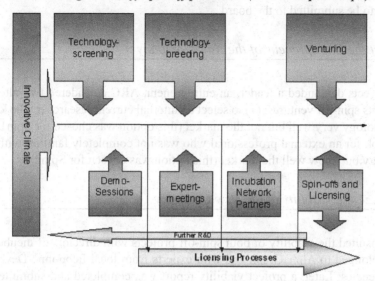

To Develop the Basic Business Idea

The idea was developed by the directors of ARC. There were two key elements at this stage of developing a business idea: sources of innovation and investors.

- **Sources of innovation (creativity):** Advancements in scientific knowledge can create new products and develop new markets. Often, a new prototype constitutes new knowledge, a source of innovation, which can be transformed into a marketable product or service yielding monopolistic rents (Drucker, 1985). The main goal of the management team of ARC for both spin-offs was to be innovative while maximizing monopolistic rents.

- **Investors (resources):** Ideas must be transformed into reality. ARC's spin-off projects were presented to venture capitalists invited by the parent firm AlphaGraph. In order to reach the market, an innovative project needs funds, expertise, and access to networks provided by venture capitalists. AlphaGraph provided ARC with its pool of venture capitalists to launch both spin off projects.

To Achieve the Approval from the Board of Directors (BoD)

Corporate governance rules were strictly enforced within ARC. The management team of ARC could not start-up both spin-off projects without the consent of the board of directors. Before a decision was reached, a complete and detailed business plan had to be submitted to the board.

To Select the Entrepreneur of the New Company

Each projects demanded a leader, an entrepreneur. ARC considered two alternatives for its spin-off ventures: (1) to select an internal current researcher who knew the technology very well but not the market (this option was chosen for Spin1), or (2) to look for an external professional who was not completely familiar with the technology but knew well the market (this option was chosen for Spin2).

To Analyze the Viability of the New Company

ARC consulted the viability of both spin-off projects with directors of incubators which belonged to AlphaGraph and with experts from local Economic Development Agencies. Later, a project viability report was completed and submitted to the Board.

To Seek Financial Support

The responsibility of each spin-off project presented an additional report explaining the funds needed for the project and the sources for obtaining the funds. An estimated cash-flow trend for the initial 3-4 years was also submitted.

To Select Partners

ARC leaded the board of directors and management team of its spin-offs. ARC's policy was to invest at least 25% in the equity of each spin-off. The owner-entrepreneur of each spin-off was also a partner and other members of AlphaGraph or BetaCom were welcome to become partners of ARC's spin offs. In the case of Spin1, ARC acted as a venture capitalist investing 90% of the equity, whereas the researcher-manager owned the remaining 10%. The partners of Spin2 were ARC, AlphaGraph, a company from the BetaCom group, and an Asian company.

To Generate an Action Plan

After receiving the approval for the project from the board, each spin-off leader started to implement their respective action plans such as the proposal and nomination of the board and key managers for each spin-off, the organization of the internal structure, culture, and key resources, and the supervision of business performance.

To Socialize the Spin-Off Project

ARC announced the creation of two spin-offs in a well known Innovation and Business Creation Award ceremony organized by local government institutions.

To Evaluate Business Performance and to Design Corrective Actions

The board of each spin-off evaluates the performance of the managers. ARC is an active and interested member of the board of its spin-offs. Although ARC develops spin-offs to capture new customers, the company is aware of the strategic relevance of its research mission. If the generation of more spin-offs increments the D of development at the expense of the R of research, a new balance is called for, which may lead to the divestiture of the spin-off firms.

Current Challenges for ARC

Even though ARC went through a successful start-up process, largely due to the constant support received from its parent firms AlphaGraph and BetaCom, there were important challenges that required a special attention from ARC's governing and management bodies. An outline of relevant issues follows:

- ARC needed to consider how to retain key human capital. Wages in the local economy were higher than the average wage in Spain. ARC trained PhD students while they worked in the organization. The ARC management team knew that the research staff of ARC could leave the company once they finished the doctorate program (i.e., they would demand a higher wage as doctors) and this could lead to a leakage of knowledge towards other firms or competitors.
- ARC was involved simultaneously in the start-up of two spin-offs. Clearly, ARC was growing internally, but also externally through these two new ventures. To ensure the survival of two new ventures at the same time is a difficult challenge. The complexity of this process added to ARC's own growth could endanger ARC's overall performance.
- In recent years, ARC was attending to an increasing number of orders from private firms. In fact, revenues from private companies increased substantially

since inception, as applied research gained significance within the organization. This *consultancy-oriented* activity caused an internal conflict since management still wanted the researchers to continue contributing to the advancement of science (i.e., publications in top scientific journals) and to developing fresh innovative ideas without being at the mercy of applied research orders from private firms.

- Another challenge for ARC was diversification. ARC was a member of international and local research networks where distinct areas of knowledge were explored. There were also domains in the local economy which demanded technological advancements, such as linguistics info-engineering. Should ARC attempt to respond to these interesting opportunities by exploring new computer graphic applications to new disciplines considering the current growth process in which the company was involved?

- ARC grew in size from 3 employees to more than 40 employees in 5 years. One of the management team members was concerned with the internal structure of the organization. Should ARC change its current horizontal structure towards a more complex hierarchical matrix structure? Would this change affect ARC's corporate values (i.e., change from an egalitarian involvement of employees in the company to a more submissive involvement)?

References

Contractor, Farok J., Kim, C.-S., & Beldona, S. (2002). Interfirm learning in alliance and technology networks: An empirical study in the global pharmaceutical and chemical industries. In F.J. Contractor & P. Lorange (Eds.), *Cooperative strategies and alliances* (pp. 493-516). Oxford, UK: Elsevier Science.

Culpan, R. (1993). Multinational competition and cooperation: Theory and practice. In R. Culpan (Ed.), *Multinational strategic alliances* (pp. 13-32). Binghamton, NY: The Haworth Press.

Culpan, R., & Kostelac, Jr., E.A. (1993). Cross-national corporate partnerships: Trends in alliance formation. In R. Culpan (Ed.), *Multinational strategic alliances* (pp. 103-122). Binghamton, NY: The Haworth Press.

De la Vega, I., Coduras, A., Justo, R., Cruz, C., & Nogueira, M.P. (2005). *Global entrepreneurship monitor: Informe ejecutivo GEM España*. Madrid: Instituto de Empresa.

Drucker, P.F. (1985). *Innovation and entrepreneurship: Practices and principles*. New York: Harper & Row.

Elfring, T., & Hulsink, W. (2001). Fighting for survival and legitimacy: Growth trajectories of high technology firms in the Netherlands. In W. During, R. Oakey, & S. Kauser (Eds.), *New technology based firms in the new millennium* (pp. 4-25). Oxford, UK: Elsevier Science.

ENTER (2006). *Digiworld España (Report 2006)*. Madrid, Spain: ENTER – IDATE Foundation.

European Information Technology Observatory Report (2006). Frankfurt, Germany: European Information Technology Observatory (EITO) - European Economic Interest Grouping (EEIG).

Gugler, P., & Dunning, J.H. (1993). Technology-based cross-border alliances. In R. Culpan, (Ed.), *Multinational strategic alliances* (pp. 123-166). Binghamton, NY: The Haworth Press.

Guth, W.D., & Ginsberg, A. (1990). Corporate entrepreneurship. *Strategic Management Journal, 11*(4), 5-15.

Hisrich, R.D., & Peters, M.P. (2002). *Entrepreneurship* (5th ed.). New York: McGraw-Hill/Irwin.

Lorange, P., & Roos, J. (1994). Interpreneurship: Technology acquisition and partnering. In M.J.C. Martin (Ed.), *Managing innovation and entrepreneurship in technology-based firms* (pp. 361-376). New York: John Wiley & Sons.

Martínez Barea, J. (2003). El proceso de creación de EIBTs: Ciclo vital y apoyos al desarrollo y crecimiento. In S.E. Katrin (Ed.), *La creación de empresas de base tecnológica: Una experiencia práctica* (pp. 61-64). Madrid, Spain: CEIN.

Morales, L., & Peña, I. (2003). Dinamismo de nuevas empresas y clusters naturales: Evidencia de la CAPV, 1993-1999. *Ekonomiaz, Revista Vasca de Economía, 53*(1), 160-183.

Mourdoukoutas, P., & Papadimitriou, S. (1998). Do Japanese companies have a competitive strategy? *European Business Review, 98*(4), 227-234.

Osland, G.E., & Yaprak, A. (1993). Process model on the formation of multinational strategic alliances. In R. Culpan (Ed.), *Multinational strategic alliances* (pp. 81-102). Binghamton, NY: The Haworth Press.

Oxley, J.E. (1999). *Governance of international strategic alliances: Technology and transaction costs*. Amsterdam: Overseas Publishers Association.

Porter, M.E. (2003). Cúmulos y competencia: Nuevos objetivos para empresas, Estados e instituciones. In M.E. Porter (Ed.), *Ser competitivo: Nuevas aportaciones y conclusiones* (pp. 203-288). Barcelona, Spain: Ediciones Deusto.

Richter, F.-J. (2000). *Strategic networks: The art of Japanese interfirm cooperation*. Binghamton, NY: The Haworth Press.

Richter, F.-J., & Teramoto, Y. (1995). Interpreneurship: A new management concept from Japan [Special issue]. *Management International Review, 35*(2), 95-104.

Wheelen, T.L., & Hunger, D.J. (2004). *Strategy management and business policy* (9th ed.). Upper Saddle River, NJ: Pearson Prentice-Hall.

Wickham, P.A. (2001). *Strategic entrepreneurship: A decision-making approach to new venture creation and management* (2nd ed.). Harlow, UK: Pearson Prentice-Hall.

Young, R.C., Francis, J.D., & Young, C.H. (1993). Innovation, high-technology use, and flexibility in small manufacturing firms. *Growth and Change, 24*(1), 67-86.

Appendix: Applied Research Areas of ARC

ARC works in applied research in the following five application areas:

Digital TV and Interactive Services

The Digital TV area of ARC explores the possibilities offered by the synergies between Digital TV and Computer Graphics. Currently, ARC is developing interactive applications and services for TV in order to bring the Information Society to a wider spectrum of citizens not necessarily familiar with PC's.

Medical Applications and ICTS for Health Care

The Medical Applications area of ARC specializes in the development of medical systems based on last generation technologies. Main research areas include 2D/3D medical image analysis (image processing, segmentation, registration, etc.), clinical information management (transmission, standards, interfaces), visualization (virtual and augmented reality), tracking, and computer vision systems. These technologies are used for the development of tools for diagnostic and surgery assistance, telemedicine, and patient tracking systems.

Virtual Reconstruction of Archaeological-Historical GIS and Tourism

The aim of this area is to support the industry of tourism and to promote both archaeological and heritage special interest sites, as well as the promotion of the GIS systems to represent, analyze, and manage geographical information data by the means of advanced computer graphics techniques (augmented reality and virtual reality), visual interaction, and communication.

Edutainment and Graphical Conversational Interfaces

This area focuses on the fields of education and leisure through the possibilities of audiovisual technologies and advanced user interfaces. Multimedia technologies, conversational 3D avatars in real time, virtual environments, and e-learning are some of the main research lines in this area.

Multimedia and Industrial Applications

ARC brings (via R&D projects) the possibility to use advanced computer graphics technologies to different sectors of the industry and the society (for example, virtual and augmented reality, image and 3D graphics processing, digital security, and multimedia interaction technologies).

Source: ARC

Endnotes

[1]   See http://www.europa.eu/rapid/pressReleasesAction.do?reference=IP/06/1319

[2]   An extensive description of applied research areas is included in the Appendix.

[3]   To preserve anonymity, we have substituted names for the management team members.

Chapter XIII

Hatching Tech Companies for a Living:
Trade Secrets We Don't Mind Telling

Paulo Rupino da Cunha, Universidade de Coimbra, Portugal

Paulo Santos, IPN-Incubadora, Portugal

Abstract

We describe a proven process to foster the creation of technology-based services, products, and companies. We start by explaining how various stakeholders—a university, an innovation and technology transfer institute, and private and public client organizations—acting in concert, create multiple opportunities for the application of technology to real-world problems, and how some of those projects originate spin-offs. We then present a real-life example of one such company that develops software for mobile applications. It spun-off from a project with a big cellular phone service provider in 2001, incubated for three years at the institute, and moved out in 2004. Its revenues continue to grow at a rate of 30% each year. We draw on our experience in assisting the creation of 70 technology-based start-ups to provide practical recommendations and point out key success factors.

Background

We share our 15 year old experience in the systematic identification and transformation of innovative technology-based ideas into new products, new services, and also new companies. We provide practical recommendations and point out key success factors when creating high-technology start-ups.

Our instrument is an innovation institute, positioned in Michael Porter's value chain (Porter, 1985), between upstream universities and downstream private companies and public institutions. Its model is acknowledged as very effective by national policy makers and by international partners. We describe its internal organization and how it relates to the other stakeholders. We further illustrate how it works by presenting the case of one of its spin-offs.

In the next section we describe how the institute came to be and how it has worked in a sustainable way since 1991. We describe the context in which new ideas can flourish and become innovative services, products, or companies. We then move on to the case of one of its spin-offs—a software development company working in the area of mobile business—to provide additional context to understand the recommendations and critical success factors presented in the last section.

Setting the Stage

Founded in the late 13th century, in 1290, our university is one of the oldest in Europe. Its population of around 22,000 students is spread throughout eight schools, 55 undergrad courses, and about 500 graduation programs, including post-grad courses, MBAs, MScs and PhDs.

In 1991, the Science and Technology School championed the creation of the innovation and technology transfer institute. The aim was to leverage the scientific knowledge held by the University in helping existing companies become more innovative, and in fostering the creation of new ones that made use of technologies that otherwise would not have been commercially exploited. The Institute was designed as a non-profit association, engaging other associates such as the city council, regional and national industrial and entrepreneurial associations, the national office for support of small- and medium-sized enterprises (SME), other higher-education schools and research labs, the national employment agency, knowledge-promotion and cooperation foundations, banks, and private companies.

The governance structure consists of a board of directors and a general assembly. Two directors—the president and vice president—are professors appointed by the University and have executive management responsibilities. The other three board positions are taken, in turn, by representatives of the other associates. Their diversity is leveraged to assemble a team with mixed profiles. Terms last for three years.

The mission of the institute—see full text in Table 1—is to act as an interface between the university and private and public organizations, fostering innovation and entrepreneurship. A distinctive characteristic is that, besides the usual business incubator, the model also includes laboratories for applied research and development in key areas, putting advanced know-how to the service of industry clients with complex problems, requiring innovative solutions.

Some international, national, and regional facts help understand the context in which the institute was created. The World Wide Web did not exist. It would only become popular two years later, in 1993, with the release of the graphical Mosaic Web browser (Wikipedia, 2006). The top Intel processor was the i486. Portugal had joined the European Union (then called European Economic Community) only 5 years earlier, in 1986. The first Portuguese cellular phone company had just been founded but network technology at the time was still analogue. The digital GSM network (Global System for Mobile Communications) would only go in operation in October 1992. The industry in our region produced ceramics, cookies, beer, photographic equipment, and textiles. The main driving force of our city was the University.

By the end of 1994 the institute's twin buildings in the University campus were ready and equipped. One of them houses the research and development (R&D) laboratories and the other the incubator. The initial investment was supported by European Union funds and one-time contribution of associates, the value being proportional to the size of their participation.

Table 1. Mission of the innovation institute

> *To leverage a strong university/enterprise relationship for the promotion of innovation, rigor, quality and entrepreneurship in private and public organizations, by acting in three complementary areas:*
> - *Research and technological development, consulting, and advanced services;*
> - *Business and ideas incubation;*
> - *Highly specialized training and promotion of science and technology.*

Figure 1. Main interactions within innovation institute and with its environment

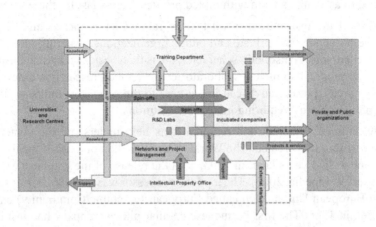

No regular maintenance grants or subsidies are received from local or central government to ensure the institute's sustainability. Everyday funding comes from services provided to customers and from national and European projects, to which the institute must apply under the same fierce competition as any other institution.

Figure 1 is a simplified representation of the current operational model of the innovation and technology transfer institute, illustrating the main interactions between its units and with its environment.

On the left side of Figure 1 we see universities and research centers, providing knowledge and technology, and on the right side we see client private and public organizations, seeking innovative services or custom products. In the following sections we describe the major units that make up the innovation institute and how they act together to satisfy those demands.

R&D Laboratories

The R&D labs are a cornerstone of the model. They represent an extension of their respective university departments or research centers—see current labs in Table 2. They provide an effective interface for industrial clients to leverage academic know-how in solving complex problems. This can involve custom research and development of a product or technology, laboratory analysis or diagnostics, consulting, or auditing.

The Networks and Project Management office acts as the interface to other university departments or research centers not physically installed at the innovation institute. It also actively monitors national and European programs for applied research and innovation.

The relationships with client organizations follow a typical business-to-business protocol. When approached with a specific problem, the innovation institute answers with a project proposal stating costs and deadlines, just like a conventional company would do. We found this to be an important means to overcome the traditional wariness of the industry in engaging academics in solving concrete problems with demanding time constrains.

Remaining administrative procedures, logistics, and staff structure are also light and project-oriented. Minimal core personnel keep the organization running and respond to less intensive demands. For larger projects, a dedicated team is assembled from a pool of experts in the required areas from among university researchers and professionals (frequently alumni from the university). Students—BSc, MSc, or PhD—are also involved under the supervision of senior staff. Besides receiving a stipend, undergrads have the opportunity to enrich their training with real-world experience, while grad students frequently find cases to study or apply the theories they are exploring. When a project is concluded, the various team elements usually return to their original duties.

Occasionally, however, after a project or a series of projects in the same area, a business opportunity to apply the know-how and technologies previously mastered may emerge. At this point, the team is encouraged by the innovation institute to create a spin-off company. For the following three years, the start-up enjoys favorable conditions to grow in the incubator.

We should note that this process, although desirable, takes its toll on the labs. First, a number of highly skilled people leave to pursue their own endeavors, thus reducing the readiness to respond to new customer demands. Second, investment must be made in training new staff and reassigning duties. Third, the labs' annual revenue is negatively affected, since the projects for which the know-how is more mature are usually the most profitable, due to a lesser need for investment in research, learning, and development.

Although technology transfer agreements with the spin-offs provide some compensation to the labs, the active promotion of new companies is essentially driven by the overarching mission of the institute.

Table 2. Labs currently installed at the innovation institute's facilities

Laboratory	Description
Informatics	Provides consulting, auditing, and custom R&D in information and communication technologies (such as information systems design, networks, or mobile computing).
Automation and Systems	Provides consulting, auditing, and custom R&D in electronics and automation (such as robotization, energy management, vision, instrumentation, and wireless technologies).
Materials	Provides consulting, auditing, and custom R&D in materials characterization and evaluation (such as failure analysis of mechanical components, materials surface modification, powder injection moulding of metallic and ceramic materials).
Pharmaceutical	Provides technical and scientific consulting in pharmacology, pharmaceutical chemistry, pharmaceutical technology and pharmacognosy.
Geotechnical	Provides consulting and specialized services in geotechnics and infrastructure foundations (such as engineering geology, inspection and control, tests, assistance with European Community certifications).
Electroanalysis and Corrosion	Performs analysis of water and effluents for toxic metals, tests of electrochemical corrosion of metallic materials, and identifies and develops appropriate coatings for metals and metallic alloys.

Business Incubator

The incubator at our facilities started its activity in 1996. By the end of that year it was housing six companies. The number rose steadily until maximum capacity was reached in 2001. See Figure 2.

Some very successful incubated companies (mainly academic spin-offs) induced an entrepreneurial attitude and a sense of confidence that is particularly evident in the evolution of the number spin-offs vs. start-ups originating in external applications. Although those high-profile cases initially benefited from the prestige of the university and of the innovation institute, they eventually contributed to that reputation by doing so well. As a consequence, the attraction of the incubator also increased.

Figure 2. Evolution of the number of companies in the incubator

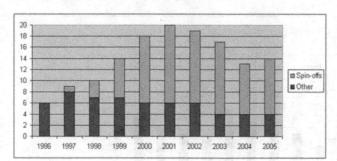

The reduction in the number of companies from 2002 onward is due solely to space constrains. As laboratories also needed to expand, a delicate balance of real-estate had to be found. We managed to avoid an even more dramatic impact on the number of incubatees by launching the virtual incubation program, suited for companies at a very early stage that still don't need physical installations other than meeting rooms to occasionally convene with customers. At a significantly lower fee, virtual incubation provides them with all the usual services and benefits except physical space. Meanwhile, a new building for the incubator is expected to be finished by the end of 2006. Using a modular design, it will house up to 50 companies, depending on the area they need. Since there are several companies on a waiting list, it is expected that the occupation will start at 50% as soon as the new building becomes operational.

The chart in Figure 3 shows the distribution of companies by sector, since the incubator started its activities. Regardless of their area, all start-ups are technology-based.

So far, 70 new companies were created. Forty-one of them already concluded their incubation periods and left for autonomous facilities. An additional 13 are physically installed at the incubator and 16 enrolled in the virtual incubation program. Twenty-eight companies work in the area of information technology and communications. Seventeen of these were spin-offs.

Nineteen additional start-ups have been formally created and are waiting for the new building to be completed. The aggregated turnover of all these companies is approximately 30 million Euros. It is estimated that some 400 specialized jobs for BScs, MScs, and PhDs have been generated.

The success rate, measured in terms of how many incubated companies keep operating, is about 80%, that is, 56 out of the 70 that were created. Slowly, the new companies have been changing the type of industry in our region. The traditional companies, some in serious difficulties due to their obsolete business models, have been ceding to these new high tech ventures.

Figure 3. Distribution of companies by area of activity

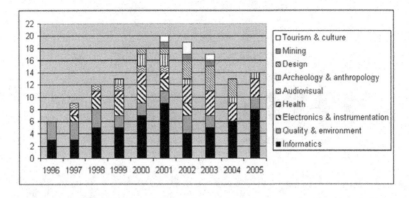

Table 3. Top mistakes made by new entrepreneurs

Inadequate market assessment
Excessive optimism
Shallow assessment of business potential
Incorrect planning of necessary investment
Conditioning investments to available co-funding by national or European framework programmes
Poor anticipation of potential obstacles
Low commitment: insufficient time dedicated to the business
Excessive number of partners and poor expectation management

The favorable conditions provided by the incubator are decisive for the healthy growth of the start-ups. Assistance begins immediately at the evaluation phase. A rigorous scrutiny of the applications is crucial. Some ideas prove too fragile and are abandoned early, saving effort, frustration, and money. Table 3 lists the top mistakes we encounter the most when dealing with new entrepreneurs.

Even the more solid ideas frequently need additional work (with our team) to evolve to a sound business plan. This is a key factor since most entrepreneurs possess strong technical expertise in their area but lack the necessary knowledge on financial issues and regulations involved in creating and running a company.

If needed, our team can also advise on funding opportunities: arrange meetings with venture capital, assist negotiations with banks, or help with applications to national or European financing programs. Legal counselling is available on generic issues and on intellectual property protection.

Providing start-ups with high-quality office space at competitive prices is another key factor. Incubation modules possess a complete communications infrastructure for phone, fax, local area network, and Internet access. Web sites can be hosted at the innovation institute's servers. Additionally, the start-ups also benefit from the use of common infrastructures, such as meeting rooms and auditorium, from administrative support, surveillance, security, cleaning, and other basic services. The location on the university campus is central and accessibility is good.

Access to knowledge networks and experts is much facilitated, thanks to the close links with the university and with international innovation organizations.

Courses on technical and management subjects, such as negotiation, entrepreneurship, innovation management, human resources management, labor regulation, project management, fiscal issues, or quality management are available from the training department.

The proximity between start-ups, R&D labs, and university research centers facilitates additional synergies. Partnerships can be easily formed to provide critical mass for bigger projects or additional competencies for interdisciplinary ones. This works for industry clients and for national and European framework programs. The latter provide excellent networking and business opportunities for the start-ups. In fact, the innovation institute is a corner stone of this network, which also involves its associates and graduated firms. The latter are starting to get involved with incubatees, namely in subcontracting, project partnerships, and even financing.

Finally, although it is an intangible factor, it is worth mentioning that being based at the incubator, the start-ups benefit from the prestige of the innovation institute and of the university in the relations with their potential customers.

In the near future, a technological park will be built in the vicinity of the innovation institute, providing real-estate for companies to install their permanent facilities.

Training Department

The training department leverages the various sources of knowledge represented in Figure 1 to build a rich portfolio of complementary knowledge areas and tutor profiles. Presently, it addresses several needs:

- Those of individual professionals seeking updates in areas that appeared or significantly evolved since their graduation
- Those of companies seeking custom training packages for their staff
- Those of industry seeking highly specialized technicians
- Those of novel, technically-oriented entrepreneurs in areas outside their expertise, such as management, accounting, and negotiation
- Those of graduates whose original training is in short demand by the market, seeking new qualifications
- Those of academics or industrialists holding innovative technologies, products, or processes seeking information on intellectual property protection

The offer thus consists of courses of variable duration, workshops, and seminars. Additionally, the training department is engaged in the promotion of science and technology.

Intellectual Property Office

The Intellectual Property Office is part of a national network of 20 offices, partially supported by public funding, installed in selected organizations throughout the country. Its mission is to explain and promote the use of intellectual property protection mechanisms, namely in those environments where significant innovation is more prone to happen: universities and tech-based companies. It does so by means of individual counselling regarding specific situations and by organizing seminars, workshops, and conferences.

The office is also equipped to help individuals or institutions throughout the complex procedures of patent claims or other forms of protection. Additionally, it can prepare applications to public funding programs designed to help cover the costs of intellectual property protection.

International Network

Although not represented in Figure 1, the institute has several international partners in the various areas in which it operates, namely:

- The European Association of Research and Technology Organizations (EARTO). EARTO is the trade association of Europe's specialized research and technology organizations. Its members make a major contribution to strengthening Europe's economic performance by supporting product and process innovation in all branches of industry and services, thereby raising the international competitiveness of European firms (EARTO, 2006).

- The European Association for the Transfer of Technologies, Innovation, and Industrial Information (TII). TII is an independent association of technology transfer and innovation support professionals. It acts as a hub for members to share professional experience and good practice, to facilitate business opportunities, and to get support in their technology transfer and innovation assignments. TII organizes conferences and training events, pursues specialist activities through dedicated sub-groups, and offers high added value Web-based tools. TII brings together innovation and technology consultants, technology brokers and intellectual asset advisors, university and research center transfer offices, regional development agencies and chambers of commerce, science parks, innovation centers and incubators, contract research organizations and engineering consultants, government ministries and agencies, and sectoral professional organizations (TII, 2006).

- The Incubator Forum. The Incubator Forum is a pan-European network of professional managers of technology incubators and incubators linked to research institutes and universities, supported by the Enterprise Directorate General of the European Commission as part of its Gate2Growth initiative (IF, 2006).

- ProTon Europe. The pan-European network of Technology Transfer Offices of Public Research Organizations (ProTon). The purpose of ProTon Europe is to support the professional development of Knowledge Transfer Offices across Europe through networking, the exchange of good practice, staff exchanges, and the delivery of appropriate training (ProTon, 2006). The innovation institute's intellectual property office is particularly involved in ProTon's work on intellectual property rights (IPR).

To further clarify the synergies in the model for innovation and entrepreneurship we have just presented, in the following section we will describe in detail how a spin-off company that develops software for mobile applications originated from the activity of one of the R&D laboratories, incubated for three years, and then moved to autonomous installations in the region where it continues to thrive.

Case Description

The stage was set in 1997. The future CEO, a professor of informatics engineering at the university upstream from the innovation institute, was asked by a research partner—a renowned multi-national corporation—to recommend a contractor for custom software development in the telecommunications area. The corporation was briefed on the relationship between the University and the innovation institute, how this type of work fitted its mission, and on the possibility of setting up a dedicated team to do the job under the leadership of the professor. The corporation found the arrangement attractive and the software outsourcing project was initiated.

The relationship progressed well and, by 1999, there were around 30 programmers working on the project. Several advantages of being based at the institute played a decisive role, namely the initial credibility provided by a close relationship with the University and the flexible logistics and administrative procedures that eased lab space allocation and hiring of team members. On the other hand, during this period, there was the opportunity to refine the software development practices in complex, real-world projects and build a knowledgeable and cohesive team. Finally, after deducting a project overhead charged by the institute, the leader was free to manage the remaining positive cash flow. Part of it was invested in the exploration of mobile phone technologies that were starting to appear promising.

In fact, by 1999, there was a growing interest from cellular phone operators in going beyond the traditional voice market into data-based services. News alerts, e-mail access, weather forecast, stock information, and games, among other services, were calling for the mastery of technologies such as the short message service (SMS)—enabling small texts to be sent and received by mobile handsets—and wireless application protocol (WAP)—providing a more interactive, Web browsing-like experience suited to the limitations of small portable devices.

As a proof of concept, the team decided to create WAP versions of the Internet portals of the two cellular phone companies operating in Portugal at the time. Both of them showed interest in the demonstrations, one of them being quick to invite the innovation institute to its exhibition stand at a major telecom expo at the time. A business relation eventually developed as the telecom company gradually contracted the development of various innovative services based on mobile technologies for its business portfolio. The original software development group was divided in two. Team 1 continued the software outsourcing project for the multinational corporation, while Team 2 was dedicated exclusively to the cellular phone operator until 2001. The credibility lent by the innovation institute and the University to the small team working for the cellular operator was crucial during the first projects, as other contractors—established Portuguese and multinational companies—represented fierce competition.

From Project to Company

Year 2001 was a turning point. By then, the team had become engaged in an increasing number of very important projects for the cellular phone operator. In this scenario, the once advantageous organization as a flexible group hosted by a non-profit institution was now seen as a handicap by the operator. This level of involvement required a more permanent structure committed to provide those services. The innovation institute had a broader mission and a governance model where the board of directors was appointed every 3 years. The cellular phone operator had concerns that a future management team did not see the collaboration as important, so it expressed the desire that the software development group become an autonomous company. This represented no problem for the innovation institute. In fact, it was consistent with its mission. The new start-up was created in March of 2001. The initial staff included the eight programmers in Team 2, the professor, and three colleagues from the Informatics Engineering Department he had invited as business partners. All partners were either PhD or PhD students in their mid-30s. The programmers were in their 20s, all BScs. It is important to note that this academic degree in Portugal took 5 years, thus being the equivalent to a MSc in most countries.

The favorable conditions under which the company was created are worthy of notice. Much of the investment in building the know-how had already been done while it was managed as a project in the R&D lab. When it spun-off, it already had an important customer and a contract backlog. It was profitable on day one. This fact enabled this limited liability firm to start without the help of venture capitalists or business angels. The initial capital was kept at 5000€, the legal minimum.

The new entrepreneurs decided to install the company in the innovation institute's incubator to leverage the various benefits previously described. Credibility was once again an issue. Customers and other stakeholders valued the fact that the young company was starting-up in a reputable and innovative environment. Physical proximity with the university was also an important factor, as it enabled the involvement of students in part-time jobs or in graduation projects, thus contributing to a more effective selection of future staff.

In spite of the close relation with the cellular phone operator and of its role in the creation of the company, there were no exclusive dedication requirements, so new clients were sought. Banks were becoming interested in the potential of SMS technology as a means to provide their clients with simple, mobile, self-service access to most common operations such as, for example, checking account balance, transferring money between accounts or ordering checks. Two financial institutions contracted this type of systems. SMS-based solutions were also developed for media companies wishing to add interactivity to TV programs for voting, opinion pooling, or contests. Tracking systems were conceived for companies that needed to distribute medical supplies.

Meanwhile, the company continued to explore new technologies such as wireless networks (Wi-Fi), Bluetooth, radio frequency identification (RFID), and cellular-based location, and broadened the range of mobile devices for which it developed software to include new generation handsets and personal digital assistants (PDAs) using the most popular operating systems: Palm OS, Pocket PC, and Symbian. The multimedia messaging service (MMS) —an evolution of SMS supporting pictures, animation, sound and rich text—together with video streaming technology, opened up new possibilities for content industries: sales of electronic postcards, phone ring tones, downloadable JAVA games, and sports alerts with pictures or video clips of highlights.

This description illustrates the key orientation of the company: to master mobile-related technologies, to provide software solutions to cellular operators or other companies wishing to have mobile data services, or to integrate enterprise applications with mobile devices. It is not a product-based company selling a specific item but rather a company selling expertise in a specific area.

Internationalization

Although the company aimed for international markets immediately after its creation, its approach changed as time progressed. Initially, Europe was the preferred target, due to geographical proximity. Although intense competition was felt, the company managed to get a contract with a big Spanish phone operator. For continued relations, however, the customer called for the installation of a local office across the street, where other companies were already present. The operator was used to discussing business opportunities with those technological partners immediately as they presented themselves. Having to arrange meetings with a company located a few hours away was considered unappealing. However, at start-up, the company was not able to open offices in other countries, so further business was not pursued.

In the second phase of its internationalization, the company looked at markets with a technological gap. These included Africa, Brazil and, strange as it may seem, the United States. In fact, by 2002, the U.S. mobile market was essentially voice-based. The sophisticated data-based services that had become commonplace in Europe, were virtually non-existent in the U.S. Keeping in mind what it learned with the European experience, this time the company looked for local partners to ensure greater proximity with end customers. Africa and Brazil proved unattractive due to either intrinsic characteristics of the markets or ineffective relations with the local partners. The approach to the U.S. resulted better with the help of a Canadian partner, although profit margins were naturally reduced.

In its third and current phase of internationalization, the company is turning back to its customer number one. The cellular phone operator is part of a large multinational group that, in this period, had undergone a worldwide restructuring. New mobile services are now planned centrally and then deployed in the various countries. The good track record the start-up had with the Portuguese branch paved the way for it to be involved in this global-scale initiative.

Although this option embodies the risk of strong dependence on one customer, this is weighed against the previous experiences of dispersing commercial efforts, dealing with local partners, or having to open offices worldwide. Expenditure on those activities decreased and margins increased once more.

Financial Data and Management Style

The company exhibits an interesting financial profile, partly due to the way it spun-off of a project. It has been profitable since day one, unlike many competitor start-ups supported by venture capital. In its first year of operation the revenues reached 320.000€. The growth rate of total revenues is roughly 30% a year. It did not suffer the effects of the burst of the ".com" bubble that affected so many technology based start-ups. Profits are not divided by the partners but rather reinvested in research and development activities and distributed by the staff as productivity prizes. There is also investment in technical and non-technical training, such as, for example, finance, behavioral, human resources management, and quality management. This hints at management style and organizational culture. The CEO and his 20 staff are young, creative, ambitious, proactive, and flexible. Team building activities are frequently organized. Relations are close, although the current organizational structure is not scalable. The company is organized in five main departments: Administration, Software Team, Quality Assurance, Technical Maintenance, and R&D Lab. Curiously, there is no marketing and sales department. The company favors a lower profile and word-of-mouth. There are no plans for growing in size, only in Earnings Before Interest Depreciation and Tax (EBIDT).

There is a heavy investment in R&D—around 30% of the profits—that, besides fitting the enquiring nature of the company and its mission, is also a way to deal with intellectual property. Although the company has the support of the innovation institute to deal with these issues, namely in filling patent claims, those processes are expensive and can become very complex if it comes to litigation. By constantly innovating, the company tries to keep one step ahead of potential contenders.

Figure 4 illustrates the company's innovation process.

New ideas are proposed using an existing template. A strengths, weaknesses, opportunities, and threats (SWOT) analysis is performed. Market potential is assessed.

Figure 4. Company's innovation process

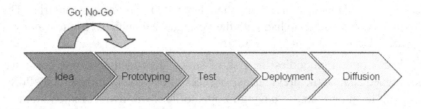

Complexity, investment, and return-on-investment are analysed. The Go/No-Go decision is taken in a session where a "proponent" (in charge of promoting the idea) and a "devil's advocate" (in charge of challenging it) try to convince a "CEO."

Future Outlook

The company left the incubator in 2004, after the regular three years, but maintained the usual close ties with the institute. It is important to note that after this period the advantages of being based at an incubator turn into hindrance, as clients start to wonder why the company is not completely autonomous yet.

As the time arrives to upgrade installations once again, the start-up looks forward to the installation of the technological park in the vicinity of the innovation institute, to leverage once more the advantages of physical proximity.

Completing the set-up of a quality management system and leader succession are the two additional challenges presently facing the company.

Quality management of products, services, and business processes is, today, a key issue in the success of most companies operating in global contexts (Cunha & Figueiredo, 2005). In fact, holding a quality certification, such as established by ISO 9001:2000 standard (ISO, 2004), is becoming a compulsory requirement for companies to play in selected markets, even as a contractor. The company initiated the project for setting up an ISO 9001:2000 quality management system in response to this state of affairs, after experiencing dismissal of a proposal merely on the grounds of not being certified. However, the staff worked closely on the project with the external consultant to avoid an excessive bureaucratization that could constrain the organization's agility, as it so often happens (Seddon, 1997). Auditing by a certification authority is expected soon.

The second challenge the company faces regards the succession of the CEO. From the onset, it was never the intention of the professor to leave the university. As he plans his return to more active academic duties, the company must now increase its autonomy from its creator.

Current Challenges

We described our process for fostering technology-based ideas and turning them into innovative products, services, and companies. Seventy companies have been created since 1996. The success rate, measured in terms of how many start-ups survive, is about 80%. A real-life account of one of those companies was provided.

The basis of our approach is an innovation institute acting as an interface between universities and private and public clients. It is organized into three areas that complement and reinforce each other: R&D laboratories capable of applying state-of-the-art university know-how to solve complex problems posed by clients, a business incubator where tech-based ideas benefit from favorable conditions to start up and grow, and a training department that serves outside customers and also addresses internal needs.

Currently, the most pressing challenge for the institution is the increase of office space to accommodate various start-ups presently on a waiting list and to expand the incubation activity. The new building is in its final construction phase and will be inaugurated soon.

A second challenge is the swift installation of the technological park in the vicinity of the innovation institute, so that the increasing number of companies graduated from the incubator no longer have to disperse.

Finally, it will be important for the labs to increase their level of services to the private and public sectors so as to further strengthen the institution.

References

Cunha, P.R., & Figueiredo, A.D. (2005). *Quality management systems and information systems: Getting more than the sum of the parts.* Paper presented at the Americas Conference on Information Systems, Omaha, NB.

EARTO (2006). Retrieved May 12, 2007, from http://www.earto.org/

IF (2006). Retrieved May 12, 2007, from http://www.thematicnetwork.com/Welcome/TN_UserWelcome.aspx?GroupID=2&CMSContentID=0

ISO (2004). Selection and use of the ISO 9000:2000 family of standards. Retrieved May 12, 2007, from http://www.iso.ch/iso/en/iso9000-14000/understand/selection_use/selection_use.html

Porter, M.E. (1985). Competitive advantage: Creating and sustaining superior performance. New York: The Free Press.

ProTon (2006). Retrieved May 12, 2007, from http://protoneurope.org/

Seddon, J. (1997). In pursuit of quality: The case against ISO 9000. Ireland: Oak Tree Press.

TII (2006). Retrieved May 12, 2007, from http://tii.org/

Wikipedia (2006). World Wide Web. Retrieved May 12, 2007, from http://en.wikipedia.org/wiki/WWW

Chapter XIV

Applying Information Technologies in Innovative Ways:
A Case Study of the Pharmaceutical Distribution Sector

Rosa Mª Muñoz Castellanos, Castilla-La Mancha University, Spain

José Luis Jurado Rincón, Castilla-La Mancha University, Spain

Abstract

The main purpose of this case study is to explain the process of discovering and application of new information technology (IT)-based opportunities developed by a Spanish enterprise whose activity is pharmaceutical distribution. It is a mature firm, which during the course of the last few years has been able to adopt information technologies in innovative ways thanks to the intrapreneurial spirit of its managers. In the analysis of this case study, after presenting the theoretical base, we describe the history of the organization, its main characteristics, and its type of business. Next, we explain the technological utilization of the company and its

managerial implications, paying special attention to its most innovative projects.
We conclude with the description of the main challenges and problems associated
with the achievement of the technological goals adopted by the organization.

Introduction

The main purpose of this case study is to explain the process of discovering and application of new information technology (IT)-based opportunities developed by a Spanish enterprise whose activity is pharmaceutical *distribution*. It is a mature firm, which during the course of the last few years has been able to adopt information technologies in innovative ways thanks to the intrapreneurial spirit of its managers. This rapid and necessary adaptation to the requirements of the new economy is positioning the company within its sector as one of the leaders. The principal method of data collection was through in-depth semistructured interviews of the managing director and IT professionals of the company. The development of the interviews took place during June and July of 2005.

First of all, it is necessary to explain some concepts related to the main issue of this case study. Various definitions of technology and technology management have been proposed. The following ones summarize their main characteristics (Probert, Farrukh, & Phaal, 2004, p.77):

1. *Technology* is broadly defined as the "know-how" of the firm, which emphasizes the applied nature of technological knowledge. While technology is often associated with science and engineering ("hard" technology), the processes which enable its effective application are also important; for example, new product and innovation processes, together with organizational structures and supporting communication/knowledge networks ("soft" aspects of technology).

2. *Technology management* addresses the effective identification, selection, acquisition, development, exploitation, and protection of technologies needed to maintain a market position and business performance in accordance with the company's objectives.

The management of technology includes the following (Durand, 2004, p. 49):

a.   Observation, identification, and assessment of competing technologies to fulfil a certain market need.

b.   Selection of the most relevant technologies from the feasible options to help the firm build a sustainable competitive advantage

c.   Access to the knowledge base required for the technologies selected, be it through internal development, research and development (R&D) partnerships, or acquisitions

d.   Management of research activities, development, feasibility studies, and, more generally, project management

e.   Subsequent implementation and improvement of product and process technologies integrated in the firm's portfolio

f.   Picking out former technologies, progressively or suddenly rendered obsolete by new technologies

As we can see, the management of technology implies several activities, the essence of which is entrepreneurship. Managers should be looking for the former and the most relevant technologies in order to help the firm in the achievement of new opportunities.

The objective of this case study is related to the study of information technology (IT), so we should also present a definition of this concept. Information technology comprises mechanical (i.e., computer-based hardware), human and knowledge technologies, coexisting to greater or lesser degrees in different systems and organizations (Roberts & Grabowski, 1999, p.164).

The European Information Technology Observatory (EITO, 2000, p.443) defines IT as the combined industries of hardware for office machines, data processing equipment, data communications equipment, and software and services.

One of the main purposes of this case study is to analyze the entrepreneurship phenomenon in combination with IT. In this sense, we can reflect upon the definition of entrepreneurship proposed by Davidsson (2005): "is about the processes of discovery and exploitation of opportunities to create future goods and services" (p. 35). Entrepreneurial people are those who establish enterprises, carry on innovations, being a crucial part of any economic system. We should compare this definition with the concept intrapreneurship. Intrapreneurs are defined as "entrepreneurs working within an existing organization" (Aaltio, 2005, p. 284). It emphasizes innovativeness, initiative, risk-taking, and diligence in the same way as entrepreneurship but without ownership of the company. Therefore, as it shall be explained, we can consider that the managers of the company we are studying behave in an intrapreneurial way. They are improving technology continuously through a flow of incremental innovations which construct and shape a technological trajectory in a company that, in this case, is an existing organization.

Innovation is at the heart of the intrapreneurial spirit of this case study. And we should consider innovation in a wider sense, as it "goes beyond the limits of technologies to address the larger scope of change in general. Innovation can indeed deal with the technological side of human activities, thus with product design and manufacturing processes, but it may also deal with the organizational and social side, for example, external interactions with suppliers, clients or partners, internal processes which became routines in the way the firm operates" (Durand, 2004, p. 49).

In this case, IT innovations are incremental (not radical) and interfunctional. They are little improvements or changes that involve new customers, new uses, new distribution and logistics, new product technology, and any combination of these.

In the analysis of this case study, we first present the history of the organization, its main characteristics, and its type of business. Next, we explain the technological utilization of the company and its managerial implications, paying special attention to its most innovative projects. We conclude with the description of the main challenges and problems associated with the achievement of the technological goals adopted by the organization.

Background

The Pharmaceutical Distribution

As already explained, the main activity of the firm we are going to analyze is pharmaceutical distribution. Therefore, it is necessary to present some characteristics of this type of business.

The pharmaceutical industry in Europe is defined as being composed of commercial enterprises engaged in the design, creation, and development of medicines to prevent or cure disease and relieve human suffering (EITO, 2000). Competitive advantage in this sector is determined largely on the basis of three key processes:

- R&D, including fundamental scientific research, development, and testing of new chemical substances
- Marketing
- Distribution

The last point is the main focus of this case study. Distribution can be defined as a variety of processes linked with delivering the pharmaceutical products needed to the right place at the right time (such as express delivery to hospitals or daily shipments to pharmacies).

The traditional channel structure in the pharmaceutical industry is three-tiered, comprising manufacturers, wholesale distributors, and the retail pharmacies. Within this structure, the distributors are well positioned for e-commerce because they would be able to offer a catalogue of more than 100,000 products, whereas the catalogue from retail pharmacies (a limited range of products) and manufacturers (their own products) would be significantly smaller. There is a trend toward concentration in the distribution channel that it is expected to lead to the emergence of a two-tiered structure comprising manufacturers and distributor/retail conglomerates.

The trend toward industry consolidation is illustrated by a number of several large mergers and acquisitions. The smaller players will find it increasingly difficult to be successful in this environment. Another important trend is supply chain restructuring by new means for sharing research, production, clinical trial, and sales information which will eventually result in the emergence of a "virtual pharmacy" that will transfigure the whole of the pharmaceutical industry.

The pharmaceutical industry is already highly automated and mechanized and, in many cases, electronic links also exist between the distributors and the pharmacies and hospitals. Use of the Internet is increasing steadily, both for internal communications within the industry and for communicating with associated sectors such as hospitals, other health care providers, payment authorities, and insurance companies. The impact that e-commerce has in the pharmaceutical sector is heavily influenced by the highly restrictive European regulation.

However, some pharmaceutical distributors in Europe have established private-access Internet sites with pharmacy partners that allow them to differentiate and gain competitive advantage.

The core impact of e-commerce in this sector will be disintermediation and a vast acceleration of the industry's globalization, which is already happening.

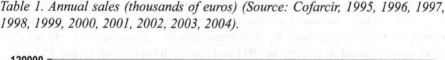

Table 1. Annual sales (thousands of euros) (Source: Cofarcir, 1995, 1996, 1997, 1998, 1999, 2000, 2001, 2002, 2003, 2004).

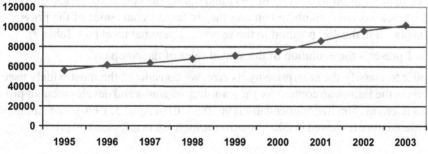

Table 2. Size of the enterprise (Source: Balance sheets of the company, several years)

Year	Number of employees (more than 250, large enterprise)*	Turnover (mill. €) (more than 40, large enterprise)*	Balance-sheet total (mill. €) (more than 27, large enterprise)*
2004	85	105	34
2003	86	102	32
2002	80	97	30

Commission Recommendation (96/280/CE) of April 3, 1996

Another potential focus for e-commerce initiatives is internal organization of a company, that is, the ability of an Internet-based system to deliver the right information to the right user at the right time. The influence on costs and key processes is significant too. We can consider, for example, the case of the procurement process: it is estimated that the cost of making a purchase order may be reduced by up to 80% through the use of efficient e-procurement processes. The largest pharmaceutical distribution companies are in the privileged position to profit the most from this environment.

The Company

Cooperativa Farmacéutica de Ciudad Real (COFARCIR) is a Spanish cooperative located in Ciudad Real, Spain, whose business is the acquisition and distribution of the pharmaceutical specialities for exclusive use by its partners (the members of the cooperative society), and, in general terms, every product related to the practice of the pharmaceutical profession.

The cooperatives can be classified in different ways depending on the chosen criteria. In this case, it is a *singular cooperative* and, considering the activity of its partners, we can class it as a *customers' cooperative* (they are associated in order to equip themselves with products with the best conditions in terms of quality and price). The company started its activity in 1931 and during the course of the last 75 years of existence has been numbered among the six largest companies of the province and is placed in the 19th position in the sector at a national level (see Table 3).

Table 1 presents the evolution of the annual sales of the company.

In order to classify the enterprise by its size, we considered the most widely used criteria in the European context for the awarding of grants and development of programs (Commission Recommendation (96/280/CE) of April 3, 1996). The amounts considered were reviewed in 2005 to show the increase in inflation and productivity.

Table 3. Market share of the pharmaceutical distributors (%) (Source: Iturrioz, 2003, p. 32)

Enterprises	1997	2000
1 COFARES	16,1	16,8
2 HEFAME	9,2	11,8
3 SAFA	8,3	9,0
4 FEDERACIÓN FARMACÉUTICA	8,4	6,9
5 CECOFAR	6,3	6,3
6 GRUPO FARMACEN	3,1	2,6
7 C.F. VALENCIANO	2,4	2,2
8 COFANO	2,4	2,1
9 COFARÁN	2,3	2,1
10 COFARCA	2,1	2,0
11 COFAS	2,1	1,9
12 HEFAGRA	1,8	1,7
13 COFAGA	1,9	1,6
14 COFARTE	1,6	1,6
15 ARAGOFAR	1,6	1,4
16 XEFAR	1,2	1,2
17 CEFANA	1,2	1,1
18 CERF CATALUÑA	1,3	1,1
19 COFARCIR	1,2	1,0
20 JAFARCO	1,0	1,0
Others	24,5	24,6
TOTAL	100	100

Considering the period of time of this study, we think that it is more appropriate to use the previous figures. Table 2 shows the figures over the last 3 years.

Considering the figures, we can class it as a medium-sized enterprise (not small, because it has more than 50 employees).

One of the most important threats that the company faces is the level of concentration of the sector in Spain, which is high. Table 3 reflects this situation.

There is a tendency toward the concentration in the sector. If we pay attention to the figures for the year 2000, it is noticeable that only five companies have more than the 50% of the market share. This is a threat for COFARCIR, as it only has the 1% of the market share. The solution may lie in the possibility of starting strategic alliances among some cooperatives. In this sense, COFARCIR has already established relationships with six companies monopolizing 25% of the pharmaceutical distribution in Spain. The result of this alliance has been the creation of the firm Organización Farmacéutica, S.A. (OFSA).

Figure 1. Productive process in the pharmaceutical distribution cooperatives (Source: Iturrioz, 2003, p. 85)

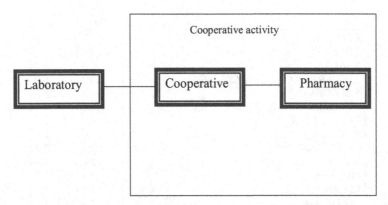

Products/Services Provided

One of the most important characteristics of pharmaceutical distribution in Spain is its wide public regulation. Patients have access to medicines in three main ways, which implies, respectively, 1%, 21%, and 78%. The national health programs fall into the first of these, which, through specific programs (vaccinations, for example), supply medicines to the users directly. Hospitals make up the second, through the medication administered to hospitalized patients. Direct shopping by the general public is the third one and it is in this process where the wholesalers (like COFAR-CIR) and the retailers (the pharmacies) participate (Juárez, 2003).

We can claim that every aspect of pharmaceutical activity is under some public regulation. Three causes explain this: the nature of the product (it can involve a health risk, so quality, security, and efficiency controls are necessary), public financing, and the necessity for intense research and development (R&D). This regulation of the sector implies that the conditions in terms of competitiveness vary from country to country and that the changes in it influence competitiveness considerably. Price is another aspect which is regulated. An industrial price is established when the medicine is authorized and registered. A fixed profit margin corresponding to the distributors and pharmacies is added to that price.

We shall now address the process developed by the enterprise. Figure 1 demonstrates this process in pharmaceutical distribution cooperatives.

As we can see, their activity as wholesalers facilitates the distribution of pharmaceutical products from the manufacturer laboratories to the pharmacies. The cooperative activity only appears in this last step, that is, the sale of the products to the partners.

Figure 2. Organization chart (Source: Cofarcir, 1995, 1996, 1997, 1998, 1999, 2000, 2001, 2002, 2003, 2004)

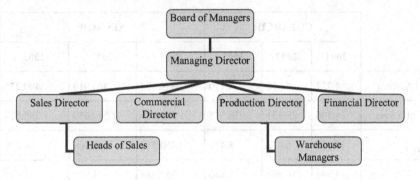

Management Structure

In the Figure 2 we can see the organization chart.

The process of decision making in pharmaceutical distribution cooperatives, considering the peculiar characteristics of their partners (the owners of the pharmacies), corresponds with the model called by Mintzberg (1989) *professional organization*, which is an organizational structure in which the hierarchical pyramid is inverted because the professionals in the base of it have a wide margin of autonomy while the managers' functions are limited to the management of the resources.

In the case of Cofarcir we can see a similar structure. There is a *strategic apex*, made up of the different controlling bodies (the General Assembly of Members, Board of Managers and Audit) and an *operating core* in which the professionals develop the guidelines set out by the organizational structure.

Financial Status

Tables 4 and 5 show some figures and ratios from the annual accounts of the company.

The figures of liquidity are good, presenting values even higher than the sector; therefore, the firm does not have any problems in facing its current liabilities.

The index of guarantee should always be superior to one because in other cases, the company would be in a situation of bankruptcy. As we can see, every figure satisfies this condition so the firm is able to honor its debts.

Table 4. Figures from the annual accounts (thousands €) (Source: Cofarcir, 1995, 1996, 1997, 1998, 1999, 2000, 2001, 2002, 2003, 2004)

	COFARCIR			SECTOR		
	2001	2002	2003	2001	2002	2003
Fixed Assets	4.227	4.910	4.110	339.598	366.919	400.275
Current Assets	24.306	28.231	30.545	1.148.489	1.249.659	1.355.574
Current Liabilities	5.052	6.452	5.475	450.718	463.360	464.228
Long-term Debt	14.594	16.896	18.880	533.886	571.919	633.605
Shareholder's Equity	8.887	9.793	10.209	503.483	581.299	658.016
Revenues	85.783	95.675	10.1059	4.614.809	5.182.358	5.776.699
Net Income	126	191	605	17.702	18.695	21.990

Table 5. Main ratios (Source: Annual Accounts, several years)

	COFARCIR			SECTOR		
	2001	2002	2003	2001	2002	2003
Liquidity (Cash+Short-term Loans/Current Liabilities)	3,25	2,77	3,41	1,44	1,55	1,60
Index of guarantee (Total Assets/Liabilities)	1,34	1,34	1,34	1,41	1,45	1,48
Working Capital (Shareholder's Equity+Long-term Debt/Fixed Assets)	5,56	5,44	7,08	3,05	3,14	3,23
ROI (Earning before interest and taxes*100/Total Assets)	0,5	0,6	1,9	*	*	*
ROE (Net Income*100/Shareholder's Equity)	1,2	2,4	6	*	*	*

* Figures not available

After the slight decrease in 2002, the increase of the working capital in 2003 is noticeable.

The Return on Investment is low, although it shows a tendency to rise. It is as well to remember that the main objective of the cooperatives is not to gain profits, but to offer an efficient service to those within it. In relation to the return on equity, all the figures are positive and the ratio is increasing which indicates sound financial management.

Setting the Stage

The pharmaceutical distribution sector, especially the company we are now analyzing, has always been a pioneer in relation to the adoption of the continuous IT developments. In the 1980s, Cofarcir gave to its pharmacies dataphones[1] for the electronic transmission of medicine orders, preceding the Internet by several years and the official definition of e-business. These orders were received by the cooperative through modems and centralized in what was, at that time, innovative Unix HP servers (series 1000 and those that followed). That initial step in the use of IT added to the robotic transformation of the main warehouse of the company, which took place in 1994, and which was an important step that allowed Cofarcir to fulfil two daily orders to each pharmacy in the region, solidifying its position as the regional leader. These first advances contributed to forming the current Spanish health system, known as the *Mediterranean model*, which is recognized worldwide for its high level of efficiency.

Case Description

Recently the company has gone one step further. Thanks to managers' entrepreneurial spirit and consideration in terms of the competitive pressure they face, Cofarcir and its pharmacies are embroider in the process of discovery and exploitation of opportunities to create new ways of developing services. We describe the main innovations that the company is adopting.

In the pharmacies, the management of stock, of orders, and of pharmaceutical services has been computerized. In addition, communication protocols at national level are used.[2] They are constantly connected to their suppliers (Cofarcir) and to the different health agents of the region through wide band connections, a channel that is used to place more than 70% of the orders received by Cofarcir.

In order to face such a huge volume of data with the necessary speed and accuracy, HP ML370 multiprocessor servers with a Linux operative system have been installed and they are connected with the rest of the servers of the system through a Gigabit ethernet network. The software that coordinates the whole activity of the enterprise is an enterprise resource plan (ERP) specifically created for the company. Due to its complexity and cost, it has been necessary for Cofarcir to form an alliance with some other cooperatives in order to be able to adapt to the changing circumstances within the sector. The core of this software is the post-relational database Cache of InterSystems[3] that provides some important features in relation to speed, flexibility, and stability of the system. The IT Department of Cofarcir has received an award in the Student Innovator Awards of InterSystems (2004) for the development, in cooperation with Castilla-La Mancha University (Spain), of a new warehouse management system through *ubiquitous computing*.

After the robotic transformation of the main warehouse of Cofarcir, the automation of the other warehouse took place as the cooperative had invested more than one million euros during 2005. The new robot, which as in the case of the main warehouse comes from Austria,[4] permits the application of the most innovative technology of the sector wide world. The use of radio frequency to prepare the orders received was also introduced in both warehouses, letting the system know which of the whole batch of units of a particular medicine had been shipped to a costumer by which employee.

All of this allows an accuracy level in the management of the orders never achieved before.

Current Challenges Facing the Organization

One of the main challenges facing medicine distribution, in relation to the accomplishment of the health requirements of the Spanish Government, is the traceability of the medicines along the whole chain from the manufacturing laboratory to delivery to the pharmacies in every Spanish city. In order to achieve this goal, the introduction of new IT will need to continue in the future. A new law[5] demands new control measures that are very difficult to apply with the existing technologies. It implies that the distributor has to identify the supplier to whom he has bought every individual unit of every pharmaceutical speciality in every warehouse and has to identify the consignee pharmacy and all of this on the basis of the manufacture batch that appears on every container. In order to be conscious of the implications of this demand, we have to consider that Cofarcir has a catalogue of more than 20,000 products and the number of units served a year is more than 6 million. The Spanish Government is currently dealing with agents of every sector looking for the best way to implement this objective. But the method that is arousing interest (mainly owing to the low cost for pharmaceutical industry), is the use of bidimensional bar code prints located on the medicine boxes; however, there are several problems associated with its use. The main difficulty is the static kind of information this method is able to save. Once the laboratory has printed the information of the batch (manufacture and date and any additional data necessary), this information can't be modified. It is not possible, therefore, to add the code of the wholesaler that delivers it or the pharmacy that sells it to the patients and this information is essential in order to have a complete knowledge of the life cycle of the product. A further problem is that there is not a developed market of electronic readers for this kind of bar codes that would allow the implementation of this system.

Despite all these difficulties, the distribution sector considers it a necessary process in order to improve the Spanish health system. Therefore, Cofarcir, along with other wholesalers, is considering an alternative to the bars codes method, such as the implantation of the *smart tags* (radio frequency identification technology) in the packing. Inside conventional tags there are memory chips that are able to store information which can be consulted and/or modified by radio frequency. The utilization of detection/writing arcs located to the entrance/exit of the products, which are able to check and save the important data of the medicines, adding supplementary information of the intermediate agents and manipulation processes to the *smart tag*, will solve the problem generated by the new law in maintaining the current quality of service. In addition to this, it is fair to say that the use of smart tags is a consolidated technology. Evidence in keeping with this can be found in the price of one of these tags. Only a few years ago, the cost of one smart tag was over one euro, but now it is only one tenth of one euro. The wholesalers think that this cost could be absorbed by the system (if compared with the price of the medicine), in order to have complete control over the life of the medicine.

As we can see, the managers of the company have shown an intrapreneurial spirit especially in light of the pressure businesses are under in today's environment to introduce new businesses and processes to maintain the level of quality and service demanded by customers.

References

Aaltio, I. (2005). Cultural change from entrepreneurship to intrapreneurship. In A. Fayolle, P. Kyrö & J. Ulijn (Eds.), *Entrepreneurship research in Europe. Outcomes and perspectives* (pp. 279-291). Cheltenham, United Kingdom: Edward Elgar Publishing Limited.

Cofarcir (1995). *Annual Reports.*

Cofarcir (1996). *Annual Reports.*

Cofarcir (1997). *Annual Reports.*

Cofarcir (1998). *Annual Reports.*

Cofarcir (1999). *Annual Reports.*

Cofarcir (2000). *Annual Reports.*

Cofarcir (2001). *Annual Reports.*

Cofarcir (2002). *Annual Reports.*

Cofarcir (2003). *Annual Reports.*

Cofarcir (2004). *Annual Reports.*

Davidson, P. (2005). Method issues in the study of venture star-up processes. In A. Fayolle, P. Kyrö & J. Ulijn (Eds.), *Entrepreneurship research in Europe. Outcomes and perspectives* (pp. 35-54). Cheltenham, United Kingdom: Edward Elgar Publishing Limited.

Durand, T. (2004). The strategic management of technology and innovation. In European Institute for Technology and Innovation Management (Ed.), *Bringing technology and innovation into the boardroom. Strategy, innovation, and competences for business value* (pp. 47-75). New York: Palgrave Macmillan.

European Information Technology Observatory (EITO) (2000). *European Information Technology Observatory 2000.* Frankfurt, Germany: EITO.

Iturrioz, J. (2003). *Las cooperativas de distribución farmacéutica en España. Diferencias con otros mayoristas.* Valencia, Spain: CIRIEC-España.

Juárez, C.A. (2003). La industria farmacéutica española. In J.E. Navas & L.A. Guerras. (Eds.), *Casos de dirección estratégica de la empresa* (pp. 80-91). Madrid, Spain: Civitas.

Mintzberg, H. (1989). *Mintzberg on management. Inside our strange world of organizations.* The Free Press.

Probert, D., Farrukh, C., & Phaal, R. (2004). Structuring a systematic approach to technology management: Processes and framework. In European Institute for Technology and Innovation Management (Ed.), *Bringing technology and innovation into the boardroom. Strategy, innovation, and competences for business value* (pp. 76-91). New York: Palgrave Macmillan.

Roberts, K.H., & Grabowski, M. (1999). Organizations, technology and structuring. In S.R. Clegg, C. Hardy & W.R. Nord (Eds.), *Managing organizations. Current issues* (pp. 159-173). London: Sage Publications.

Endnotes

[1] Autonomous devices for data transmission through a telephone line which permitted the communication of orders to a central server. The first models, like Azurdata, MSI o Micronic, transmitted to a speed of 300 bps.

[2] The first standardized protocol for sending and receiving orders was known as MSI. Now, FEDICOM is the most widely used by the Spanish distribution sector. Cofarcir has developed pioneering protocols in Spain, devised to achieve value-added services in the communication between distribution and the pharmacies.

[3] The first database used in the health sector. It can be found in the best hospitals of the United States (Massachussets General Hospital, UCLA Medical Center of California, Stanford University Hospital, etc.) and in some Spanish hospitals.

[4] Knapp, a company located in Graz (Austria), is a leader in automation worldwide. One of its last innovations, applied for the first time by Cofarcir, is called DABA. It makes the identification and locking of the packing of the orders, guaranteeing the security of the product from the warehouse to its destiny.

[5] Law 29/2006, 26th July, Article 87.

About the Authors

Jose-Aurelio Medina-Garrido, PhD, is a lecturer at the University of Cadiz, Spain. His research interests include the enabling role of information systems for strategic networks and dynamic capabilities development. He was a visiting fellow at the University of Warwick (UK) and at Real Colegio Complutense at Harvard and has contributed to several books on IT. Dr. Medina-Garrido has published articles and papers in *International Journal of Information Technology,* Investigaciones Europeas de Dirección y Economía de la Empresa, International Conference on the Dynamics of Strategy (University of Surrey), European Academy of Management International Conference, and AEDEM and ACEDE Conferences. He is a member of Regional Entrepreneurship Monitor in Andalusia, Spain, which is part of the Global Entrepreneurship Monitor (GEM) international project developed by Babson College and the London Business School. He participates in several research groups on "Dynamic Capabilities and Strategic Change," "Strategic Management and Human Resources," and "Creation of Cultural Firms." Dr. Medina-Garrido has been a consultant for several firms.

Salustiano Martínez-Fierro, PhD, is a lecturer at the University of Cadiz, Spain. His research focuses on strategic alliances and entrepreneurship. He received his PhD in management from the University of Cadiz. His articles and papers have been published by Academy of Management Meetings, International Conference of Iberoamerican, Academy of Management, European Academy of Management, Anales de Economía y Administracion de Empresas, *International Journal of Cross Cultural Management*, International Society for the Study of Work and

Organizational Values (ISSWOV), AEDEM and ACEDE Conferences, and Meeting Luso-Espanholas de Gestao Científica. He has contributed to three books on strategic alliances and work values. He is a member of the Entrepreneurial Session of ACEDE and AEDEM and participates in several research groups on "Strategic Management and Human Resources" and "Creation of Cultural Firms." He is a member of Regional Entrepreneurship Monitor in Andalusia, Spain, which is part of the Global Entrepreneurship Monitor (GEM) international project developed by Babson College and the London Business School. He was reviewer of the ACEDE Conference (2003, 2005) and the 4th International Meetings of Iberoamerican Academy of Management.

Jose Ruiz-Navarro, PhD, is a professor of management and dean of the Faculty of Business Administration at the University of Cadiz, Spain. He has been a visiting professor at Purdue University Kranner School of Management. Dr Ruiz-Navarro has been a consultant for the Chamber of Industry and Commerce in Cadiz, as well as for the following industries: automotive (Ford), aeronautic (Construcciones Aeronauticas, now EADS), food, and shipping. He has been CEO at ZUR (a promotion office of the Spanish Ministry of Industry), Gestion 1 (Consultancy), Free Zone Port of Cadiz, INI (Spanish Industrial Public Holding), and Astilleros Españoles, S.A. (Shipyard Industry). His articles and conferences have been published by Long Range Planning, Eastern Academy of Management, International Conference on the Dynamics of Strategy (University of Surrey), European Group of Organizational Studies (EGOS), Strategic Management Society, Conference of Management and Organizational Cognition, and *Strategic Management Journal*. He is an expert evaluator of the European Commission DG XII. He was reviewer of the International Congress of Academy of Management - Organization and Management Theory Division, 2000, Iberoamerican Academy of Management, 1999, I, II & III Workshops on Human Resources and Strategy in Spain, and Revista Europea de Direccion y Economia de la Empresa.

* * *

Jose Ariza Montes, JA, has a PhD in economic and business science and is principal lecturer of the Human Resources Area in the School of Business and Economic Science (ETEA), Universidad de Córdoba. A researcher and professor, Dr. Montes has published numerous articles in scientific magazines and is author of several books: *Gestión Integrada de Personas, Una perspectiva de organización* (in collaboration) (Desclée De Brouwer, 1999), *El reto del equilibrio: Vida personal y profesional* (Desclée De Brouwer, 2002), and *Dirección y Administración Integrada de Personas* (in collaboration) (McGraw-Hill, 2004).

Andrea Bikfalvi is a lecturer within the Business Administration and Product Design Department at the University of Girona. She is an active member of the research group, Gradient. Her research interests include management of innovation, new venture creation, and university-industry links. Bikfalvi has business administration studies complemented with a PhD in the same area. She has experience working on international projects in research and teaching.

Alicia Coduras Martínez, PhD, is an associate research professor in the Department of Entrepreneurship and Family Business (Instituto de Empresa, Spain). She is an expert in quantitative methods. In recent years, her research has focused on entrepreneurship and she heads the Global Entrepreneurship Monitor Project (GEM) in Spain. Professor Coduras holds a PhD in political sciences from the University of Pompeu Fabra and a degree in economic and business sciences from the University of Barcelona. She was a professor at the University of Barcelona and at the University of Pompeu Fabra. She has contributed to several books on entrepreneurship, presented papers in major international forums, and published articles in prestigious specialized journals.

María José Crisóstomo-Acevedo is a physical therapist at Jerez Hospital, in Southern Spain. She has a BS in physical therapy from the University of Seville and an MS in sports physical therapy. Her research interests include the enabling role of information systems for telemedicine and telerehabilitation. She has contributed to several books on IT and telemedicine. Her papers have been published in *Encyclopedia of IS&T* (2nd ed.), *Handbook of Research on Virtual Workplaces and the New Nature of Business Practices*, and *Encyclopedia of Human Resources Information Systems: Challenges in e-HRM.*

Cristina Cruz received her PhD in business administration and quantitative methods at Carlos III University in Madrid. Currently, she is a professor of entrepreneurial studies at the Entrepreneurship Department at Instituto de Empresa Business School where she also studied the Executive Development Program in Family Business. Professor Cruz is also a member of the research team of the Global Entrepreneurship Monitor (GEM) Project in Spain and an expert in family business management. She has co-authored several business cases studies, two of which (Mecca Cola and Workcenter) have been awarded as the best cases by the instituto de Empresa in 2005 and 2006 respectively.

Guillermo de Haro has a PhD in business organizations (specialized in technology and strategy), telecommunication engineer, and MBA *cum laude* from Instituto de Empresa Business School, where he also studied the Executive Program in Managing and Audiovisual Sector. He has been a consultant in IBV Corporation, and operations manager at Workcenter. At the moment, he is director of digital technicolor in the Department of Entertainment Services in Spain. He is a member of the European Committee ECIME and an associate member of the Arts and Science Academy. de Haro is also an associate professor of Instituto de Empresa. Dr. de Haro is author and co-author of businesses studies as Ing Direct, Casadellibro.com, Buongiorno! MyAlert or Workcenter, being last one awarded as best study of 2005 and multimedia case most innovative of 2006.

Ignacio De la Vega is a professor of entrepreneurship, director of strategic development, and director of International Center for Entrepreneurship at Instituto de Empresa Business School, work that he combines with his business and consultancy activities. As businessman he has taken part in numerous business initiatives. Professor de la Vega has been new projects director and responsible of corporative projects in various national and multinational businesses. He has also contributed to the business development from the administration as trading, consumer and exterior promotions managing director and manager of IMADE. Professor de la Vega has a degree in law with Honors, an MA in international affairs of law and diplomacy (Harvard-Tufts). He is the director of the GEM Project in Spain and co-author of numerous books regarding business creations, including *Crea tu propia empresa* (MacGraw-Hill).

Veerle De Schryver is a business consultant at Tools for Growth Decision Support (TforG), Belgium. TforG is a marketing consultancy company specializing in supporting Global Medical Technology Companies in acquiring the right insights for further business development. Her main professional expertise is in strategic B-2-B marketing and international market research. Prior to TforG, she worked as a scientific researcher at Vlerick Leuven Gent Management School, Belgium, where she dedicated her time to the European Center for E-Business Studies.

Andrew Garman is an associate professor and associate chair of the Department of Health Systems Management, Rush University, Chicago. His research program focuses on leadership assessment and development. He teaches graduate courses in organizational analysis, governance, and health care entrepreneurship.

Antonia Mercedes García-Cabrera is a professor of strategic management and organizational development and change at the University of Las Palmas de Gran Canaria, Spain. She received her PhD in management in 1994. Her areas of academic interest include organizational identity, cross-cultural studies, and entrepreneurship. Her research involves issues of entrepreneurship including studies of the personal characteristics of the individual and the national cultural dimensions as factors influencing the decision to create a venture, taking into account the existence of cultural differences within a single country. She has also undertaken research into the different components that affect the business opportunity recognition stage from a cognitive, holistic, and dynamic perspective.

María Gracia García-Soto is a professor of strategic management at the University of Las Palmas de Gran Canaria, Spain. She received her PhD in management in 2003. Her areas of academic interest include corporate governance, cross-cultural studies, and entrepreneurship. Her research in the field of entrepreneurship has centered on the study of the psychological and sociological variables that determine entrepreneurial behavior from a dual perspective. First, and from an evolutionary perspective, she has analyzed how those variables affect the recognition of a technology-based business opportunity. Second, she has undertaken studies of individual characteristics and the national culture as key factors in the entrepreneurial behavior of the individual in developing countries.

María Teresa Garrido-Álvarez is an associate professor of general management in the Department of Business Administration, Accounting, and Sociology at the University of Jaén, Spain. She has an MS in financial markets from the Autonomous University of Madrid. She has taught several courses at the postgraduate level at the Spanish Open University (UNED), the Andalusian Institute of Public Administration, and the Andalusian Public Security School. She is member of the research team "Organization Jaén" and has participated in international research projects granted by the European Union related to the impact of new technologies on local development. Her research interests include human resources management, local development, e-learning, and collaboration.

José Luis González is a PhD candidate and works for the Technology Center at Universidad de Deusto, Spain. He holds an MS in business administration from the same university. Mr. González is conducting research on issues related to technology management and young venture performance. He is a member of the Global Entrepreneurship Monitor (GEM) research consortium and collaborates with the Basque research group in this project.

Aard Groen is scientific director of Nikos, the Dutch Institute for Knowledge Intensive Entrepreneurship at the University of Twente, the Netherlands. Groen's research interest focuses on knowledge-intensive entrepreneurship in networks. He is published in journals and books on entrepreneurship, marketing, university-industry interaction and innovation, and technology dynamics. Groen is also head of department, Nikos from the Faculty of Management and Governance, in which the chairs of entrepreneurship strategic management, marketing, and international management are positioned. Groen received his MS in public administration from the University of Twente, and his PhD in business administration from the University of Groningen.

Rod Hart has over 15 years of experience in health care operations and IT design. His expertise includes system strategy and planning, system selection, system re-design, project leadership, and system implementation. He was previously a senior manager with Cap Gemini Ernst & Young, a leading consulting and technology firm. Mr. Hart has worked in the health care system of four countries (the United States, Canada, New Zealand, and Malaysia) and has an MBA and MHSA from the University of Michigan.

Arzu İşeri-Say is an associate professor of management and organization at the Department of Management, Boğaziçi University, Turkey. She received her PhD from the University of Bradford Management Center, UK, in the area of organizational analysis. She teaches organization theory and behavior, organizational change, strategy, and disaster management. Her published work covers topics such as culture, managerial work values, consumer power, virtualization of services, globalization, decision support systems for disaster mitigation and response, and social and organizational aspects of disaster management. She is currently interested in risk perception, sense-making in disasters, storytelling perspective of organizing, and innovative management research methods.

José Luis Jurado Rincón was born in Ciudad Real, Spain, on February 11, 1974. He has a degree in administration and business management and is a professor in the Mathematics Department at the Faculty of Law and Social Sciences of Ciudad Real, Castilla-La Mancha University, Spain, where he has been delivering classes for 9 years. He is also the financial director of Cooperativa Farmacéutica de Ciudad Real (COFARCIR), a Spanish pharmaceutical company.

Paul Kirwan is a doctoral candidate at the Dutch Institute for Knowledge Intensive Entrepreneurship (Nikos) at the University of Twente, the Netherlands. His research focuses on high-tech and international entrepreneurship. He specifically examines the entrepreneurial process of "global-start-ups" and investigates the role networks and support networks play in allowing these firms to realize their global potential. Prior to being admitted to the doctoral program, he spent a year working as a researcher with Nikos. Born in Cork, Ireland, he graduated from University College Cork, with an MSc (research) in management in 2001.

Edurne Loyarte is the financial and quality manager of Vicomtech, located in San Sebastian, Spain. She received her bachelor's degree in business management and administration from the University of Deusto with a speciality master in strategy. She holds a PhD in economics and business administration from the University of Deusto, San Sebastian. She has published several articles in the field of communities of practices and collaborates in research projects with the University of Deusto.

Alfonso Miguel Márquez-García is an associate professor of general management in the Department of Business Administration, Accounting, and Sociology at the University of Jaén, Spain. He also serves as virtual tutor at the Catalonia Open University (UOC). He is member of the research team "Organization Jaén" and has participated in international research projects granted by the European Union. His research interests include cooperation and strategic alliances, trust, local development, IT, and e-learning. Some results have been published in *Revesco, ICADE, RELATEC*, books chapters at IGI Global and Kluwer Academic Publishers, Workshop on Trust Within and Between Organizations (EIASM), and Conference Proceedings of the European Academy of Management (EURAM).

Alfredo Romeo Molina has a major in finance by the St. Louis University in the United States in 1997. Mr. Molina was a financial analyst at the Commerce Bank of St. Louis for two and a half years and has entrepreneurial experience in different projects related to the Knowledge Society. He is also author of the book *La Pastilla Roja, Software Libre y Revolución Digital*, the first book written in Spanish on free software and the digital revolution. Mr. Molina is Blobject's founder and partner is responsible of the technology consulting area of the company.

Alfonso Carlos Morales Gutiérrez is principal lecturer of organization and nanagement of business and human resources in the School of Business and Economic Science (ETEA), Universidad de Córdoba. He has written several books, among them: *Empresas y emprendedores en Córdoba. 30 casos de éxito* (2000, Diputación); *Análisis y Diseño de Sistemas Organizativos* (2004, Thomson-Civitas) y *Dirección y Administración Integrada de Personas* (in collaboration) (2004, McGraw-Hill), *Análisis Económico de la Empresa Autogestionada* (2004-CIRIEC). Since 1990, he has led the research group SEJ-148 Estudios Cooperativos y ENL (ETEA), subsidized by the Junta de Andalucía.

María del Carmen Moreno-Martos is an associate professor of general management in the Department of Business Administration, Accounting, and Sociology at the University of Jaén, Spain. She also served as an economist at a regional government agency (Junta de Andalucía). Now she is working on her PhD in environment prospective. She has taught several courses at the postgraduate level at the Spanish Open University (UNED). She is a member of the research team "Organization Jaén" and has participated in international research projects granted by the European Union. Her research interests include local development, e-learning, and collaboration.

Rosa Mª Muñoz Castellanos was born in Toledo, Spain, on July 4, 1968. She attained a degree in administration and business management in 1991 and worked as the managing director of the Spanish Red Cross in Pontevedra during 1992 and 1993. She is currently a professor at the Faculty of Law and Social Sciences of Ciudad Real, Castilla-La Mancha University, Spain, where she works in the Enterprise Organization Department and has been delivering classes for 13 years. She attained a PhD in economy in 2000.

Steve Muylle, PhD, is an associate professor and chairman of the Competence Center Marketing at Vlerick Leuven Gent Management School, Belgium. He is also a visiting professor at Ghent University, Belgium. His research interests are in the area of electronic commerce, electronic supply management, and Web site interface design. His research has been published in various journals, including *Communications of the ACM, Decision Support Systems, Information & Management,* and *IEEE Computer Society Proceedings.* He has worked with many companies, both large corporations and SMEs, on various education and research projects, and serves frequently as a trainer in executive education programs for leading multinational companies across Europe.

Mayur Patel has over 15 years of experience as a health care planner and consultant and has conducted a broad range of strategic planning and performance improvement engagements for hospitals and physician groups throughout the U.S., Eastern Europe, and East Africa. Mr. Patel was previously a senior manager in the PricewaterhouseCoopers health care consulting practice. He holds an MS in health systems management from Rush University.

Iñaki Peña is an assistant professor of management at Universidad de Deusto, Spain, and a senior researcher of the Basque Institute of Competitiveness. He holds a PhD from Purdue University, Indiana. Dr. Peña has collaborated on several books and published numerous articles on entrepreneurship, innovation, and firm start-up policies. Some of his articles have been published in international journals such as *Small Business Economics, International Journal of Technology Management, Journal of Intellectual Capital,* and *Journal of Knowledge Management.* Dr. Peña is a member of the Global Entrepreneurship Monitor (GEM) research consortium and the team leader of the Basque research group.

Paulo Rupino da Cunha is an assistant professor of information systems at the University of Coimbra, Portugal. He holds a PhD and an MSc in informatics engineering. He is the vice president of Instituto Pedro Nunes, an innovation and technology transfer organization and business incubator. For a period of 3 years he was the coordinator of the Informatics Engineering Chapter for the center region of Portugal, of the Portuguese Engineering Association. For a two-year term he held the vice presidency of the Department of Informatics Engineering of the University of Coimbra. He is the author of various papers and serves on the program committee for several conferences.

Paulo Santos holds an undergraduate degree in economics and a specialization in financing and investment projects from the University of Coimbra, Portugal. He started his career as a junior consultant in investment and competitiveness projects in regional and national development associations. Since 2001 he has been the executive director of Instituto Pedro Nunes' Business Incubator.

Christian Serarols is a senior lecturer within the Business Economics Department at Universitat Autònoma de Barcelona and a member of the Research Group, High-Tech E Entrepreneurs in Catalonia. Research interests include entrepreneurship and small business management, e-business, and electronic commerce. Serarols has an industrial engineering background, a PhD in business economics, and industrial experience in technical research, consulting, and management. He has founded a high-tech enterprise in the field of content aggregation.

Ayşegül Toker received her PhD in industrial engineering at the Middle East Technical University (METU). She is now an associate professor at the Department of Management, Boğaziçi University, Turkey, where she teaches courses on MIS, e-business models, customer relationship management, information and technology based marketing, and customer analytics. She has articles published in the areas of decision support systems, business excellence, total quality management, and production management. Her current research interests include e-business models and applications, customer relationship management, data-mining applications, customer-knowledge management, and customer-focused strategies.

Peter Van der Sijde is the senior project manager/researcher/lecturer at the Dutch Institute for Knowledge Intensive Entrepreneurship (Nikos), is on the Faculty of Management and Governance of the University of Twente, and is a lecturer (associate professor) for knowledge innovative entrepreneurship at the Saxion Universities for Professional Education, both located in Enschede, the Netherlands. His research interests are in student entrepreneurship, high-tech and international entrepreneurship as well as the interaction between knowledge institutes. Van der Sijde is trained as an educational psychologist (Free University Amsterdam – 1982) and a theoretical psychologist (Free University Amsterdam – 1985). He received his PhD from the University of Twente (1987: Training the teaching script).

Index